Behavioral Research on
Exceptional Children

Behavioral Research on Exceptional Children

EDITORS

SAMUEL A. KIRK, PH.D.

Director, Institute for Research on Exceptional Children,
University of Illinois, Urbana

BLUMA B. WEINER, ED.D.

Assistant Professor, Department of Special Education and
Rehabilitation, University of Pittsburgh, Pennsylvania

Authors

LEON CHARNEY, Ph.D., is Professor of Special Education, Newark State College, Union, New Jersey.

MIRIAM L. GOLDBERG, Ph.D., is Associate Professor of Education, Teachers College, Columbia University, New York City.

NORRIS G. HARING, Ed.D., is Associate Professor of Pediatrics and Education, and Education Director, Children's Rehabilitation Unit, University of Kansas Medical Center, Kansas City.

RICK F. HEBER, Ph.D., is Professor of Special Education, University of Wisconsin, Madison.

CLIFFORD E. HOWE, Ph.D., is Supervisor of Special Education, Long Beach Unified School District, California.

LAURA J. JORDAN, Ph.D., is Assistant Professor of Education, Department of Special Education, University of Illinois, Urbana.

KENNETH R. MANGAN, Ed.D., is Superintendent, Illinois School for the Deaf, Jacksonville.

CARSON Y. NOLAN, Ph.D., is Director, Department of Educational Research, The American Printing House for the Blind, Louisville, Kentucky.

A. HARRY PASSOW, Ed.D., is Professor of Education, Teachers College, Columbia University, and Director, Talented Youth Project, Horace Mann-Lincoln Institute of School Experimentation, New York City.

HERBERT C. QUAY, Ph.D., is Associate Professor of Psychology, Northwestern University, Evanston, Illinois.

STEPHEN P. QUIGLEY, Ph.D., is Associate Professor, Institute for Research on Exceptional Children, University of Illinois, Urbana.

L. LEON REID, Ph.D., is Associate Professor, Department of Special Education and Rehabilitation, School of Education, University of Pittsburgh, Pennsylvania.

RICHARD L. SCHIEFELBUSCH, Ph.D., is Professor of Speech Pathology and Director, the Bureau of Child Research, University of Kansas, Lawrence.

Table of Contents

Preface

During the past two decades, the field of special education has undergone an "explosion" both in services and in knowledge. The development of programs for exceptional children, particularly since World War II, has been so rapid that few professional workers have been able to keep up with the expanding scene. Because of the heterogeneity of this field, which includes so many kinds of deviant development, and because of the multiplicity of disciplines concerned with services and research, information processing has broken down. It is becoming increasingly difficult, if not impossible, for one individual to keep abreast of literature which is so widely dispersed in numerous professional and technical journals. For this reason we have seen the appearance of various compilations of abstracts, readings, and reviews, most of which have been highly specialized.

The present monograph is one of a series of publications of the Council for Exceptional Children dealing with contemporary problems and issues in the education of children and youth who require a variety of special services. It provides selected reviews of relevant studies in each major category of exceptionality and can serve as a supplement to basic textbooks in the field.

Much of the early literature on exceptional children pertained to physiological aspects of disability. Valuable as these findings were, there was little in them which had direct relevance to problems of school learning and social adjustment. With more recent advances in theories of perception, learning, and personality, there has emerged greater interest in, and a greater need for, information bearing upon the *behavioral* aspects of exceptionality. Responsible instruction, program development, and guidance depend upon such knowledge. The focus of this monograph, therefore, is specifically upon behavioral research on exceptional children.

The contributing authors and reviewers were invited to participate in the production of this volume because of their active interest and current professional responsibilities in the respective areas. They were asked to be selective in their choice of materials and to be guided by regard for those investigations which represent significant advances in procedure or results.

The sequence of chapters calls attention to the relatedness of the several categories of exceptionality and acknowledges their overlap. Chapters I, II, and III deal with research in the traditional areas of *cognitive functioning*—the gifted and the mentally retarded. Chapters IV, V, and VI are concerned with research on children with primary *sensory disorders*—the visually and auditorily impaired. Chapters VII and VIII give consideration to children with *cerebral dysfunctioning* and *orthopedic* and *special health problems*—children who were often undifferentiated as "crippled children" in the early literature. Chapters IX, X, and XI present reviews on behavior which may be described as *communicative* and *adjustive*—speech and language impairment, emotional disturbance, and delinquency. Chapter XII is concerned with research on the *administration* of special educational services.

The structure of the chapters facilitates the identification of specific kinds of information. Each one is organized into sections which are appropriate to the particular area of exceptionality. Each chapter includes a definition of the subject to be covered, a description of the topics reviewed, the reviews of research for each topic, and—in most cases—a final summary comment on the status of research in the area under consideration and on problems which need investigation. The separate studies which are reviewed are treated briefly but specifically according to the following headings: (a) author and title, (b) purpose, (c) subjects, (d) method or procedure, (e) results, and (f) comments by the chapter author where the findings appeared to warrant some extension of the presentation.

It is hoped that persons who use the monograph will not only be interested in the chapters which deal with their established areas of concern, but will also develop a critical curiosity about the state of research in other areas of special education. As awareness of interdependent conditions and multiple disabilities in children and youth becomes more prevalent, earlier notions of "types"—or stereotypes—of exceptional children will be corrected. A more comprehensive body of knowledge creates heavier professional obligations for understanding and practice, and thus provides impetus for improved services for all exceptional children.

In any review of research it is inevitable that the authors would select literature which is, at the time, most relevant to them, and all of them would admit that other very important studies could also have been selected. Due to the limited space allotted for this monograph, it was necessary to omit many excellent references which otherwise would have been included.

In format, the reviews of the literature presented in this publication have been set up as independent entities. In this way the monograph lends itself to easy revision, since the major topics need not be altered when new studies are added. It will therefore be possible for this publication to be revised every three to five years, with the addition of important studies reported during the interim and possibly the elimination of some studies which were originally included. It is requested that readers of this monograph assist with its revision by sending any and all criticisms, errors noted, or references which should have been included to Editor, CEC Monographs (Council for Exceptional Children, 1201 Sixteenth Street, Northwest, Washington 6, D.C.).

SAMUEL A. KIRK AND BLUMA B. WEINER

Behavioral Research on Exceptional Children

1

The Gifted

A. Harry Passow and Miriam L. Goldberg

A gifted child is one who has the capacity for superior achievement in some area of human endeavor which has consistently made an outstanding contribution to civilization. Such a broad definition would include academic fields such as languages, social sciences, natural sciences, and mathematics; arts fields such as music, graphic and plastic arts, performing arts, and mechanical arts; and the field of human relations. However, the studies included below, reflecting the state of the field itself, are limited to the areas of intellectual, creative, and scientific talent. The studies are organized under the following topics:

1. Characteristics of the gifted.
2. Identification of the gifted.
3. Achievement, motivation, and underachievement.
4. Educational programs.

The studies included in this chapter were selected from a rather extensive body of research on the nature and education of the gifted. Other equally significant studies might have been included were more space

Reviewed by James J. Gallagher, University of Illinois.

The authors wish to express their appreciation to Floyd E. Waterman, Research Assistant, Horace Mann-Lincoln Institute of School Experimentation, for his help in the preparation of this chapter.

available. The authors have tried to select studies which tackled the more fundamental issues and in which sound research methodology was employed.

CHARACTERISTICS OF THE GIFTED

Much of the basic information about the characteristics, backgrounds, and development of the gifted has come from Terman's longitudinal studies and Hollingworth's studies of children with unusually high IQs. Their findings have been confirmed generally and added to by the studies of large groups of intellectually able children by such researchers as Paul Witty, Merle Sumption, Willard Abraham, Gertrude Hildreth and Walter Barbe.

> Terman, L. M., and Oden, Melita H. *The Gifted Group at Mid-life: Thirty-five Years Follow-up of the Superior Child.* Vol. V. *Genetic Studies of Genius.* Stanford: Stanford University Press, 1959.

Purpose: To determine what intellectually superior children are like, how they differ from average children, how they develop in youth and as adults, and what some of the factors are that influence their later achievement.

Subjects: 1528 subjects (857 males and 671 females) selected in 1921 on the basis of high intelligence. The average age at inception of the study was 11 years; the mean IQ was 151. Subjects came from every ethnic and racial group then represented in California and from every socio-economic level. However, the majority were the offspring of intellectually superior parents from above-average homes. They were superior to the generality in physique and health, educational history, variety and depth of interests, character traits, and emotional stability.

Procedures: A field follow-up was made in 1950-52. The procedures used in this follow-up included: administration of a revised form of the Concept Mastery Test (devised in 1939 as an individual adult intelligence test), personal interviews, questionnaires for subjects and spouses, and testing of offspring with the Stanford-Binet. This battery was administered to 1004 gifted subjects and 690 of their spouses.

Results: Follow-up studies in 1927, 1940, and 1946 revealed that the gifted group remained superior to the generality in all areas tested. The 1950-52 follow-up, given when the mean age of the gifted group was 44, revealed the following results:

4

Two percent of the gifted had CMT scores in the 180-189 interval (perfect score 190) and only 10 subjects (approximately one percent) scored below 60. The spouse group itself was a superior group. A comparison of CMT scores for gifted subjects in 1950-52 with their childhood Stanford-Binet IQs showed that the higher the CMT scores, the higher were the Stanford-Binet IQ levels. There was a positive relationship between CMT score and the level of education. Over 90 percent of the group had married; over three-fourths reported no serious sex problems. The typical family had 2.4 children. Divorce rate was lower than for the generality. College graduates had lower divorce rates than those who did not graduate from college.

Of those who failed to graduate from college, more women than men were rated as having *some* or *serious* difficulties in adjustment. Eighty-seven percent of the men and 83 percent of the women entered college, and 70 percent of the men and 67 percent of the women graduated. In the generality in the decade 1930-1940, less than eight percent of those of comparable age were graduated from college. Two-thirds of the men and almost three-fifths of the women who completed college entered graduate school, and over half of the men and one-third of the women took one or more advanced degrees. The academic record for the college graduates was superior to the generality of college students. About 80 percent made an average grade of "B" or better. Over one-third won honors. Almost half of the men took undergraduate majors in the social sciences; the rest were divided among the physical sciences, engineering, and letters. Of the women, over one-third majored in social science and the same number in letters; less than 10 percent went into education and about as many into the physical and biological sciences.

Occupationally, almost 90 percent of the men were in the professions, higher business or semi-professions. None were in semi-skilled or unskilled jobs. Law was the most frequently chosen profession, followed by university teaching and engineering. The median income of the men was $9640. Of the women, half were housewives, eight percent had part-time jobs and the rest were in full-time employment. Of the married women, less than one-third held full-time jobs and about 10 percent worked part-time. Those women who took advanced degrees were more apt to be employed than those with only a bachelor's degree. The median income of the employed women was $4875.

Politically, the group viewed itself as slightly right of center on a conservative-radical scale. There was a shift toward conservatism from 1940 to 1950. General health was rated as good or very good by 90 percent of the men and 80 percent of the women. Handicapping physical defects were infrequent. Both men and women were not only taller than the generality, but also taller than the average for college students. The incidence of hospitalization among gifted men was slightly below the expectancy for the male population of comparable age. The incidence of hospitalization among gifted women was slightly above the expectancy for the female population of comparable age. The incidence of alcoholism in the gifted population was one percent of gifted men and one-half of one percent for women, contrasted to generality of seven percent and one percent.

As adults, the gifted remained superior to the generality in nearly every aspect tested, most strikingly in intellectual ability, scholastic attainment and vocational achievement. Over 100 are listed in *American Men of Science* or *Who's Who in America*, but no great composers or creative artists have come out of the group.

Comment: Volume I of the *Genetic Studies* deals with the early mental and physical traits of the children from the 1922 study. Volume II contains an analysis of the early mental traits of 300 geniuses. Volumes III and IV contain the data from the follow-up study of 1927-28 and those of 1936, 1940 and 1945.

Although the *Genetic Studies of Genius* are the classic longitudinal studies in this area and much of our present knowledge about the intellectually gifted stems from Terman's findings, there are some limitations which must be kept in mind when projecting these findings to present-day conceptions about gifted children. The need to keep the study within manageable proportions resulted in a sampling bias. By Terman's own estimate, at least 10 percent of those in the population samples who would have qualified as gifted were not included because they were not nominated by teachers. As a result, pupils of high intelligence who were already "underachieving" in the elementary school were omitted from the sample.

Secondly, the study was restricted to a population drawn chiefly from California's large and medium-sized urban areas. As a result, the characteristics attributed to gifted children may well be representative of urban gifted children rather than of gifted children in general. Thirdly, the relationship between intelligence and various physical and personality traits needs to be examined more carefully in view of the consistently high relationship between general intelligence and the socio-economic status of parents. It may well be that some of the characteristics which are ascribed to intellectual giftedness are, instead, related to socio-economic status. For example, Bonsall and Stellfre (M. R. Bonsall and

B. Stellfre. The Temperament of Gifted Children. *California Journal of Educational Research*, 1955, 6, 195-199.) found that when socioeconomic background was held constant, very few significant differences remained between the temperamental characteristics of gifted and average students. Differences in emotional stability, sociability, friendliness, or cooperation were related to social class rather than to intelligence. A similar approach to the analysis of physical characteristics of gifted children as well as to the values they hold, may find differences previously attributed to intelligence to be more significantly related to socioeconomic status.

Having followed the group to maturity at mid-life, Terman found a paucity of really outstanding, creative individuals in the group. This raises some questions as to the validity of the term "genius" which Terman originally applied to his subjects. However, the group as a whole achieved professionally and vocationally at a far higher level than the general population and maintained intellectual superiority at least through mid-life. Perhaps Terman's conclusion that gifted people are socially and personally at least as well adjusted as the average would have had to be modified had the group contained a greater proportion of "true geniuses," since it is in such individuals that problems of social or personal adjustment have been found by other researchers in the field. (See, for example, P. A. Witty and H. C. Lehman. Nervous Instability and Genius: Poetry and Fiction. *Journal of Abnormal and Social Psychology*, 24, 77-90 and Nervous Instability and Genius: Some Conflicting Opinions. *Journal of Abnormal and Social Psychology*, 24, 486-497.)

Hollingworth, Leta S. *Children Above 180 IQ*. Yonkers-on-Hudson, New York: World Book Company, 1942.

Purpose: To determine the characteristics of children with IQs of above 180.

Subjects: 12 children who tested above 180 on the Stanford-Binet test (mean IQ 186.72), found by Hollingworth and associates over a 20-year period.

Procedure: Individual case studies were made. Data were obtained on each subject's family background, educational achievement, intelligence test scores, and college attendance. Adult intelligence data were gathered. Generalizations about children with high IQs were based in part on these data and in part on an earlier study.

Results: Ten of the subjects were firstborn, one was fourth-born and one was sixth. Five subjects were only children; five were from families with one other child; one came from a family of three siblings, all of whom had died at birth; and one subject had six siblings. All of the parents were from either the professional, clerical, or business-proprietor classes. Four children started to read at age three; two started at age four; and three of the remaining six read "before kindergarten." General health was always reported as good and physique as superior. There was no apparent pattern in the parental age at the time of the child's birth.

The students seemed to "go through the ceiling of available tests for adult intelligence by the time they are 21 years old." One-third of the subjects showed notable signs of creativeness; another third showed indications to a moderate degree, and the remaining third gave no indications of marked constructive originality.

These children presented educational problems from their entrance into school. The problems were not only those of school personnel but of the children themselves. Depending on the solution of their problems, the children either were well articulated to school and society or developed a distaste for school, obstinacy, and recalcitrance, perhaps accompanied by bitterness. Although all 12 children were identified fairly early in their lives, there were very different degrees of adaptation to school and society, ranging from opposition to rapt and enthusiastic preoccupation. The children who had achieved most contented and socially useful adaptation were those whose parents, teachers, and principals had made prompt use of special gift identification, and sought educational guidance or taken advantage of such experimental classes for exceptional children as were available at the time. The children of superior intelligence were not, as a group, socially annoying.

Comment: The basic limitation of the Hollingworth study lies in its use of the case study method, necessitated by the restricted number of children with IQs above 180. The study provides some valuable hypotheses regarding the special characteristics and problems of children with unusually high intelligence. Hollingworth's most significant contribution was not in specific research studies but rather in her efforts to provide special educational opportunities for intellectually gifted pupils. (See, for example, Leta S. Hollingworth. *Gifted Children: Their Nature and Nurture.* New York: Macmillan, 1926, and An Enrichment Curriculum for Rapid Learners at Public School 500: The Speyer School. *Teachers College Record,* 1938, 39, 296-306.)

D'Heurle, A., Mellinger, Jeanne C., and Haggard, E. A. Personality, Intellectual, and Achievement Patterns in Gifted Children. *Psychological Monographs*, 1959, 73, 1-28.

Purpose: To delineate the organization or structure of a variety of factors that determine patterns of academic achievement.

Subjects: 76 pupils enrolled in the third grade during the year 1950-51, all in the 90th percentile or above on national norms for both intellectual ability and achievement, were studied until the ninth grade.

Procedures: Reading, arithmetic, and spelling achievement scores were correlated with a series of personality variables derived from the Rorschach, the Children's Apperception Test (CAT), and behavioral observation. On the 27 personality and parent-attitudes variables, relatively high ($\rho = .98$ to .78) interjudge reliabilities were obtained. Stanford-Binet IQs and Primary Mental Ability scores were partialled out of these correlations between achievement and personality factors to remove the effects of general mental ability on personality variables. Achievement profiles were prepared.

Results: High general achievers (i.e., children achieving high scores on arithmetic, reading, and spelling tests) were sensitive and responsive to socialization pressures, accepted adult values, and strived to live up to adult expectations. In school they showed a higher level of adjustment and developed good work habits. High arithmetic achievers presented personality structures similar to the high general achievers but tended to be more spontaneous and creative, skilled in the manipulation of abstract symbols, more aggressive, independent, and self-confident. High reading achievers were withdrawn, reacted negatively to parental authority, and were insecure in relation to the adult world. They found difficulty expressing feelings openly in relations with others but showed a great deal of freedom and expansiveness in their fantasy. Their mental approach was strikingly abstract and theoretical except when dealing with objective, quantitative data or organizing problem material, in which case they were markedly inferior. High spelling achievers were passive, dependent on adult authority and sought approval by submission and strict adherence to rules.

Comment: The two assumptions that (a) academic achievement and intellectual abilities are associated with nonintellective factors; and (b) cognitive processes emerge within the personality organization of the individual and are meaningful in terms of his generalized effort to deal with his world as he sees it, were borne out by the findings. The results support the view that "learning," "memory," "intelligence," and "personality" are by no means isolated and independent processes, but rather that they involve various aspects of the person's attempt to deal with and adapt to reality as he sees it.

Warren, J. R., and Heist, P. A. Personality Attributes of Gifted College Students. *Science*, 1960, 132, 330-337.

Purpose: To make an appraisal of the behavioral characteristics of gifted college students as measured by objective personality inventories.

Subjects: The 918 (659 males, 259 females) National Merit Scholars. For purposes of comparison, 841 students (388 from University of California and 453 from Michigan State University) representing all four undergraduate years were used. The estimated mean IQ of the Merit Scholars was 150; the minimum IQ was 130.

Procedures: The two groups were compared on (a) College Entrance Examination Board tests, (b) Omnibus Personality Inventory, and (c) Allport-Vernon-Lindzey Study of Values.

Results: The higher Ego-strength scores of the National Merit Scholarship subjects suggest that they operate at a higher level of personal effectiveness and that they are more self-confident, resourceful, and independent than the less intelligent. The higher Complexity scores indicate greater intellectual independence and a tendency toward original, unconventional ways of responding to the environment, as well as greater tolerance of ambiguity and greater potential for creativity. The personality structure of the gifted student and his ways of thinking (intellectual rebelliousness, originality, ego-strength and potential for creativity) are conducive to intellectual achievement. The gifted students value the theoretical and aesthetic orientations relatively higher and the economic or utilitarian relatively lower than do the students in the comparative samples.

Accompanying the high scholastic aptitude of the gifted is a strong attraction to intellectual activity combined with high levels of aesthetic awareness and appreciation. High Aesthetic scores, exhibited particularly by the gifted women, indicate a receptive orientation toward sensory experiences and possibly a predilection for their harmonious organization.

The attribute that most sharply differentiates the gifted of both sexes from unselected college students is a strong disposition toward intellectual activity: liking for reflective and abstract thought; interest in ideas and conceptualization; a rational, cognitive approach to reality; and a positive, functional approach to scholarly pursuits.

Gifted students are independent, confident, and generally mature in their interactions with the external world. As compared to the normative groups, they have more complex perceptions and reactions. They are less authoritarian and less rigid, to the extent that many are free to become "risk-takers" in the world of ideas. Most of them react with greater originality, imagination and resourcefulness to the stimulation they receive.

Comment: Descriptive studies of the achievement, aptitudes, and personality attributes of National Merit Scholars and Certificate of Merit winners have been reported in several articles. (See, for example, J. L. Holland and R. C. Stalnaker. A Descriptive Study of Talented High School Seniors: National Merit Scholars. *Bulletin of the National Association of Secondary School Principals,* 1958, 42, 9-21, and J. L. Holland. The Achievement, Aptitudes, and Personalities of National Merit Scholars and Certificate of Merit Winners. *Bulletin of the National Association of Secondary School Principals,* 1960, 44, 100-104.) It should be noted that despite the fact that the basis of the selection for the National Merit Scholars and Certificate winners consisted primarily of tests of aptitude and acquired knowledge—generally considered of a "convergent thinking" nature—the population which was selected by these instruments had many characteristics in common with groups selected on the basis of "divergent thinking" tests. Is the similarity due to the fact that the subjective element in the selection process (interviews with candidates) tended to single out those individuals who possess the more creative traits associated with intellectuality, or does the selection of those who achieve the very highest scores on tests of aptitude and acquired knowledge and who have been highly successful in high school as measured by grades, of itself result in the selection of students who resemble those rated high on divergent thinking and creativity?

Getzels, J. W., and Jackson, P. W. The Study of Giftedness: A Multidimensional Approach. The Gifted Student. *Coöperative Research Monograph,* U.S. Government Printing Office, 1960, No. 2, 1-18.

Purpose: To discover the significant variables differentiating the creative from the intelligent person.

Subjects: The total population of 449 pupils in a private secondary

11

school from which a high intelligence group of 28 and a high creativity group of 26 were selected.

Procedures: The entire population was tested on five measures of creativity (adapted from Guilford and Cartell), as follows: word association, uses for things, hidden shapes, fables, and make-up problems. A Stanford-Binet, a WISC and a Henmon-Nelson score were available for each pupil (the latter two were converted to comparable Stanford-Binet IQs). On the basis of these measures two experimental groups were formed. The high creativity group consisted of 26 students (15 boys and 11 girls) who had scored in the top 20 percent of the total group in creativity but not in the top 20 percent in intelligence. The high intelligence group included 28 students (17 boys and 11 girls) who had scored in the top 20 percent in IQ but not in the top 20 percent in creativity.

The two groups were compared to each other and to the total school population on school performance, teacher preferences on having them in class, and n-Achievement as measured by the McClelland stimulus-pictures test scored conventionally and rated "blind" for creativity.

Results: The mean IQ of the high intelligence group was 150; of the high creative group, 127; and of the total population, including experimentals, 132. The school achievement mean for the total population was 49.91; for the high intelligence group, 55.00; and for the high creative group, 56.27. There were significant differences in teacher preference ratings, favoring the high intelligence group. No significant differences were found in the n-Achievement scores. Systematic differentiation of protocols by content-analysis found that the high creative group was significantly higher in fantasy production categories of stimulus-free theme, unexpected ending, presence of humor, presence of incongruity, and playful attitude toward theme.

Differences between the two groups appeared in both quality and quantity of occupational goals. The quantity of possibilities mentioned was significantly greater for the high creatives. When the quality of occupations mentioned was categorized as conventional (lawyer, doctor, professor) and unconventional (adventurer, inventor, writer), the high creative group mentioned a significantly greater proportion of unconventional occupations than did the high intelligence group (18 percent of the high intelligence group and 62 percent of the high creative group mentioned at least one unconventional occupation as a possibility).

The essence of creativity appears to lie in the ability to produce new forms, to conjoin elements that are customarily thought of as independent or dissimilar; not merely in the propensity for seeing the bizarre but rather in the aptitude for achieving new meanings having social value. Failure to distinguish between convergent and divergent talent in schools may have serious consequences for society.

Comment: Credit for the pioneering efforts in viewing creativity as the intellectual process of divergent thinking and in developing instruments for its measurement is due to Guilford's work. The above study represents one of the first systematic efforts to investigate the characteristics and achievement of youngsters who score high on tests of divergent thinking. Although these tests measure intellectual abilities other than those measured by the standard tests of general intelligence, and although pupils who score high on such tests of creativity tend in general to show high academic attainment, it is still uncertain what kinds of intellectual, academic, and artistic performance these tests actually predict. There is as yet little evidence to show that outstanding practitioners in areas of creative endeavor in the arts or sciences score consistently high on these instruments or that a high score on these instruments is a sufficient condition for outstanding creative attainment. However, the refinement of these instruments through continuous and varied experimental use should open new areas of talent identification and study. A future longitudinal study such as Terman's, using instruments which assess various aspects of intellectual ability, especially those dealing with divergent thinking, might discover a significant number of gifted individuals who would not be identified were the presently available intelligence tests used as the sole criterion for giftedness. For more details, see J. W. Getzels and P. W. Jackson, *Creativity and Intelligence.* New York: John Wiley and Sons, 1962.

Torrance, E. P. Explorations in Creative Thinking in the Early School Years: IQ and Creativity in School Achievement. *Research Memorandum,* University of Minnesota, Bureau of Educational Research, 1959. No. 11.

Purpose: To determine if creative thinking plays an important role in academic learning among elementary pupils in the fifth and sixth grades.

Subjects: 75 subjects representing all pupils in grades four to six (25 per grade) in the University of Minnesota Elementary School.

Procedures: Wechsler Intelligence Scale for Children, Gates Reading Test, and Iowa Achievement Battery scores were obtained from school records for the year 1958. An achievement index was derived by dividing achieved grade equivalent by the student's present grade. A battery of creative thinking tests (adapted from Guilford) was administered. These included uses of common objects, impossibilities, consequences, situations, problems, and improvements. Correlations between achievement quotients, creativity scores, and IQ were computed separately for each grade and for all grades taken together. Correlations were also computed between creativity and achievement with IQ partialed out.

Results: For the fourth grade all correlations between creativity and achievement were significant and ranged from .52 with Gates Reading to .67 with Iowa Reading. In that grade, the correlation of creativity with IQ was .63. For the fifth grade, all achievement tests but arithmetic were significantly correlated with creativity. The correlation of creativity with IQ in that grade was only .12, not significantly different from zero. For the sixth grade only Iowa Reading Skills tests correlated significantly with creativity. No significant correlation of IQ and creativity was found.

For all grades combined, correlations between creativity and all other measures were significantly different from zero, ranging from .26 with IQ to .53 with Iowa Reading Skills. Correlations between IQ and achievement scores were significant for all subjects in each grade; correlations were highest in fourth grade, lowest in sixth. For all grades combined the range was from .52 for English skills to .63 for work study skills.

With IQ held constant, correlation between achievement and creativity remained significant for Iowa Reading in fourth grade, for all subjects but arithmetic in fifth grade, and for Gates Reading and Iowa Reading in sixth grade. For all grades combined, significant correlations with creativity were obtained for all subjects. The relationship between creativity and achievement, holding intelligence constant, suggests that the creative thinking ability plays an important role in learning, especially in the fifth and sixth grades.

> Torrance, E. P. Educational Achievement of the Highly Intelligent and the Highly Creative: Eight Partial Replications of the Getzels-Jackson Study. *Research Memorandum,* University of Minnesota, Bureau of Educational Research, 1960, No. 18.

Purpose: To provide data on clues to determine when the Getzels-Jackson results are likely to hold.

Subjects: 25 pupils in each of grades three to six in a university laboratory school; 128 pupils in grades four and five of an elementary school in a small college town; 238 fifth and sixth graders in a metropolitan parochial school; 110 fifth and sixth graders in a metropolitan public school; 272 students in grades 9 to 12 of a laboratory high school; 70 teachers and counsellors in a summer guidance institute; and 85 students in a summer educational psychology class.

Procedures: Data were collected on intelligence and achievement using standardized tests. Creativity scores were obtained by a battery of tests of divergent thinking. In each of the eight studies the highly creative groups consisted of those ranking in the upper 20 percent of the sample studied on the measures of creative thinking but not in the upper 20 percent on the measure of intelligence or scholastic aptitude. The highly intelligent groups consisted of those ranking in the upper 20 percent on the measure of intelligence or scholastic aptitude but not in the upper 20 percent on the measures of creative thinking. Those ranking in the upper 20 percent on both measures were not considered. The two groups in each situation were then compared on achievement test scores.

Results: In all eight samples significant differences were found in the mean intelligence scores of the highly intelligent and highly creative groups. The amount of overlap between the groups identified as gifted by the two kinds of measures showed that, in most of the groups studied, about 70 percent of the most creative would have been eliminated if the selection of a "gifted" group were based solely on intelligence test scores (cut-off: 135). Two exceptions were an elementary school which used the California Test of Mental Maturity, and a high school which used the Lorge-Thorndike. In these two schools the highly creative group tended more often than in the others to coincide with the highly intelligent. Coefficients of correlation between creativity scores and intelligence scores computed within each grade of each school tended to be positive but low.

Comparisons of achievement of the highly intelligent and the highly creative were made. Only in the small town and parochial elementary schools, where the mean IQs of the highly creative groups fell considerably below 115, were the mean achievement scores of the highly creative significantly lower than those of the highly intelligent groups. In all other schools the differences in achievement were not statistically significant. There was a tendency for the highly creative groups to be superior to the highly intelligent groups in reading and language skills, but not in work-study and arithmetic skills.

Among the college students, the mean achievement scores of the highly intelligent and the highly creative showed no significant differences, but the means for the highly creative were consistently higher on Creative Applications, Evaluation, and Self-Initiated Learning; the highly

15

intelligent group had higher means on recognition and recall of subject matter.

Terman, L. M. Scientists and Nonscientists in a Group of 800 Gifted Men. *Psychological Monographs*, 1954, 68, No. 7 (Whole No. 378).

Purpose: To study retrospectively the characteristics of 788 male members of a gifted group to determine items which might differentiate those who became scientists from those who did not.

Subjects: 788 male members of the gifted group (selected on the basis of childhood IQs in the top one percent for their ages) whose careers were followed for 30 years.

Procedures: The educational and vocational records of all subjects were examined and the men were classified into eight groups for comparative study: Physical Science Researchers—PSR (N = 51); Engineers —E (N = 104); Medical-Biological Researchers—MB (N = 61); Physical or Biological Majors, Non-Researchers—PBS (N = 68); Social Scientists—SS (N = 149); Lawyers—L (N = 83); Humanities Majors—H (N = 95); and Non-College Graduates (N = 177). Five hundred items of information obtained for each subject between 1921 and 1951 were recorded on IBM cards and sorted on each variable for the seven groups (Non-College Graduates excluded from evaluation of group differences). The items included ratings and traits from childhood and family background, case history information from the 1928, 1940, and 1950-51 follow-ups and Strong Vocational Interest Test scores.

Results: The MB and PSR groups were the ones with the most favorable home backgrounds; the E and PBS groups, the least favorable backgrounds; the SS, L and H groups were in an intermediate position. Early ability or interest in science was far more common among children who later became physical scientists, engineers, or biologists than among those who entered nonscientific fields.

Strong Vocational Interest tests were scored for six kinds of scientists. The Physical Science Researcher group was either highest or second highest in frequency of superior scores for all six scientific occupations. The Engineer group was highest or second on three; the Medical-Biological Researchers, highest or second on two. The relative permanence of an individual's interest patterns after the date of high school graduation was confirmed.

There were some 18 variables that yielded significant group differences on matters related directly or indirectly to social adjustment. On

16

a majority of these, the nonscientists made a better showing than did the scientist group. Data obtained in the 1922 study on interest in play and games, average or parent-teacher composite ratings on social, moral, and volitional traits showed the L group highest on all four. The E's were lowest. Data from the 1940 follow-up showed similar results. The L and H groups participated most actively in high school activities. The self-ratings on interest in social life showed groups SS and MB almost equally high and the E group the lowest. From the biographical data completed for the 1950 follow-up, the science groups tended to rate significantly lower than the nonscience groups on matters of social adjustment and good personality. On matters of occupational success and life satisfactions, the PSR's scored highest on five of the eight variables. The SS group was lowest on four of the eight.

Compared to the college-going men, the non-college men came from less cultured homes, achieved less in school, tested lower in intelligence as adults, and were less successful vocationally.

In Review

Several smaller but highly informative studies of the personal and social characteristics of gifted youngsters have been done since Terman began his monumental efforts in the 1920s. (See, for example: W. Abraham. A Hundred Gifted Children. *Understanding the Child*, 1957, 26, 116-120; M. R. Sumption. *Three Hundred Gifted Children*. Yonkers-on-Hudson, New York: World Book Company, 1941; P. A. Witty. *A Study of One Hundred Gifted Children*. Lawrence: University of Kansas, 1930.) As a result of these works we know a great deal today about the characteristics of intellectually gifted children. As mentioned earlier, there are some limitations inherent in all these studies, but even with these restrictions our picture of the highly intelligent child is fairly complete. However, we have only the beginnings of knowledge of the characteristics of children or youth who would qualify as gifted, not on the basis of high IQ, but on the basis of special talent or outstanding performance on tests of divergent thinking. With some of the new concepts of giftedness, the research in the next decade should provide as much information on various other talents as we now have available on the attributes of the individual of high IQ.

IDENTIFICATION OF THE GIFTED

The findings from Terman's studies contribute support to the value of childhood intelligence for predicting superior adult attainment. School identification procedures now usually involve some assessment of general intellectual ability. The Getzels and Jackson and the Torrance studies reported above represent efforts to broaden the concept of giftedness and to include creativity and divergent thinking as additional cognitive variables to be sought in identifying the gifted. The Quincy Youth Development Project and the Gifted Child Project of the Portland Public Schools have defined talent broadly and sought to identify the upper 30 and the upper 10 percent, respectively, of the intellectually most able pupils and the most talented in art, music, creative dance, creative writing, creative dramatics, mechanical talent, and social leadership. The techniques and procedures employed by the Quincy Youth Development Project are described in P. H. Bowman, *et al.* Studying Children and Training Counselors in a Community Program. *Supplementary Education Monograph*, University of Chicago Press, 1953, No. 78. Those used in the Portland Project are described in Portland Public Schools. *The Gifted Child in Portland.* Portland, Oregon: The Public Schools, 1959. A discussion of some of the questions involved and cautions to be exercised in detecting gifted pupils is found in Ruth A. Martinson and L. M. Lessinger. Problems in the Identification of Intellectually Gifted Pupils. *Exceptional Children*, 1960, 26, 227-231, 241.

Pegnato, C. V. Identifying Mentally Gifted in Junior High Schools. *Pittsburgh Schools*, 1959, 33, 215-223.

Purpose: To determine which of the commonly used identification procedures in the junior high school would be best in selecting pupils for referral to the school psychologist for identification as mentally gifted (Stanford-Binet IQ score of 136 or higher).

Subjects: 1400 students in grades seven, eight, and nine of a Pittsburgh junior high school.

Procedures: The group was screened for giftedness, using a variety of methods including teacher nomination, group intelligence tests, group achievement tests, honor roll listings, tests of mathematical ability, nominations of students with art or music talent, and membership on student council. The lists obtained from all the methods were combined and analyzed, and 781 students (394 boys and 387 girls) were referred for individual intelligence examinations. Of those referred, Stanford-Binet IQs had already been obtained for 368 children in tests administered in the elementary schools, and 68 had IQs of 136 or above. Of 413 other students who were given individual tests, an additional 23 stu-

dents were identified as having IQs of 136 or above. Thus a total of 91 students (55 boys and 36 girls) was identified as intellectually gifted.

The *effectiveness* (defined by the percentage of gifted children correctly identified) and the *efficiency* (defined by the ratio between the total number of children referred by a screening device for individual examination and the number of gifted children identified) were then determined for each screening method.

Results: Of the 450 students referred on the basis of scores above 115 on group intelligence tests, 84 were identified as mentally gifted, representing 92 percent of all the intellectually gifted in the school. When a cut-off of 130 IQ group intelligence tests was used, only 21.9 percent of the gifted were located; at IQ 125, 43.9 percent were located; at IQ 120, 71.4 percent were located, and at 115, 92.3 percent were located. The three other major screening methods, teacher selection, group achievement, and honor-roll, contributed only five other names (after 190 individual Stanford-Binet examinations). Screening on special aptitudes failed to locate any of the gifted not previously screened.

The achievement test results contributed the second largest number of children (50) properly selected as mentally gifted. Although three-fourths of the 91 gifted children were on the honor roll, 304 other children were also on the honor roll. Mathematical aptitude as a screening procedure had high relative efficiency, but almost half of the mentally gifted were not located by that list, and at least twice as many nongifted were included. A screening procedure based on recognition by peers for political and social leaders had little promise in locating mentally gifted children. Teachers did not locate gifted children effectively or efficiently enough to place much reliance on them for screening. Although group intelligence tests are the most effective (if IQ 115-120 is used as a cut-off point) and the most efficient method of identification, they cannot be relied upon to discriminate among the brighter students because of low ceilings. Besides, some pupils scoring above IQ 130 on such tests fail to reach this score on the Stanford-Binet. The second best procedure was group achievement test results followed by honor roll lists and then teacher selection. To find all of the gifted at a school, a combination of procedures should be utilized. Children who do not score high on group intelligence tests but who rate high according to teacher judgment and who show objective evidence of superior achievement should be referred for individual testing.

Comment: The above study defined giftedness as the attainment of a Stanford-Binet IQ score of 136 or higher. If we assume that this is a valid

19

definition of giftedness, then the study is a valuable analysis of the extent to which techniques and procedures other than the individual Stanford-Binet contribute to identifying youngsters who meet this criterion. There is, of course, nothing in the study or in the literature to defend this particular cut-off point as the minimal criterion for giftedness. The study is valuable in pointing out the limitations of group intelligence tests, school grades, or teacher selection for locating those who would qualify as gifted on the Stanford-Binet and especially for discriminating among the brightest students. However, reliance on a very narrow definition of giftedness restricts the usefulness of the findings for practical school identification programs.

Justman, J. Selecting Pupils for Placement in Special Progress Classes in Junior High School. *High Points.* 1956, 38. No. 2, 58-62.

Purpose: To describe the varying results obtained when three different commonly used intelligence tests serve as the basis for recommending placement in a special progress class.

Subjects: 560 students in 25 sixth-grade classes in three New York City elementary schools.

Procedures: The Pintner Intermediate Intelligence Test was administered to the subjects in October 1955; the Henmon-Nelson Test of Mental Ability a month later; and the Otis Quick-Scoring Test, Beta Form, six months later. The results from the Metropolitan Intermediate, administered city-wide, were also available.

Results: Admission to special progress classes is based on an average IQ of 130 or above on two group intelligence tests and a reading achievement of 8.5 or better. The number and percentage of pupils meeting the IQ standard for admission using the varying results were as follows:

	Number	Percent
130 IQ on all three tests	21	3.8
130 IQ on Pintner alone	35	6.3
130 IQ on Otis alone	44	7.5
130 IQ on Henmon-Nelson alone	76	13.6
130 IQ average of Pintner and Otis	33	5.9
130 IQ average of Pintner and Henmon-Nelson	37	6.6
130 IQ average of Otis and Henmon-Nelson	51	9.1

Using the results of the Metropolitan Intermediate Test as an additional criterion for selection did not change this pattern. All of the pupils who met the requirement of an average IQ of 130 on two group tests also succeeded in obtaining a reading grade of 8.5 or better, and qualified for admission in this respect as well.

Among the factors contributing to the wide variation in test results are: differences in the abilities tapped by the several tests, differences in standardization groups used in arriving at the norms for the several tests, and differences in the degree to which the several tests are affected by the reading ability of the pupils to whom they are administerd.

Comment: Since schools across the country rely on various group intelligence tests as a measure of intellectual ability, it is important to recognize, as this study points out, that the several commonly-used tests do not all measure the same things for the same youngsters in the same way. These differences are present even though most of these tests report comparably high reliabilities and validities. Use of a single group intelligence test for categorizing youngsters as intellectually gifted is a highly suspect procedure, especially as the proportion of youngsters thus identified would vary considerably depending upon the particular test used.

Davis, F. B., Lesser, G. S., French, Elizabeth G., *et al.* Identification and Classroom Behavior of Gifted Elementary School Children. The Gifted Student. *Coöperative Research Monographs,* U. S. Government Printing Office, 1960, No. 2, 19-32.

Purpose: To answer the following questions: (a) Are there intellectual abilities independent of, and/or loosely related to verbal reasoning ability in which some children as young as 4-6 to 5-6 years might prove to be outstanding regardless of their verbal reasoning ability? (b) Can young children who are outstanding in such abilities be identified by means of a suitable test? (c) What differences can be observed in the classroom behavior of first grade children selected as outstanding in at least one of several loosely related intellectual abilities?

Subjects: 263 children who applied in spring 1958 for admission to the first grade of the Hunter College Elementary School, a school for gifted children. From this population, 57 were selected for purposes of validating two forms of the identification instrument. Members of the experimental and control groups (26 and 27, respectively) were later selected from the 263 applicants.

Procedures: Information from a series of preliminary Science-Reasoning *t*ests was used to construct two parallel forms of the Hunter Aptitude Scales for Gifted Children. The five scales covered the following areas: Space, Number, Reasoning, Science, Vocabulary. The scales were tested for reliability and intercorrelations were computed.

To organize the experimental class, those who scored in the top seven on one of the five scales of the preliminary tests were included if they met the social and emotional maturity requirements of the school's admission policy and if they had not taken the Stanford-Binet prior to the Hunter Tests. The control class was composed of children who met the standard requirements for admission to the Hunter College Elementary School. (Same as above and 130+ on the Stanford-Binet.) In the fall of 1958 both the experimental and control classes were tested with the SRA Primary Mental Abilities Test (5 to 7 years) and the Hunter Preliminary Tests of Reasoning and Science. The Stanford-Binet was administered to the experimental group.

To compare the effects of instruction in a special area on the children gifted in that area with the effects on children gifted in other areas, special instruction related to each of the five mental abilities was provided all pupils in the experimental class. Each child received four times as many training sessions in his own area of giftedness as in the other four areas. At the end of first grade both groups were tested on five specially designed achievement tests, one in each area of ability. Observations (two 45-minute periods per week) were coded and analyzed; student participation in the regular class was rated. The PMA (7 to 11 years) was administered to both classes. Two forms of the Hunter Aptitude Scales for Gifted Children were administered.

Results: The mean IQ of the control group (152.9) exceeded the mean IQ of the experimental group (131.7) by 21.9 points. However, in each of the five areas tested, the special aptitude group in the experimental class exceeded the scores of the higher IQ control group. When the means of the two total classes were compared in each of the five special areas, the differences consistently favored the experimental class, but only in science was the difference statistically significant. As a result of the special instruction, four of the five aptitude groups (all but science) gained significantly more in their special area than did the rest of the experimental class on the PMA tests. Special instruction in science was more effective for those gifted in the verbal area than for those gifted in science or number. On the Hunter Scales the gifted groups did significantly better than the experimental class as a whole only in vocabulary and number.

Comments and responses relative to each of the five areas as coded by observers were more often and more consistently given by those gifted in each area, both during regular class time and during the special instruction sessions. On the basis of the criteria used, the preliminary tests were moderately successful in differentiating among young children of diverse aptitudes.

Comment: In view of the generally accepted belief that there is little differentiation of intellectual abilities in young children, these findings are of particular interest since they demonstrate that even before first grade, children who are outstanding in one or two but not necessarily all such special abilities as verbal ability, numerical facility, spatial orientation, and logical reasoning can be reliably identified. However, the conclusion that children with outstanding ability in one area will benefit more from special instruction in that area than will pupils whose intellectual strengths are in other abilities is not adequately supported by the data. Even the few significant differences which are reported are open to question, since the youngsters with particular strengths in an area received four times as much direct instruction in that area as did the other groups. It must be kept in mind that this is a pilot study and that the number of subjects involved in each of the subcategories was too small for any conclusive findings.

ACHIEVEMENT, MOTIVATION, AND UNDERACHIEVEMENT

The fact that intellect and achievement are far from perfectly correlated caused Terman to comment: "To identify the internal and external factors that help or hinder the fruition of exceptional talent, and to measure the extent of their influences, are surely among the major problems of our time." Underachievement in school and college is the most obvious manifestation of the gap between ability and attainment. To date, there have been few experimental studies which attempt to assess the effectiveness of special educational or psychological provisions for underachievers, nor have the childhood antecedents of secondary school underachievement been fully explored. Research into the causes of underachievement and the means by which the individual can be motivated to realize his potential may help stem the loss of talent.

Shaw, M. C., and McCuen, J. T. The Onset of Academic Underachievement in Bright Children. *Journal of Educational Psychology,* 1960, 51, 103-109.

Purpose: To determine the specific grade level at which academic underachievement can be said to begin and at which the subsequent pattern of achievement may be determined.

Subjects: 144 subjects in grades 11 and 12 were selected. Students in the upper 25 percent (over 110 IQ) of the school population with regard to ability were classified as achievers or underachievers on the basis of cumulative grade-point averages in grades 9 to 11. A student whose IQ placed him in the upper 25 percent and whose grade-point average (GPA) fell below the mean of the class was classified as an "underachiever." A student whose IQ was above 110 and who earned a GPA above the average of his class was classified as an "achiever." Those who fell exactly at the class average (2.40 on a 4-point scale) were not included in the study. Only students who had lived in the same school district for their entire school career were included in the study. The final selection of subjects resulted in four groups: 36 male achievers, 36 male underachievers, 45 female achievers, and 17 female underachievers.

Procedures: Following the selection, the academic record for each student from grades 1 to 11 was studied and grade-point averages at each grade were computed.

Results: Comparison of the male underachievers and achievers showed a significant difference from the third grade on, a difference which increased in significance at each grade level up to grade 10, where it decreased somewhat, but remained significant. A difference in GPA in favor of the achiever group actually existed at grade one and became larger at grade two but it was not significant below grade three.

Up to and including grade five, the female underachievers actually exceeded the achievers in GPA, although not at a significant level. At grade six female achievers obtained a higher mean GPA for the first time, and from that point until grade 10 this difference increased every year although it did not reach significance until grade nine. At this point through grade 11 the difference was significant.

The male underachiever appeared predisposed to underachieve academically upon entry into school; his problem became steadily more serious until grade 10 at which time it became only slightly less serious, due primarily to a drop in GPA on the part of the achiever group. The timing of the drop in GPA (sixth grade) in the female underachiever coincided with the beginning of puberty. It was hypothesized that females do not display their self-directing tendencies to the extent that males do until they approach adolescence. Underachievement in these subjects was not a temporary phenomenon but was rather chronic in nature.

Comment: The findings on early onset of underachievement reported in this study contradict findings from Terman's work and from other studies reported in this chapter (Goldberg, *et al.*). The general consensus seemed to have been that overt underachievement does not become apparent until the end of the junior high school years, whereas this study finds many of the pupils achieving far less than expected in the elementary years. It may be that the difference between these findings and those reported in other studies is due to differences in the population samples. Terman dealt with students of IQ of 140 and above; the Goldberg work dealt with students with IQs of 125 and above. It may be that in a population such as that of Shaw and McCuen, where pupils with IQs as low as 110 are included, underachievement is observable earlier. It is possible that for the more highly gifted youngsters the demands of the elementary school are not sufficiently taxing to make for overt underachievement.

Conklin, Agnes M. *Failures of Highly Intelligent Pupils: A Study of their Behavior by Means of the Control Group.* New York: Bureau of Publications, Teachers College, Columbia University, 1940.

Purpose: To study the behavior of highly intelligent students who fail in high school.

Subjects: Two groups selected from 128 high school students with IQs of 130 or higher. One group consisted of 32 boys and 13 girls who were failing in one or more major school subjects, and the other of 27 boys and 15 girls of equal intelligence who had not experienced school failure. The IQ range was from 130 to 163 in each group. The mean of the unadjusted or experimental group was 136.07; the mean for the adjusted or control group was 135.8.

Procedures: Case studies were made of each of the subjects. Physical, psychological, and psychiatric examinations were completed and data gathered on home and family background.

Results: There were no significant differences between the groups in terms of age at school entrance, number of grades skipped or repeated, preference among school levels, attitude toward schooling, and choice of high school.

The control group participated significantly more often in high school clubs. Term after term, the unadjusted group maintained average teacher grades of 69 percent; the adjusted of 81 percent. In the year and one-half in which the data were being gathered for this study, 76 percent of the unadjusted group and only five percent of the adjusted group were referred to the Student Welfare Committee as "problems."

The groups were found to be alike on many aspects of home and family backgrounds. The parents of almost 70 percent of both groups were immigrants, having resided in America for about the same length of time. The children of both groups were native-born, urban children, 80 percent of whom had been brought up in New York City. Foreign languages were spoken in homes of both groups to the same extent. There were no differences on the scales which rated material or cultural possessions. The size of family income was the same for both groups. The groups were identical in their propensity to choose similar places for recreational activities. Both groups engaged in out-of-school activities. The unadjusted group more often devoted its time to paid work; the adjusted group to the study of Hebrew.

The groups were reliably different in number of physical disabilities, with the adjusted group exceeding the unadjusted group in number and severity of handicaps. The only significant difference between the groups in developmental history was that the members of the unadjusted group had had more unwholesome relationships with their companions and more unsatisfactory relations with their parents. The use of cruel and ineffectual punishment by parents, and unfortunate attitudes toward discipline by the child, were found significantly more often for the unadjusted group. These unfortunate circumstances probably contributed to their poor schoolwork. Psychiatrists working without foreknowledge of how the individuals were classified, after comparatively brief and incomplete examinations, were still able to distinguish the two groups unmistakably.

In general, there was considerable overlapping in the data for the two groups. Three clinicians expressed the judgment that only 35 to 40 percent of the psychiatric items and less than 20 percent of the physical and psychological findings could be dealt with successfully by the schools. The group felt that schools as now organized could not eliminate most of the maladjustments.

Pierce, J. V. and Bowman, P. H. Motivation Patterns of Superior High School Students. The Gifted Student. *Coöperative Research Monograph,* U.S. Government Printing Office, 1960, No. 2, 33-66.

Purpose: To differentiate between able high-achieving and able low-achieving high school students on a number of nonintellectual variables.

Subjects: 229 subjects (109 twelfth-grade students and 120 tenth-grade students) in the top 30 percent in intellectual ability who were in the Quincy Public Schools in 1957-58. Subjects were included in the study on the basis of scores on any three of seven group intelligence tests. Girls and boys were ranked separately on ability at each grade level.

Procedures: To obtain a student's achievement-ability rank, a weight value was assigned to each course of study and to each letter-grade earned by the students. The grade weights were multiplied by the course weights and the students were then ranked separately by grade-level and sex. The grade-course ranks were multiplied by two and the ability rank then subtracted to provide an achievement rank. Students whose achievement rank placed them below the median for their total group were identified as low achievers; those above, as high achievers. Data were collected on achievement motivation, achievement values, socio-economic status, adult identification, parent attitudes toward child rearing, psychological inventory, sociometrics, and teacher rating.

Results: On McClelland's n-Achievement, the high-achieving boys at tenth- and twelfth-grade levels scored higher than the low-achieving boys. However, among the girls the low achievers both in tenth and twelfth grades scored higher than the high achievers. When all of the high-achieving boys were compared with all the low-achieving boys on the involvement categories—the ability to become self-engaged in achievement tests—the high-achievers scored significantly higher.

The high-achieving tenth grade boys scored significantly higher than did the low-achieving tenth grade boys on Strodtbeck's Value Scale (V Scale). However, at the twelfth grade the two groups did not differ significantly from each other, although the scores of the low-achieving boys tended to be somewhat higher. At both the tenth and twelfth grade the high-achieving girls scored higher than did the low-achieving girls.

Strength of educational motivation was assessed on such factors as peer identification, reading index, educational goals, grades desired, monetary goals, school subjects liked, and identification with adults important to the subject. Student interview measures differentiated in all cases, with high-achieving students scoring higher. All the high-achieving boys and the high-achieving tenth grade girls were found to be better adjusted than the low-achieving students. The high-achieving twelfth grade girls appeared less well adjusted than the low-achievers. High-achieving students scored higher on leadership skills but not on friendship. Low-achieving students in the tenth grade scored significantly higher on aggression and maladjustment. At the twelfth grade level, the boys in the low-achieving category were seen as more aggressive by their peers. High achievers reported that they had been more active in school-related activities at the junior high level. They valued schoolwork and imagination more highly than did the low achievers. High achievers described the concepts school, self, student, and competition as significantly more positive than did the low achievers.

High achievers named fathers as having been important influences in their lives significantly more often than did their low-achieving peers. They were more active than the low achievers in religious activity.

The high achievers more often came from small families where they were either the first born or only child, and more of their parents had attended college; their mothers more often had college aspirations for them and more often reported that their children engaged in educationally related hobbies.

When comparisons were made on the authoritarian-control factor, the mothers of high-achieving girls were rated significantly higher than the mothers of low-achieving girls. But the mothers of the low-achieving boys were rated significantly higher than the mothers of the high boys (whose mothers were significantly higher on the democratic attitudes factor).

Comment: This study, as compared to some of the others, presents an important example of differences in findings that occur due to differences in populations sampled, even when the names given to the populations are the same. As in the Shaw and McCuen study, it is important to keep in mind the very large proportion of pupils whom this study identified as "superior." Whereas most other studies have dealt with the top one to 10 percent of the population and have investigated some of the causes and characteristics of underachievement in high ability groups, the Pierce and Bowman study is concerned with the upper third of the total high school population. Just as one must guard against generalizing about the characteristics of the top 20 or 30 percent of the population from findings such as Terman's, which investigated only the top one percent, so one must be careful not to particularize from this study, which dealt with the top third of the population, to the correlates of underachievement for those whose intelligence places them in the top one to 10 percent.

Nason, L. J. Academic Achievement of Gifted High School Students: Patterns of Circumstances Related to Educational Achievement of High School Pupils of Superior Ability. *Educational Monographs*, University of Southern California Press, 1958. No. 17.

Purpose: To study the circumstances and conditions which influence some high school pupils of superior ability to achieve a high level of academic attainment while others of equal ability fail to realize proportionate accomplishment.

Subjects: The group consisted of 237 superior students (125 girls and 112 boys; 106 tenth graders, 72 eleventh graders, and 59 twelfth graders) selected from three high schools on the basis of an IQ of 125 or above, a Cooperative Reading Test score of 66 or above, and a complete record of grade-point average (GPA). The mean IQ of the group was 126.86. Academic achievement was defined in terms of grade-point averages in all subjects other than physical education. Students with a GPA of 3.00 or less were labelled "low achievers"; those with GPA of 3.75 or higher were considered "high achievers." Twenty-two pairs of boys and 22 pairs of girls matched on IQ but discrepant on school GPA were selected for further study.

Procedures: Data were collected from the following sources: cumulative records, Confidential Data Sheets, personality tests, teacher ratings, and pupil's self-evaluation on a check sheet of information about special abilities, hobbies, likes and dislikes, attitudes toward school and schoolwork, work, future educational and vocational plans, parental attitudes and sources of inspiration to succeed.

Results: Relationship between IQ and GPA for the 237 students was found to be 0.344 for girls, 0.391 for boys. The group enjoyed all or most things about school and schoolwork and felt that the courses they were taking were good preparation for their futures. Ninety-four percent of the boys and 90 percent of the girls planned to go to college.

Although a greater proportion of the high-achieving boys than low-achievers indicated parental expectation of their going to college, and the high-achieving girls scored higher than low-achieving girls on school and community relations and social adjustment, no single circumstance or trait was found which would distinguish the individual pupils as to membership in the high- or low-achievement group.

However, a pattern of circumstances was found which seemed to be closely related to high-level achievement of superior pupils. The pattern was made up of six circumstances. The pupil associated with the complete pattern of circumstances could be described as one who (a) is satisfactorily adjusted personally and socially, (b) includes college in his plans for the future, (c) has a fairly specific vocational choice or plan, (d) indicates that his parents expect him to go to college, (e) feels no parental disagreement with his vocational plans, and (f) senses a source of inspiration or encouragement to succeed. Such a pupil was in all cases a high achiever.

The achievement level of superior pupils was not determined by their relative intelligence within the group. Pupils of both relatively high and low IQs were found in each level of achievement. The high-achieving pupils tended to achieve more satisfactory status with their peers than the low achievers. However, peer acceptance did not consistently predict the achievement level of an individual student. Academic and vocational planning appeared to influence the achievement of superior pupils at all grade levels of the senior high school. Low achievement seemed to be associated with a lack of one or more of the positive circumstances described above rather than with the presence of negative influences. In some cases high-achieving pupils faced negative influences as strong as those associated with low-achieving pupils.

Comment: Perhaps the most important contribution of this study lies in its attempt to find correlates of underachievement through a pattern of circumstances rather than through a series of independently observed factors. Although the pattern of circumstances may vary from one locality to another and from one group of underachievers to another, methodologically, the attempt to identify a series of interrelated concurrent circumstances may prove to be a sound approach to studying underachievement.

Goldberg, Miriam L., *et al.* A Three Year Experimental Program at DeWitt Clinton High School to Help Underachievers. *High Points*, 1959, 41, No. 1, 5-35.

Purpose: To determine social and personal factors associated with underachievement and to experiment with school procedures which would provide special attention to the problems of underachievers.

Subjects: Students who entered the tenth grade of DeWitt Clinton High School in New York City in 1956-1957. One hundred two entering tenth-grade boys with IQs of 120 or higher and ninth-grade junior high school grade averages below 80 were tested with the California Test of Mental Maturity. Seventy students were identified as underachievers (U). In addition, a group of high-ability high achievers (H) was identified. These students had IQs comparable to those of the underachievers, but their ninth-grade averages were above 85 percent. No special provisions were made for this group beyond those normally made by the school for able students.

Procedures: The underachievers were arranged into 35 pairs, matched on IQ and ninth-grade average. One student from each pair was assigned to the special class and the other became part of the control group. The controls (unidentified to any of the teachers) were randomly distributed throughout the remaining homeroom sections.

In the spring of 1956, each of the U's and the H's took the Iowa Test of Educational Development. Early in the school year a self-attitudes inventory, an attitude towards school inventory, an academic aspiration level questionnaire, and the Kuder Preference Record were administered to all the groups of students, and interviews were conducted.

The special class was assigned to a specially selected teacher as section officer as well as social studies teacher. The members of this class were informed that they were part of a group of high-ability students who needed to raise the level of their school performance.

Results: At the end of the first year the experimental group, though slow in improving, exceeded the control in almost all subject areas. The following year they remained with their initial teacher for homeroom, but were placed for social studies with a highly qualified but rather rigid teacher who was inflexible in her demands for high standards both in work and in behavior. At the end of one semester the group fell well below the controls in all areas, especially in social studies. They became highly supportive of one another in their negative behavior and tested the limits to such an extent that little teaching could go on. Reassignment of the group to an accepting, flexible male teacher for the next year did little to raise the academic level of the group. By graduation, the majority were not accepted by the colleges of their choice; many had dropped out of the academic stream and made no educational plans beyond high school; a few dropped out before graduation. These patterns were no different for the control group. In each, about 10 percent of the students improved greatly and achieved honor school status. The experimental effects, though apparently significant after one year, showed no carry-over into the upper grades.

In the second year, 35 students with IQs above 120 who were failures or near-failures in first-year algebra were placed in a special geometry class with a "master" teacher. Here, too, a control group was identified. It was hypothesized that the achievement of success in a major area of failure would result in improved performance in all academic areas. Although about half of the special group, as compared to about one-fourth of the control group, achieved high scores on an objective geometry test after one semester, they did not show a comparable improvement in other subjects. On the contrary, those who were most outstanding in the math class received lower grades in the other subjects than they had before. When, in the second semester, programming problems necessitated a change of teachers, the special group, at the end of the year, showed no differences from the controls in teacher grades or in geometry Regents marks.

Evaluation of the effects of the two approaches revealed that the greatest need of these boys was to be able to identify with a teacher and to have ample opportunity for help with both personal and academic problems. In view of these findings, in 1958-59 two groups of underachievers were identified (25 per group) and were programmed for a consecutive daily homeroom and study hour to be continued for the three years of high school. This arrangement allowed time for individual conferences, help with work-study skills, group discussions of common problems, and individual help in specific subject areas. Evaluation of the grades of students in the special classes at the end of one year showed no differences from the grades of the control group.

Twenty-one improvers from the first study were compared with an equal number of nonimprovers. The two groups differed significantly with respect to composite and correctness of writing scores on the Iowa Test of Educational Development (the improvers were higher) and on the self-attitudes inventory (nonimprovers showed a greater discrepancy between their perception of abilities and their wished-for abilities status). The large discrepancy suggests that nonimprovers see their ability to perform in various areas as too far from what they would like it to be to warrant making an effort to improve. There were differences in other areas as well, but these did not reach statistical significance. For example, the incidence of divorces was greater among the parents of the nonimprovers; fewer nonimprovers had reached a decision on vocational goals, and where they did state a preference it was less often above the level of their father's present occupation; fewer were only or oldest children; fewer had older siblings in college who could act as achievement models for them.

Comment: This study represents one of the few attempts reported in the literature to modify the academic behavior of the underachiever through school efforts. The negative results reported here as well as those of other researchers who attempted to provide special counselling or guidance services to such groups suggest that, as yet, there is little concrete help that research can give schools in planning special provisions for the underachiever. (See, for example, M. M. Ohlsen and F. C. Proff. The Extent to Which Group Counselling Improves the Academic and Personal Adjustment of Underachieving Gifted Adolescents. College of Education, University of Illinois [mimeographed report]; and

Talent Preservation Project: Interim Report. Columbia University School of Engineering, 1959 [mimeographed report].)

It well may be that such efforts as those described in this study as well as other attempts at guidance and therapy are effective in redirecting the self-concepts and attitudes of the underachiever, but that the period in which these services are provided is too short to allow for such changes to be reflected in improved grades. What is needed in this area is a longitudinal study following up those students who received various kinds of special assistance to see whether and which kinds of assistance resulted in later improvement in academic behavior and attitudes.

Tannenbaum, A. J. *Adolescents' Attitudes Toward Academic Brilliance.* New York: Bureau of Publications, Teachers College, Columbia University, 1962.

Purpose: To ascertain whether reactional differences of adolescents toward academic brilliance are stimulated by ability characteristics or other personal attributes.

Subjects: 615 eleventh graders in a New York City comprehensive high school.

Procedure: Subjects were asked to respond to written descriptions of stereotyped students. Three dichotomized characteristics (brilliant-average, studious-nonstudious, and athletic-nonathletic) appeared in eight possible combinations in sentences describing the stimulus characters. The subjects then indicated for each of 54 traits whether or not it typified each of the eight stimulus characters.

Results: The students ranked the characters in the following order of desirability:

Brilliant-Nonstudious Athlete
Average-Nonstudious Athlete
Average-Studious Athlete
Brilliant-Studious Athlete
Brilliant-Nonstudious Nonathlete
Average-Nonstudious Nonathlete
Average-Studious Nonathlete
Brilliant-Studious Nonathlete.

Of the four possible comparisons between students described as average and those described as brilliant who were alike on studiousness and sportsmindedness, the only significant difference was between the Average and the Brilliant Nonstudious Athlete, favoring the Average character. The mean ratings for the four Average characters did not differ from those for the four Brilliant characters. Both the Brilliant-Athletes and the Brilliant-Nonathletes were rated significantly higher when they were described as nonstudious than when they were described as studious. In every case the Athletes rated significantly higher than the Nonathletes. There was no significant linear relationship between the intelligence and parental education status of the respondents and their ratings of the various characters.

Insofar as verbal stereotypes reflect face-to-face relations, these results suggest that academic brilliance per se, as compared to average ability, is not a stigma among adolescents, but when combined with relatively unacceptable attributes such as studiousness or nonathleticism, it can penalize its possessor. The Nonstudious Athlete may demonstrate outstanding brainpower without fearing social derogation by peers. However, a display of brilliance by one who is studious and indifferent to sports constitutes a definite status risk.

Educators should consider the possible effects of these adolescent values upon the gifted youth's desire to excel. The brilliant student may be an exceptionally prominent target for teenage pressures to conform to certain behaviors and values. If so, there is danger of his deliberately masking his talent in order to relieve these pressures.

Comment: The above study highlights the importance of considering the attitudes of adolescents towards outstanding academic or creative achievers in present school efforts to raise scholastic standards and to foster the "pursuit of excellence." These findings are supported by Coleman's research (J. S. Coleman. *The Adolescent Society.* Glencoe, Illinois: Free Press, 1961) which found that high academic attainment is far from first in determining the adolescent's status in the peer culture of the American high school. The Coleman research found this situation to be true even in college-oriented suburban school situations. Wilson found that the lower-class school was more detrimental to outstanding achievement and college aspirations among intellectually talented students than the middle-class school, even when the students came from professional and middle-class family backgrounds. (See A. B. Wilson, Residential Segregation of Social Classes and Aspirations of High School Boys. *American Sociological Review,* 1959, 24, 836-845.) To what extent the negative attitudes toward academic excellence will be modified by societal demands for more people in professional and academic pursuits is not yet clear.

In Review

Despite the extensive literature in the area of motivation of gifted students—some bibliographies include as many as several hundred titles—variance in achievement among intellectually gifted students is far from fully understood. It can be stated as a fact that many students of high IQ and/or aptitude as measured by standardized tests do poorly in school. Sometimes this poor performance is apparent as early as the elementary school. In most instances, however, it becomes marked during the secondary school years (especially for the high IQ groups). To what extent this phenomenon is a result of the limited predictive validity of existing aptitude and intelligence measures for actual academic performance, to what extent it can be explained in terms of social factors which influence the attitudes of some gifted students, or to what extent individual and personality factors are at the root of the problem is as yet far from clear. Certainly the few reported efforts in assisting gifted underachievers through either school programs, counselling, or group therapy have not found these methods effective in raising academic performance.

EDUCATIONAL PROGRAMS

Over the years, schools have used many different plans and program modifications for educating the gifted. Research has focused on studying the effects of specific administrative arrangements such as various kinds of special grouping or acceleration. From these studies, the advantages and disadvantages of such arrangements have emerged, but no single adaptation has yet provided a conclusive method of providing for all kinds and degrees of giftedness. The educational process by which talent potential is best transformed to talented performance still presents problems for research.

> Gallagher, J. J., and Crowder, Thora. The Adjustment of Gifted Children in the Regular Classroom. *Exceptional Children*, 1957, 23, 306-319, 353-363, 396-398.

Purpose: To discover the extent to which highly intelligent children have difficulty adjusting to a regular classroom situation academically, intellectually, socially, and emotionally.

Subjects: 35 students (20 boys and 15 girls) in grades two through five in a midwestern city, with a highly favorable social, economic, and educational level. About half of the fathers were college professors or con-

35

nected in some academic capacity with a university; 11 percent were skilled or semi-skilled workers; 34 percent had professional backgrounds or were in business. Over half of the mothers finished college and over three-fourths had attended college. There were no histories of divorce in any of the subjects' families. The subjects had Stanford-Binet IQs of 150 or better.

Procedures: Intelligence and achievement tests were administered and data gathered on Rorschach tests, teacher ratings, and sociometrics. Total data on each child were evaluated and areas identified where the child was not developing to the limit of his potential.

Results: The children tended to score higher on WISC verbal than on performance subtests. The median for the verbal was 143; performance, 138; and full scale, 144. The median reading, social studies, and science scores on the Stanford Achievement tests and Intermediate and Advanced Battery for the 23 children in the intermediate grades were more than four grades above placement. Only in one or two subjects were scores as low as grade level; the median arithmetic computation score was only .7 grade units above grade placement. Thirty-three of 34 children obtained higher arithmetic reasoning than arithmetic computational scores. The performance of the 12 children in grade two and lower three who took the elementary battery showed less deviation between achievement and grade placement. The median gain over grade level was between one and two grade units for each subject.

On the sociometrics, over half of the gifted group ranked in the top quartile in social popularity. Over 80 percent of the group was above the median for their class in the number of choices received, and only two pupils fell in the bottom quartile. On the Rorschach, as rated by two judges (with high interjudge reliability), five cases were ranked as having marked disturbance, while 30 of the cases were rated as producing a predominantly healthy record. The same results held for the characteristics of anxiety and hostility.

In contrast to the other findings, the judges were not positively impressed with the creative aspects of the records. Only seven cases were rated as showing high creativity, 11 cases yielded some creative responses, and 17 revealed no originality or creativity in their records. Corroborating these data, the teachers rated only nine cases as spontaneously developing new ideas and 11 as not having creative work as a strong point. Ten of the children were rated as being the leaders and another 18 placed as potential leaders although they might have been personally disinclined to leadership. Seven seldom or rarely attempted leadership roles.

Of the 16 primary children, seven were rated as having "no outstanding problems"; while only three of the 19 intermediate-grade children were so classified. Nine of the 19 in the intermediate group were identified as showing intellectual inflexibility as compared to one of the 16 in the younger group. Seven children in each of the groups were rated as having problems of motivation.

Social adjustment turned out to be less of a problem than other areas of adjustment. Even where social adjustment problems were present, these did not seem to relate to intellectual status. It seemed possible that some children were deliberately restricting their intellectual activity in order to insure their social status.

Goldberg, Miriam L., Justman, J., Passow, A. H., and Hage, J. *The Effects of Ability Grouping: A Comparative Study of Broad, Medium, and Narrow-Range Classes in the Elementary School.* Horace Mann-Lincoln Institute Interim Report. New York: Teachers College, Columbia University, 1961.

Purpose: To explore the differences in achievement and learning patterns, social and personal relations, motivational structure, and attitudes toward self and school of intermediate-grade children when grouped in classes with various ranges of intellectual ability. To test the hypothesis: Neither the range of abilities in any given classroom, nor the relative position of a particular ability level within the range, nor the presence or absence of gifted pupils will affect the attainments of elementary school pupils. Data on attainment of social and personal development as well as teacher ratings are presently being analyzed. These will be reported later.

Subjects: 3000 fifth-grade pupils in 45 elementary schools were classified according to five IQ levels varying from low-average to gifted; 86 classes were organized on the basis of 15 ability-grouping patterns, some of which were narrow (one or two ability levels), some medium (three ability levels), and others broad-range (four or five ability levels).

Procedures: The classes remained intact for two years. The pupils were tested at the beginning of the fifth and at the end of the sixth grade. Measurements were taken of academic achievement, interests, self-appraisal, attitudes toward school, friendship, and leadership status, attitudes toward more and less endowed peers, and creative writing. In addition, each pupil was rated by both his fifth and sixth grade teachers on a variety of traits. No attempt was made to influence or modify instruction in any way; the study involved administrative groupings only.

37

Results: Achievement tests provided measures in nine areas, including reading, language, arithmetic, social studies, science, and work-study skills. On all but the science, social studies, and arithmetic computation tests, the increments in achievement were seriously limited for the higher ability students by the test ceilings. For all five ability levels taken together, achievement increments in social studies, reading, vocabulary, and the three areas of arithmetic were significantly greater in the broad-range than in the medium- and narrow-range classes. However, the differences were generally small and for no one group were they significant in more than two or three of the subjects tested. In general, if the data for the five ability levels are considered as a whole, the indications are that the broad-range patterns (four or five ability levels) show the largest mean increments in achievement, followed by the narrow-range patterns (one or two ability levels). The smallest increments were observed in the medium-range (three ability levels) groups.

A class-by-class analysis of the relationships among achievement increments in various subjects indicated that for any class (for each ability level), high achievement in one area was not necessarily accompanied by comparably high achievement in others. These findings suggest that teachers tended to emphasize one or two subjects because these represented either their own strengths or perceived student weaknesses.

On the other hand, success of one ability level (within each subject) tended to be significantly correlated with success of other ability levels in the classroom. This finding held most often for reading, language usage, and arithmetic; it held least often for science. In general, teachers seemed to be more successful in handling several ability levels simultaneously in any one subject than they were in treating several subjects with equally satisfactory results.

For the three intermediate ability levels (IQ 100 to 129), being at the top, in the middle, or at the bottom of the ability range in a classroom had no significant effect on achievement.

The presence of gifted students (IQ 130 or above) in the classroom, regardless of the ability range of the class, affected the achievement of the other ability levels in science and, to a lesser extent, in social studies. Where there were gifted students, the other ability levels scored higher in these two subject areas than in classes of equal range where the gifted were absent. Conversely, the presence of the low-average tended to have a positive effect on the arithmetic computation scores of the other ability levels. These findings may shed some light on the general superior attainments of all ability levels in the broad-range classes.

Interest scores in all areas tested tended to go down for all ability levels. However, for the gifted, the narrow-range ability groups reversed this tendency in some interest areas. There was no significant relationship found between interest and IQ or between interest and achievement in a given subject.

Comment: On a large scale this study supports the findings of many earlier studies that ability grouping per se does not make a difference in the school achievement and adjustment of either gifted or non-gifted children. However, an important limitation of this study as well as of many others lies in the sole use of standardized achievement tests to assess academic attainment. Learnings which are not measured by standardized achievement tests but which may be of great significance to the intellectual development of the students remain unassessed. It is possible that ability grouping may have effects on achievement which do not show up on standardized instruments.

The finding that for any one class success in one subject did not necessarily imply comparable success in another subject was especially true for the gifted pupils. This finding raises questions about the ability of any one teacher to provide adequate instruction for gifted children across all the elementary subject areas.

Mann, H. How Real Are Friendships of Gifted and Typical Children in a Program of Partial Segregation? *Exceptional Children*, 1957, 23, 199-201, 206.

Purpose: To examine the contention that gifted children in a partially segregated program have opportunity to develop and maintain friendships with typical children in their regular classrooms.

Subjects: 281 students in grades four to six of the Colfax School, Pittsburgh, Pennsylvania. Children with Stanford-Binet IQs of 130 or more spent half their school day in regular classrooms with typical children and the remainder in workshops with gifted children doing only enrichment work.

Procedures: The first sociometric test was given to 281 children, including 67 gifted children in the intermediate and senior workshops. The intermediate workshop group consisted of 31 gifted children from the fourth and lower half of the fifth grade. The senior workshop consisted of 36 gifted pupils drawn from the sixth and the upper half of the fifth grade. The instrument was designed to measure the social position gifted children held among gifted as well as typical classmates. Three acceptance-oriented and three rejection-oriented questions were asked.

A second sociometric test was designed to examine the choices of gifted children in the regular classroom and workshops. Two accept-ance-oriented and two rejection-oriented questions were asked only of the 67 gifted children. A questionnaire was sent to their parents asking which children the gifted child chose to invite to his home, which he invited to stay overnight, which he invited to help him on studies, and which he called upon when he wanted someone with whom to play. This questionnaire also asked parents to identify the meeting place of out-of-school friends. A 93 percent return was received on the question-naire.

Results: On the first sociometric test, gifted children in the intermedi-ate workshop chose other gifted children 181 times more than typical children. The gifted children in the senior workshop chose other gifted children 124 times more than typical children. Typical children from the intermediate regular classes chose other typical children 524 times more than gifted children. In the senior regular classes they chose other typical children 806 times more than gifted children.

Gifted children in the intermediate workshop rejected other gifted children 153 times more than typical children. In the senior workshop the gifted children rejected other gifted children 102 times more than typical children. Typical children rejected other typical children 607 times more than gifted children in the intermediate regular class. In the senior regular classes typical children rejected other typical children 921 times more than gifted children.

The second sociometric test showed that in the intermediate work-shop gifted children preferred other gifted children to criticize their work in music and art 71 percent of the time; in the senior workshop they preferred gifted children to criticize their work 65 percent of the time. When the acceptance choices of workshop children on the first sociometric test were compared with the children listed by the parents as their child's most frequently chosen associate in each of the three situations, a correlation of +.42 was found for intermediate workshop children and +.39 for senior workshop children. The gifted children chose to play with children in the neighborhood 51.79 percent of the time. They chose to study with children from within the workshop 87.04 percent of the time; with typical classroom children 1.81 percent of the time; with children from the neighborhood 5.99 percent of the time; and with children within the family 4.56 percent of the time. When in-viting children to their home, the gifted children selected from within the workshop group 44.20 percent of the time.

There was a substantial relationship between the friends the gifted children had in school and those they had in the community. The higher the school acceptance score the more frequent the mention of the child's name on the parent questionnaire. The workshop provided the most frequent locale for meeting the friends gifted children made. While the workshop, the room in which gifted children work together, helped to develop and reinforce friendships in and out of school, the regular class, which provided a place where gifted and typical children mingled, did not actually produce relationships significant enough to be classified as friendships.

Comment: The above findings must be considered in view of the fact that the sociometric instruments were administered while the youngsters were in their separate special programs. Had the friendship choices been made at the time when the average and gifted children were together, both the acceptance and rejection patterns may have been different since proximity exerts a significant influence on such choices.

Justman, J. *A Comparison of the Functioning of Intellectually Gifted Children Enrolled in Special Progress and Normal Progress Classes in Junior High Schools.* New York: Board of Education, Bureau of Educational Research, 1952. (Mimeographed)

Purpose: To appraise the comparative functioning of intellectually gifted pupils drawn from special progress (SP) classes in which the three years of junior high school are completed in two years, with that of gifted pupils from normal progress (NP) classes.

Subjects: 83 pairs of students matched on school attended, grade, sex, mental age, chronological age and IQ, drawn from the seventh grade entering NP and SP classes. All subjects met the criteria for admission to the SP program: IQ of 130 or higher on two group tests, reading level of 8.0, arithmetic level 8.0, good health, and minimum age of 11.

Procedures: All subjects were evaluated on a variety of achievement, attitude, interest and social adjustment instruments near the beginning of seventh grade and again 14 school months later. Achievement test results were treated in two ways: (a) comparison of results on total tests; (b) comparison of results only on those items which were related to the seventh- and eighth-grade courses of study. All items dealing with ninth-grade content were eliminated.

Results: There were no significant differences in increments in reading skills or arithmetic computation between SP and NP students. However, as a group, the SPs were initially higher on reading. The SP group made significantly greater gains in mathematics, science, social studies and work-study skills when compared on the total tests. When the groups were equated on reading and only seventh- and eighth-grade items considered, the superiority of the SP group remained significant in some aspects of mathematics, in work-study skills and in science. Differences in social studies became minor and nonsignificant.

A test of personality yielded no consistent differences between the groups. The three sociometric techniques utilized yielded conflicting results. On the Friendship Nominations and the Modified Ohio Social Acceptance Scale, SP classes showed better social adjustment than their matched pairs. The reverse was true on the Casting Characters test. There was no conclusive indication of differences in personal and social adjustment.

On none of the interest measures did the two groups differ significantly. Intellectually gifted pupils in SP classes generally showed academic achievement superior to that normally attained by equally gifted pupils.

Comment: The significant implication of the Justman study is that, despite the year's difference in chronological age, the accelerated pupils did at least as well in most areas of academic and personal adjustment as those pupils who had spent the full three years in junior high schools. In addition to having done as well as their older classmates on the material of the seventh and eighth grade, the accelerants managed to cover a considerable amount of the material for the following (ninth) year. This study stresses the importance of acceleration in this area as usually measured by standardized achievement tests.

Abramson, D. The Effectiveness of Grouping for Students of High Ability. *Educational Research Bulletin.* 1959, 38, 169-182.

Purpose: To investigate the relationship between the grouping of high school pupils on the basis of ability and their subsequent progress in college.

Subjects: The subjects were drawn from a sample of 318 students who were graduates of four New York City high schools which practiced different kinds of grouping. School A grouped high-ability pupils heterogeneously with other pupils from all levels of ability. School B selected high-ability students for honor classes in one or two major subjects only. School C grouped high-ability pupils in an honor school so that they were in special honor classes for most of their major classes. School D selected only high-ability pupils for admission on the basis of a special examination. Each sample consisted of 16 students (8 males and 8 females) drawn from each of three levels of intelligence: Level 1, IQ 115 to 124; Level 2, IQ 125 to 134; and Level 3, IQ 135 to 160. The total of 192 students were equally distributed (by sex and intelligence level) between New York City municipal and other colleges.

Procedures: Students were compared on subsequent academic achievement through the sophomore year of college. Overall grade-point averages, honors, and grades in specific courses were used as criteria of achievement. The comparisons were made for each criterion for both the total group and for those attending the New York City municipal colleges.

Results: There were no statistically significant differences in the grade-point averages earned by students who had been members of ability groups and those who had not. Variations in the extent to which ability grouping had been employed failed to produce any significant differences in the tests applied to each year of college work or to the grade-point averages for the combined two years for either the total or municipal college group.

When the grade-point averages were considered according to the three levels of intelligence and without regard to the particular high school attended, statistically significant differences were obtained in five of the six tests which were applied. In four instances, Level 3 students were superior to those of Levels 1 and 2, while in the fifth instance they exceeded significantly only Level 1 students. Women attained grade-point averages significantly superior to those of men in the total group but not in the municipal college group. Consideration of the possible effect of the interactions of the variables of sex, school, and level of intelligence produced consistently negative results. No evidence was found to support the possibility that any significant effects could be attributed to the working together of any two or more of the three main variables.

There were no significant differences of any kind in either the number of honors won or the number of students who won them among the specific high schools which had used the several methods of grouping. No differences in honors were observed between men and women, but the level-of-intelligence categories showed statistically significant differences in honors won. In no specific subject were the effects of school or sex significant. The effects of level of intelligence, however, were significant in two of the eight testing situations.

College freshmen and sophomore grade-point averages, honors, and course grades were not influenced by patterns of high school ability grouping. The overall achievement of students, as judged by grade-point averages and honors, seemed to be associated with level of intelligence rather than with the grouping patterns used in the particular high school attended.

Comment: Caution must be exercised in generalizing from this study. The limited sample and the lack of comparability in college curricula raise certain questions. The chief issue, however, is the criterion problem: whether college grades are an adequate measure of the effectiveness of various kinds of high school programs. To this criterion problem must be added the fact that even though the differences in grade-point averages earned by the students in the various groupings were not statistically significant, in all comparisons they followed the same direction (highest for the specialized school, lowest for the ungrouped situation). The consistency of the direction suggests that factors other than chance may be operating in the effects of the various grouping arrangements.

Hobson, J. R. Scholastic Standing and Activity Participation of Underage High School Pupils Originally Admitted to Kindergarten on the Basis of Physical and Psychological Examinations. Paper read at American Psychological Association, Division 16, September, 1956. (Mimeographed)

Purpose: To compare scholastic performance in high school, participation in school activities, and college admissions success of underage children originally admitted to kindergarten by test, with the performance of others who graduated in their class.

Subjects: 550 high school graduates, 1946 to 1955, who were originally admitted to school underage and 3891 other graduates admitted at the regular age.

Procedures: The two groups were compared on numbers who graduated with honors and numbers elected to an honor society based on both participation and prominence in extracurricular activities as well as scholarship. A more detailed study of the classes of 1946 and 1947 included a comparison of high school scholastic performance of 94 underage children with 764 others as to marks and average rank in class; extracurricular activities for the four-year period including a frequency distribution and informal analysis of these activities; and percentages of college admissions with an appraisal of the colleges to which admission was gained.

44

Results: Both the underage boys and girls exceeded their older controls in the percentage who graduated with honors in each one of the 10 years, usually by a large margin. One-fourth of the underage girls graduated with honors. For both sexes combined, 22.7 percent of the underage students as compared to 11.9 percent of the older group graduated with honors. For the 10-year period the percentage of the underage group admitted to Alpha Pi honor society was twice that of the other students. The four-year academic point ratings of the underage group in the class of 1946 was 2.49 compared with an average of 2.10 for the other children. The average rank in class for the underage boys in the class of 1946 was 167 (out of 387) and 219 for the other boys.

The scholastic superiority in elementary school of underage children originally admitted on the basis of physical and psychological examinations continued and was somewhat increased through the high school years. Underage accelerates engaged in a significantly larger number of extracurricular activities over the four-year period than did their classmates of the same sex. In the matter of honors, awards, and distinctions at graduation, the underage boys and girls exceeded their fellows by a ratio of about two to one. A significantly larger percentage of underage graduates sought and gained admission to accredited four-year colleges of superior standing than did their classmates of the same sex.

Keys, N. The Oakland Study. The Underage Student in High School and College: Educational and Social Adjustments. *University of California Publications in Education*, 1938, 7, No. 3, 229-255.

Purpose: To compare the adjustment in senior high school of markedly younger bright pupils with that of students of normal age having similar ability and social background.

Subjects: Four groups of students were selected: an experimental group of 46 students with IQs of 120 to 137, graduating at 16 years, 8 months or younger; a control group of 46 students graduating at 17 years, 6 months or older, matched for IQ, sex, race, and socio-economic status with the experimental group; a high IQ group consisting of 24 accelerates with IQs of 136 to 151, too high to permit matching with controls; and a Low IQ group (IQ 93 to 119) consisting of 43 pupils accelerated from two to five semesters. The mean age of the control group was 19 months above that of the experimental group.

45

Procedures: The students were compared on activities, honors, student offices, rating by school counselors, scores on the Bernreuter Personality Inventory, and questionnaire responses covering opinions and personal adjustments.

Results: The mean high school grade-point average for the experimental group was 3.15; for the controls, 3.07; for the high IQ group, 3.64; and for the low IQ group, 2.84. The differences between the high and low IQ groups and between the experimental and control groups were significant. In the percentage within the groups receiving honors and prizes, the high IQ group led with 63 percent; the experimentals had 61 percent; controls, 50 percent; and the low IQ group, 28 percent. The difference between the high and low IQ groups was statistically significant.

The younger boys had no disadvantage in athletics. The experimental group had four times as many boys on the football team as the control group. While the difference was not significant, the experimental girls also exceeded the controls. Eighty-four percent of the high IQ students participated in one or more extracurricular activities as compared with 72 percent of the experimental group, 61 percent of the controls and 65 percent of the low IQ group.

There were no significant differences among the groups with respect to physical health. Without knowledge of groupings, counselors rated the high IQ students slightly lower on personality than the control students, although the difference was not significant. More than twice as many control students were rated "timid," "shy," and "reserved" by counselors as were experimental students. Data from the Bernreuter Personality Inventory indicated that the neurotic tendency mean for the experimental group was 49.9 as compared with the 54.1 for the controls, 51.4 for the high IQs and 45.7 for the low IQ group. The differences between the experimental and control groups and between the high and low groups were significant. The difference between the experimental and control groups on the Sociability Scale was not significant. The high IQ group scored significantly higher on Sociability than the low IQs.

The study suggests that acceleration, far from contributing to maladjustment, may actually be helpful to the social relations of bright students. To judge from the age of companions preferred, 78 percent of the accelerated boys and girls were appropriately placed in high school as against 55 percent of the normal age boys and girls.

Comment: The Keys study was one of the first attempts to compare the adjustment and achievement of accelerated high school pupils to the academic and social adjustment of an equally able group of non-accelerants. Although the sample was relatively small, the differences between groups were sufficiently great to reach statistical significance.

The Fund for the Advancement of Education. *They Went to College Early.* Education Report No. 2. New York: Author, 1957.

Purpose: To study the results of early admission to college in selected universities.

Subjects: 860 college students who were admitted to 12 different colleges or universities before completion of high school and were approximately two years younger than the average college freshman at the time of admission. A carefully selected group of comparison students, matched with the early admittees on academic aptitude, were included as a control group. A total of 1350 students were admitted early between 1951 and 1954, but the report focused primarily on the 860 graduates admitted in 1951 and 1952.

Procedures: Each of the 12 colleges kept detailed records on the Scholars (early admittees) and the comparison students. A 34-item questionnaire with information about family and school backgrounds, experiences in college, and plans for the future was completed by the students. Each of the participating colleges reported on its own experience with the program. An appraisal of the social and emotional adjustment of the 1951 Scholars was made by a team of trained psychiatrists. An analysis was made of essays written just before graduation by the 1951 and 1952 Scholars on their college experiences and their views of early admission.

Results: Three-fourths of the Scholars were males. At the time of entrance to college, 29.3 percent were under 16, 56.4 percent were 16, and 14.3 percent were 17 or older. About half of the Scholars had completed grade 11 of high school; 41.9 percent finished grade 10 only; and 7.1 percent went through grade 12. The bulk of the Scholars (76.6 percent of the 865 tested) had total scores of 110 and above on the ACE psychological examination. Approximately three-fourths came from city public schools, 11.1 percent from suburban schools, 6.5 percent from rural schools, and 9.2 percent from private schools. The parents were primarily engaged in professional and business occupations; 22.0 percent were laborers.

Academically, the Scholar groups outperformed their classmates as a whole and their comparison students. The rate of failure among the first two Scholar groups was somewhat higher than among the comparison group (11.2 and 11.9 percent for the Scholars; 8.2 and 9.0 percent for the comparison students), but it was lower than among the classes as a whole. The reasons for failure were no different than for the college students in general. The Scholars encountered more difficulties in initial adjustment to campus life than the older comparison students but these problems were minor ones which soon disappeared. In the two institutions in which separate dormitory facilities and other special services were provided, the Scholars had more difficulties of a social nature than in those schools which provided no special treatment.

Among the first two groups of Scholars who graduated, the proportion planning to go on to graduate work was substantially higher than among the comparison students. Eleven of the 12 colleges incorporated the early admission idea into their regular admissions policy, the twelfth had taken no action.

In all but a few cases where data were available, the Scholars' parents and their high school principals expressed themselves as favorably disposed to early admission. The students themselves responded favorably: 75 percent of the 1952 group said they felt early admission had been profitable to them and 66 percent felt that early admission should become a regular part of the admission policy of American colleges.

Comment: Despite the positive findings from this study as well as those of other researchers, early admission to college has not become a popular means of providing for academically gifted students. The reasons for this are not clear: it may reflect the resistance on the part of the high school principals and staffs to losing their most able students to the colleges and, to some extent, the existing prejudice against the underage college student on the campus.

> Portland Public Schools. *The Gifted Child in Portland: A Report of Five Years of Experience in Developing a Program for Children of Exceptional Endowment.* Portland, Oregon: The Public Schools, 1959.

Purpose: To develop and refine procedures for identifying outstanding intellectual ability and talent in creative, artistic, mechanical, and social areas; to evaluate the results of experimentation with teaching methods, materials, school and class organization; and to determine the characteristics of gifted and talented pupils.

Subjects: Pupils in the various phases of the Portland Cooperative Program for Students and Exceptional Talent. Programs were in both elementary and secondary schools. Approximately 10 percent of the total pupil population in 14 elementary schools and four high schools were involved.

Procedures: A variety of studies was carried out during the second to the fifth year of the program which began in 1952-53. The studies were in eight areas: identification and talent testing, attitudes of gifted students, qualities of leaders, achievement and adjustment of gifted elementary school pupils, follow-up in college of high school graduates, underachieving high school students, and ability grouping in ninth grade combined English-social studies classes.

Results: Talent screening devices for identifying pupils gifted in art, music, creative writing, creative dance, social leadership, and mechanical talent were developed and tested.

Questionnaire responses by high school students indicated that 85 percent felt that inclusion in a special program made no difference in their social status, 10 to 15 percent felt it had given them prestige, and only one to two percent reported that the program made them unpopular.

A study of the personal qualities children value in their peer leadership involved 750 pupils, grades six to eight. The pupils nominated leaders and gave reasons for their choices. There was a shift between the sixth and eighth grades from "mental ability and effort" to "likeable personal characteristics" as determining their selection. Such a shift may be typical of adolescents in general.

Three studies were undertaken to evaluate the effects of the elementary school program on the pupils' achievement and adjustment. The results of these studies indicated that the pupils who participated in the program had made, and were continuing to make, greater gains in intellectual achievement than comparable youngsters not participating. There seemed to be no ill effects on the general adjustment of participating pupils. Their attitudes and activities suggested that they were making more constructive uses of their superior ability than the matched pupils.

The effects of special classes and seminars on student performance and adjustment in college were examined in two studies. The experimental group achieved a significantly higher total grade-point average during the freshman year than did the control group. In general, the studies indicated that the special classes in high school prepared students for college better than did the regular classes.

Three studies related to creative thinking abilities were undertaken. Teachers developed methods for stimulating creativity in the fifth- and sixth-grade classrooms. However, the results of such instruction were not significantly related to scores on tests of creative thinking. In another study, it was found that pupils expressing authoritarian attitudes showed less sensitivity to problems, less improvising ability, and less originality than equally bright peers who showed nonauthoritarian attitudes. In a study of the relationship between creative thinking and conformity, it was found that students scoring high on originality placed greater emphasis on independent thinking and less on "going along with the group."

An intensive study was made of 49 high-achieving boys and an equated group of 49 underachieving boys in terms of educational, personal and social adjustment, vocational aspirations, and family relations. Information was obtained on some 200 variables. High achievers characterized themselves as more accomplishing and studious and less lazy than did underachievers. Underachievers more often viewed academic achievement as incompatible with enjoying life and having fun. Most high achievers had an accurate conception of their own high scholastic ability, while most underachievers, though correctly recognizing that their ability was above average, underestimated their ability. More underachievers expressed relatively negative attitudes regarding school, teachers, and studying. Significantly more underachievers indicated that they would like to be in occupations involving adventure or excitement. High achievers and underachievers did not differ in their expressed satisfaction with life in general, and the majority of each group expressed themselves as moderately to well satisfied. Somewhat fewer high achievers were satisfied with their relationships with girls; underachievers reported having more dates. In describing the immediate group of friends with which they spent the most time, underachievers significantly more often described their cliques as negative toward school achievement. High achievers much more often enjoyed emotionally supportive family relations.

A study of the effects of ability grouping as compared to broad-range grouping in ninth grade combined English-social studies classes indicated that students in both situations made significant gains on most tests used, but neither arrangement proved significantly better than the other. Analysis of teacher logs revealed that generally teachers were not successful in using different content or methods of instruction with the selectively grouped students.

Comment: No brief summary can really do justice to the variety of studies undertaken in connection with the development of the Portland Gifted Child Project. For four of the five years, research and evaluation were integral parts of program development. Most significant were the attempts to identify youngsters with special talent in addition to intellectual aptitudes, the arrangements which brought specialized instruction into the elementary grades, and the program modifications which resulted from careful assessment of on-going experiences.

Simpson, R. E., and Martinson, Ruth A. *Educational Programs for Gifted Pupils: A Report to the California Legislature Prepared Pursuant to Section 2 of Chapter 2385, Statutes of 1957.* Sacramento: California State Department of Public Instruction, 1961.

Purpose: To study the need for special programs for gifted pupils, to determine the costs of such programs, and to analyze the special benefits to be derived from such programs.

Subjects: 929 pupils took part in one of 17 different special programs. Each of the pupils was selected on the basic criterion of a Stanford-Binet IQ of 130 or above. The mean IQ scores were approximately 140 for the various groups. Each of the experimental pupils was matched with a control pupil of same intelligence (within five points), age (within six months), sex, and socio-economic status.

Procedures: Programs were established in school districts of varied sizes. The 17 plans, ranging from grades 1 to 12, involved various kinds of enrichment in the regular classroom, acceleration, and grouping. At the first-grade level, for example, there was enrichment in the regular class, acceleration, ungraded curriculum, and cluster groups. At the twelfth-grade level, there were honors classes and acceleration to university and junior college. The effects of the special programs were evaluated using tests of academic achievement, social relationships and psychological maturity, attitudes, teacher reaction forms, and evaluations of pupils and programs by teachers, parents and pupils. While each of the specific programs was evaluated, they were not compared for relative effectiveness.

Results: The gifted pupils in the special programs attained an achievement level which was unusually high, compared with the total and control populations. The control gifted made gains comparable to the average population but remained as they had begun at the higher level. The gifted in special programs made gains commensurate with their high level of ability—i.e., they started at a higher level of achievement and maintained growth in accordance with expectations based on this unusual ability. All of the achievement data supported the merits of special, individualized programs for the gifted. No adverse effects

51

were found in the friendship choices of pupils who were in special programs. The total group of first, fifth and sixth grade pupils made significant gains in friendship choices when compared with the control pupils. Proper educational opportunity seemed to aid in improving classroom status.

The gifted pupils had desirable personal and social characteristics paralleling their high intelligence and achievement ratings. On retests on the California Psychological Inventory, the experimental pupils gained on 19 scales and lost on three, despite high initial ratings. The control gifted gained on nine scales and lost on eight. The students in special groups seemed to have avoided deleterious effects in personal-social-psychological areas. The ratings of pupil attitudes towards school learning (including study habits, critical thinking ability, motivation for learning and self-understanding) were highly favorable in all the special programs and at all grade levels.

Ninety-six percent of the pupils saw the special program as having been beneficial. The greatest value was perceived as providing pupils with an opportunity to progress at their own rate. Ninety-two percent of the parents and three-fourths of the pupils strongly favored continuation of the programs. The teachers revealed favorable attitudes toward the various programs in which they had participated. They pointed up a number of problems, but indicated that they had benefited from in-service activities designed to increase their teaching skills and academic knowledge. Total costs and cost per pupil for each district were determined, including the cost of identification and of implementing the program.

Comment: Although the study concludes that gifted students enrolled in special programs excelled those who were in regular classes, no attempt has been made to compare one kind of special program with another. In view of the many kinds of special adaptations involved in this research, the difficulty for even a statewide study to make comparisons of the effectiveness among the various provisions is underscored. However, this lack of comparative evaluation represents a limitation in the research design since it leaves the school administrator and program planner without help as to which of the various special programs are most effective for which kinds of youngsters and under what circumstances.

In Review

Reviews of research on educational programs for gifted students can be found in the following: K. E. Anderson (Ed.) *Research on the Academically Talented*. Washington, D.C.: National Education Association, 1961; J. J. Gallagher. *Analysis of Research on the Education of Gifted Children*. Springfield: State of Illinois, Office of the Superintendent of Public Instruction, 1960; Miriam L. Goldberg. Research on the Gifted. In B. Shertzer (Ed.), *Working with Superior Students*. Chicago: Science Research Associates, 1960, 41-66; and A. H. Passow. Enrichment of Education for the Gifted. In N. Henry (Ed.), Education for the Gifted. *Yearbook of the National Society for the Study of Education*, 1958, 57, Part II, 198-221.

Research on educational programs has dealt primarily with administrative adaptations and curriculum modifications. Relatively little is known about the relationship between specific educational experiences and the nourishment of individual talents. McClelland, the chairman of the Social Science Research Council's Committee on the Identification of Talent (D. C. McClelland, *et al. Talent and Society: New Perspectives in the Identification of Talent*. Princeton, N.J.: Van Nostrand Company, 1958) urges that the *process by which talent becomes actual* should be the focus of experimentation and research. Until more is known about "what we are measuring, how it develops under different circumstances, and how it is related to the ultimate criteria of talented performance which we want to predict," there will remain "an outstanding gap in current talent research."

2

The Educable Mentally Retarded

Rick F. Heber

The term "educable mentally retarded" refers to a heterogeneous group of children who have in common: (a) general intellectual functioning which is below the average range of the general population; (b) a predicted or demonstrated inability to cope with the regular school curriculum at the typical age; (c) a potential for achievement of a minimal but significant level of basic academic skills when provided with a curriculum and teaching techniques appropriate to their level and rate of intellectual development; and (d) a potential for achievement of those social and occupational skills essential to independent adult living. The specific administrative criteria governing placement of pupils in special classes for the educable mentally retarded vary from community to community and from state to state. As a consequence of the great variations in criteria governing placement in classrooms for educable mentally retarded children, any experiment or survey which used subjects whose IQ scores generally range from 50 to 85 on an individual test of general intelligence was considered eligible for inclusion in this review, irrespective of age, etiological considerations, or type of placement of the subjects. The reader, in interpreting and generalizing research findings re-

Special acknowledgement is due Mr. Herbert J. Prehm for his assistance in searching and reviewing the literature.

ported in this review, must take into consideration the possible relationship of these and other characteristics of the experimental subjects to the results.

In selecting studies for review, an effort was made to select those studies which have been most frequently cited in publications and which are representative of the various kinds of investigations being undertaken and the various methodologies being utilized in this field of research. The studies are grouped according to four major categories of research relevant to education of retarded children.

1. The influence of environmental factors on intellectual development.
2. Learning and performance.
3. Educational methods, achievement, and pupil characteristics.
4. Socio-occupational adjustment of the educable mentally retarded as adults.

THE INFLUENCE OF ENVIRONMENTAL FACTORS ON INTELLECTUAL DEVELOPMENT

A substantial proportion of all educable mentally retarded children derives from adverse environmental circumstances and from families in which one or more parents or siblings are also retarded in intellectual development. Opinions conflict regarding the extent to which intellectual development is retarded in these children as a result of deprivation of adequate opportunities for learning verbal and other intellectual skills. Consequently, studies pertinent to this issue are of critical importance.

Many of the findings reported in this section must be considered tentative rather than conclusive. The studies reviewed are initial inquiries which have pinpointed important variables for further study, rather than precise, methodologically refined experiments. Identification of the specific intellectual abilities which are modified adversely by stimulus deprivation or positively by stimulus enrichment will have important implications for educational treatment of the retarded child.

Clarke, A. D. B., Clarke, A. M., and Reiman, S. Cognitive and Social Changes in the Feebleminded—Three Further Studies. *British Journal of Psychology*, 1958, 49, 144-157.

Purpose: To study the effect of environmental changes on intellectual functioning of persons who are mentally retarded. A series of studies was undertaken as a follow-up of earlier studies by the authors which had demonstrated substantial increases in the measured intelligence of retarded persons removed from extremely impoverished environments.

Study I: 28 institutionalized subjects of an original study group of 59 were available for re-study after a six-year period. Mean CA at time of retesting was 27.9. These persons tended to be the less competent members of the original group since the more competent were more likely to have been discharged or on work-leave from the institution to which they had originally been committed. These subjects were retested on the same test which had been administered six and three years earlier (Wechsler, Form I).

Those subjects who had originally come to the institution from homes which were judged independently (on a 12-point rating scale) to be extremely impoverished showed a mean increment in IQ from 59.6 to 75.8 over the six-year interval. Those coming from somewhat less adverse circumstances increased in IQ from 62.3 to 72.5, approximately one-third of a standard deviation less than the other group. Range of changes was from −2 to +21 points with 53 percent of the subjects showing increases of 10 points or more, and 26 percent of the subjects showing increases of 15 points or better.

Study II: All patients admitted to the institution in a given year were retested approximately four and one-half years later to determine whether changes in measured intelligence were a direct function of length of time between test and retest.

Subjects coming from very bad homes showed an increase of 11.5 IQ points while those rated as coming from somewhat less adverse circumstances showed a gain of 7.2 points. In an earlier study over a two and one-half year test-retest period, "bad home" subjects gained 9.7 points and subjects from less adverse conditions gained 4.1 points. The slight gain between the two and one-half and four and one-half year retest interval for the "bad home" group could not be directly accounted for on the basis of time between testings. On the other hand, changes in the "less adverse" group seemed to be more directly a function of test-retest interval.

Study III: Subjects in the institution were given a program of intensive vocational preparation to determine whether this enrichment of the institutional environment would have any positive effect on measured intellectual functioning. Comparison of positive changes in Wechsler scores with those reported in Study II indicated little, if any, effect of the training program beyond that produced by transfer from the "bad home" conditions to the regular British institution environment.

Comment: These data suggest that removal of retarded persons from an extremely impoverished environment may result in positive gains in intelligence test scores which do not appear to be explained by "unreliability of measurement." These findings further suggest that the effects of any habilitative measure taken on behalf of a retarded person may vary as a function of the prior environmental circumstances of that individual (i.e., retardates coming to the institution from homes judged as the most inadequate showed the greatest gains in test scores as a result of the change in environment).

Kephart, N. C. Influencing the Rate of Mental Growth in Retarded Children through Environmental Stimulation. *Yearbook of the National Society for the Study of Education*, 1940, 39, Part II, 223-230.

Purpose: To determine if intelligence test scores of retarded children who present no evidence of CNS pathology (a) decrease while the children remain in their own homes, (b) increase as a result of institutional placement, or (c) increase as a result of a specialized training program within the institution.

Subjects: For Part I, 50 institutionalized retardates (CA 4 to 16, mean IQ—67.6). For Part II, 16 institutionalized boys (CA 15 to 18, mean IQ —66.3).

Procedure: Changes in intelligence test scores were determined over a period of time in which the boys had resided in their own homes (average interval of 3.8 years) and over a period of time in which the boys had resided in the institution (average interval of 4.8 years). Changes in intelligence scores were also determined for 16 boys over a period of time in which they took part in a specialized training program within the institution (average interval of 1.5 years).

Results: The retarded children showed a decrease in intelligence test score over the period of time they remained at home. This contrasted with an average gain in test score of 4.0 points for these same children over the period they were studied in the institution. The 16 boys participating in the specialized training program showed an average gain of 10.1 points (from 66.3 to 76.4) in test score over the period of their participation.

Comment: The author infers that the children studied came from undesirable homes and that the institution is, therefore, a relatively more favorable environment, but he fails to provide any description of home conditions or of conditions within the institution. A major defect in this study is the possibility that a decline in intellectual performance while in the community may have been one of the factors leading to institutionalization. Children living in similar kinds of homes and not coming to the attention of the institution may have maintained or raised their level of intellectual performance.

Pasamanick, B. A Comparative Study of the Behavioral Development of Negro Infants. *Pedagogical Seminary and Journal of Genetic Psychology*, 1946, 69, 3-44.

Purpose: To compare the development of motor skills, adaptive behavior, language behavior, and personal-social behavior in Negro and white children.

Subjects: 53 Negro babies and 99 white babies (57 illegitimate and in foster homes, 22 illegitimate and in an institution, and 20 nursery school applicants) from New Haven, Connecticut were studied.

Procedure: The behavioral development of infants in the four groups was evaluated using the Yale Developmental Schedule. In addition, some Negro subjects were also evaluated using the Tables of Individual Behavior Items as developed by Gesell and Amatruda. Data from these scales were computed on the basis of half-years of life.

Results: No differences were found initially in the behavioral development of white and Negro babies with the exception that the Negro infants were somewhat superior to the white infants in gross motor development. Environmental impoverishment was shown to have a detrimental influence on the behavioral development of the group of institutionalized white children. An incipient downward trend beginning at the third half-year of life was noted for the Negro infants and was attributed to a lack of environmental stimulation.

Comment: Although this study does not deal specifically with retardates, it is of importance in that it demonstrates that group differences in behavioral development begin to appear at about 18 months. The authors cite these differences as evidence of the effect of sociocultural factors on intellectual development. The design of the study does not, however, preclude the possibility that the findings could be a function of inherent Negro-white differences in rate of development.

58

Skeels, H. M. A Study of the Effects of Differential Stimulation on Mentally Retarded Children: A Follow-up Report. *American Journal of Mental Deficiency*, 1941-42, 46, 340-350.

Purpose: To follow up the subjects of a previous study (Skeels and Dye, 1939) designed to determine the effects of a radical shift in environment on the intellectual development of preschool-age mentally retarded children.

Subjects: The experimental group was comprised of 13 retarded children (all under age three, with a mean IQ of 64.3) and the contrast group of 12 children (all under age three, with a mean IQ of 86.7). All subjects were or had been residents of an institution for dependent children regarded as providing an impoverished, non-stimulating environment.

Procedure: At a mean age of 19 months the experimental subjects were transferred from the orphanage to a residential center for the retarded where they were placed, either singly or in pairs, in wards with mildly retarded adolescent or adult females. It was assumed that this environment would be more stimulating (the retarded females were described as giving great attention to the infants placed with them) than that of the orphanage. The contrast group remained in the orphanage environment. All subjects were tested (Kuhlman-Binet or Stanford-Binet) before and after the experimental period (approximately two years) and again two and one-half years later.

Results: The mean IQ of the experimental group increased from 64.3, initially, to 91.8 at the close of the experimental period and to 95.9 on the follow-up test. The mean IQ for the contrast group decreased from 86.7, initially, to 60.5 at the close of the experimental period and then increased to 66.1 on the follow-up test two and one-half years later.

Comment: Since the contrast group in this study was selected *post hoc* (i.e. after observations on the experimental group had been made), we have no assurance that the groups did not differ on relevant variables, and this circumstance represents a serious limitation of the study. Because of this problem of methodology and the small number of subjects employed, interpretation of the findings must be tentative. The obvious, striking differences in intellectual growth between the experimental and contrast groups cannot be ignored, however. The study demonstrates the upward shift in level of functioning which may be effected by removal from an environment destitute of stimulation, and the deterioration in functioning level which may result from prolonged exposure to such conditions.

Skeels, H. M., and Harms, Irene. Children with Inferior Social Histories: Their Mental Development in Adoptive Homes. *Journal of Genetic Psychology*, 1948, 72, 283-294.

Purpose: To study the intellectual development of children of parents with inferior social histories.

Subjects: Three groups of children (most of whom were illegitimate) whose true parents were socially inferior. In one group of 87 children the true mothers were identified as mentally retarded on the basis of psychometric tests. In a second group of 111 children, the true fathers were in the lowest occupational level, and in a third category, 31 children had a retarded mother along with a father who was in the lowest possible occupational bracket.

Procedure: Prior to age two, all subjects were placed in foster homes which were considered superior to the homes of their true parents. They were tested on either the Kuhlman-Binet or the 1916 Stanford-Binet at an average age of 5-3 years.

Results: The three groups achieved mean IQ scores ranging from 102.2 to 113.4, an intelligence level comparable to that which would be predicted for true children of the foster parents. The prevalence of mental retardation in these groups was no greater than that to be expected on the basis of frequency for the general population.

Comment: As with other foster parent studies, interpretations of the results must be tempered as a result of methodological problems such as the failure to assign all available infants to foster homes at random and the lack of adequate data pertaining to status of true parents. It cannot be disputed, however, that the available data on true parents did indicate that they tended toward sub-average intellectual and occupational performance. This sub-average status was not obviously reflected in the intellectual performance of their children being reared in foster homes.

Skodak, Marie, and Skeels, H. M. A Final Follow-up Study of One Hundred Adopted Children. *Journal of Genetic Psychology*, 1949, 75, 85-125.

Purpose: To determine the effect of environmental change on the development of intellectual ability in adoptive children.

Subjects: 100 children who were placed before the age of six months in adoptive homes of a higher or potentially higher socio-economic level than that of their true mothers.

Procedure: The intellectual and academic progress of the subjects was evaluated over a 10-year period. The IQs, current state of development, and educational achievement of the children were compared with those of the true mothers.

Results: In each case the socio-economic, educational, and intellectual level in the adoptive home was higher than the level from which the child was taken prior to adoption. The adopted children had a mean IQ level 20 points higher than the measured intelligence of their true mothers. In almost all instances the children reached and maintained a functioning level compatible with the environment in which they were placed.

Comment: This study, along with other of the "environmental" studies, is difficult to interpret because of the many methodological problems inherent in this type of research (for example, in this study, lack of knowledge of the intellectual level of the true fathers, many of whom were unknown; lack of random assignment of infants to foster homes; questions regarding reliability of the assessments of the intellectual levels of the true mothers, etc.). This study suggests that one may not predict an outcome of mental retardation for illegitimate children reared in foster homes solely on the bases of the social, intellectual, educational, and occupational performance of the natural parents. By contrast, other studies have shown that many retarded children come from homes where they are reared by parents who present inferior social histories.

Speer, G. S. The Mental Development of Children of Feeble-minded and Normal Mothers. *Yearbook of the National Society for the Study of Education,* 1940, 39, 309-314.

Purpose: To compare the intellectual development of children of mentally retarded and nonretarded mothers.

Subjects: 68 physically normal children whose mothers were identified as retarded and 57 physically normal children whose mothers were not mentally retarded were subjects for this study. Both groups of children were legally dependent.

Procedure: When a mother died, deserted, or was declared incompetent, all children in the family under 16 years of age were declared dependent and placed in boarding homes. Intelligence tests were administered to all children (prior to placement for those over 12; within three months of placement for those over age three, and several years after placement for those under age three) and their age at placement was noted.

Results: The data indicated a consistent decrease in the IQ of children of retarded mothers as a function of the length of time the children had spent in their own homes. The median IQ for this group of children fell from 100.5 for those placed in foster homes when two years or younger to 53.1 for those placed when between the ages of 12 and 15. This relationship did not appear for children of nonretarded mothers.

Comment: Despite a number of methodological questions which cloud interpretation, the dramatic differences in intellectual level obtained as a function of age at time of placement suggest a direct relationship: the longer the exposure to adverse environmental conditions, the greater the deterioration in level of intellectual function.

In Review

Many critical problems of methodology have plagued researchers who have attempted to study the effects of environmental factors on intellectual development. Some of the major problems bearing on interpretation of the environmental studies are: (a) lack of random assignment of infants or children to the various conditions of environment being studied (e.g. own home vs. foster home); (b) changes in the aspects of behavior typically measured by general intelligence tests from early infancy to later childhood, and differences in the social concept of mental retardation from infancy to childhood to adult life; (c) inadequate psychometric data on the natural parents of the children under study; and (d) lack of precise measures of various components of environment (e.g., impoverishment of the environment is usually rated on the basis of such gross measures as parent occupation, education, and income, or parental breaches of the legal or moral code). As a consequence of these and other critical problems of methodology, our knowledge of the environmental determinants of intellectual deviations is still quite limited. The trend of the findings of studies reported in this section suggests that intellectual development is modified by psychological and social factors within the environment, and that retrogressions or progressions in level of intellectual functioning sometimes are brought about by substantial changes in environmental conditions.

The difficult problems of methodology which were not surmounted in the early studies have resulted in a neglect of this area of investigation by researchers during the past few years. However, no area of knowledge is of greater importance in education of the mentally retarded than that concerning the question of the extent to which the various intellectual abilities may be influenced by various components of the environment. The more sophisticated experimental designs and techniques available

62

today must be brought to bear on this area of research in mental retardation.

LEARNING AND PERFORMANCE

In the past decade a great number of basic experimental studies have been conducted which have been aimed at uncovering the role of specific variables in the performance or achievement deficit of the retarded child. As we achieve a better understanding of the role played by such variables as incentive motivation, incidental learning, retention, verbal mediation, stimulus-attending, etc., it will become possible to devise educational methods which will take into account the specific deficits of the retarded pupils.

Eisman, Bernice S. Paired Associate Learning, Generalization and Retention as a Function of Intelligence. *American Journal of Mental Deficiency*, 1958, 63, 481-489.

Purpose: To compare paired-associate learning, stimulus generalization, and retention in intellectually retarded, normal, and superior children.

Subjects: Groups (23 subjects each) of high (IQ 120 to 134), average (IQ 91 to 108), and low (IQ 46 to 77) ability were selected from the same junior high school and matched on chronological age.

Procedure: The paired-associate learning task consisted of seven pairs of pictures of common objects (basket-hammer, auto-jack, etc.). The learning task was repeated until a criterion of four correct trials was achieved. Following the learning task a stimulus generalization task was given. Short-term recall (for half the subjects) was measured one week after the learning task and long-term recall was assessed after a one-month interval.

Results: No significant differences between groups were obtained in learning, stimulus generalization or retention.

Comment: The findings of this study are highly provocative in indicating that educable retarded subjects develop new associations of already well-differentiated stimuli and responses as rapidly as their age peers of normal or superior intelligence. It is possible, however, that the findings may be an artifact of the methodology of using highly familiar pictorial stimuli, with the task being too simple to be sensitive to group differences in learning and retention. Additional studies of paired as-

63

sociate learning using nonmeaningful stimuli and tasks of different
difficulty levels are obviously needed before definitive conclusions may
be drawn.

Griffith, B. C., and Spitz, H. H. Some Relationships Between
Abstraction and Word Meaning in Retarded Adolescents.
American Journal of Mental Deficiency, 1958, 63, 247-251.

Purpose: To study the relationship between verbal abstraction and
the ways in which nouns are defined.

Subjects: 26 institutionalized, mentally retarded boys (mean IQ 66,
range 48 to 83) ranging in age from 14 to 20 with a mean age of 17-2.

Procedure: Subjects were given an abstraction test which involved the
abstraction of a common property from each of a series of groups of
three nouns (e.g. carrots, peaches, meat). These same nouns were also
embedded in a list of nouns which subjects were required to define individually. The order of presentation of the definition and abstraction
tasks was counterbalanced with a 24-hour interval between tests.

Results: Most retarded subjects failed to produce an acceptable abstraction *unless* they had also defined on the definition test at least two
of the three nouns comprising the triad by the common characteristic
(e.g. "eat" for at least two of the triad "carrots, peaches, meat"). On the
other hand, normal children matched with the retarded group on mental age were highly successful in giving a correct abstraction if they had
defined only one of the three nouns by the common characteristic on
the definition task.

Comment: The study suggests that retardates have difficulty in ab-
stracting unless specific verbal mediators are available. It illustrates that
retardates tend to be inferior to normal children of the same overall
mental age in activities which require verbal abstraction. (See comment
under Griffith, Spitz, and Lipman.)

Griffith, B. C., Spitz, H. H., and Lipman, R. S. Verbal Mediation and Concept Formation in Retarded and Normal Subjects. *Journal of Experimental Psychology,* 1959, 58, 247-251.

Purpose: To study the role of verbal mediators in the formation of
concepts.

Subjects: 44 institutionalized retardates were divided into high (mean
CA 17-9, mean IQ 74) and low (mean CA 16-9, mean IQ 56) groups.

64

The normal subjects were divided into two groups of 31 (mean CA 9-3, mean IQ 109) and 25 (mean CA 7-0, IQ "average") subjects.

Procedure: The procedure used was the same as that in the Griffith and Spitz (1958) experiment.

Results: The findings for the retardates and young normal subjects confirm the findings of the earlier experiment; i.e., in order to produce an acceptable abstraction these subjects had to define two of three nouns in a triad by a characteristic common to all three. The older normal subjects were able to obtain acceptable abstractions when defining only one word of the triad in terms of a common characteristic.

Comment: The findings of this experiment are in agreement with the earlier findings of Griffith and Spitz which suggest that retardates have difficulty in abstraction unless specific verbal mediators are available. However, more than availability of a verbal mediator must be involved in the results. That is, the subject who defined one word of a given triad by a common characteristic actually had an appropriate mediator available. In such cases the problem was the failure to use an available mediator rather than the absence of one. It would be interesting to determine whether these differences between retarded and normal groups would obtain where subjects were required to recognize (using a multiple-choice technique) rather than produce, an appropriate mediator. Since there is the possibility that institutionalized subjects have had less experience calling for verbal abstraction than the noninstitutionalized, it is important that this study be repeated comparing noninstitutionalized retarded children with normal subjects.

Deficits in verbal abstraction abilities have long been implicated as a primary determinant of the subaverage achievement of retarded children. Studies such as this aimed at elucidating the role of verbal processes in the performance deficits of retarded children are of great importance.

Johnson, G. O. Memorization, Recognition, Recall, and Savings. In *Comparative Studies of Some Learning Characteristics in Mentally Retarded and Normal Children of the Same Mental Age.* Syracuse: Syracuse University Research Institute, 1958, 22-39.

Purpose: To study the learning and retention characteristics of groups of retarded and normal children of the same mental age.

Subjects: 30 normal (CA 8-6 to 11-0, mean IQ 100.43, range 80 to 119)

65

and 30 retarded children (CA 11-3 to 16-11, mean IQ 70, range 61 to 76) were matched on sex and equated for mental age.

Procedure: Using the anticipation method with a memory drum and one-second exposure, a serial learning task consisting of six nonsense syllables was presented to each subject. Recognition, recall, and relearning tests were administered one and two weeks after initial learning.

Results: No significant differences between the retarded and normal groups were obtained for original learning, recall or relearning. On the first recognition test (one week after learning) a significant difference in favor of the normals was obtained. No significant difference was found on the second recognition test (two weeks after original learning).

Comment: This study indicates that serial verbal learning is equally rapid for retarded and normal groups of comparable mental age. The use of a CA control group of normal children in this study would have provided evidence concerning the relative importance of low MA and low IQ in serial learning.

Johnson, G. O. Generalization (Transfer of a Principle). In *Comparative Studies of Some Learning Characteristics in Mentally Retarded and Normal Children of the Same Mental Age.* Syracuse: Syracuse University Research Institute, 1958, 75-98.

Purpose: To compare mentally retarded and intellectually average children on their ability to transfer an applicable principle learned on one task to a second, unique task.

Subjects: Groups of 36 normal (CA 8-1 to 10-11, mean IQ 105) and 36 retarded (CA 12-1 to 15-7, mean IQ 69) subjects, each divided into subgroups of 18 subjects each.

Procedure: All subjects disassembled and reassembled an assembly task and were then timed on rate of reassembly for 10 items. The retarded and normal control groups then received additional practice on assembly over a four-day period. The experimental groups were given instruction in a principle which would facilitate assembly and were then given practice. A unique assembly task was finally administered to all subjects as a test of transfer of the principle.

Results: The performance of both retarded and normal experimental groups was superior to that of the control groups on the unique task. The mentally retarded experimental group showed a significantly greater degree of transfer than the intellectually normal group.

Comment: The results of this study are in opposition to the common belief that mental retardates demonstrate substantial deficits in ability to transfer.

Kaufman, M. E., and Peterson, W. M. Acquisition of a Learning Set by Normal and Mentally Retarded Children. *Journal of Comparative and Physiological Psychology,* 1958, 51, 619-621.

Purpose: To study differences between retarded and normal children in the acquisition of an object-quality discrimination learning set.

Subjects: Eight educable retarded subjects (Stanford-Binet IQ 50 to 75, CA 9 to 12) matched with six normals on sex and age.

Procedure: A modified version of the Wisconsin General Test Apparatus was used to observe the formation of a learning set. Eight problems per day were presented, with three trials permitted per problem.

Results: With 90 percent correct on the second trial as the learning set criterion, five of the six normal and one of the eight retarded subjects reached criterion on the first block of 48 problems. The remaining normal and five of the eight retarded subjects reached criterion with training on 48 additional problems. The retarded subjects made a greater percentage of perseverative errors (an error following an error).

Comment: Since the retarded and normal groups varied on MA (being matched on CA), it is not certain whether the results are attributable to the retardation factor or to absolute mental age. The study does demonstrate learning set formation in retarded subjects.

Kounin, J. S. Experimental Studies of Rigidity. Part I. The Measurement of Rigidity in Normal and Feebleminded persons. *Character and Personality,* 1941, 9, 251-272.

Purpose: To test the hypothesis (based on Lewinian field theory) that the older and more mentally retarded a person, the greater the degree of rigidity present.

Subjects: Three groups of 21 subjects, old mentally retarded (CA 29 to 43, mean 41.7), young retarded (CA 10-10 to 17, mean 14-6) and normals (CA 7 to 8-9 mean 7-10) were matched on mental age. All retarded subjects were institutionalized.

Procedure and Results: The general hypothesis regarding greater rigidity in older and more retarded subjects was tested by specific predictions that increased rigidity would facilitate performance on tasks where interference between the psychological situations would be detrimental, and that performance efficiency would be lowered on tasks requiring integration of behavioral situations. These predictions were tested on a number of specific experimental tasks.

Experiment I—Satiation and cosatiation: Subjects were asked to draw four different objects successively. Each subject was asked to draw the second, third, or fourth object after he had become satiated on the preceding object. As predicted, there was the least amount of cosatiation in the case of the older retarded subjects and most among the normals.

Experiment II—Transfer of habit: Subjects were given 20 trials depressing a lever which released a marble. Subjects were then required to raise the lever for a 30-trial period. As predicted, there was less interference from phase I to phase II in the case of the retarded subjects, with the normals making the most errors on phase II.

Experiment III—Card sorting in simple and overlapping situations: Subjects were required to perform simple and complex (overlapping) card-sorting tasks. Moving from the simple tasks to the complex, overlapping tasks was more difficult for the normal than for the young retarded and old retarded subjects.

Experiment IV—Integration by classification: Subjects were required to sort into categories cards which varied in shape and color.

The old retarded subjects found this task extremely difficult, tending to respond to differences among immediately perceived cards rather than to the total group.

Experiment V–Restructuring by classification: Subjects were required to sort cards as in experiment IV but were asked to shift their basis of sorting. Old retarded subjects had the greatest degree of difficulty in shifting the basis of sorting.

Comment: While these findings support the rigidity hypothesis, there are other explanations which should be investigated. For example, the apparent greater rigidity in the retarded group could, in part, be a function of institutionalization rather than retardation. This study should be replicated adding groups of older and institutionalized normals, and groups of noninstitutionalized retarded.

Luria, A. R., and Vinogradova, O. S. An Objective Investigation of the Dynamics of Semantic Systems. *British Journal of Psychology*, 1959, 50, 89-105.

Purpose: To study the regulating function of speech and language in motor performance of mentally retarded children.

Subjects: Children from 15 to 17 years of age who presented varying degrees of mental retardation ("high-grade morons," "low-grade morons" and "imbeciles").

Procedure: Subjects were required to press a button in response to a signal word (e.g. *koshka*—cat), and were tested with words of similar sounds (e.g. *okoshko*—window) and words of similar meaning (dog, kitten, etc.).

Results: While normal and "moron" subjects actually pressed the button only to the signal word, "imbecile" subjects frequently pushed the button in response to similar sounding words. A measure of the tendency to press the button indicated that normals generalized almost exclusively on the basis of meaning; "high-grade morons" showed generalization both to words of similar meaning and sound; "low-grade morons" showed semantic generalization only to the word "kitten" but showed considerable generalization to sound; and imbeciles showed an extreme generalization to sound. While the high-grade morons were able to learn increased semantic generalization and decreased sound generalization with continued reinforcement, fatigue tended to disinhibit the generalized inhibition to sound.

Comment: Comparison and interpretation is made difficult by a lack of precise description of the experimental subjects. The study tends to support the authors' hypothesis that, in the mentally retarded, language fails to develop to the point where it assumes an efficient regulating function over motor behavior.

Plenderleith, M. Discrimination Learning and Discrimination Reversal Learning in Normal and Feebleminded Children. *Journal of Genetic Psychology*, 1956, 88, 107-112.

Purpose: To test the hypothesis that retarded subjects as compared with subjects of average intelligence will perform more poorly on a discrimination reversal learning task.

Subjects: A group of retarded children (Stanford-Binet IQ range from 50 to 69) and a group of normal children, matched on mental age. The retarded and normal groups were divided into two subgroups matched on mental age, chronological age, and IQ.

Procedure: The stimuli used consisted of pairs of pictures. Each pair was presented six times only. New pairs were presented until the subject learned that his first response for each newly presented pair was always the incorrect one. The learning criterion was five correct trials after the initial trial on each of three successive pairs of pictures plus verbalization of the principle involved in the correct solution. In the reversal learning situation the subject was required to respond according to one principle for a varied number of trials and was then required to change the basis of selection of the correct response for six trials. The reversal learning test was administered 24 hours or six weeks after original learning.

Results: Retarded and normal subjects learned the original discrimination problem equally well. Mentally retarded children presented with the discrimination reversal problem after six weeks took longer to reach the criterion than the comparable normal group. All groups, however, showed considerable positive transfer from original to reversal learning task.

Comment: The finding of a significant difference in reversal learning between retarded and normal groups after a six-week interval but not after a 24-hour interval suggests the possibility of a delayed retention deficit in retarded children when compared with the performance of normal children of comparable mental age. While not classed as such, the original learning task was quite comparable to learning set tasks. The results on original learning do not support the notion of a learning set deficit in retarded children and are not consistent with the findings of the previously discussed Kaufman and Peterson study. However, an MA control was used in the present study while a CA control was used in the Kaufman and Peterson study.

Stevenson, H. W., and Iscoe, I. Transposition in the Feeble-minded. *Journal of Experimental Psychology,* 1955, 49, 11-15.

Purpose: To determine if transposition by retarded persons will decrease as the stimuli become increasingly remote from the training pair.

Subjects: 44 institutionalized retardates, ranging in CA from 9 to 40, with an average MA of 7 years.

Procedure: All subjects were trained to choose the smaller of two stimulus squares. The stimuli were presented in a random sequence with the criterion of learning being nine correct choices out of 10. Approximately 60 trials were given each day until the criterion was met.

The subjects were then assigned at random to one of three groups for the test trials which began at the end of the training period. Test trials were continued until four consecutive correct responses were made or until 40 trials had been given. Each group was tested for transposition (i.e. choosing the smaller of the test pair rather than the one nearest in size to the correct stimulus of the training pair) on test stimuli which differed in the amount by which they were discrepant from the size of the training pair.

Results: No decrease in transposition with increasing remoteness of the test stimuli was found. Only three subjects were able to verbalize the principle (i.e. selecting the smaller of the pair presented) in the transposition from one set of stimuli to another.

Comment: This study is important in demonstrating that retarded persons will transpose (on the basis of a relational principle) even though they are unable to verbalize the principle involved.

In Review

Perhaps the most notable change characterizing the field of research in mental retardation over the past decade has been the great increase in basic experimental studies of learning, motivational, and perceptual processes relevant to the education of the mentally retarded. These studies, methodologically, have been among the most sophisticated of the investigations conducted since, typically, they have not encountered the administrative problems of research which beset workers researching applied problems (e.g. the problems consequent to carrying out extreme manipulations of educational and other environmental experiences of children). There are, nevertheless, a few problems which have characterized some of the basic research on learning and served to restrict generalizations of findings.

Occasionally, researchers have viewed the retarded as occupying an intermediate position on the phylogenetic scale between rats and humans. This sometimes has resulted in a restricted conceptualization of researchable problems and a mechanical translation of methodologies, designs, and hypotheses appropriate in animal studies to research with the mentally retarded.

Many studies have compared institutionalized retarded with noninstitutionalized normals, with the factor of institutionalization contaminating the results.

Many studies have used only CA or MA normal controls rather than both. Where only one of these variables is controlled, it is impossible to draw definite conclusions concerning whether obtained differences are a function of low MA, low IQ, or low MA plus low IQ.

Interpretation and generalization of results and integration of findings of different studies often have been impossible, due to extreme variability in the distribution of causes of mental retardation between experimental samples.

71

The studies of learning reviewed here have served to demonstrate that retarded children do not necessarily have a deficit, or equal deficits, in all aspects or types of learning. They have served to focus attention on the specific nature, as opposed to the general nature, of the retarded child's deficit. As compared to research on learning variables, relatively little attention has been directed, as yet, to the role of motivation and perception variables in the performance of retarded children.

EDUCATIONAL METHODS, ACHIEVEMENT, AND PUPIL CHARACTERISTICS

Public school special classes for the educable mentally retarded have existed for more than half a century. It is only in the past decade that we have begun to give considerable attention to evaluating the effectiveness of plans and methods of educating retarded pupils and to studying the educational characteristics of retarded children.

Blatt, B. The Physical, Personality, and Academic Status of Children Who Are Mentally Retarded Attending Special Classes as Compared with Children Who Are Mentally Retarded Attending Regular Classes. *American Journal of Mental Deficiency*, 1958, 62, 810-818.

Purpose: To compare academic achievement, personal adjustment and physical status of mentally retarded pupils enrolled in special classes with that of retarded pupils enrolled in regular classes.

Subjects: 75 retarded pupils (mean CA 13-9, mean IQ 66) enrolled in special classes and 50 retarded pupils (mean CA 13-6, mean IQ 69) enrolled in regular classes in a school system having no special classes. The two groups were comparable in CA, MA, and IQ.

Procedure: Evaluations were made of physical characteristics, physical defects, motor skills, personal and social maturity, academic achievement and interests.

Results: The physical status of the groups did not differ except that uncorrected or permanent physical defects were more prevalent in the special class group. No differences were found between groups in educational achievement. Data from the New York City Scales of Social Maturity and Emotional Stability indicated greater emotional stability and social maturity in special class pupils. Scores on the California Test of Personality, however, indicated no differences between groups in personal and social adjustment.

Comment: The conflicting findings on personal and social adjustment may be accounted for on the basis of the dependency of the New York City Scales on teacher ratings. The obtained differences in favor of special class pupils may have been an artifact of attitudinal differences between regular and special class teachers. Blatt attempted to control the selection factors operative in determining which retarded pupils are placed in special classes by drawing his "regular class" sample from a school system having no special classes. This cannot be considered a satisfactory control over the selection factor since, undoubtedly, some retarded pupils remained in regular classes in the school system from which the "special class" sample was drawn.

Cassidy, Viola M., and Stanton, Jeannette E. *An Investigation of Factors Involved in the Educational Placement of Mentally Retarded Children: A Study of Differences Between Children in Special and Regular Classes in Ohio.* U.S. Office of Education Cooperative Research Program, Project No. 043, Columbus: Ohio State University, 1959.

Purpose: To compare academic achievement and personal-social adjustment of mentally retarded children in special and regular public school classes.

Subjects: Subjects were 100 pupils from special classes for the mentally retarded from 16 different school systems and 94 mentally retarded pupils in regular classes from 20 school systems having no special class services. Subjects ranged in age from 12-0 to 14-11, and in IQ from 50 to 75.

Procedure: A four-hour battery of tests was employed to measure (a) language recognition, (b) visual-motor coordination and perception, (c) visual-motor expression, (d) mental ability, (e) visual perception, (f) academic skills, and (g) personal adjustment.

Results: Mentally retarded pupils in regular classes showed a higher level of academic achievement than retarded pupils in special classes. Special class pupils demonstrated greater personal and social adjustment as evidenced by the California Test of Personality and teachers' ratings. Special class teachers indicated that in working with pupils they placed greater stress on development of personal-social skills than on academic achievement.

Comment: This study suffers from the methodological problem common to this type of investigation; that is, there is no assurance that the special class and regular class pupils were equivalent initially. Never-

73

theless, the study does raise questions as to the efficacy of special classes as far as academic achievement is concerned. It supports the belief that retarded pupils are apt to achieve a more adequate personal and social adjustment in special classes.

Cruickshank, W. M. Arithmetic Ability of Mentally Retarded Children: II. Understanding Arithmetic Processes. *Journal of Educational Research*, 1948, 42, 279-288.

Purpose: To determine whether there are differences in the abilities of retarded and normal children, matched for general mental and arithmetic ages, to solve arithmetic problems and to understand various arithmetic processes.

Subjects: 15 retarded boys (mean CA 14.29, mean IQ 73.33) and 15 intellectually normal boys (mean CA 9.09, mean IQ 110.4), matched on mental and arithmetic ages.

Procedure: A test consisting of 20 problems was presented to each group. In the first administration, subjects were told which arithmetic processes would be used to solve the problems. A slightly different form of the test was administered to subjects 24 hours later to determine whether the previously stated processes would be used. Tests consisted of three types of problems: the first consisted of presentation of necessary plus superfluous facts; the second presented only the needed facts; and the third provided only the computational facts ($5 \times 2 = ?$).

Results: Retarded subjects experienced greater difficulty than normals in naming the arithmetic process involved and in actual solution of the problem. The mentally retarded were significantly less able to use the pertinent facts when they were imbedded in superfluous material, and were less able to solve the problem when the necessary facts were printed in verbal form. They were more nearly like the normals in straight computation.

Comment: This study is one of the few extensive analyses of arithmetic ability in retarded pupils.

Dunn, L. M. A Comparison of the Reading Processes of Mentally Retarded and Normal Boys of the Same Mental Age. I. Studies of Reading and Arithmetic in Mentally Retarded Boys. *Monograph of the Society for Research in Child Development*, 1954, 19, 7-99.

Purpose: To compare educable retarded boys in special classes with intellectually normal boys of the same mental age on various aspects of the reading process.

Subjects: 20 retarded boys (IQ 50 to 79, MA 8-0 to 10-0) enrolled in special classes and 30 normal pupils (IQ 95 to 112) of comparable general mental ages were used as subjects.

Procedure: An extensive battery of tests of various aspects of reading was administered to all subjects. (e.gs., Gates Advanced Primary Reading Tests, Monroe Diagnostic Reading Examination, Monroe Word Discrimination Test, Gray Oral Paragraphs Reading Test, Keystone Visual Survey Tests, Harris Test of Lateral Dominance.)

Results: In reading, the retarded group averaged one year below the normal group of comparable mental age. In reading errors, the retarded group had more faulty vowels, sound omissions, and words aided and refused. They had fewer repetitions and additions of sounds and made less use of context clues. There were no differences between groups in frequency of faulty consonants, reversals, or other types of errors.

Normal pupils presented fewer visual problems and were superior in basic auditory acuity. No significant differences between groups were found on handedness, eye dominance, or mixed lateral dominance. No differences between retarded and normal subjects were found in sound-blending skills. On the basis of teacher ratings, more personal-social maladjustments were found in the retarded group.

Comment: This study is the most extensive analysis of reading skills of educable retarded pupils that has been conducted. The findings of greater prevalences of visual and auditory defects and social-emotional problems in the retarded group suggest that these may, themselves, be factors related to below-expectancy reading skills among educable retarded pupils.

Francis, R. J., and Rarick, G. L. Motor Characteristics of the Mentally Retarded. *American Journal of Mental Deficiency,* 1959, 63, 792-811.

Purpose: To study gross motor abilities of educable mentally retarded children.

Subjects: 284 educable mentally retarded children (IQ 50 to 90, CA 7-6 to 14-6) from special public school classes.

Procedure: A battery of 11 motor performance tests was administered to each subject. These tests included measures of Static Strength, Running Speed, Dynamic Strength, Agility, and Balance.

Results: The mentally retarded children were significantly inferior to normal children on all motor proficiency tests, with scores ranging from two to four years below published age norms. Further, the discrepancy between the performance of the retarded and normals tended to increase with advancing age.

Comment: This study convincingly refutes the common belief that non-organic educable retarded children do not show deficiencies in motor skill development.

Gallagher, J. J. A Comparison of Brain-Injured and Non-Brain-Injured Mentally Retarded Children on Several Psychological Variables. *Monograph of the Society for Research in Child Development,* 1957, No. 2 (Whole No. 65).

Purpose: To investigate differences in behavior characteristics between brain injured and familial mentally retarded children.

Subjects: 48 institutionalized mentally retarded children (CA 6-9 to 14-5, Stanford Binet IQ 35 to 76) were used as subjects. One-half of the subjects were diagnosed as cultural-familial mentally retarded and the other half as brain injured on the basis of the Riggs and Rain classification system, EEG findings, and individual neurological examination.

Procedure: Subjects were administered a wide variety of tests of verbal and nonverbal intelligence, language development, quantitative conceptualization, personality factors and perceptual ability. The measures used ranged from standardized tests to tests developed specifically for use in the experiment.

Results: Significant differences between brain injured and familial groups were not obtained for any of the measures of perceptual ability. Wide variability in the performance of the brain injured group was noted, however, with some subjects doing well on perceptual tasks and others very poorly. There was, likewise, little evidence of differences between groups in the development of quantitative concepts or in basic learning ability. On subtests of the language scale used, however, brain injured subjects were inferior to familials on objection association, visual form tracing, and vocal "cloze" meaning. On the other hand, the brain injured subjects were superior on picture series description and two subtests which demanded a type of verbal imitative behavior. On personality measures, the brain injured group was more hyperactive, demanding, anxious, distractible, showed a greater need for affection, and was less able to postpone gratification.

Comment: For a number of years educators and psychologists have tended to generalize a number of behavior attributes (disorders of perception, in particular) to those mentally retarded receiving a general medical designation of brain injured. The findings of this carefully designed study clearly indicate that *not all* brain injured children are characterized by perceptual disturbances or other behavior disorders; that some do is not questioned. The results suggest that educational programs should be based on the specific behavioral abilities and disabilities presented rather than on a designation of brain injury.

Gallagher, J. J. *Tutoring of Brain-Injured Mentally Retarded Children.* Springfield, Illinois: Charles C. Thomas, 1960.

Purpose: To study the effects of tutoring on the intellectual and personal-social development of children diagnosed as brain injured.

Subjects: 42 institutionalized brain injured children (CA 8 to 12) matched on Stanford-Binet MA, and assigned at random to experimental and control groups.

Procedure: The experimental group was tutored on tasks designed to facilitate development of intellectual skills for one hour a day for two years and then received no tutoring for one year. The control group received tutoring only in the third year. A number of tests were administered and re-administered over the experimental period to measure changes in behavioral skills.

Results: Brain injured children improved in intellectual functioning as a result of tutoring, with younger children making greater gains than older children. Gains in verbal skills were greater than in nonverbal skills. Cessation of tutoring resulted in a tendency for the child to regress in developmental level.

Comment: The author's findings provide a basis for some optimism regarding the potential response of brain injured children to specialized education. This study represents the only objective evaluation of the effectiveness of special educational techniques in facilitating the development of this type of pupil. Whether even more positive results would be obtained with noninstitutionalized children or with a more extensive teaching program are follow-up questions which merit study.

Hegge, T. G. Special Reading Disability with Particular Reference to the Mentally Deficient. *Proceedings of the American Association of Mental Deficiency*, 1934, 39, 297-343.

Purpose: To study the effectiveness of a remedial reading program based on principles of learning for mentally retarded pupils with special reading difficulties.

Subjects: An experimental group of 14 pupils (mean CA 13-4, IQ 71, reading grade 1.6) and a comparison group of 100 unselected institutional pupils of approximately the same chronological and mental age distributions.

Procedure: The experimental group was exposed to a method of remedial reading instruction which utilized a systematic series of reading drills (30 minutes of individual daily instruction).

Results: The experimental group, after a 22-month period, showed an average reading gain of 2.6 grades, an advancement several times greater than that of the comparison group (average increment .43 grades), and greater than that to be expected in the general population of normal children.

Comment: This study served to demonstrate the value of a systematic program of remedial reading training for retarded children.

Johnson, G. O. A Study of the Social Position of Mentally Handicapped Children in the Regular Grades. *American Journal of Mental Deficiency*, 1950, 55, 60-89.

Purpose: To determine whether mentally retarded pupils in regular classes are accepted, isolated, or rejected by their classmates.

Subjects: 659 typical and 39 retarded pupils from 25 regular public school classes, each of which contained at least one retarded pupil. Retarded pupils were selected on the basis of a Stanford-Binet IQ score below 70 and other criteria.

Procedure: A sociometric rating technique was used to determine "stars," "isolates," and rejected pupils.

Results: Results of ratings were as follows;

	Retarded pupils	Typical pupils
Stars	5.13%	17.45%
Isolates	69.23%	39.00%
Rejectees	46.15%	4.40%

Reasons for isolation and rejection of retarded pupils by their age peers appeared to be associated with antisocial behavior rather than poor academic achievement.

Comment: This study demonstrates that retarded pupils can be psychologically as segregated from their age peers in regular classes as in special classes.

Kirk, S. A. The Effects of Remedial Reading on the Educational Progress and Personality Adjustment of High-Grade Mentally Deficient Problem Children: Ten Case Studies. *Journal of Juvenile Research*, 1934, 18, 140-162.

Purpose: To evaluate effects of remedial reading on educational progress and personal adjustment of retarded pupils.

Subjects: 10 children (CA 11 to 17, IQ 65 to 90) who had been committed to an institution for high-grade mentally deficient children.

Procedure: Case studies based on psychological and educational evaluations, on behavior reports, and on daily reading records were completed for each subject.

Results: Case study findings suggested that in some cases therapeutic effects accompany remediation of special reading difficulties. Based on approximate averages, the case study group progressed 1.2 grades on a battery of reading tests and .6 grades on the complete Stanford Achievement Test over a five-month period of training with standard remedial reading lessons. By comparison, a group selected from the total population at the institution school progressed only .43 grades in reading level over 10 months of schooling. Over a five-month period following remedial reading instruction, the case study group showed approximately twice as much progress on the total Stanford Achievement Test as the comparison group from the general school program of the institution. In addition, success in reading tended to be correlated with a reduction in classroom behaviors associated with maladjustment.

Comment: This study represents one of the earliest efforts to demonstrate the efficacy of providing mentally retarded pupils with a systematic program of reading instruction based on established principles of learning.

Kirk, S. A. *Early Education of the Mentally Retarded.* Urbana: University of Illinois Press, 1958.

Purpose: To determine the effect of preschool education on the social and mental development of young educable mentally handicapped children.

Subjects: Four groups of educable mentally retarded children (CA three to six at time of initial examination, IQs from 40 to 80) were utilized as follows:

Community Experimental Group: 28 preschool mentally handicapped children from the community who were given a six hours per day enriched nursery school environment until entering first grade or a special class at the age of six years.

Community Contrast Group: 26 preschool mentally handicapped children from the same or neighboring communities who were not exposed to preschool experience. This group was called a "contrast group" because of the inability to randomize subjects due to the difficulty in securing a sufficient number of children.

Institution Experimental Group: 15 institutionalized retarded subjects who were taken from the wards for six hours per day and exposed to an enriched preschool program.

Institution Contrast Group: 12 children who were similar to the experimental group but from another institution, and who were never exposed to a preschool program. In addition, data on a group of 10 institutionalized cases who had been tested and retested at the preschool-age level were taken from the files and used for a sub-contrast group.

Procedure: All groups were administered intelligence and social maturity tests before, during, and after the preschool experience. Contrast groups were tested over the same periods as the preschool groups. On the basis of these test data plus data from case studies, all children were classified according to level of social and mental development into one of the following categories: (a) uneducable, (b) questionable educability, (c) low educable, (d) high educable, (e) borderline, (f) low average, (g) average. A comparison of relative changes in social and intellectual level between the experimental and contrast groups was made.

Results: Children receiving preschool education in both the community and institution made significantly greater changes in IQs and SQs on the Binet, Kuhlmann, and Vineland tests than did contrast group subjects.

In the community, the experimental group had made significantly greater gains on all tests by the end of the preschool period than the contrast group. While the experimental group gained in both IQ and SQ during this period, the contrast group made little if any gain. However, after the community contrast group entered first grade or special education classes at ages six to seven, their IQs and SQs also tended to show increments. The experimental group tended to retain the gains already made, without further acceleration.

For the institutional groups, the preschool subjects showed significant gains in IQ and SQ whereas the contrast group tended to drop in IQ and SQ. The experimental group retained the gains already made but evidenced no further acceleration after leaving preschool. The contrast group did not show any further decrement in function after entering the institution school program.

Changes in rate of growth were greatest for retarded children coming from the most culturally deprived conditions and evidencing no CNS pathology. They were least for organically impaired children, while children who were both organically impaired and culturally deprived occupied an intermediate position.

Comment: This is perhaps the study of greatest significance in the education of the mentally retarded which has been conducted in the past several years. Kirk has demonstrated the importance of providing early enriched environmental opportunities for the mentally handicapped, particularly for children being reared under subcultural conditions. Kirk encountered great difficulty in identifying preschool-age educable retarded who did not present organic components. Therefore, his sample for that group was small. This study should be extended using a larger group of children being reared under adverse environmental circumstances who have a high probability (as determined by test and family history data) of being placed in special classes as they enter and progress through school.

Thurstone, Thelma G. *An Evaluation of Educating Mentally Handicapped Children in Special Classes and in Regular Grades.* U.S. Office of Education Cooperative Research Program, Project No. OE-SAE-6452. Chapel Hill: University of North Carolina, 1960.

Purpose: To compare the intellectual growth, academic achievement, social development, and gross motor skills of educable mentally handicapped children enrolled in regular and special classes in North Carolina.

Subjects: 1273 children with IQs between 50 and 79, of whom 769 were in special classes and 504 were in the regular grades.

Procedure: The subjects were evaluated on the Stanford-Binet Test of Intelligence, the Stanford Achievement Test, the Primary Mental Abilities Test, various sociometric devices, and a test of gross motor skills.

Results: On the first administration of the Stanford Achievement

Test, the regular class retardates had significantly higher achievement scores than the special class children in all areas except arithmetic computation. On the second year's administration of the test, there were no significant differences between the gain scores for regular and special class children. However, for the lower IQ (50 to 59) group, the gain scores, except in arithmetic computation, were significantly higher in favor of the special class children.

The mentally handicapped children in the regular grades were found to be rejected and social isolates. The special class children seemed to be better adjusted in school and to have more friends than the regular class retardates. In gross motor skills, the retardates were consistently inferior in their accomplishments to normal children of comparable age.

Comment: As with other studies comparing achievement of retarded pupils in regular versus special classes the results are difficult to interpret due to the lack of control over assignment to special classes and maintenance in regular classes. This study cites evidence of superior social adjustment among special class pupils. However, mutual acceptance of each other within the special class is not evidence that these children are not as maladjusted as retarded pupils remaining in regular classes in the area of relationships with normal siblings and peers.

Weiner, Bluma B. A Report on the Final Academic Achievement of Thirty-seven Mentally Handicapped Boys Who Had Been Enrolled in a Prolonged Pre-academic Program. *American Journal of Mental Deficiency*, 1954, 59, 210-219.

Purpose: To determine the effects of a prolonged pre-academic program (emphasizing socialization, language and concept development, arts and crafts, and play and recreation skills) on final academic status of retarded pupils.

Subjects: 37 experimental subjects and 31 comparison subjects, all males, ranged in IQ from 60 to 79. Average age at time of enrollment in the pre-academic program was 8-10.

Procedure: Children in the experimental group were enrolled in the pre-academic program from an average age of 8-10 to 11-2, at which time they were transferred to the general academic program of the Wayne County Training School. Children in the comparison group were enrolled in the general academic program throughout. Final academic achievement of both groups was assessed at an average age of 15-6.

Results: There were no significant differences between groups on final academic status in reading, arithmetic or overall achievement.

Comment: This report raises a question as to the most appropriate level for initiation of teaching of traditional academic subjects. The study should be repeated and related investigations conducted in public school settings.

In Review

A number of studies have attempted to compare the effectiveness of special classes and regular classes in facilitating academic learning and social adjustment of educable retarded children. However, conclusions must be held in abeyance since in none of the studies were retarded children assigned at random to special or regular classes, and no study investigated effectiveness of special classes as a function of the nature of the special class curriculum or teacher qualifications.

Most of the educational studies have been retrospective; that is, the pupils were already assigned and participating in the educational treatment to be evaluated (e.g., institution vs. public school education, regular class vs. special class). In retrospective studies of this type it is quite probable that unspecified selective factors which operated to determine the pupil's placement also related to his educational achievement. As a consequence of unspecified selective factors, definitive conclusions from retrospective studies are hazardous. A second defect of much educational research is that it has studied the effects of educational treatments for retarded children *in general.* It is quite possible that the effects of given educational treatments may differ among groups of retarded children showing different behavioral characteristics. There is a great need for educational research in which pupils are assigned to experimental treatments at random and in which effects are studied as a function of specific intellectual and personal-social characteristics.

SOCIO-OCCUPATIONAL ADJUSTMENT OF EDUCABLE MENTALLY RETARDED AS ADULTS

The ultimate criterion of success of all educational efforts on behalf of the educable retarded is the adequacy of the social and vocational adjustment achieved by these persons in adult life. Therefore, many surveys have been conducted relative to the adult adjustment of mentally retarded persons.

Baller, W. R. A Study of the Present Social Status of a Group of Adults Who, When They Were in Elementary Schools, Were Classified as Mentally Deficient. *Genetic Psychology Monographs*, 1936, 18, 165-244.

Purpose: To investigate the adult personal, social, and vocational adjustment of persons who had been enrolled in special classes for the mentally retarded in the Lincoln, Nebraska public schools.

Subjects: 206 pupils formerly enrolled in special classes for the mentally retarded in the Lincoln, Nebraska public schools selected on the basis of IQ of 70 or less, clinical evaluation which indicated mental retardation, one or more years of special class attendance, and CA greater than 21 years at time of the study. Control subjects with group-test IQs from 100 to 120 were matched with the former special class pupils on the basis of age, sex, and nationality.

Procedure: Information regarding the subjects was obtained through personal contacts and by examination of pertinent records of all community and state agencies to whom subjects might have been known.

Results: Ninety-five percent of the mentally retarded subjects and 98 percent of the normal control subjects were located for follow-up study. The average age of subjects at the time of follow-up was 27 (Range 21 to 34). Only 11.22 percent of the mentally retarded subjects had been institutionalized at any time. Approximately seven percent of the retarded subjects, as compared with one percent of the control subjects, were deceased at follow-up.

Thirty-three percent of the male retarded subjects and 59 percent of the females were married and had an average of 1.32 children per marriage as compared with .84 per marriage for control subjects. There were from three to seven times more breaches of the law among the retarded than among normal controls (percentage of violations varied from 25 to 1.5 percent depending upon category). During the depression years (1931 to 35), two and one-third times more retarded than normal subjects were added to relief rolls.

Forty-eight of the 196 retarded subjects followed up were making a completely acceptable adjustment as judged by the fact that they were totally self-supporting and had no record of violation of the legal or social standards of their communities. Eighty-three percent of the retarded had been self-supporting to some extent for some period of time. (See comment under Charles, below.)

Charles, D. C. Ability and Accomplishment of Persons Earlier Judged Mentally Deficient. *Genetic Psychology Monographs*, 1953, 47, 3-71.

Purpose: To study the current adjustment (1950) of former pupils in special classes for the mentally retarded who had been studied 15 years earlier (1935) by Baller.

Subjects: 151 of the 196 former mentally retarded pupils originally located by Baller (see previous review). These subjects appeared to be representative of the total original group. Current ages varied from 36 to 49.

Procedure: Intensive efforts were made to locate as many of the original Baller group as possible. Current status information was obtained by interview of subjects and by examination of agency and institutional records.

Results: Follow-up in 1950 revealed: (a) a continued slightly higher mortality than the general population, (b) slightly lower average number of children per family for married subjects than the national norm, (c) institutionalization at some time for 10 percent of the total group, (d) a slightly lower marriage rate than the national norm, and (e) a divorce rate about equal to that of the general population. Three-fourths of the subjects lived in single family units and over half owned or were buying homes. In the post-war period, 66 percent of the subjects were totally self-supporting, 25 percent were receiving some economic assistance, and 9 percent were receiving considerable aid. Thirty-eight percent of the group had a record of law violation, the majority being instances of traffic and minor civil cases. The majority of the 183 children of the married subjects were progressing through school without evidence of retardation. The distribution of their intelligence test scores approximated that of the general population (mean 95; SD 16.5).

Comment: Charles' follow-up of Baller's investigation indicates the importance of economic conditions to the adjustment achieved by retarded adults: a far more optimistic picture of vocational status is presented in the Charles study (post-WW II period) than in the Baller report (depression period). Charles' study suggest that retarded persons may be expected to progress in their level of adjustment as they move from their early 20s to their 30s and 40s. This report dispels the notion that the retarded invariably produce large families of retarded offspring. This study fails to consider the significance of legal violations, moral deviations, public assistance, etc., in relation to the sociocultural milieu in which the low-income retarded adult finds himself. A highly informative study would be one in which retarded adults were compared on these variables with nonretarded persons of equivalent incomes.

Fernald, W. E. After-care Study of the Patients Discharged from Waverly for a Period of Twenty-five Years. *Ungraded,* 1919, 5, 25-31.

Purpose: To study the community adjustment of mentally retarded patients who had been discharged from the Massachusetts School for the Feebleminded over a 25-year period from 1890-1914 inclusive.

Subjects: Of the 1537 patients discharged during this period, 646 (470 males and 176 females) were available for the purposes of this study. While accurate reports on intellectual status of this group of 646 were not reported, there is indication that all levels of retardation were represented.

Procedure: Current community adjustment of the former patients was ascertained by means of correspondence and interviews with parents, friends, and others having relevant information concerning former patients.

Results: Of the 176 females studied, 62 had been re-admitted or committed to other institutions and 24 had died. Of the 90 remaining in the community, 27 were married (with a total of 50 offspring), 8 (unmarried) were completely self-supporting, 32 were providing substantial help in their homes, and 23 were living at home but not performing useful service. Over the 25-year period, 48 of the 176 women had a history of sex violations, and four had been sentenced to penal institutions.

Of the 470 males, 111 had been re-admitted or committed to other institutions, 54 had died, 55 had been arrested, and 32 of these committed to penal institutions. Among the remaining 250 cases, 28 were completely self-supporting and without supervision, 86 were earning wages but receiving supervision at home, 77 were providing help in the home only, and 59 were living at home without providing any help.

Comments: This study is of historical significance in that it represents the first important follow-up of mentally retarded patients released from institutions. The belief prevailing at the time of this study was that the mentally retarded were predisposed to antisocial and immoral behavior and that they were always incapable of contributing to their own support. Solution of the problem from society's viewpoint was felt to be found through segregation in institutions which emphasized custody and physical management. As Fernald, in reporting his study, stated:

"The relatively small number of discharges for so long a period . . . shows that the policy of long-continued segregation was consistently followed during the entire period. We honestly believed that nearly all of these people should remain in the institution indefinitely. Some were allowed to go because they seemed to have no vicious tendencies, and their friends were intelligent and able to look out for them, but the *majority were dismissed under protest*" (italics mine). Fernald's follow-up study demonstrated that some retarded persons were capable of useful work and contributing to their support, and that they were not necessarily criminally or morally degenerate. Fernald's findings contributed to a modification of the pessimistic view of the era and to a shift in emphasis of institutions from physical management to habilitation.

> Kennedy, Ruby J. R., *et al. The Social Adjustment of Morons in a Connecticut City.* Hartford: Commission to Study Resources of the State of Connecticut, in Collaboration with the Carnegie Institute of Washington, 1948.

Purpose: To study the community adjustment of mentally retarded adults.

Subjects: 256 mentally retarded (IQ 45 to 75) adults and 129 normal controls. The two groups were matched on sex, age, birthplace, religion, and nationality, and derived from the same socio-economic background.

Procedure: Occupational and social status were determined through interviews with subjects and their employers and through study of public records.

Results: A larger percentage of the retarded subjects as compared with the controls were unemployed, married, on relief, had come to the attention of police and courts, and had parents who themselves had records of legal or moral violations. A smaller percentage of the retarded subjects owned their own homes, participated in community recreational activities, or had served in the military. In general, the above and other similar differences tended to be small but significant. The most striking differences obtained between groups were in types of occupations and in educational achievement. Occupational attainment and educational status were distinctly superior for the normal controls.

Comment: Differences in adjustment of retarded and nonretarded adults, though significant in most categories, tend to be smaller than some perhaps would anticipate. These findings thereby engender optimism concerning the potential of retarded persons to lead satisfactory lives in the community. Comparison studies of retarded and nonre-

87

tarded adults have typically failed to take into consideration differences in social characteristics which may be created by differences in socio-economic level achieved. Many of the differences obtained may be a function of differences in sociocultural circumstances rather than the factor of mental retardation per se.

Krishef, C. H., and Hall, M. A. Employment of the Mentally Retarded in Hennepin County, Minnesota. *American Journal of Mental Deficiency,* 1955, 60, 182-189.

Purpose: To study occupational characteristics of employed retardates and to determine the relationship of intelligence level to job category and salary level.

Subjects: 177 employed retardates under guardianship of a county welfare board. Subjects were divided into high IQ (60 to 79) and low IQ (50 or lower) male and female groups.

Procedure: Vocational status was classified according to the Dictionary of Occupational Titles.

Results: No differences in salary level, type of job, or length of time on the same job, were noted for the two male IQ groups. The high IQ group of females held a number of types of jobs (maids in private homes, nurses' aides, practical nurses, and waitresses) which were not represented in the lower IQ groups. As with the males, no differences in salary or length of time on the job existed between high and low IQ groups.

Conclusion: The study is consistent with a number of similar status studies in finding measured intelligence—within the traditional educable retarded range—to be a relatively unimportant variable in vocational adjustment.

Peckham, R. A. Problems in Job Adjustment of the Mentally Retarded. *American Journal of Mental Deficiency,* 1951, 56, 448-453.

Purpose: To identify important factors related to job adjustment of mentally retarded workers.

Subjects: A sample of 80 representative mentally retarded clients of the Michigan Division of Vocational Rehabilitation.

Procedure: The rehabilitation counselors made independent studies of the clients whom they had served for the purpose of identifying the client's problems in initial efforts to adjust to the job and the methods used by the counselor in assisting the client to meet these problems.

Results: Acceptance by fellow workers was viewed by counselors as the most important single problem. Each counselor reported ridicule and teasing by co-workers as a frequent basis for job termination. General lack of social sophistication as reflected in disregard of rules for punctuality, proper dress, and general deportment was also reported by all counselors as a frequent source of difficulty in work adjustment. Dissatisfaction with salary, difficulties in management of finances, lack of initiative, and unrealistic aspirations and assessment of abilities on the part of parents and clients were also identified as frequent problems.

Counselors felt that many of these problems could be solved by conferences with clients, parents, and employers, and by on-the-job training programs. Counselors perceived superimposed physical disabilities and serious personality problems as complicating problems which frequently proved unsolvable.

Comment: It is important to recognize that the results of this study are based, in large measure, on *post hoc* opinions of the counselors who worked with the clients involved. The study highlights, however, the importance of extrapersonal variables (employer, co-worker attitudes, etc.) and accessory job skills (personal-social attributes) in the vocational adjustment of the mentally retarded.

In Review

Research on socio-occupational adjustment of retarded persons has tended to focus on status surveys in which current status (income, type of job, length of time on job, police record, marriage record) are related to a few simple variables (IQ, physical appearance, age, length of prior institutionalization). Investigators, typically, have failed to consider the effects of the sociocultural milieu of low-income families in reporting and interpreting findings of these status surveys. Consequently, little can be said regarding the relationship of intellectual retardation to community adjustment independent of the factors of socio-economic circumstances.

Studies are needed of the social adjustment of retarded adults in comparison with the adjustment of nonretarded adults living in comparable socio-economic circumstances. Research attention must be directed to the relationship of specific educational treatments (e.g., curricula emphasizing job skill training vs. curricula emphasizing traditional academic achievement) to adult adjustment, and to the relationship of extra-personal variables (e.g., employer, co-worker, and community attitudes) to adult community adjustment.

89

3

The Trainable Mentally Retarded

Leon Charney

The trainable mentally retarded are those children who are ineligible for classes for the educable mentally retarded, but who possess potentialities for training in self care, social adjustment in the home or neighborhood, and economic usefulness in the home or in a sheltered environment. On an individual psychometric examination such children usually fall in the 30 to 50 IQ range. At maturity they may attain a mental age range from approximately four to eight years.

The material contained in this chapter is organized under the following topics:

1. Surveys and evaluations of school programs.
2. Physical and behavioral characteristics.
3. Learning.
4. Follow-up studies.
5. Family adjustment and parental counseling.

SURVEYS AND EVALUATIONS OF PUBLIC SCHOOL PROGRAMS

> Connor, Frances P., and Goldberg, I. I. Opinions of Some Teachers Regarding their Work with Trainable Children: Implications for Teacher Education. *American Journal of Mental Deficiency*, 1960, 64, 658-670.
>
> *Purpose:* To provide information concerning the composition of

Reviewed by I. Ignacy Goldberg, Teachers College, Columbia University.

classes organized for trainable children, and to assess the attitudes of teachers of these children.

Procedure: A questionnaire was sent to 200 teachers in 46 states. Ninety-two responses were received which supplied information concerning 1307 pupils. Responses were received from 44 public day schools, 20 private day schools, 23 state residential centers and five residential schools.

Results: for the total group of pupils CA ranged from three to 36 years. The median CA for the group was 11 years. The median IQ for the public day school children was 47. Children in private day schools revealed a median IQ of 38, while those in public residential schools and private residential schools obtained median IQs of 35 and 41 respectively. Twenty-three percent of the entire group were reported to be above 50 IQ. Of the public day school group, 34 percent of the children were reported to have IQs above 50 compared to 17 percent above IQ 50 for the children in public residential schools. Fifty-two percent of the 1307 pupils were reported as falling into the clinical categories of mongolism, cerebral palsy, brain injury or epilepsy. Teachers did not support the contention that mongoloids were docile or placid. Teachers indicated a need for more carefully defined screening standards and for adequate housing. They also indicated a need for specific preparation in the area of the trainable child, including techniques to facilitate parent communication.

Comment: The differences in median IQs of children in the various programs emphasize the dangers involved in generalizing from research conducted with children enrolled in a particular type of facility. The survey confirms the impression that this is generally a multiply handicapped group. The high percentage of children manifesting IQs above 50 (particularly in public day school classes) indicates that factors other than intellectual ability are considered in placement.

Bonham, S. S. *Report on the National Survey of Community Class Programs for the Trainable Mentally Retarded Child.* Report of the Governor's Committee for the Mentally Retarded, State of Ohio, 1960.

Purpose: To secure data concerning legislation, state standards, criteria, and policy regarding programs for the trainable mentally retarded child.

Procedure: Direct communication was undertaken with each of the 50 states and the District of Columbia. A work sheet was designed and worked out for each of the 51 units. This work sheet was then returned to each state for validation. The validated work sheets were then tabulated.

Results: The survey revealed that 38 states and the District of Columbia had a program of day classes. Of the 12 states reporting no public day school program, six indicated that the question was under study. In 37 instances, administration of these programs was under the state department of education. In Ohio the program was under the Department of Mental Hygiene. Twelve states indicated employment of IQ limits between 30 and 50. Twenty states indicated employment of criteria other than IQ. In 38 instances some form of teacher certification was required. Statewide enrollments ranged from under 100 to over 2500.

Comment: The survey indicates a rapid growth of programs for trainable children under the auspices of the state departments of education.

Kirk, S. A. *Public School Provisions for Severely Retarded Children: A Survey of Practices in the United States.* Special Report to the New York State Interdepartmental Health Resources Board, July 1957.

Purpose: To survey the current status of school programs for severely retarded children in selected communities in the United States and to analyze and evaluate existing legislative provisions and state and local policies and practices.

Procedure: Information was obtained from numerous sources, including the general literature in the field, a study of legislative acts and state regulations, research projects, and on-the-spot visits to many classes and programs in various parts of the United States.

Results: A composite conceptualization of the trainable child stressed potential for self care, social adjustment, and economic usefulness. Studies of incidence indicated one or two severely mentally retarded children in the community for every 1000 school age population. In most cases programs were under the department of education. Annual costs were approximately $900 per child. No specific training programs for teachers of trainable children had been established.

Comment: This is the most comprehensive survey of public school programs available.

Goldstein, H. *Report Number Two on Study Projects for Trainable Mentally Handicapped Children.* Springfield: Illinois Department of Public Instruction, January 1956.

Purpose: To report the results of a two-year pilot study of special classes for trainable mentally handicapped children in local school districts in Illinois. The study undertook to gather facts, to explore problems and procedures related to the instruction of these children, and to evaluate the contribution which the public schools could make toward their training.

Procedure: Study projects were organized in 12 school districts. The projects consisted of 22 classes, 24 teachers and a total enrollment of 198 children. During the first year of the study, data were gathered on a total of 173 children. The children were tested and retested on the Kuhlman Test of Mental Development and either the Ontario School Ability Examination or the Merrill-Palmer Scale. In some cases the Stanford-Binet was used in place of the Kuhlman. The Vineland Social Maturity Scale was administered to all of the children. Teachers and parents rated the children on the Behavior Check List which had been especially devised for use with trainable children.

Results: Consideration of psychometric data for the two-year period revealed a slight increase in IQ by the end of the first year of training. By the end of the second year of training, IQs had declined to that level which obtained at the time of admission. Analysis of teacher and parent ratings on the Behavior Check List revealed that, although the teachers recorded considerable progress during the first year, they recorded no progress during the second year. The parents, on the other hand, recorded less progress than the teachers during the first year, but saw some improvement during the second year.

Analysis of data on 22 children excluded from the program revealed that children with Kuhlman IQs below 24 were eventually dropped from the program. Children with IQs of 35 and above were retained in the program. The Vineland Social Maturity Scale was less discriminating than the Kuhlman IQ in distinguishing those who were eventually dropped from the program from those who were retained.

Parents continued their favorable expectations for the program. There was a decrease in the percentage of parents anticipating that their children would eventually become self supporting. Many also revised their biases against institutions. Survey of three counties and two urban centers revealed at least one or two trainable children per 1000 children of school age in each community.

Comment: This major study failed to reveal any pronounced changes in the intellectual or social behavior of the children as a result of two years of training in a public day school. However, the short-term nature of the study and the absence of control groups prevents the development of definite statements concerning the value of such classes.

Guenther, R. J. *Final Report: The Michigan Demonstration Research Project for the Severely Mentally Retarded.* Lansing: Michigan Department of Public Instruction, August 1956.

Purpose: To establish a demonstration project to explore programs for the severely retarded of varying age levels and to develop an evaluation method for these programs.

Procedure: Three centers were selected: a preschool, a school, and a postschool program. During 1953-54 all three centers were activated in accordance with the plans and procedures of the project and continued in operation for about three years. Changes in the behavior of the children were evaluated by means of the Behavior Check List and a Behavior Check List Supplement. Children were also evaluated on the Stanford-Binet, the Vineland Social Maturity Scale and the Kuhlman Test of Mental Development. Directed interviews were held periodically with each mother and father. Complete case study data were reported on nine children in one center. To determine prevalence, a survey was made in the three centers in which the project was active.

Results: Over the two-year period most children maintained their initial rate of mental growth. The Vineland Social Maturity Scale showed substantially higher scores for seven out of the nine children on the retest in the school center. Similar data were not available for the preschool center or the postschool center. Some gains were noted on the Behavior Rating Scale. By the final interview, parents were somewhat more realistic in their expectations and attitudes toward school.

The survey revealed the prevalence of trainable children in the community living at home to be 1.7 per 1000 school-age children. This compared favorably with the figure of 1.49 per 1000 noted in the Illinois study.

Comment: The value of the psychometric and behavioral data reported is restricted, due to the small number of children for whom complete data were available. However, the survey results are of value in shedding light on the prevalence of trainable mentally retarded in the community.

Johnson, G. O., Capobianco, R. J., and Blake, Kathryn A. An Evaluation of Behavioral Changes in Trainable Mentally Deficient Children. *American Journal of Mental Deficiency*, 1960, 64, 881-893.

Purpose: To assess changes in behavior of trainable mentally retarded children over a two-year period, and to evaluate the usefulness of various tests with trainable children.

Subjects: Children enrolled in seven public school classes and 10 institutional classes were evaluated. The children ranged in CA from 7 to 15 years. They were ineligible for classes for the educable mentally retarded, were ambulatory and toilet trained, and were free of severe personality problems.

Procedure: During the first year the children were evaluated twice on the 1937 Revision of the Stanford-Binet; the Vineland Social Maturity Scale; Behavior Check List; Fels Child Behavior Rating Scale; California Pre-Test of Vision, Hearing, and Motor Coordination; a language scale, and an articulation test. Included in the second year were a large number of tests of intelligence. A trend analysis was undertaken to assess changes in behavior as measured by the Vineland Social Maturity Scale, Fels Child Behavior Rating Scale, and the Behavior Check List.

Results: The Stanford-Binet was considered the best single test, with the Merrill-Palmer, the Minnesota Pre-School Scale, and the Kuhlman Test of Mental Development considered applicable to this group. Results of the trend analysis revealed significant increments in scores on all three measures from first to final administration.

Comment: As with a number of other reported studies, the absence of control groups does not make it possible to attribute observed changes to the program of training. The authors note that while changes were statistically significant, these changes were not of any particular clinical significance.

Hottel, J. V. *An Evaluation of the Tennessee Day Class Program for Severely Retarded (Trainable) Children.* Nashville: George Peabody College for Teachers, 1958.

Purpose: To compare trainable children enrolled in day class programs to trainable children at home in terms of change in behavior and change in parent-child relations.

Subjects: 21 children enrolled in special public school day classes for the first time in 1956-57 were matched on the basis of sex, etiology, CA, MA, and SA to 21 children remaining at home. All children were between CA 6 to 16, and had Stanford-Binet IQs between 30 and 50. The experimental group had a mean CA of 8.7 years and a mean MA of 3.5 years. The mean Stanford-Binet IQ of this group was 41.1. The control group had a mean CA of 8.6 years, and a mean MA of 3.4 years. The mean Stanford-Binet IQ of this group was 39.9.

Procedure: The 1937 Revision of the Stanford-Binet, Form L, and the Vineland Social Maturity Scale were used as criterion measures for matching and as indicators for development of behavioral skills. In addition, a Rating Scale of Child Behavior and a modified Fels Scale of Parent Behavior were utilized. Children in the experimental and control groups were tested on the Stanford-Binet and Vineland within 30 days of the beginning of the 1956-57 school year. A psychological examiner visited the home and interviewed the parents utilizing the Rating Scale of Child Behavior. The examiner rated the home on the modified Fels Scale. At the end of the 1956-57 school year all measures were repeated.

Results: Comparisons of the total experimental and control groups showed that the day class group did not differ significantly from the control group in rate of development of MA, IQ, SA, and SQ.

No significant differences were noted on the Rating Scale of Child Behavior or on the Fels Scale of Parent Behavior. *Post hoc* analysis revealed that children with IQs between 40 and 50 made significantly greater gains in mental age than either children with comparable intelligence who remained at home or children with lower intelligence who attended the special classes.

Comment: This is the only research currently available which utilized a control group. The results tend to confirm the research by Goldstein and by Johnson and Capobianco in that children with IQs in the 40 to 50 range appear to make the most progress in classes for trainable children. The study is limited, however, by its short term nature and the utilization of instruments which were, in general, not sensitive to small changes in the behavior of the children or in parent-child relations.

In Review

In spite of continuing controversy concerning the role of public school education in our society, responsibility for programs for trainable children has been allocated to state departments of education. Short-term studies lacking control groups have failed to demonstrate clinically significant intellectual or behavioral changes in children that might be attributed to the program. The single study utilizing controls indicated that children of 40 to 50 IQ made significant gains in intellectual growth.

PHYSICAL AND BEHAVIORAL CHARACTERISTICS

Capobianco, R. J., and Cole, Dorothy A. Social Behavior of Mentally Retarded Children. *American Journal of Mental Deficiency*, 1960, 64, 638-651.

Purpose: To gather information to provide a better understanding of the functioning social levels of the mentally retarded and to compare the free play behavior of trainable and educable children in institutional and noninstitutional environments.

Subjects: 101 educable mental retardates from public schools and institutions between the ages of 7 and 12-5, and 75 trainable children of similar CAs from private day schools and institutions were utilized. A group of normal children between the ages of 2 and 4-5 was utilized for comparative purposes.

Procedure: Subjects were rated on a social participation scale developed by Parten and Newhall. The socio-economic status of each child was computed on the Warner, Meeker, Eells Index. During a five-month pilot period, three observers rated the children. Following agreement on procedure, they undertook a series of 80 observations of each child.

Results: Educable mental retardates displayed a significantly higher degree of social participation than did the trainable mental retardates. There was no significant difference between institutional and noninstitutional mental retardates in degree of social participation. Females were significantly higher in social participation than were males. The normal children whose MAs were similar to those of the trainable group were rated higher in social participation. For both educables and trainables there was a non-consistent relationship between CA and level of play behavior. MA did not appear to influence significantly the pattern of social participation. Of the three measured variables, CA, MA, and IQ, the last appeared to influence most the play behavior of the mentally retarded child within this chronological age range.

97

Comment: This study is important in that it illustrates a lack of consistent relationship between MA and play behavior. There has been a tendency to equate the retarded child with the normal child of similar mental age. This study did not yield data in support of this tendency. In addition, the study failed to reveal anticipated differences between an institutional and day school group. This is provocative, since it is generally assumed that an institutional environment often has an inhibiting effect upon social behavior.

Semmel, M. Comparison of Teacher Ratings of Brain Injured and Mongoloid Severely Retarded (Trainable) Children Attending Community Day School Classes. *American Journal of Mental Deficiency,* 1960, 64, 963-971.

Purpose: A review of research revealed a lack of conclusive evidence regarding the hypothesis that specific clinical types among the trainable mentally retarded are characterized by unique differences in qualitative psychological functioning. The specific purpose of the study was to explore the differences in teacher ratings of observed functioning of mongoloid and brain injured trainable mental retardates within a community school setting and to determine how mongoloid and brain injured children differ in respect to self-help skills, social skills, motor skills, and academic and vocational skills.

Subjects: 59 pairs of mongoloid and brain injured children were selected from a total day school population of 170 trainable children. The subjects were matched on the basis of CA, MA, and IQ. The Cassel and Riggs criteria were applied in the selection of brain injured children.

Procedure: 17 teachers from the school observed the children in their classes over a period of one month. They rated the children on the Stoddard and Rosenzweig Behavior Rating Scale for Severely Mentally Retarded Children.

Results: There was no significant difference between the groups in total ratings for the five areas contained in the instrument. In toto, teacher ratings of trainable children functioning within the environs of a public school building were not differentiated by the clinical classification of the children observed.

Comment: This study sheds some light on the feasibility of placing mongoloid and brain injured children in the same classroom. The results of this study tend to indicate that such placement is feasible.

Blessing, K. R. The Middle Range Mongoloid in Trainable Classes. *American Journal of Mental Deficiency*, 1959, 63, 812-821.

Purpose: To investigate the attitudes of teachers of the trainable towards mongoloid children enrolled in public school classes.

Procedure: A questionnaire was sent to all 23 of Wisconsin's teachers of the trainable who conduct 38 half-day units. Nineteen out of the 23 teachers responded to the questionnaire. They provided detailed information on 83 mongoloid children out of a total of 225 trainable mental retardates.

Results: Consideration of the behavioral picture reported indicated that mongoloid children run the full gamut of emotional and social responses and that their behavioral responses did not fall into any neat, tight compartment of "docility" and "amenability" as reported earlier in the literature. They were, however, ranked easiest to manage and instruct.

Comment: This study is of importance in that it tends to confirm a growing recognition that characteristics generally attributed to mongoloids may not be as universal as had been earlier assumed.

Cantor, G. N. and Girardeau, F. L. Rhythmic Discrimination Ability in Mongoloid and Normal Children. *American Journal of Mental Deficiency*, 1959, 63, 621-625.

Purpose: To investigate the generalization that mongoloids tend to be characterized by unusual sensitivity to rhythmic stimulation.

Subjects: 44 mongoloids enrolled in trainable classes in 12 Tennessee communities and 24 normals from the Peabody demonstration school were compared. The groups were not equivalent in mental age; the mongoloids had a mean MA of 3 years, while the normals had a mean MA of 4-8.

Procedure: All subjects were required to distinguish between sounds produced by metronomes beating at different rates.

Results: Normals did significantly better than mongoloids. The results seem to indicate that, in the absence of objective evidence to the contrary, trainable-level mongoloids cannot be said to be characterized by a marked sense of rhythm.

Comment: Although this study cannot be considered definitive due to the mental age difference, it does shed some light on the need for an

99

investigation of commonly accepted generalizations concerning the characteristics of mongoloid children.

Gibson, D., and Gibbins, R. J. The Relation of Mongolian Stigmata to Intellectual Status. *American Journal of Mental Deficiency*, 1958, 63, 345-348.

Purpose: To detect any systematic relationship obtaining between the number of mongoloid physical stigmata and degree of amentia.

Subjects: 32 mongoloids, 16 males and 16 females, of mean CA 9.4 were utilized.

Procedure: Subjects were tested on the 1937 Stanford-Binet, Form L, and were examined against 14 diagnostic signs.

Results: Stigmata occurred randomly within the age range of the sample. There was no evidence of a significant linear relationship between CA and physical stigmata. Regression analysis of IQ on number of stigmata yielded a regression coefficient of .63 which was statistically significant. Thus, a positive relationship between intelligence and the number of physical stigmata was demonstrated.

Comment: This study contradicts the popular conception that there is a negative relationship between physical stigmata and intellectual ability in mongoloids. If this study is supported by future research, attention will have to be given by educators to the problem of determining the degree to which mongoloids are placed in classes for trainable children on the basis of stigmata rather than intellectual ability.

Murphy, Mary M. Comparison of Developmental Patterns of Three Diagnostic Groups of Middle Grade and Low Grade Mental Defectives. *American Journal of Mental Deficiency*, 1956, 61, 164-169.

Purpose: To ascertain whether the intellectual development of the mongoloid follows the pattern of the exogenous etiological group or that of the endogenous group.

Subjects: All subjects were residents of three cottages for severely retarded males at Woodbine Colony. The brain injured group consisted of 38 subjects with histories of birth trauma, intracranial infection, etc. The familial group consisted of 40 subjects with no known brain injury. There were 40 subjects in the mongoloid group. These groups were equated on the basis of CA and IQ.

Procedure: The mongoloids were compared with two equated groups of brain injured and familial children in the areas of verbal production and concrete performance. Performance on the Stanford-Binet or Cattell Infant Intelligence Scale was considered an index of verbal production and performance on the Draw-a-Man Test was treated as a measure of concrete performance ability. MAs derived from the Stanford-Binet and Cattell were compared and correlated with drawing test scores.

Results: The results indicated that all three groups had developed equally in verbal and performance areas. Quantitatively, the average developmental levels of the brain injured and mongoloid groups were similar. Qualitatively, the mongoloid pattern of performance was more similar to the familial group.

Comment: Although mongolism is generally considered to be exogenous in etiology, the study indicates that caution must be employed in applying the characteristics typical of exogenous mental retardates to the mongoloid group.

Gardener, W. I., Cromwell, Rue L., and Foshee, J. G. Studies in Activity Level. II. Effects of Distal Visual Stimulation in Organics, Familials, Hyperactives, and Hypoactives. *American Journal of Mental Deficiency*, 1959, 63, 1028-33.

Purpose: Noting that Strauss and Lehtinen described the brain injured child as one who is extremely responsive to stimuli, the authors undertook to determine the effects of change in amount of visual stimulation upon the activity level of various groups of mentally defective individuals.

Subjects: 24 organic and 24 familial residents at the Tennessee Cloverbottom Home, matched on the basis of CA and MA. The mean IQ of the organics was 47.5. The familials had a mean IQ of 45.4. Subjects who had previously been identified as hyperactive and hypoactive were compared.

Procedure: The subjects were tested for a five-minute period on a ballistograph designed to record human activity under conditions of reduced and increased visual stimulation.

Results: No significant differences were discovered in the degree of total activity by organics and familials. Both groups were significantly more active under the condition of reduced visual stimulation. The results are not in agreement with the notion that increased distal stimulation promotes higher activity.

Comment: Although the results have no direct bearing on the findings of Strauss and Lehtinen, the findings do indicate the need for caution

101

in reference to generalizations concerning the behavioral characteristics of brain injured children.

In Review

The research studies reported on the characteristics of trainable children throw some doubt on the generality of those characteristics commonly attributed to mongoloids or brain injured children. The differences have not been borne out, due either to a discrepancy between impressionistic reports and research data, or to the lack of precision in the instruments used to find these differences.

LEARNING

Studies of various aspects of the learning process (motivation, set, nature of stimuli, etc.) with trainable-level retarded children are few in number and generally have utilized institutionalized subjects. Reported below are some of the major contributions concerned with the learning characteristics of trainable-level children and adults. Because of the paucity of studies, significant research utilizing groups with mean IQs above 50 are also reported.

Ellis, N. R., and Distefano, M. K., Jr., Effects of Verbal Urging and Praise Upon Rotary Pursuit Performance in Mental Defectives. *American Journal of Mental Deficiency*, 1959, 64, 486-490.

Purpose: To investigate the effects of social influences, verbal urging, and praise upon the acquisition of rotary pursuit skill in mental defectives.

Subjects: 28 institutionalized defectives, males and females, divided into an experimental and control group. Subjects were matched on the basis of previous rotary performance, Stanford-Binet IQ, CA, and sex. The experimental group had a mean CA of 17.8, mean IQ of 51.7. The control group had a mean CA of 16.4, mean IQ of 53.3.

Procedure: All subjects were required to keep a pointer on a target. Control subjects were simply told their score. Experimental subjects were urged and praised.

Results: The verbally urged and praised group performed significantly better than the controls. The data demonstrate the facilitative effects of verbal urging and praise upon psychomotor performance in mental defectives.

Comment: Although these groups do not fall precisely into the trainable category, the study does demonstrate the effectiveness of urging and praise with an institutionalized group. Whether similar findings would result with a day school group has not been ascertained.

Metzger, R. Probability Learning in Children and Aments. *American Journal of Mental Deficiency,* 1960, 64, 869-874.

Purpose: To explore the probability learning behavior of retardates.

Subjects: Normal subjects and familial and non-familial retardates matched on the basis of MA and divided into high and low MA groups. Each group consisted of three subgroups of 30 subjects each. The mean MA for the high MA group was 9.2; for the low MA group the mean was 6.3. Retarded subjects were residents of the Dixon State School for the Retarded.

Procedure: A classical two-choice light-guessing task was employed. The subjects were required to predict which of two lights would appear. Each of the lights was presented in a fixed proportion of the total number of trials, but in random sequence.

Results: Significant differences occurred between high and low MA groups and between mental status groups on the overall stereotype of response. The results appear to be in accord with the concepts of Kounin and Lewin who postulate mental retardates to be more rigid than normals. Analysis of the response data in terms of stereotype showed significantly more stereotype for mental retardates than for normals; significantly less stereotype for the high MA group than the low MA group; and no significant difference for groups differentiated on the basis of etiology.

Comment: This study is of importance in that it serves to reinforce the concepts of Kounin and Lewin. However, questions may be raised concerning the relationship between institutional life and rigidity of response.

House, Betty J. and Zeaman, D. Visual Discrimination Learning in Imbeciles. *American Journal of Mental Deficiency,* 1958, 63, 447-452.

Purpose: In studies comparing the performance of normal children to those of monkeys and chimpanzees on discrimination problems, it has been found that children between two and four years of age may be roughly equivalent to the subhuman primates. It was the purpose of this study to provide data on visual discrimination learning of imbeciles and compare these data with published data based on studies of monkeys.

Subjects: 37 subjects from the Mansfield State Training School ranging in age from six to 19 years were selected. The mean IQ of the group was 31. The mean MA was 3-6. Seventeen females and 20 males were utilized. Thirteen subjects were mongoloids; 17 were cerebral palsied.

Procedure: Two stimuli were presented for 25 trials per day until a criterion of 20 out of 25 correct choices was reached during a single daily session. A candy reward was always under a particular stimulus. The position of the correct stimulus varied with each presentation.

Results: The median number of errors for the group was 119. Previous research with monkeys reported a median number of errors of four. No relationship was found between performance and IQ, MA, or CA, because of the restricted range of these variables. It was concluded that imbeciles with MAs between 2 and 4-6 were inferior to monkeys in this type of discrimination problem and, by implication, inferior to normal children of ages 2 to 4, since normals of this age have been shown to be equal to or better than monkeys in such a learning situation.

Comment: This study is of importance since educational procedures often involve presentation of materials assumed to be within the grasp of the child's ability as measured by MA.

The results of this study are, however, restricted by the assumption of constancy of motivation. Further research is needed in reference to the relationship between motivation and the performance of imbeciles.

Kolstoe, O. P. Language Training of Low Grade Mongoloid Children. *American Journal of Mental Deficiency,* 1958, 63, 17-30.

Purpose: Noting that mongoloids are markedly deficient in language, the author undertook to determine whether or not low-grade mongoloid children were trainable in language functions when given individual instruction.

Subjects: 30 mongoloids from the Lincoln State School were selected and divided into experimental and control groups. The groups were matched on the basis of CA, MA, and Kuhlman IQ. The children were free of crippling defects and ranged in age from 5-6 to 14-6 years. The minimum MA was 1-6 years. Only white subjects were utilized.

Procedure: The children in the experimental group were assigned in groups of five to three instructors. The children were instructed individually in 45-minute periods five days per week for five and one-half months. Experimental and control groups were pretested and post-tested on the Illinois Language Test. Observational Rating Scale, and a composite of items taken from the Kuhlman and Stanford-Binet.

Results: Both groups dropped in IQ, although the control group dropped more than the experimental group. Significant differences in favor of the experimental group were noted on portions of the Illinois Language Test. No differences were found on the Observational Rating Scale or the Composite Scale. The results indicated that those children of higher MA (above two years) benefitted slightly from the program. Those with MAs under two years showed no such tendency.

Comment: This study sheds light on the feasibility of a program of language training in programs for trainable level children. The results do not indicate that such a program will result in marked improvement in low-grade mongoloid children. However, since the subjects were an institutionalized sample, the results cannot be directly applied to children in community day school programs.

Zeaman, D. H., House, Betty J., and Orlando, R. Use of Special Training Conditions in Visual Discrimination Learning with Imbeciles. *American Journal of Mental Deficiency*, 1958, 63, 453-459.

Purpose: The authors note that there is evidence that mental deficiency may be associated with deficiency in ability to solve visual discrimination problems. A higher proportion of failures is evidenced among imbeciles than would be expected on the basis of mental age. The purpose of this study was to investigate whether the relationship between additional cues, familiarity, and novelty results in cognition and discrimination learning.

Subjects: 14 institutionalized imbecile subjects with an MA range of two to six years.

Procedure: Three experiments were conducted. In the first experiment children were trained in color naming and then presented with a visual discrimination task utilizing colored stimuli. The second experiment was concerned with the degree of facilitation occurring if one of the stimuli had the property of familiarity and the other of novelty. In the third experiment, subjects who had previously failed were trained on a much easier task and then re-examined on the original discrimination task.

Results: Those subjects who were trained in color naming performed significantly better than those subjects who did not receive such training. The results imply that teaching verbal labels will facilitate learning nonverbal discrimination. A measurable improvement occurred with the introduction of a novel positive or negative stimulus. No significant improvement occurred in the performance of those subjects who were retrained on an easier task.

Comment: This study suggests a number of approaches to facilitating the visual discrimination learning of imbeciles.

Barnett, C. D., and Cantor, G. N. Discrimination Set in Defectives. *American Journal of Mental Deficiency*, 1957, 62, 334-337.

Purpose: To investigate the phenomenon of transfer of training in mental retardates with specific regard to discrimination set.

Subjects: 40 institutionalized males of mean CA of 34.1 and mean IQ of 42.6 were selected. All subjects had failed to learn a previously administered discrimination problem.

Procedure: Experimental and control groups consisting of 20 subjects each were established. The experimental groups learned a visual discrimination task with the assistance of verbal comments from the experimenter. Upon reaching a criterion of 15 correct trials out of 16, they were given a similar transfer task. The control group engaged in color-naming and conversation and then was given the transfer task.

Results: The performance of the experimental group was significantly better than that of the control group. Subjects of higher MA (above 6.3 years) exceeded subjects of lower MA (below 6.3 years).

Comment: Adult imbeciles are apparently able to benefit from specific training and transfer such training to new tasks of a similar nature.

Gordon, S., O'Connor, N., and Tizard, J. Some Effects of Incentives on the Performance of Imbeciles on a Repetitive Task. *American Journal of Mental Deficiency*, 1955, 60, 371-377.

Purpose: Previous research with normal subjects has revealed that the incentive provided by knowledge of the results of one's efforts is most effective. Three experiments were undertaken to determine the ability of imbeciles to respond to incentives of different types and to study the effects of such incentives upon subsequent performance of a repetitive task.

106

Subjects: 40 institutionalized imbeciles between the ages of 17 and 35 years. The mean Stanford-Binet IQ of the group was 36.4.

Procedure: The task employed involved the placement of nails in a pegboard. The subjects were ranked on the basis of average performance and then the four subjects with highest scores were grouped and assigned at random to one of four experimental conditions. There were 10 subjects in each experimental group. The incentive conditions were Goal (knowledge of results), Cooperation (two teams competing against each other), Competition (one subject encouraged to beat another), and Control (a neutral condition). On the thirty-first day of the experiment, subjects under Cooperation, Competition, and Control situations were changed to the Goal condition. After six weeks without practice, the subjects were retested.

Results: The first experiment revealed that performance was highest under the Goal incentive, with Competition, Cooperation, and Control following in that order. When the groups were shifted to the Goal incentive, significant improvement occurred. The results indicated the positive incentive value of knowledge of results and the establishment of comprehensible goals.

Comment: The study indicates that imbeciles can and do respond differently to variation in incentive conditions and indicates maximum performance when goals are based upon knowledge of previous level of performance.

Tizard, J., and Loos, F. M. The Learning of a Spatial Relations Test by Adult Imbeciles. *American Journal of Mental Deficiency*, 1954, 59, 85-90.

Purpose: To determine how well imbeciles succeed in carrying out a fairly complex laboratory task after practice, and the measure of transfer of training to a similar task.

Subjects: Eight male institutionalized imbeciles of mean IQ 34.1.

Procedure: After a training period, all subjects were tested on all four boards of the Minnesota Spatial Relations Test.

Results: All subjects showed rapid improvement and considerable transfer of training. The subjects were retested one month after the final practice period and their scores remained much higher than their initial scores. The results indicated that a subject's initial score on the test which was used is likely to give a poor estimate of his actual ability to do the test after practice.

Comment: Although employing small numbers, this study is of interest in that it raises questions regarding the relationship between initial score and performance ability after training.

Hermelin, E., and O'Connor, N. The Rote and Concept Learning of Imbeciles. *Journal of Mental Deficiency Research*, 1958, 2, 21-27.

Purpose: To determine whether imbecile children can use simple concepts in problem solving.

Subjects: 20 institutionalized children of mean IQ 40.7.

Procedure: The subjects were presented with a series of pictures and rewarded upon selection of the correct picture. The first series consisted of pictures of random items and thus involved rote memory. The second and third series utilized pictures containing items of class and quantity. Selection of the correct items in these latter cases involved utilization of the concept of classification and quantity.

Results: The performance of the group indicated ability to utilize the concept of classification and quantity. Performance on these series was superior to performance in the rote-learning series.

Comment: This study indicates that imbeciles can utilize simple principles in a learning situation. Further studies are needed concerning the relationship of this ability to level of motivation, complexity of task and previous training.

In Review

There is a paucity of reported studies dealing with the learning characteristics of trainable level mental retardates. Further, much of the reported research is characterized by utilization of institutionalized subjects. Study of various aspects of the learning process utilizing trainable children from community day schools is sorely needed.

FOLLOW-UP STUDIES

Because of the comparative newness of community programs for the trainable mentally retarded, few follow-up studies are available. Long-term longitudinal studies comparing children who have received community day school training and those who have not constitute a most pressing need.

Tisdall, W. J. A Follow-up Study of Trainable Mentally Handicapped Children in Illinois. *American Journal of Mental Deficiency*, 1960, 64, 11-16.

Purpose: To study the adjustment of children who, five years previously, were enrolled in special public school classes for the trainable mentally retarded.

Subjects: 126 subjects of mean IQ 33 who had been in special classes for the trainable.

Procedure: Interviews were conducted with teachers, directors, and parents.

Results: Results revealed that 11.9 percent of the group had been institutionalized, 25.4 percent of the group were not in school but were at home, 23.8 percent were still in public school classes, and 18.3 percent were in parent-sponsored classes. Thus, five years after the commencement of a public school training program, approximately 80 percent of the group were in the community. Parents indicated that skills derived from training were retained. Major needs were for post-school programs and parent guidance and counseling.

Comment: The question of post-school services for the trainable is one which is becoming increasingly intense as more and more such children complete their schooling. An unmet need also exists in reference to parent guidance and counseling.

Saenger, G. *The Adjustment of Severely Retarded Adults in the Community.* Albany: New York State Interdepartmental Health Resources Board, October 1957.

Purpose: To study the adjustment of severely retarded adults outside and inside their homes and to determine the extent to which such persons contribute to the home and secure employment. Adjustment was related to the characteristics of the retarded and his family.

Procedure: The study was based on interviews of 520 severely retarded adults conducted by trained social workers. The sample interviewed was chosen from a list of 2640 former pupils of all classes conducted by the Board of Education of the City of New York for the trainable retarded from 1929 to 1955.

Results: Two-thirds of all former pupils were found to be living in the community. Twenty-six percent had been institutionalized. Of those interviewed, the large majority were able to dress and feed themselves and care for their bodily functions. Only one out of nine could read even simple passages. Parents exhibited a high degree of acceptance of the retarded child. One-third of the group was able to leave the immediate neighborhood unaccompanied. Twenty-seven percent were working for pay. An additional nine percent had worked but were currently unemployed. Most worked at simple chores. Jobs were most often found by the parents. Most parents had more or less definite arrangements to keep the child in the community.

Comment: This is the most comprehensive follow-up study available. Some caution must be exercised, however, in generalizing from these findings to currently existing classes for trainable children which usually include children of greater degrees of retardation than those reported upon in this study. In general the IQs of the children in this study were about 10 points higher than those found in current classes for the trainable mentally retarded.

Delp, H. A., and Lorenz, Marcella. Follow-up Study of 84 Public School Special Class Pupils with IQs Below 50. *American Journal of Mental Deficiency*, 1953, 58, 175-182.

Purpose: To assess the post-school adjustment of 84 former members of public school classes for trainable children.

Procedure: Interviews were conducted with parents, teachers, social workers, and the children themselves.

Results: Of the 84, 30 had been institutionalized. Of these 30, 17 had been excluded from public school prior to commitment. Of 41 children located at home, 10 had been gainfully employed, and 25 more were reported as helpful around the home. Parents felt that many benefits had been derived from training.

Comment: This study revealed a higher rate of institutionalization than either of the studies reported above. However, due to differences in locale and the availability of educational programs and community facilities for adult retardates, this study cannot be directly compared with the later studies by Saenger and Tisdall.

In Review

The few follow-up studies available indicate surprisingly good adjustment for those children in the 40 to 50 IQ range. Most trainable children appear to remain in the community. Every study reports that parents feel that benefits are derived from public school training programs.

Few research studies are available dealing with the impact of the retarded child upon the family, although many articles of a general nature are to be found. Three major contributions in this area are reported below. In the area of parent counseling, only one research project reports on the effectiveness of different types of parent education programs.

Farber, B. Effects of a Severely Mentally Retarded Child on Family Integration. *Monographs of the Society for Research in Child Development*, 1959, 24, No. 2.

Purpose: To describe the various conditions influencing the effect of a severely mentally retarded child on family integration.

Subjects: 240 families were studied; 179 families had a retarded child at home; 49 families had a child in a state institution; and 16 had a child in a private residential school.

Procedure: Interview procedures were established. An index of marital integration, a sibling role tension index, a modified Vineland scale, and a neighborliness scale were devised.

Results: Generally the marital integration of parents of mentally retarded boys at home was lower than that of parents of mentally retarded girls. Presence of a retarded boy in lower-class families had a more acute effect on the parents' marriage than the presence of a retarded girl. This was not true for middle-class families. On the average, the normal sister but not the normal brother was helped by institutionalizing the retarded child. Participation in the Catholic Church appeared to be supportive.

Comment: This study is an outstanding contribution and indicates the multiplicity of factors which determine the degree and nature of the impact of the retarded child upon the family.

Farber, B. Family Organization and Crisis: Maintenance of Integration in Families with a Severely Mentally Retarded Child. *Monographs of the Society for Research in Child Development*, 1960, 25, No. 1.

Purpose: To study the ways in which families deal with the crisis of having a severely mentally retarded child.

Subjects: Information pertaining to 233 families was analyzed. Each family had one child who was severely mentally retarded.

Procedure: Parents were interviewed twice. Included in the second interview was an index of marital integration, a sibling role tension index, a marital prediction index, a modification of a Vineland Social Maturity Scale, a social mobility scale, and a neighborliness scale, in addition to questions on family and personal background.

Results: When parents who used consistent parent-oriented, child-oriented, or home-oriented strategies were compared with those who did not, the parents who utilized one of the three consistent orientations were found to have a higher marital integration score than the others. The results indicated that type of family orientation rather than institutionalization per se seems important for the marital integration of the parents. The degree of marital integration is a function of a combination of the severity of the crisis situation and the strategies used by the family. Normal sisters (but not brothers) are given parent-substitute responsibilities and are seen by the mother to be affected adversely by the presence of the retarded child.

Comment: This study further demonstrates the complexity of factors affecting family adjustment and demonstrates the fallacy of the concept that institutionalization is the only solution to family crisis resulting from the presence of a severely retarded child.

Harris, D. B. *A Study of the Modification of Parental Attitudes Toward an Understanding of Mentally Retarded Children.* Institute of Child Development and Welfare, College of Education, University of Minnesota, 1959. Contract 7774, United States Office of Education.

Purpose: To investigate the effectiveness of three methods of parent education in developing parental attitudes and understandings in reference to retarded children.

Subjects: The families of 30 trainable level children attending a day care center were utilized.

Procedure: The general method was to compare three methods of parent education: (a) incidental and informal counseling by the staff of the day care center; (b) small group discussion; (c) formal programs dealing with some aspect of mental retardation. Pretesting and post-testing was undertaken. Observations of parent-child behavior were made and the following instruments were employed: (a) a measure of

Common Knowledge about Children; (b) a Mental Retardation Information Test; and (c) the Parents' Attitudes Research Instrument.

Results: No significant differences were noted on any of the measures employed. However, field work impressions suggested that parents do gain from attempts to help them face their problem.

Comment: Many public school programs for trainable level children recognize the need for parent education. Further study is needed of the most effective method of facilitating change of parental attitudes.

In Review

Major contributions have recently appeared dealing with the impact of severe retardation upon family life. Further research is needed concerning the most effective approaches to facilitating family adjustment.

SUMMARY

The recent growth of public school programs for the trainable level mentally retarded has precipitated a new interest in educational, psychological and sociological research concerned with the characteristics of these individuals and their families.

Published surveys of the current status of school programs for the trainable level retardate indicate that the nationwide trend has been in the direction of placing responsibility for such programs under the auspices of the state departments of education.

The composition of public school classes for trainable children reveals a high percentage of children falling in one or another clinical category and thus indicates that the group may be considered to be multiply handicapped. Public day school programs are further characterized by inclusion of children with IQs above 50 in such programs.

Surveys concerned with the incidence of trainable children living in the community are in substantial agreement that this incidence is between one and two such children per 1000 school age population.

Evaluations of the behavioral changes which occur when children are placed in a public school program have, at the present writing, failed to reveal definite results. There are indications, however, that children with IQs below 25 tend to be dropped from such programs, and that children with IQs in the 40 to 50 range benefit most from such training. Long-term longitudinal studies are very much needed in order to evaluate the effectiveness of such programs.

Studies concerned with investigation of common generalizations concerning the characteristics of mongoloid children have failed to support the contention that such children are universally "docile" or "amenable," or that such children are characterized by a marked sense of rhythm. When teachers compared the behavior of mongoloids with brain injured children, no significant differences obtained in reference to performance related to self care, social, and motor skills.

Performance of mongoloids on the Stanford-Binet, Cattell Infant Intelligence Scale and Draw-A-Man Test revealed qualitative performance similar to the familial group. When mongoloid stigmata were related to intellectual status, a significant positive correlation was obtained, thereby contradicting the popular conception of a negative relationship between the physical stigmata and intellectual status of mongoloids. The results of an intensive language training program with mongoloid children were essentially negative.

Studies of motivational variation and performance in a learning situation have been characterized by the use of institutionalized subjects. The reported studies indicate that adult imbeciles are capable of transfer of training and that variation in incentive conditions does affect their performance.

Follow-up studies of trainable children are few in number. However, these studies reveal that most trainable children remain in the community, and that those children with IQs in the 40 to 50 range exhibit surprisingly good adjustment to home and neighborhood.

Results of studies of the impact of the trainable child upon family integration strongly suggest that recommendations concerning institutionalization must take cognizance of the multiplicity of factors affecting family integration. Research concerned with the effectiveness of three methods of parent education failed to yield definite results.

Further research is needed in all areas of work with the trainable child. Of particular importance to educators are studies dealing with the effectiveness of public school programs and the relationship between such programs and adult performance of the retardate. Studies of the effectiveness of variation in incentive conditions as they affect learning may have a direct impact upon classroom practices and procedures.

4

The Visually Impaired

Carson Y. Nolan

SECTION I—BRAILLE READERS

The material described in this section emphasizes results of studies applicable to those groups among visually handicapped children who characteristically employ braille as an educational medium. From the communication standpoint, these groups predominantly utilize tactile and auditory channels. As of January 1, 1960, 8503 such children were enrolled in public school programs.*

The research covered varies widely in quality of design, execution, analysis, and description. To a great extent, this variability in quality reflects the historical fact that research in this area has been largely a product of opportunity. While several schools and organizations have supported continuous investigation over long-term periods, the bulk of published reports describes a single effort made by a single individual. This condition appears to be the greatest single factor contributing to the present lack of integration of research in the field.

* M. S. Hooper. The Preparation and Distribution of Textbooks for Blind Children. Louisville, Kentucky: American Printing House for the Blind, 1960. Unpublished.

Reviewed by Samuel C. Ashcroft, Peabody College for Teachers, Nashville, Tennessee.

Research areas are described in the following order:

1. Sensory and perceptual factors relevant to education.
2. Educational media and their uses.
3. Intelligence and its measurement.
4. Educational development and its measurement.
5. Personality and social development and their measurement.
6. Physical performance and its measurement .

The reference cited for any given study is that which the author believes to be most widely available.

SENSORY AND PERCEPTUAL FACTORS RELEVANT TO EDUCATION

Because blind children are restricted in sensory input, interest arose early in describing the effects of this condition from a dynamic perceptual standpoint. The implications of restriction of visual sensitivity for the functioning of other sense avenues have held wide interest. Investigations have been made of sensory and perceptual processes important to specific behavioral areas such as communication, learning, and mobility.

> Seashore, C. E., and Ling, T. L. The Comparative Sensitiveness of Blind and Seeing Persons. *Psychological Monographs,* 1918, 25, 148-158.

Purpose: To compare blind and seeing groups for auditory, tactual. and kinesthetic sensitivity.

Subjects: 16 high school students (ages 16 to 26 years) who had been totally blind for more than five years and 15 seeing high school students (ages 14 to 19 years).

Procedure: The groups were compared on ability to (a) identify the direction of a sound source in a horizontal perimeter, (b) discriminate the intensities of pairs of tones, (c) discriminate weights using the method of constant stimuli, (d) discriminate passive pressure, and (e) discriminate active pressure. The two-point threshold on the tip of the first finger and the inside of the forearm was also determined.

Results: No differences existed between blind and seeing groups in any of the measures obtained. Development of the use of a sense consists not in the heightening of sensitivity or sensory discrimination but in the development of complexes and meanings in terms of these.

Comment: This study represents an early attempt to test the theory of "sensory compensation" and its implications for behavior of the blind.

116

Broadly conceived, this theory holds that loss in one sense area is compensated by development of hypersensitivity in other sense areas. The study did not uphold the theory.

Axelrod, S. *Effects of Early Blindness. Performance of Blind and Sighted Children on Tactile and Auditory Tasks.* New York: American Foundation for the Blind, 1959.

Purpose: To compare the performance of early-blind, late-blind, and seeing children on simple and complex tactile and auditory tasks.

Subjects: 82 children blind before 18 months of age (ages nine years to 19-8 years, IQ range 79 to 162) were matched with 82 seeing children. A group of 20 late-blind children (ages 9-3 to 20-8 years, IQ range 80 to 147) was also studied.

Procedure: Early-blind and seeing groups were compared on (a) light-touch and two-point thresholds on the right and left index fingers and the ring finger of the preferred hand, (b) performance on two complex tactile tasks and one complex auditory task involving the ability to derive relationships among objects or stimuli presented, and (c) ability to transfer a solution from a problem presented in one sense modality to its analogue presented in another. The late-blind group was included in the latter two comparisons.

Results: The early-blind had lower two-point limens than seeing children, although this difference was related to sex and finger. Such increased sensitivity (on the right index finger) did not appear related to braille reading habits.

Early-blind subjects were inferior in performance to seeing subjects when (a) required to abstract a characteristic common to rewarded members of pairs of objects, (b) required to solve matching problems in which the correct choice among three palpated objects or three auditory stimuli was the object or stimulus identical to the one intermediate in space or temporal sequence, and (c) presented with a learning set task involving the transfer of a principle of solution from the matching problem presented haptically to an analogous one presented aurally or vice versa.

No differences existed between performance of the late-blind and that of the other groups except in the case of the tactile matching test where performance of the late-blind was significantly better than that of the early-blind.

Comment: The differences in two-point threshold found in this study raise again the question of sensory compensation. Questions of more

117

importance are raised by the finding of consistent superiority of the seeing group in the learning tasks: What are the effects of early sensory deprivation, particularly visual deprivation, for later learning and problem solving?

Nolan, C. Y. Roughness Discrimination among Blind Children in the Primary Grades. *International Journal for the Education of the Blind,* 1960, 9, 97-100.

Purpose: To study variation among blind children in kindergarten through fourth grade in the ability to discriminate degrees of difference in roughness.

Subjects: 94 children from four schools for the blind who read braille or were considered potential braille readers. These included 54 boys and 40 girls, ages 5-4 to 13-6.

Procedure: The stimuli consisted of 4-inch squares of 14 grades of sandpaper which were paired to make 27 test items. No pair of papers for any item was more than three grades apart. The test was administered individually to children who were required to identify the rougher square. One group of 31 children was retested after one year.

Results: The ability to discriminate roughness was found not to be related to chronological age. Significant differences among the mean scores for grades were found, with means increasing with grade assignment. A significant mean increase in score was found for the group retested after one year.

Comment: These results concerning a basic sensory dimension (tactile sensitivity) may have important implications for understanding readiness in braille reading. If, in addition to required mental age, the minimum tactual development level necessary for successful introduction to braille reading can be specified, this part of education may be made more efficient.

Schlaegel, T. F., Jr. The Dominant Method of Imagery in Blind as Compared to Sighted Adolescents. *Journal of Genetic Psychology,* 1953, 83, 265-277.

Purpose: To determine the role of visual acuity and of age at onset of blindness in the imagery employed by blind and seeing adolescents.

Subjects: 67 blind students from the Indiana School for the Blind (ages 12 to 24 years) and 78 seeing high school students (ages 14 to 18 years).

118

Procedure: Groups were administered the Griffitts test of "concrete imagery" which consists of 125 words or phrases given orally. The subjects responded by writing down the type of their first image (visual, auditory, kinesthetic, tactual, thermal, olfactory, or gustatory.)

Results: When averages of the blind and the seeing groups were considered as wholes, they were equal, and the relative dominance of imagery was the same for both in the following decreasing order: visual, auditory, kinesthetic, tactual-thermal, and olfactory-gustatory.

When the blind were divided on the basis of present vision and visual history, these differences were found: (a) those subjects with poorest vision had the least number of visual and the most number of auditory responses, (b) as visual acuity increased, there was an average increase in visual imagery responses to an extent even greater than that of normal controls, and (c) if the onset of visual loss took place before age six, visual imagery tended to disappear, this being most pronounced in those subjects with poorest vision.

Comment: The consequences for behavior of the mode of imagery employed in perception have barely been touched upon. These results have important implications for research and education in that they identify an important factor contributing to heterogeneity among the blind, i.e., whether an individual's mode of imagery is characteristically visual, haptic, or auditory.

Worchel, P. Space Perception and Orientation in the Blind. *Psychological Monographs*, 1951, 65, No. 15.

Purpose: To determine the role of visualization in the ability of the blind to perceive and manipulate spatial relations tactually and to orient themselves spatially.

Subjects: 33 totally blind and 33 seeing pupils matched for sex and chronological age.

Procedure: Experiment 1. The methods of reproduction (drawing) and of verbal description were used in testing perception of simple geometric forms when handled by one hand and both hands. Recognition of a stimulus form (using both hands) from among four response forms was required.

Experiment 2. The subjects were given two stimulus forms (one in each hand) and required to indicate which of four response forms would result from their combination.

Experiment 3. The subjects were required to return to an initial starting position via a straight path after having been led along a right-angle path (right-angle isosceles triangle) and via a right-angle path after having been led along a straight path.

Results: The seeing subjects were superior to the blind in tactual form perception as measured through reproduction by drawing and verbal description, in the imaginal manipulation of space relations, and in space orientation. The blind did as well as the seeing in the recognition of tactual form. The accidentally blinded surpassed the congenitally blind in tactual form perception (reproduction and verbal report) and in the space relations test. They equaled the congenitally blind in the recognition of tactual form and in space orientation. There was a significant and high correlation between age at onset of blindness and (a) tactual form reproduction and description, and (b) the manipulation of space relations.

Sex differences were in favor of the males, but the differences were not significant in any of the tests. For the blind subjects, chronological age was significantly related to performance in the space relations test; in all the other tests, there was no relationship between chronological age and performance. The ability to translate tactile-kinesthetic impressions into visual imagery gave significantly better scores in all of the tests of form perception except recognition and space orientation. In the space orientation tests, visual imagery was important in directional orientation, but the estimation of time was fundamental in distance orientation for both the blind and the seeing subjects.

Comment: This comparative study of abilities of blind and seeing groups in spatial relationships and spatial orientation points out the importance in perception of the modes of imagery available to the individual. Possession of visual imagery appears to be a marked advantage. The implication for education is that the age at onset of blindness and the degree of visual handicap seriously affect the manner in which perceptual processes become organized.

Supa, M., Cotzin, M., and Dallenbach, K. M. "Facial Vision": The Perception of Obstacles by the Blind. *American Journal of Psychology,* 1944, 57, 133-183.

Purpose: To determine the necessary and sufficient conditions for the perception of obstacles by the blind.

Subjects: Two blind and two seeing adults. The blind subjects possessed the ability to perceive obstacles from a distance and daily utilized this ability. At the start of the experiments the seeing subjects lacked this ability.

Procedure: In Experiments 1 to 6, the blindfolded subject was placed at varying distances in front of an obstacle (A 4' 10" x 4' masonite board with lower edge 2' from the floor served as the obstacle in Experiments 2 to 6. In Experiments 1 and 7 a wall served as the obstacle). He was instructed to walk toward it, to respond when the obstacle was first perceived, and then to approach as near as possible without touching and respond again. Distances at response points were recorded. The first five experiments were repeated twice, once with the subject wearing shoes and walking on a hardwood floor, and once in stocking feet on a soft carpet runner. The order of the repetitions was counterbalanced. Each experiment consisted of 25 successful trials (no contacts with obstacle) or 50 consecutive failures. When failures were interspersed with successes, trials were continued until the successes reached 25. Four preliminary experiments were run to familiarize the subjects with the experimental conditions and to teach seeing subjects obstacle perception. False trials (no obstacle) were introduced in Experiment 3. For Experiment 4, all exposed areas of the skin were covered; for Experiment 5, the ears were plugged and the pinna was securely covered; and for Experiment 6, the subject was stimulated aurally (earphones) by a continuous 1000-cycle tone. For Experiment 7, the subject was placed in a sound-proof room, and judged the experimenter's approach to the obstacle through sound transmitted from a microphone held by the experimenter to earphones on the subject.

Results: Stimulation of the face and other exposed areas of the skin by air and sound waves was neither a necessary nor sufficient condition for perception of obstacles by the subjects. Stimulation of the skin by reflected breath was neither a necessary condition nor, as far as "facial pressure" was concerned, a sufficient condition for determining extreme nearness of the obstacle. The pressure theory of the obstacle sense, insofar as it applies to the face and other exposed areas of the skin, appeared to be untenable. Aural stimulation appeared to be both a necessary and a sufficient condition for the perception of obstacles by the subjects.

Comment: Although this particular study does not employ children as subjects, it has an important bearing on development of methods of teaching children mobility. This study was the first of a series (carried out principally by Worchel and his co-workers) that clearly defined the role of hearing in obstacle avoidance.

In Review

The studies above are examples of the many diverse topics in this area

121

which have attracted the fleeting attention of research workers. However, much more information describing basic sensory and perceptual processes of the blind is needed before many educational problems can be solved. Too many times in the past these processes have been assumed to be direct analogues of visual processes. Many of the wrong turns taken down the educational path can be attributed to such thinking. A number of issues in this area as well as much past research are effectively described in the monograph by Axelrod reviewed earlier.

EDUCATIONAL MEDIA AND THEIR USES

As indicated earlier, the tactile and auditory senses are the major avenues of communication for the education of blind children. It is only to be expected that a significant area of research should concern media for these two channels. Braille and recorded materials constitute the principal media used for textbooks. The following studies deal principally with these media.

Meyers, E., Ethington, Doris, and Ashcroft, S. Readability of Braille as a Function of Three Spacing Variables. *Journal of Applied Psychology*, 1958, 42, 163-165.

Purpose: To compare the readability of braille in which the spacings between dots within cells, between cells, and between lines were varied over three distances for each.

Subjects: 108 blind children in grades five to 12 were divided into 27 groups of four, each matched on reading ability for braille with standard spacing.

Procedure: Each subject read silently from eight chapters of *The Black Arrow* for two 50-minute periods on successive days. Time to read each page was recorded for each subject. At the end of the second day, a 30-item comprehension test was administered. Each group read one of 27 possible combinations of braille produced by varying the space between dots (.080″, .090″, .100″), the space between cells (.123″, .140″, .160″) and the space between lines (.163″, .220″, .300″). (Underlined values represent those of standard braille.)

Results: Average reading speed for standard braille was found to be 68 wpm (range 5 to 195 wpm). Dot spacing of .080″ was inferior to .090″ or .100″, there being no difference between the latter two. Cell spacing of .123″ or possibly .140″ was more readable than .160″. Line spacing of .220″ was more readable than either of the other values.

Comment: The configuration of punctiform writing was the subject of violent and bitter controversy during the first two decades of this century. Some points regarding the contraction of braille and its technical specialization for subjects such as mathematics and arithmetic have yet to be resolved. This study effectively demonstrates, however, that there is little room for improvement in the dimensions of braille printing.

Holland, B. F., and Eatman, Pauline F. The Silent Reading Habits of Blind Children. *Teachers Forum (Blind)*, 1933, 6, 4-11.

Purpose: To discover the differences in performance of good and poor braille readers and to analyze the reading procedures of individual subjects.

Subjects: 28 children—four each from grades 3, 4, 6, 7, 8, 9, and 11. Two from each grade had been rated as good readers and two as poor readers by teachers of reading.

Procedure: A constant-speed camera was used to photograph the hands of readers at the rate of one frame/.20 sec. These pictures were projected on the reading material, the position of fingers marked, and the reading rate calculated. The subjects read a selection from the Stanford Achievement Test at the eight-year-old level of difficulty. They were directed to read the material once and, at the end, to pronounce or call out a word left out of the selection. This response was used as a comprehension check. Total time required was approximately 10 minutes per subject.

Measures taken were: (a) the total number of exposures per line; (b) the average number of braille cells read by the left and right hands independently; (c) the time spent by subjects at the beginning and the end of each line; (d) the number of regressive movements; and (e) the time spent by subjects making "return sweeps."

Results: The performance of poor readers was more variable than that of good readers. Great variability existed in hand preference and finger preference and in coordination of hand movements. The left and right fingers read a large amount of material independently. Good readers read more material with the right hand, and the amount of material read by the left finger was less than that read by the right. More time was spent at the beginning than at the end of lines; good readers spent less time at the end than at the beginning; poor readers spent more time at the end than at the beginning. More regressive movements were made by the left hand than the right; good readers made fewer regressive movements than did poor readers. Six to seven percent of the time was spent making return sweeps. Good readers spent less time than poor; good readers spent less time making return sweeps with the left hand than the right; the reverse was true for poor readers.

Holland, B. F. Speed and Pressure Factors in Braille Reading. *Teachers Forum (Blind)*, 1934, 7, 13-17.

Purpose: To investigate the relation of pressure to speed in braille reading.

Subjects: 17 slow and 17 fast readers, grades four to 10, selected on the basis of photographic records of finger movements while reading.

Procedure: The subjects read a practice selection and an experimental selection taken from the Stanford Achievement Reading Test under instruction to read as usual. Time and pressure were recorded using a kymograph.

Results: Fast readers tended to use less pressure while reading braille than did slow readers. Correlation between pressure and speed was rho= .27. Amount of pressure varied within a given line. Pressure at the beginning of a line was less than at the end. Fast readers showed less variation. Poor readers tended to increase the amount of pressure as they read through a paragraph.

Fertsch, Pauline. Hand Dominance in Reading Braille. *American Journal of Psychology*, 1947, 60, 335-349.

Purpose: To investigate the problem of handedness and hand dominance in braille reading.

Subjects: 33 blind boys and 30 blind girls of average or above average intelligence who scored in the upper or lower thirds on the Monroe test of reading comprehension.

Procedure: Determination of hand dominance: Using the Shank Test of Reading Comprehension, the reading performance of each hand was tested separately. Measures of both reading time and comprehension were obtained.

Determination of the method of reading: Motion picture records of reading performance were obtained during both oral and silent reading. Comprehension was tested.

Determination of handedness: A hand dynamometer was used to determine handedness through the correlation of hand-strength and hand preference. Not enough left-handed persons were available for study.

Results: On the basis of performance when the hands read separately, blind readers may be classified into "right-dominant," "left-dominant," and "hands equal" groups.

The "hands equal" group read a larger number of braille cells with the hands functioning independently, read faster, and contained fewer poor readers than the other two groups. The "right-dominant" group read almost as many braille cells with the hands separate, read almost as fast as the "hands equal" group, and contained an equal number of good and poor readers. The "left-dominant" group read a small amount of material with the hands functioning independently, read slowest of the three groups, and contained twice as many poor readers as good readers.

Good readers read a substantial amount of material with the hands functioning independently and of this about twice as much with the right hand as the left. Poor readers kept the right and left fingers close together and consequently read very little with the hands independently.

Comment: The previous three references are examples of studies carried out for the purpose of describing the mechanics of braille reading. These reports demonstrate a research method which has as its goal finding the best methods for performance of a skill, i.e., comparing the methods used by poor and highly skilled performers.

Ashcroft, S. C. Errors in Oral Reading of Braille at Elementary Grade Levels. Unpublished doctoral thesis, University of Illinois, 1960.

Purpose: To study the oral performance of children reading braille in order to identify errors and classify these according to type, frequency, and grade level.

Subjects: 748 tactual braille readers of both sexes in grades two to six who did not possess additional handicaps that would seriously affect their reading behavior.

Procedure: Subjects were required to read 12 simple passages of graded reading difficulty which were designed to include almost all of the 185 signs, abbreviations, and contractions of braille as they commonly occur. The material was presented individually and errors made were recorded verbatim according to a standardized procedure.

Results: Eight types of errors were found relating to the use of braille by the subjects. The types of errors together with their percentage of occurence were: missed dots, 16 percent; ending problems, 15 percent; reversals, 13 percent; added dots, 13 percent; association, 12 percent;

125

gross substitutions, 12 percent; up and down alignment, 10 percent; and left and right alignment, 9 percent.

From the standpoint of mode of braille spelling (orthography), order of categories of orthography involving most to least number of errors was: short form words, multiple cell contractions, combinations of orthography, lower contractions, upper contractions, full spelling, and alphabet abbreviations. The first three categories above included only 28 percent of the total number of the words but contributed 46 percent of the total number of errors made.

From the behavioral standpoint, the eight error types could be classified as arising from problems of perception (missed dots, added dots, and ending problems); problems of orientation (reversals, vertical alignment and horizontal alignment); and problems of memory (association errors and gross substitutions).

Comment: This study is an example of descriptive and analytical research which has as its primary purpose the identification of specific problems for future study. Most experimental studies are based upon hypotheses derived from the description and analysis of complex behavior patterns. Ashcroft suggests a number of pregnant hypotheses concerning braille reading which could be tested experimentally.

Enc, M. A. and Stolurow, L. M. The Effect of Two Recording Speeds on Learning. *New Outlook for the Blind,* 1960, 54, 39-48.

Purpose: To test the hypothesis that comprehension of auditory information is positively correlated with word rate within limits due to effect of temporal contiguity.

Subjects: 23 seventh and eighth grade blind children, ages 13 to 17 years, IQ range 89 to 144.

Procedure: Ten 1300-1400 word stories were recorded at slow (174 wpm) and fast (211 wpm) word rates. A 20-item multiple choice comprehension test was available for each. The subjects were divided into three groups. Groups I and II alternated in hearing the fast or slow version of an identical story which was changed on each of 10 days. Group III heard no story. Retention for story content was tested immediately and 24 hours after hearing. Group III was tested similarly at the same time.

Results: The groups which heard the stories scored significantly higher on the test than the group which heard no stories. For nine out of 10

126

stories the group hearing the faster story received a significantly higher test score immediately after hearing. For 13 out of 14 children the means based on the fast stories were higher than those based on the slow stories. Results for retention after 24 hours were the same as for immediate retention.

Comment: A major problem for blind children is the restriction in rate of communication imposed by use of braille (average 68 words per minute) or recordings (average approximately 150 words per minute) for presentation of textbook materials. In this study, the authors examined the relationships between rate of communication and the efficiency of comprehension and retention for a series of stories. The findings indicate that further research in auditory communication and listening techniques could be fruitful.

Merry, R. V., and Merry, Frieda K. The Tactual Recognition of Embossed Pictures by Blind Children, *Journal of Applied Psychology*, 1933, 17, 148-163.

Purpose: To determine how well blind children can recognize two- and three-dimensional embossed pictures and to investigate the effects of training in perspective and graphic representation upon this ability.

Subjects: 49 boys and 49 girls with no useful vision. Subjects were from six to 24 years of age, with IQs from 61 to 146, in kindergarten to twelfth grade.

Procedure: Experiment 1. The subjects were presented with five two-dimensional designs and 10 three-dimensional objects embossed in paper, and were asked to name them. Experiment 2. The subjects were given one or more months training in comparing objects with their two- and three-dimensional embossed representations.

Results: Experiment 1. The ability of children to recognize tactually simple embossed designs and pictures was quite limited (16 got 0 scores on pictures). Simple embossed designs (square, circle, etc.) were recognized more often than were embossed pictures of three dimensional objects (house, table, etc.). Positive relationships were found between (a) speed of response and total score and (b) IQ and the ability to recognize two-dimensional designs. The age at which vision was lost was not related to this ability.

Experiment 2. Instruction in designs representing two-dimensional objects resulted in improvement for most children (range 0 to 95 percent, median 20 percent). Instruction in recognizing embossed representations of three-dimensional objects resulted in improvement ranging from –20 percent to 50 percent, median 20 percent. The greatest improvement occurred for older children (range 10 to 50 percent).

Comment: Since the beginning of embossed printing, there has been an interest in developing means of presenting pictorial information to the blind. Most attempts have employed tactual analogues of visual techniques for doing this. Generally, results were comparable to those of the above study. This is one of many examples of research in which application of visual models for perception in developments for the blind has had negative results.

In Review

If a few superficial studies of arithmetic media were included, the topics above would exhaust the variety of research under this heading. Unfortunately, developments in media are often dependent upon rather exact information concerning sensory and perceptual processes. As indicated earlier, little specific data on these topics are available with respect to the blind. Advances in graphic communication methods for the tactual sense modality are particularly impeded by this lack.

The existence of educational media implies that educational methods for teaching children to use them are available. No major research on development or evaluation of educational methods for blind children has been conducted.

INTELLIGENCE AND ITS MEASUREMENT

Interest in measuring the intelligence of blind children arose as early as 1914 with adaptation of the early Simon-Binet scales. Then, as now, problems of validity were major among those faced by the researchers. Items in tests designed for sighted persons often lacked content (face) validity for the blind. Necessary changes in methods of test administration, together with item changes as a consequence of lack of content validity, meant that sighted norms were no longer usable. Therefore, tests lacked concurrent validity also. The studies described below are representative of the types of research efforts made in this area.

Hayes, S. P. A Second Test Scale for the Mental Measurement of the Visually Handicapped; the Interim Hayes-Binet Intelligence Tests for the Blind, 1942 Revision. *Outlook for the Blind*, 1943, 37, 37-41.

Purpose: To describe results of the early use of the 1942 Interim Hayes-Binet Intelligence Tests for the Blind.

Subjects: 119 children in grades seven to 12 from the Upper School at Perkins Institute.

Procedure: The scale is a tentative selection of test items from the 1937 Revision, Stanford-Binet. It includes items from both forms L and M and is arranged, administered, scored, and interpreted similarly.

Results: The IQ distribution for blind children approached a normal distribution. The corrected split-half reliability was .91. IQs obtained correlate .95 with IQs obtained from the Wechsler-Bellevue Verbal Scale. IQs were highly related to school status and achievement test scores.

Comment: The Interim Hayes-Binet remains the most widely used intelligence test adapted for blind children. One of the aims in adapting this test was to achieve, at each age level, a distribution of intelligence quotients with a mean of 100. In order to achieve this, age levels for some items were changed from those assigned in the 1937 Revision, Stanford-Binet. This means, of course, that scores for the two tests do not have the same meaning.

Hayes, S. P. Alternative Scales for the Mental Measurement of the Visually Handicapped. *Outlook for the Blind*, 1942, 36, 225-230.

Purpose: To describe the adequacy of the Wechsler-Bellevue Scale, Form I, when used with the blind.

Subjects: Approximately 120 pupils, 14 years of age and above, from the Perkins School for the Blind.

Procedure: Pupils' scores on the Wechsler-Bellevue verbal scales were compared with their scores on other tests and with test scores obtained by other groups. Validity and item statistics of the Wechsler were studied.

Results: IQs obtained with this test were normally distributed with a range from 50 to 138. IQs obtained from the Wechsler verbal scales were correlated .85 with scores obtained with the Hayes-Binet and were correlated .70 with scores obtained from the Stanford Achievement Tests. No reliability estimate was obtained, but between subtest correlations were comparable with those obtained by Wechsler and ranged from .54 to .78. Some items appeared to be at different levels of difficulty for the blind than for the sighted.

Comment: Although some questions concerning the validity for the blind of certain test items have arisen, the Wechsler Intelligence Scales in their various forms have been widely employed in testing blind children. A further criticism of the use of these tests is that the performance aspects of intellectual functioning are ignored.

Wattron, J. B. A Suggested Performance Test of Intelligence. *New Outlook for the Blind,* 1956, 50, 115-121.

Purpose: To construct an adequate adaptation of the Kohs-type blocks which could be manipulated conveniently by blind subjects; to compare scores of a blind group on this test with a known criterion of intelligence; and to compare scores on this test of a blind group and a seeing group.

Subjects: 10 male and 10 female totally blind students (seven to 17 years old) and 20 seeing subjects matched with the first group on sex and age.

Procedure: The test used duplicated the Kohs-blocks except that red surfaces were rough and white surfaces were smooth. The subjects duplicated the designs employing four and nine blocks. Interim Hayes-Binet scores were obtained on blind students. Seeing students duplicated the designs through a screening device which eliminated visual cues.

Results: The adapted test materials were found to be practical for handling by blind subjects in preliminary trials. Correlations between scores on the block tests and those derived from the Interim Hayes-Binet were .84 with a standard error of .067. No significant differences were found between scores of the blind and sighted groups.

Comment: Because most performance test items included in standard intelligence tests require vision for their solution, the number of performance items which can be used to test blind children is small. Generally speaking, no good performance tests of intelligence for blind children are presently available. As this study shows, development of such tests is possible. Currently, efforts are underway to develop and standardize performance scales for use with this group.

Sargent, Ruth F. The Otis Classification Test, Form A, Part II, Adapted for Use with Classes of Blind Children. *Teachers Forum (Blind),* 1931, 4, 30-33.

Purpose: To describe the adaptation of the Otis Test for use with blind children.

Subjects: 210 pupils from Pennsylvania Institution for the Instruction of the Blind and from Perkins Institute (ages 10 to 36 years and grades five to 11). IQs ranged from 69 to 145, and were obtained using the 1923 Irwin-Hayes Binet Tests.

Procedure: Items were eliminated if (a) they could not be done conveniently without the aid of vision, (b) they involved visual experience as a background, or (c) a large percentage of failure among blind children known to be normal indicated that they were abnormally difficult for the blind. Forty-one items of the original 75 were retained.

Results: Scores showed a correlation of .59 with IQ and .76 with MA. "The curves of median scores by grades, by chronological age, and by mental age all show a fair upward trend . . . . the curve (s) and correlation (s) seem quite satisfactory and indicate this adaptation will probably function well in surveys of general intelligence in classes for the blind . . ."

Comment: Good group tests of intelligence are not available for use with blind children. A reason may be the length of time required for administration because of slowness of braille reading. This study illustrates the problem of content validity in the adaptation of standardized tests for use with the blind. Modification of sighted tests to the extent illustrated by this study renders scores obtained meaningless unless new norms are developed.

Komisar, D., and MacDonnell, Marian. Gains in IQ for Students Attending a School for the Blind. *Exceptional Children,* 1955, 21, 127-129.

Purpose: To analyze differences among test-retest scores for intelligence obtained at varying lengths of time from the blind.

Subjects: 89 students from Oak Hill School, Hartford, Connecticut.

Procedure: The subjects were tested with the Hayes-Binet or WISC and at some later interval retested with either of these tests.

Results: The group showed a significant gain in IQ (6.3 points) upon retesting after at least one year (range one to four years). Gains tended to increase with length of time of attendance. Children in lower IQ categories showed most gain, but substantial gains were shown by some children in other categories. Results are interpreted to result from the enriched program for blind children available at a residential school.

Comment: Stability of IQ is a much greater problem with blind children than with seeing children. This is particularly true with very young blind children. Because many such children spend their preschool years in environments which may be deprived culturally, emotionally, and physically, early test scores may significantly underestimate their potential. The results of this study illustrate the results of exposure to a favorable environment on the stability of intelligence quotients.

In Review

In spite of validity problems, adaptations of intelligence tests have played an important role in the education of blind children over the last four decades. Use of such tests makes possible a reliable ranking of blind children, from high to low, along an intellectual continuum. Norms relative to this particular group have been roughly determined and, in the case of the Wechsler scales, a direct comparison with the performance of seeing groups can be made. Therefore, such tests can be of great use in the tasks of educational placement and educational planning. Successful use of tests in this manner has led to a general complacency over the validity problem. Testers lose sight of the fact that the IQ of a blind child derived from an adapted test often does not have the same meaning as an equivalent IQ of a seeing child derived from the original standardized version.

Educational Development and its Measurement

Research on educational development of blind children was started about 1920. Although most subject areas have been touched upon at one time or another, the area of language development has been of major interest. Major vehicles for such research have been standardized achievement tests which have been adapted for use by the blind. While most achievement tests have content validity for this group, the concurrent validity of many of them is open to question. Adaptation of achievement tests for the blind requires changes in mode of administration, test format, and test timing. Thus, results of a direct comparison of achievement of blind groups and seeing groups upon the basis of test scores may be ambiguous. In spite of this difficulty, achievement tests can contribute valuable information when blind children serve as their own norms under conditions of repeated testing.

Hayes, S. P. Stanford Achievement Tests for the Blind; New and Old. *Teachers Forum (Blind)*, 1941, 14, 2-18.

Purpose: To describe results of use of Forms V, W, X, Y, and Z with blind children and give directions for use of Forms D, E, F, G, and H.

Subjects: 600 pupils in grades four to nine from nine residential schools for the blind tested during 1935 to 1940.

Procedure: Tests were administered routinely to classes during this period. Braille adaptations were used.

Results: Test-retest reliabilities ranged from .92 to .96. Achievement-mental age correlations ranged from .75 to .95. Intercorrelations between subject matter tests ranged from .66 to .93. Achievement curves for all subject matter tests closely follow those for the sighted norm group, except for arithmetic computation where the blind fall considerably below the sighted standards.

Comment: The Stanford Achievement Tests have been the most widely used of all tests for this purpose. These tests have been adapted to braille administration by multiplying standard time limits, where appropriate, by a factor of two and one-half. This is done to compensate for the slow rates at which braille is read. Some tests have been adapted for oral administration in which the examiner reads all the items to all students taking the test. In this case, variations among scores resulting from speed factors are eliminated.

Hayes, S. P. Factors Influencing the School Success of the Blind. *Teachers Forum (Blind)*, 1934, 6, 91-99.

Purpose: To determine if the cause of blindness, age of incidence, and other factors influence school success.

Subjects: Groups of from 60 to 500 students tested at large residential schools at all grade levels.

Procedure: Students were tested using standardized tests on various common school subjects.

Results: Cause of blindness was not related to school success. Age of incidence did not appear correlated with school success. Age of entrance into school appeared negatively correlated with school success. There were no significant sex differences in school success.

Comment: Attempts to predict school success from biographical and physical data have met with little success. The dynamics determining academic and other kinds of success for blind children are exceedingly complex; hence it is necessary to consider each blind child as a distinct individual and plan education accordingly.

Merry, Frieda K. A Survey of the Problem Solving Ability of Pupils in Six Residential Schools for the Blind. *Teachers Forum (Blind)*, 1931, 3, 12-15.

Purpose: To determine the ability of blind children to analyze simple

133

arithmetic problems; to compare these results with those obtained with seeing children; and to indicate outstanding difficulties of such children in problem solving and to suggest types of remediation.

Subjects: 170 pupils in grades four to six from six representative residential schools.

Procedure: The Stevenson Arithmetic Reading Test I, Form 2 (Problem Analysis) was brailled and administered by teachers in the schools. The test required no calculation, but the child was required to answer questions about (a) the facts given, (b) what to find out, (c) how to select the most reasonable answer, (d) what process should be used in solving the problem.

Results: Blind children compared favorably on this test with seeing children in the same grade. However, blind children were older than seeing children in the same grade. Both blind and seeing children did well at determining what is to be found out in the problem and the process necessary to its solution, but needed instruction in enumerating facts given and estimating answers.

Comment: The problems experienced by blind children in arithmetic achievement were indicated in the results above. The results of this study indicate that such difficulty is not a consequence of lack of ability in the type of comprehension and reasoning required to attack arithmetic problems.

Nolan, C. Y. Achievement in Arithmetic Computation. Analysis of School Differences and Identification of Areas of Low Achievement. *International Journal for the Education of the Blind,* 1959, 8, 125-128.

Purpose: To make an analysis of differences in achievement in arithmetic computation among several schools for the blind, and to identify tentatively types of arithmetical operations where achievement is low.

Subjects: Braille adaptations of Form J of the Stanford Achievement Computation Tests were administered to children in nine residential schools for the blind. The Primary Level Test was taken by 77 children in grade 3.2; the Elementary Level Test by 70 children in grade 4.2; the Intermediate Level Test by 57 children in grade 6.2; and the Advanced Level Test by 78 children in grade 8.2.

Procedure: The adapted tests consisted of two forms administered on successive days by the classroom teachers. The two lower level tests required the child to record his answer on a separate sheet of paper with a braillewriter. The two upper level tests were a multiple choice type which required the student to underline the most appropriate of four answers. Braille problems were presented exactly as in the print edition. Time for each form was set at 45 minutes.

Results: Significant differences in mean achievement existed among schools at each grade level. The extent of school differences increased with grade level. The rank order of achievement for schools appeared stable over all four grades. Specific arithmetic operations giving difficulty for at least 60 percent of the pupils at each grade level were identified.

Comment: The results of this study seem to indicate that the problem in arithmetic achievement stems from some other source than mental ability. The great differences in achievement among schools indicate that research in arithmetic teaching methods may be a fruitful approach to this problem.

Hayes, S. P. Words are Wise Men's Counters (Hobbes): How Rich Are the Blind? *Teachers Forum (Blind),* 1938, 10, 94-103, 108.

Purpose: To determine how efficient blind children are in the understanding of words.

Subjects and Procedure: 443 individuals (ages 10 to 23+) were tested using Terman's English Group Vocabulary Test. 180 children in grades four to nine were given the Stanford Achievement Test, No. 2, Word Meaning.

Results: The results indicated an inferiority in the understanding of words among the blind about equal to their retardation in the early grades, with a progressively greater inferiority in later adolescence where longer words and specialized, abstract terms form a larger proportion of standard vocabularies.

Comment: Since blind children must acquire many more concepts vicariously than must seeing children, and since auditory and tactile communication is slow, growth of vocabulary has long been a matter of interest. This study, as well as others, demonstrates the extent of the effects of the above factors in vocabulary growth.

Payne, Sarah. Free Association in Blind Children. Unpublished master's thesis, Columbia University, 1931.

Purpose: To compare free association of blind and partially seeing children with those of normal children.

Subjects: 41 children (ages seven to 15 years, grades one to four) in school at the New York Institute for Education of the Blind. None could see well enough to travel in strange surroundings.

Procedure: The Kent-Rosanoff word list as modified by Woodrow and Lowell was used. Children were required to respond to a stimulus word with the first word that occurred to them following stimulation (free association).

Results: Blind children tended to give fewer specific common reactions to the words. Blind children gave almost three times as many individual responses as did normal children. Perseveration reactions were especially apparent. Blind children showed definite limitation in their fields of association. They gave fewer adequate associations than did normal children.

Comment: Not only is vocabulary growth affected in extent but also in the kind of conceptual relationships formed. Some studies have indicated that the latter effects can be extreme. This research demonstrates a technique that can be used effectively to explore this problem further.

> Rowe, Emma D. *Speech Problems of Blind Children: Survey of the North California Area.* New York: American Foundation for the Blind, 1958.

Purpose: To determine the percentage of significant speech defects to be found in the speech of blind children enrolled in schools in northern California.

Subjects: 73 boys and 75 girls (grades one to six, ages six to 16 years) were studied. Ninety children were enrolled in a residential school while 58 were enrolled in public day schools. All were legally blind, with 74 being totally blind or having light perception only.

Procedure: Measures used included a speech inventory filled out by teachers, a tape-recorded individual speech test which consisted of naming objects which covered sounds in initial position in words and counting to 10, and a sample of connected speech where the child was encouraged to talk freely. The results obtained were rated by two trained public school speech therapists.

Results: The percentage of speech defects was low when compared with most school surveys. All defects found were considered to be minor and in no case was the speech defect severe enough to interfere markedly with effective communication.

Comment: Research in speech development has long been of interest in this field. The results of this recent study are in conflict with those of earlier studies where many more speech difficulties were discovered. This paper contains a comprehensive review of earlier work in this area.

In Review

With the exception of arithmetic, achievement of blind children appears to approach that of seeing children at the same grade level. However, blind children are often older than seeing children in comparative grades. Reasons for retardation in terms of age-for-grade are not clear. This may be a consequence of slower rates of communication, differential rates of perceptual development between blind and seeing children, inadequate methods of instruction, or a combination of these and other things. So far as the author has been able to determine, no studies comparing the effectiveness of educational methods for blind children have been made in any subject area.

PERSONALITY AND SOCIAL DEVELOPMENT AND THEIR MEASUREMENT

Studies in these areas have important, if indirect, implications for education because education is a social process in which the child's success depends, at least in part, on the degree of his personal integration and maturity. Major research interests in this area have been the adaptation of standardized tests for use with the blind, comparison of development of personality between blind and seeing groups, and investigation of some of the dynamics of personality development.

Efforts to adapt personality tests for use with the blind have compounded the problems intrinsic to these tests with those of content and concurrent validity for the blind as discussed previously.

Maxfield, Kathryn E. and Fjeld, Harriet A. The Social Maturity of the Visually Handicapped Preschool Child. *Child Development,* 1942, 13, 1-27.

Purpose: To determine the usefulness of the Vineland Social Maturity Scale as a measure of the general social competence of visually handicapped children.

Subjects: 101 visually handicapped children (ages nine months to 6-10 years).

Procedure: The first 77 items of the Vineland Social Maturity Scale were used as a basis for this study. The effects of differing degrees of

137

blindness and intelligence upon total scores and individual item scores were investigated.

Results: Twenty items were found useful without revision, 31 with revision, and 36 new items were included to constitute a revised scale. The results definitely indicated that these children, as a group, were retarded on specific items, and appear to be more docile, less active, and have less initiative than seeing children of corresponding ages.

Comment: A major problem for early education is identifying that point in life when young blind children have reached a level of development which will permit them to enter school. This research describes the adaptation of a scale which may be used for this purpose. Implied in the results is the extent of the problem of content validity for revision of this test.

Scholl, Geraldine. Some Notes on the Use of Two Personality Tests with Visually Handicapped Students. *New Outlook for the Blind*, 1953, 47, 287-295.

Purpose: To describe the use of the Bell Adjustment and Bernreuter Personality Inventories with the blind and to summarize results of their use.

Subjects: 62 students were given the Bernreuter and 52 students were given the Bell. All students were enrolled in grade 11 of a residential school for the blind.

Procedure: Both tests were recorded and administered by means of a tape recorder. Individual administration was used with the subject responding by putting numbered cards in appropriate boxes.

Results: Bernreuter: Blind girls appeared better adjusted than blind boys on the scales measuring neurotic tendency, self sufficiency, and dominance-submission (B1-N, B2-S, and B4-D).

Bell: Blind children averaged within the normal range for the Home, Health, Social, and Emotional scales. Boys appeared superior to girls on the Home Scale and Emotional Scale. On the Total Scale the median for both boys and girls fell within the Average norm category.

Comment: A number of paper and pencil personality tests have been adapted for use with the blind. Such tests have been read orally to groups, brailled, or recorded and presented individually or to groups. Test scores have been analyzed to describe personal adjustment of blind groups in terms of test norms. Findings of such studies have varied widely, with little consistency among the several studies reported in the literature.

Hayes, S. P. An Interest Inventory for the Guidance of the Blind. *Outlook for the Blind*, 1948, 42, 95-104.

Purpose: To describe an adaptation of the Kuder Preference Record and give results of its use.

Subjects: 58 boys and 33 girls (CA 13 to 22 years, MA 12 to 22 years) enrolled in the Upper School at Perkins School for the Blind.

Procedure: The test was given orally to groups; subjects responded by making pencil marks on appropriate dots on a braille multiple choice answer sheet. Some individual items were changed to conform with capacities of the blind.

Results: The interests of boys were high in the Musical and Clerical areas, low in the Mechanical and Computational areas, and below the median of norms for other areas. The interests of girls were high in the Persuasive, Literary and Musical areas, and at or below the median for other areas. No reliability estimates were available. High agreement existed ($r = .62$ to $.95$) between teachers' ratings on possible success and interest scores of students for the Musical, Mechanical, Computational, and Literary areas. Low agreement ($r = .08$ to $.24$) was found for the Persuasive and Clerical areas.

Comment: This is one of the few studies representing test adaptations in the interest and aptitude areas. Lack of availability of large numbers of subjects entering specific educational or vocational areas has prevented research on the predictive validity of the various standardized interest and aptitude tests.

Sommers, Vita S. *The Influence of Parental Attitudes and Social Environment on the Personality Development of the Adolescent Blind.* New York: American Foundation for the Blind, 1944.

Purpose: To evaluate the influence of parental attitudes and social environment on the behavior and personality development of the adolescent blind.

Subjects: 68 boys and 75 girls with no useful vision who lost their vision before six years of age. Subjects ranged in age from 14 to 21 years, and in grade level from eight to 12. Intelligence ranged from low average to very superior.

Procedure: All subjects were administered the California Test of Personality (CTP) and a questionnaire on attitudes and adjustment. Seventy-two mothers filled out a similar questionnaire for their children.

For 50 subjects, intensive interviews were conducted both with parents and children.

Results: Results from the CTP indicated that blind adolescents as a group fell below the norms of the seeing with respect to personal and social adjustment, and blind girls seemed to be slightly better adjusted than blind boys. However, the author concluded that, due to the nature of many of the test items, these findings lacked validity.

Answers to questionnaires indicated that "frustrations or maladjustments or emotional disturbances result more frequently from the social attitudes and conditions surrounding the blind person and brought about by the presence of the handicap, than from the sensory disability itself."

"Interviews with parents disclosed that the majority of mothers studied experienced frustrations or feelings of conflict because of having given birth to a blind child . . . [these] seemed to arise from a sense of unfulfillment resulting from the fact that the birth of a child with a handicap as apparent as blindness failed to meet the concept of the kind of child which the mother had expected; while the contradiction between maternal devotion and an irrepressible sense of repulsion caused by the blindness seemed to create feelings of irreconcilable conflict. These . . . feelings . . . [resulted in] a sense of guilt which frequently was associated with self-consciousness or a sense of inferiority."

Reactions of parents to children fell into five fairly distinct categories: (a) genuine acceptance of the handicap and devotion to the child, (b) an attitude of denial that either parent or child is affected by the handicap, (c) overprotectiveness and excessive pity, (d) disguised rejection, and (e) overt rejection.

Adolescents displayed a variety of adjustive behavior closely related to the reactions of their parents (particularly mothers) to their handicap. These included: (a) wholesome compensatory and hypercompensatory behavior, (b) denial reactions, (c) defensive behavior, (d) withdrawing tendencies, and (e) nonadjustive reactions.

Verrillo, R. T. A Study of Adjustment and the Relationship Between Parental Attitudes and Adjustment in Visually Impaired and Sighted Adolescents. Unpublished doctoral thesis, University of Rochester, 1958.

Purpose: To determine the relationship between the attitudes of parents and the adjustment of groups of visually handicapped and sighted adolescent offspring.

Subjects: The visually handicapped group included 12 totally blind, 28 legally blind, and 31 partially seeing children who were living with their parents. These were matched in age, grade placement, intelligence, and socio-economic status with a group of 40 normally seeing children. Mothers were also contacted. All children had attended public schools for at least three years prior to the study.

Procedure: Two measures of adjustment of children were obtained: the self-ideal sort of attitude items by children and a teacher's behavior rating scale. Perceived attitudes of parents were indicated by the children on a Situations Projective Test – B. Parents completed a master scale which measured parental child-rearing attitudes. Attitudes of children as perceived by parents were tapped through the Situations Projective Test – A.

Results: No significant differences in adjustment were found between visually impaired and normally seeing groups or between sexes within or between groups. For the handicapped group, no significant relationships were found between publicly expressed maternal attitudes and adolescent adjustment. Adolescent adjustment in both groups was significantly related to children's perception of attitudes of rejection and acceptance in parent figures. Children's perceived attitudes and parental attitudes were significantly related. High socio-economic status was positively related to degree of adjustment of children and to maternal acceptance of children in both groups. Low status was related to attitudes of overprotection, dominance, rejection, anti-minority, and authoritarianism. In the visually handicapped group, attitudes toward blindness became significantly more negative as ages of children increased.

Comment: The last two studies represent attempts to define and relate factors important to personality development. These studies of intrafamily relationships and their implications for personal adjustment demonstrate the effects of these factors and also that such effects are not confined to the blind. The Q-sort method demonstrated is an example of one of the more rigorous experimental approaches to the problem of personality development.

Kent, H. R. The Effect of Repeated Praise or Blame on the Work Achievement of Blind Children. Unpublished doctoral thesis, Columbia University, 1956.

Purpose: To determine if motivational needs differ among sighted children, blind children in public schools, and blind children in residential schools.

Subjects: Three groups matched for age included 60 pupils from residential schools for the blind, 43 blind pupils from New York City schools, and 60 seeing children from the same schools. A control group included 30 blind children from residential schools.

Procedure: All subjects in the first three groups were given the Introversion-Extroversion Scale of Aspects of Personality by Pintner, *et al.* Those scoring above median were classed as extroverts and those below as introverts. Half of the extroverts were randomly chosen to receive praise and half to receive blame while given a series of trials on a cancellation test. Similar conditions were applied to the introverted group. The control group took the cancellation test but received neither praise nor blame.

Results: Either incentive was more effective than none for residential school blind children, but only praise was effective for public school blind children. The effect for the latter group was less intense. Regardless of personality type, praise was found to be a more effective motivator than blame for all groups. Degree of achievement, in response to either motivational variable, proved to be the same for the seeing and residential blind groups. Both of these groups significantly exceeded the public school blind.

The major conclusion was that blind children could not be considered a homogeneous group with respect to the motivational processes investigated, and, like seeing children, they were influenced by environmental circumstances.

Comment: The social implications of the various types of educational programs for the motivation, social integration, and self-concept development of blind children have not been explored. This study is of interest because of the question it leaves unanswered. Why did blind children in public school classes react as they did?

In Review

There are no indications that the dynamics of personality development in the blind differ from those of other groups. Social factors within the home and school environments appear important in the personality development of blind children.

PHYSICAL DEVELOPMENT AND ITS MEASUREMENT

The physical development of blind children has received little study. However, physical development with its implications for general health

142

and better mobility are of tremendous importance to the overall well-being of blind children.

Buell, C. Motor Performance of Visually Handicapped Children. *Outlook for the Blind*, 1950, 44, 256-258.

Purpose: To measure the gross motor performance of blind and partially seeing children.

Subjects: 865 children in 12 residential schools and eight braille classes served as subjects: 36 percent had no useful vision; 25 percent of these had lost vision after six years of age; more than 50 percent had attended a special school for at least six years; 27 percent of the blind and 11 percent of the partially seeing were classified as over-protected.

Procedure: The children were given a battery of tests including the 50-yard dash, the basketball throw for distance, the standing broad jump and the Iowa Brace Test.

Results: Visually handicapped children scored far below seeing children. No one factor—body control, static balance, coordination, or agility—seemed responsible. Limited physical activity (due to lack of vision and over-protection by parents) appeared to be the major reason for this finding. Physical performance by the blind was as consistent as that of the seeing. The partially seeing, in general, exceeded the totally blind on all tests; this difference usually disappeared at the high school level. Over-protected children scored lower than those from normal environments. Children who lost their vision after age six had less difficulty adjusting to physical activities than those who lost their vision earlier.

Comment: This study is characteristic of initial researches in that its purpose is to explore and to define, for further research, specific aspects of a more general problem area. As such, the approach to the problem area is generalized and normative.

SUMMARY

With few exceptions, lack of integration characterizes previous research in the education of blind children. As is implied by the articles reviewed, much research has been of a normative nature comparing the blind with the seeing for numerous types of behavior. The quality of research in terms of design, execution, statistical analysis, and reporting has often been quite disappointing. Many studies have involved groups that were too small and did not represent the populations for whom inferences were to be made.

These criticisms exemplify the necessity for establishing long-range integrated research programs. Such programs should be under the direction of social scientists who have thorough training in research techniques and in the subject matter specific to their areas of study. In order to solve the problem of sampling, research programs must have resources that will enable them to draw subjects from throughout the United States as required. General research problems which need further study are indicated below under the appropriate area.

Sensory and perceptual factors relevant to education: Further studies of haptic perception of form are urgently needed. Space perception as a function of auditory and haptic cues should be explored further in order to better understand and solve problems in mobility. The effects of sensory deprivation upon the development of perceptual processes appears an important problem for study.

Educational media and their use: Perceptual factors in braille reading such as cues in recognizing whole words and tactual span have yet to be investigated. Description is needed of perceptual and learning factors in listening which are related to the educational process. Problems in graphic communication which are closely related to those of tactual form perception need intensive study. Development of satisfactory devices for arithmetical computing and description of methods for their use are important. Study should be made of the applicability of teaching machines to the visually handicapped population.

Intelligence and its measurement: Verbal intelligence tests, both individual and group, which have content and concurrent validity for both blind and seeing groups, are needed. Also needed are performance scales of intelligence for blind children.

Educational development and its measurement: Further research on problems of concurrent validity of achievement tests should be undertaken. Research to identify the best teaching methods for reading, arithmetic, and geography has yet to be carried out. Concept development and vocabulary development in preschool and primary level children need further study.

Personality and social development and their measurement: The implications of the various types of educational programs for the social integration and self-concept development of blind children should be explored. Research in this area particularly needs improvement in sampling procedures, control procedures, and instrumentation.

SECTION II—LARGE-TYPE READERS

The material in this section describes studies of groups among visually handicapped children who characteristically employ large-type as a principal medium of education. These children are often termed "partially seeing" children. The vision of children falling within this group may range from approximately 20/70 in the better corrected eye down to visual acuities of 20/200 or lower, which fall within the legally accepted definition of blindness. Such children are educated as seeing children. It is estimated that approximately 78,000 potential large-type readers are enrolled in public schools in the United States; however, only 11 percent of these are receiving special help.*

Specific research studies dealing with factors in the education of large-type readers are few. Causes for this are not clear. Some explanation for lack of research with this group may lie in the manner in which they are perceived. In accounting for lack of research on the large-type reader, Lowenfeldt† aptly states, "He is, for all practical purposes, a seeing child, and his handicap, if it is one, does not affect him in any different way from other children who slightly deviate from 'the normal'."

For the convenience of the reader, the material has been organized under the following research categories:

1. Educational media.
2. Intelligence testing.
3. Educational development.
4. Personality and social development.

EDUCATIONAL MEDIA

A variety of special media is utilized in the education of partially seeing children. However, empirical research on media has dealt almost entirely with legibility of textbook materials. Type size and style have been the principal subject of interest. No unanimity of opinion exists to this day concerning the size of type most satisfactory for large type books. Types used in the past have included 18-point, 24-point, and 32-point sizes (approximately 72 points make an inch). The following summaries deal with textbook legibility.

* APHA discussions of eye problems. *Sight-Saving Review*, 1959, 29, p. 96.

† B. Lowenfeld. Psychological problems of children with impaired vision. In W. M. Cruickshank (Ed.). *Psychology of Exceptional Children and Youth.* Englewood Cliffs, N. J.: Prentice-Hall. 1955, p. 273.

Fortner, Ethel N. Investigation of Large Type Books. *Proceedings, American Association of Workers for the Blind,* 1943, 78-81.

Purpose: To compare ease of reading for material in 18- and 24-point type under standardized conditions.

Subjects: 39 normally seeing public school children, grades four to six, ages nine to 14, and 56 children with defective vision (grades four to 12, ages nine to 18). Visual defects included myopia, cataract, astigmatism, albinism, corneal opacities, optic neuritis, retinitis pigmentosa, chorioretinitis, amblyopia, optic atrophy, dislocated lens, strabismus, coloboma, microphthalmia, and hyperopia. Range of vision was from less than 20/200 to 20/20.

Procedure: Children were required to read 521-word selections from a fourth grade cleartype reader printed in 24- and 18-point Goudy bold print under standard light conditions. Eye blink-rate was used as a criterion of ease in seeing. Reading time was recorded.

Results: No significant difference in involuntary blink-rate for 24- and 18-point type was found; therefore it was concluded both were equally legible. Seventy-five percent of the children approved 18-point type because it permitted a greater eye span.

Nolan, C. Y. Readability of Large Types: A Study of Type Sizes and Type Styles. *International Journal for the Education of the Blind,* 1959, 9, 41-44.

Purpose: To determine the comparative readability of type of two styles and of two sizes.

Subjects: 264 children of both sexes (grades four to 12, ages eight to 20 years) whose IQs exceeded 69. Half the group was legally blind with vision in the better corrected eye ranging from 20/200 to 2/200. Range of vision for the remainder was from 20/40 to 20/160. The children were enrolled in sight-saving classes in 47 public schools and residential schools for the blind in Ohio, Illinois, and Kentucky.

Procedure: A treatments x treatments x levels design was used. The treatments consisted of comparison of 18- and 24-point type and of comparison of a common type face (Antique with Old Style) with an experimental type. Two visual levels were employed: legally blind children and non-legally blind children. The criterion used was reading speed which was measured by a 30-minute test based on the 1942 edition of Gates Basic Reading Test, grades three to eight.

Results: Groups of both legally blind and nonblind large-type readers read 18-point and 24-point type with equal speed. A common schoolbook type was found to be more legible than an experimental type. Average reading speeds were 91 wpm for the legally blind group and 106 wpm for the non-legally blind group.

Comment: The two studies reviewed above give results which support the view that 18-point type is as legible as 24-point type. (From the cost standpoint, 18-point type is more desirable because of lower cost of texts.) Studies which support the greater legibility of 24-point type are said to have been made. However, these were not available in published form at the time of writing. Criteria other than reading speed and eyeblink rate may be pertinent in evaluating relative legibility of types.

The low reading speeds reported emphasize the need for exploring the efficiency of other media for communicating educational information to this group.

Nolan, C. Y. A Study of Pictures for Large Type Textbooks. *International Journal for the Education of the Blind,* 1960, 9, 67-70.

Purpose: To evaluate a method of legibly reproducing colored pictures in black and white for use in large-type books.

Subjects: 28 boys and 12 girls who were large-type readers (age 11 to 20 years, grades five to 10.) Visual acuities in the better corrected eye ranged from 20/50 to 10/200. Seventy percent of the group was legally blind.

Procedure: Black and white tracings of five different colored pictures were made according to three general rules: (a) Contour was emphasized as a cue to form perception, (b) figure-ground relations were emphasized where possible, and (c) extraneous detail or clutter was omitted from pictures where possible. Four variations in black and white tracings were made for each picture: (a) a simple line drawing, (b) a line drawing with areas blacked in for contrast, (c) a line drawing with blacked areas and light shading, and (d) a line drawing with blacked areas and heavy shading. The method of paired comparison was used to compare each variation of each picture with every other variation as well as with a black and white photo-offset print of the original colored picture.

Results: A traced picture consisting of a line drawing with areas blacked in for contrast was judged more legible than other modes of presentation 75 percent of the time. Any mode of black and white tracing of colored pictures was judged to be more legible than its black and white photo-offset counterpart.

Comment: Large-type reproduction of regular textbooks is accomplished through the photo-offset process and books are printed in black ink on a lightly-tinted buff or off-white paper. High costs prohibit complete reproduction of textbooks in color. Results of attempts to reproduce originally multicolored pictures or maps in black and white have ranged from pictures where clearness of contour and distinctiveness of figure-ground relationships were slightly diminished, to those where the whole picture appeared one area of almost equally dark grays. The above study describes the evaluation of methods of inexpensively reproducing legible pictures.

INTELLIGENCE TESTING

Standard individual intelligence tests with both verbal and performance scales can be used with many partially seeing children. Loss of validity can result for timed tests of both verbal and performance abilities when individual visual loss is sufficient to seriously impair rate of visual or manual behavior and their coordination. No special adaptations of intelligence tests are currently available for use with large-type readers.

Pintner, R. Intelligence Testing of Partially-Sighted Children. *Journal of Educational Psychology*, 1942, 33, 265-72.

Purpose: To compare regular and enlarged forms of the Revised (1937) Stanford-Binet Tests of Intelligence in the testing of partially seeing children.

Subjects: 602 partially seeing children, most of whom were 10 to 12 years old.

Procedure: The children were tested and retested using both regular Stanford-Binet materials and enlarged materials for this same test.

Results: The mean IQ for the group when tested with enlarged materials was 95. However, the author comments that this may be an underestimate because of the larger numbers of children in the sample who came from bilingual homes. When divided into groups according to measures of visual acuity, no difference was found between a group having 20/70 to 20/200 and a group with better acuity. No differences were found between test results obtained by regular forms and enlarged forms of the test. However, a study of previous IQs obtained from many different kinds of tests showed, on the whole, lower IQs than those obtained by the enlarged Binet.

Livingston, J. S. Evaluation of an Enlarged Test Form Used with the Partially Seeing. *Sight-Saving Review*, 1958, 28, 37-39.

Purpose: To discover clues to intelligence strengths and weaknesses of partially seeing children and to determine whether enlarging the Revised (1937) Stanford-Binet Scale would increase their scores.

Subjects: 60 partially seeing children (ages eight to nine years, vision of 20/70 to 20/200, and mean IQ of 98.6) were compared with 407 normally seeing children with mean IQ of 103.3.

Procedure: Visually handicapped groups were split, matched, and compared on Form L of the Stanford-Binet, with the experimental group being tested on a photographic enlargement of the tests. The visually handicapped were compared with the sighted on 11 categories of mental functioning developed from the test.

Results: No difference was found among IQs of partially seeing groups compared on the basis of scores from regular test forms and a photographic enlargement of these. The partially seeing were inferior to the normally seeing in visual motor coordination but were superior on two abstract word tests. The general conclusion drawn was that no major differences existed between these two groups in several categories of mental functioning.

Comment: The two studies just reviewed demonstrate the usefulness of standard test materials with most partially seeing children. No great direct relationships have been found between intelligence and visual acuity. However, in testing partially seeing children it is important to consider each child individually in determining what specific measures are most applicable. Attempts to adapt group intelligence tests for this subpopulation are not reported in the literature.

EDUCATIONAL DEVELOPMENT

Attempts to describe the educational achievement of large-type readers have been few. Most of these attempts were made in the 1920s. An example of these efforts is provided below. The principal reason for lack of recent effort to study educational development appears to be the absence of measuring instruments for this purpose. Since 1958, a series of standardized achievement tests in large-type has been available from the American Printing House for the Blind. The growing use of these tests opens the way for large-scale study in this area.

Peck, Olive S. Reading Ability of Sight-Saving Class Pupils in Cleveland, Ohio. *Sight-Saving Review,* 1933, 3, 115-126.

Purpose: To determine the reading ability of large-type readers.

Subjects: Approximately 234 children in grades two to nine who were enrolled in Sight-Saving Classes in Cleveland, Ohio, during the years 1932 to 1933.

Procedure: The subjects were tested and retested after one year. The Stanford Achievement Test in Reading, Form A, was reproduced in large type for this purpose. Scores recorded were based on time limits allowed children in regular classes as well as a limit allowing one and-one-half times regular time.

Results: Median reading achievement for all grades was close to the respective norms for each grade.

PERSONALITY AND SOCIAL DEVELOPMENT

Studies in this area are predominately comparisons of the personal adjustment of partially seeing children with that of other groups, or studies of attitudes of others toward such children. Problems of validity equivalent to those described for intelligence tests may occur in use of standardized personality tests with some members of this group. No specially adapted tests of personality or social development are currently available for use with this group.

Pintner, R., and Forlano, G. Personality Tests of Partially Sighted Children. *Journal of Applied Psychology,* 1943, 27, 283-87.

Purpose: To determine if differences in personality exist between groups of children enrolled in sight-conservation classes and groups enrolled in regular classes.

Subjects: 874 partially seeing children in elementary, junior high, and high school classes.

Procedure: Children were administered the Aspects of Personality Test and Pupil Portraits Test. These group tests were reproduced in large type for this purpose.

Results: Generally, partially seeing children showed no marked average deviations from normal children in factors of ascendance, extroversion, emotional stability, school adjustment and home adjustment. The most probable group deviation was shown by partially seeing girls who seem to be more introverted than normal girls.

Comment: No general or marked differences in personality development have been found among partially seeing groups and others. Comparisons on this topic have been few and the measuring instruments used inadequate. In the general literature, however, belief is often expressed in the existence of significant numbers of personality problems within the partially seeing group.

Underberg, Rita P. The Relationship Between Parental Understanding and Child Adjustment in the Visually Disabled Adolescent. Unpublished doctoral thesis, University of Rochester, 1958.

Purpose: To test the hypothesis that good parental understanding is related to good child adjustment, high child perception of acceptance, and low child perception of rejection in groups of visually disabled and seeing adolescents. In addition it was hypothesized that the seeing group is characterized by better adjustment, higher perceptions of acceptance and better parental understanding.

Subjects: 40 seeing, 12 totally blind, 28 legally blind, and 31 partially seeing children and their mothers. Children were from grades seven to 12 in public schools in cities in New York State. Groups were closely matched on sex, age, educational level, IQ, and socio-economic status.

Procedure: All children were administered two tests that measured adjustment, a measure of self-concept, and a projective test which measured child perceptions of pity, overprotection, rejection and acceptance. Teachers' ratings of children's adjustment were obtained. Parental understanding was measured by the magnitude of the difference between parental prediction and the actual response of their children to the measures of self-concept and the projective test. Parents also predicted self-concept for an "average" child.

Results: For seeing children, accurate parental prediction of self-concept was significantly related to all measures of adjustment and perceived acceptance and rejection as predicted. For the experimental groups, significant relationships appeared between accurate parental prediction of self-concept and the self-concept measures of adjustment. Group differences in child adjustment, child perception, and parental understanding were generally not significant. However, the partially seeing group might possibly be characterized by somewhat greater child perception of pity and somewhat poorer parental understanding.

Parental predictions of self-concept for the "average" child were closely related to those made for their own child except for the partially seeing group whose mothers, as opposed to the others, perceived their children as being different from the average. Generally it is believed that the study findings support the idea that the parent-child relationship is a fundamental influence upon adjustment, the operations of which are similar for both seeing and visually disabled adolescents.

Comment: The findings of this study indicate that less understanding may exist between partially seeing children and their parents than is usual in similar relationships involving normally seeing or blind children. Lack of understanding between partially seeing children and others in a variety of situations is frequently mentioned in the literature. This is believed to result from differences which occur between the expected and observed behavior of these children. Since from outward appearances many such children seem normal, parents and others have normal expectancies for the child's behavior and its growth. When expression of the handicap prevents normal growth or causes aberrant behavior, this is judged to result from lack of intelligence, clumsiness, or sheer perversity on the part of the child.

Force, D. G., Jr. Social Status of Physically Handicapped Children. *Exceptional Children,* 1956, 23, 104-107, 132-133.

Purpose: To compare physically handicapped and normal children in integrated classes at the elementary school level, to determine the effect of physical disability upon social position among peers.

Subjects: 63 physically handicapped and 361 normal children of average intelligence in 14 elementary classes (grades one to six) of three Michigan schools, including seven visually handicapped children.

Procedure: A near-sociometric instrument was used to reveal choice behavior on three criteria—friends, playmates, and workmates. Teachers rated all children for outstanding positive and negative behavior traits. Data were analyzed using deviation-from-chance-expectancy techniques.

Results: Physically handicapped children were not as well accepted as normal children in integrated classes at the elementary school level. Visually handicapped children received significantly lower numbers of choices on all criteria than did normal children. Psychological identification of subgroups of normal children and physically handicapped children was made by elementary school children in their choice behavior. Physical disabilities have varying social values with cerebral palsy ranking lowest on the value scale (visual disability ranks next lowest). The individual physically handicapped child who is highly accepted by a peer group manifests many socially desirable traits and relatively few negative traits. Few such children have enough positive assets to offset completely the negative effect of being labelled as handicapped by normal peers.

Comment: Much has been said and written in the last three decades concerning the necessity for integrating the visually handicapped in the mainstreams of society. Many educators have naively assumed that the simple juxtaposition of the visually handicapped and seeing within an educational setting would assure this occurance. The above study amply demonstrates that placing handicapped children within regular classes is only the initial step in their integration.

Murphy, A. T. Attitudes of Educators Toward the Visually Handicapped. *Sight-Saving Review,* 1960, 30, 157-161.

Purpose: To measure the attitudes of educators toward groups of exceptional children.

Subjects: 100 elementary classroom teachers, 32 elementary school principals, 46 special educators, 100 college freshmen in teacher training, and 31 speech clinicians.

Procedure: Teachers ranked eight categories of exceptionality according to the type they would prefer to teach and the type about which they knew most. Categories included the visually handicapped, mentally retarded, emotionally disturbed, crippled, hearing handicapped, gifted, speech disordered, and delinquent.

Results: Children with visual handicaps were ranked lowest or next to the lowest in preference and knowledge by all teacher groups except the special educators. Special educators ranked the visually handicapped near the middle of the preference range. Other nonpreferred groups were the delinquent and hearing handicapped.

Comment: Negative attitudes toward visually handicapped individuals prevail throughout all strata of our society, including educators. The impact of such attitudes upon the visually handicapped individual is likely to have negative effects. The educational implications of such effects can be great.

153

SUMMARY

Twenty years ago, Pintner* commented on the lack of research on the partially seeing and upon our almost total ignorance of the psychology of these children. Today, these comments have almost the same degree of applicability. Within the last several years, groups have discussed and identified a number of educational research problems relative to this group. As nearly as can be determined, at present there are no concentrated or even sporadic efforts being made to supplement our knowledge of partially seeing children. Some major problems for research in the education of large type readers are listed below.

Educational Media: Further studies in the legibility of text materials need to be made. These should include studies of graphic material, pictures, and type. For print, factors such as line length and leading need study. Use of auditory communication in the education of this group should be explored. The implications of the growing use of optical aids for design of text materials need analysis.

Intelligence testing: Development of group intelligence tests and study of validity problems arising in the use of standard individual intelligence tests with these children are needed.

Educational development: Collection and analysis of achievement test results should be made in order to evaluate educational progress. It is likely that results of such an analysis will generate a host of specific research problems in this area.

Personality and social development: Further identification of specific problems in personality and social development arising from visual handicaps is needed. Further test development in this area would be useful. Basic information stemming from these activities could lead to further research on means to help solve problems confronting this group in the personality and social realms.

* R. Pintner, J. Eisenson, and M. Stanton. *The Psychology of the Physically Handicapped.* New York: Crofts & Co., 1941, p. 260.

5

The Hard of Hearing

Stephen P. Quigley

Very few studies dealing with the behavioral effects of hearing loss have appeared in recent years. Most of the recent literature on the hard of hearing has been contributed by the varied specialists and disciplines represented within the profession of audiology. The bulk of this literature is concerned with the processes and disorders of hearing rather than with the effects of the disorders on the achievement and adjustment of individuals. Because the emphasis in this review is on behavioral research, the extensive literature on audiology has been treated in only a cursory fashion.

The material in this review is organized under the following topics:
1. Definitions.
2. Identification.
3. Aural rehabilitation.
4. Intelligence.
5. Educational achievement.
6. Personal and social adjustment.

Reviewed by Alice Streng, University of Wisconsin in Milwaukee.

Within special education there is a tendency to consider the hearing impaired as forming two distinct groups: the deaf and the hard of hearing. There is a further tendency to regard each of these groups as being relatively homogeneous. These tendencies also are reflected in the research literature in which groups of subjects often are designated as being deaf or hard of hearing without further subclassification based on the degree of hearing impairment and other variables. This may be one of the causes of conflicting research findings in studies dealing with the hard of hearing. There appears to be considerable agreement that individuals with sensory-neural hearing losses exceeding 75 or 80 decibels may be classified as deaf and that those with hearing losses of a lesser degree may be classified as hard of hearing. Thus, the hard of hearing can hardly be considered as a homogeneous group either for educational or research purposes since the degree of hearing loss within this group may vary from relatively mild losses of 20 db to relatively severe losses of 70 db. Research studies need to consider this wide variance in degree of hearing impairment as an important variable. It is not unlikely that two identical studies of the personality of hard of hearing persons, one using a sample with an average hearing loss of 30 db and the other a sample with an average loss of 60 db, would present conflicting results if the behavioral consequences of hearing impairment vary with the degree of impairment.

There are two definitions which consider the hearing impaired as forming two groups: the hard of hearing and the deaf. The first of these definitions was proposed by the White House Conference on Child Health and Protection.*

> The *deaf* are those who were born either totally deaf or sufficiently deaf to prevent the establishment of speech and natural language; those who became deaf in childhood before language and speech were established; or those who became deaf in childhood so soon after the natural establishment of speech and language that the ability to speak and understand speech and language has been practically lost to them.
>
> The *hard of hearing* are those who established speech and ability to understand speech and language, and subsequently developed impairment of hearing. These children are sound-conscious and have a normal, or almost normal, attitude towards the world of sound in which they live.

* White House Conference on Child Health and Protection. *Special Education, The Handicapped and the Gifted: Report of the Committee on Special Classes* (Section III, Education and Training) Vol. III—F, New York: Century Company. 1931, p. 277.

156

The Committee on Nomenclature of the Conference of Executives of American Schools for the Deaf* proposed in 1937 the following definitions:

The *deaf:* those in whom the sense of hearing is non-functional for the ordinary purposes of life. This general group is made up of two distinct classes based entirely on the time of the loss of hearing: (a) the congenitally deaf—those who were born deaf; (b) the adventitiously deaf—those who were born with normal hearing but in whom the sense of hearing became non-functional later through illness or accident.

The *hard of hearing:* those in whom the sense of hearing, although defective, is functional with or without a hearing aid.

Each of these definitions attempts to define deafness in terms of a single variable: the White House Conference definition in terms of the time and the method of establishing speech and language, and the Conference of Executives definition in terms of the present functional auditory status of the individual. For the purposes of this review the important fact is that each of the definitions classifies the hard of hearing as a single group and makes no mention of subclassifications within this group.

More recent attempts at definition have included the audiological concept of degree of hearing loss as measured in decibels. One such definition and classification is that of Streng† who establishes five classifications of hearing impairment:

Class 1. They are the children with *mild* losses (20-30 db in the better ear in the speech range). They learn speech by ear and are on the borderline between the normally hearing and those with significant defective hearing.

Class 2. They are the children with *marginal* losses (30-40 db). They have difficulty in understanding speech by ear at a distance of more than a few feet and in following group conversation.

Class 3. They are the children with *moderate* losses (40-60 db). They have enough hearing to learn language and speech through the ear when sound is amplified for them and when the auditory sense is aided by the visual.

The children in these first three categories may be considered as being hard of hearing.

* Conference of Executives of American Schools for the Deaf. Report of the Conference Committee on Nomenclature. *American Annals of the Deaf,* 83, 1938, p. 3.

† Alice Streng, *et al., Hearing Therapy for Children.* New York: Grune and Stratton, 1958, p. 164.

157

Class 4. They are the children with *severe* losses (60-75 db). They have trainable residual hearing but their language and speech will not develop spontaneously, so they must learn to communicate through the use of specialized techniques. They are on the borderline between the hard of hearing and the deaf, and may be considered the "educationally deaf" or partially deaf.

Class 5. They are the children with *profound* losses (greater than 75 db). They cannot learn to understand language by ear alone, even with amplification of sound.

The distinguishing feature of this definition, which is representative of similar definitions recently proposed,* is that it does not classify the hard of hearing as a single, homogeneous group. It recognizes that the hard of hearing may be divided into subgroups, each presenting varying problems and requiring differing educational programs. There is need for similar recognition of this in designing research studies dealing with the hard of hearing. One major problem with establishing such classifications is defining the criteria which separate one category from another. It is likely that most of these classifications are based on authority or experienced judgment rather than on research. It might be possible, with the presently existing research techniques and instrumentation, to establish criteria for defining such classifications of hearing impairment that the behavioral consequences in the various categories would differ from each other in degree or in kind.

Three major variables which would be of importance are:

Degree of loss. This is the traditional psychoacoustic variable for measuring deafness. The degree of loss usually is measured in decibels. The hard of hearing individual can be described in terms of his degree of loss of awareness of, and response to, sound.

Age at onset of hearing loss. The age at which an individual loses his hearing is of crucial importance in the educational process and in his psychosocial and vocational adjustment. Two individuals might have exactly the same degree of hearing loss as measured in decibels with an audiometer; yet, if one individual suffered hearing impairment at birth and the other at age 15, there is likely to be considerable difference between them in such factors as educational achievement, language development, and speech development.

Type of hearing loss. The likely behavioral consequences of hearing impairment are related to the type of impairment. For example, purely

* S. R. Silverman, Clinical and Educational Procedures for the Hard-of-hearing. In L. E. Travis (Ed.), *Handbook of Speech Pathology*. New York: Appleton-Century-Crofts, 1957, 426-435.

conductive hearing losses, which involve injury only to the part of the hearing mechanism whose primary function is to conduct sound to the inner ear and thus to the brain, usually can be greatly aided by sound amplification systems. Sensory-neural impairments, on the other hand, are less amenable to such treatment.

It is recognized that for clinical and educational purposes it is desirable to consider each child as an individual and not as a member of a classification. For practical purposes, however, children are grouped and classified; and for the researcher who often deals with the mythical average such classifications are useful. The use of research to devise relatively homogeneous and meaningful classifications of the hard of hearing would provide an aid for the improvement of design and controls in research studies. Such classifications would serve to emphasize that the findings of a research study using a sample of children with an average hearing loss of 20 db are not necessarily applicable to children with hearing losses of a greater degree or a different type.

The following is an example of the type of study which might serve to devise meaningful behavioral definitions of subclassifications of the hard of hearing.

Silverman, S. R., Thurlow, W. R., Walsh, T. E., and Davis, H. Improvement in the Social Adequacy of Hearing Following the Fenestration Operation. *Laryngoscope*, 1948, 58, 607-631.

Purpose: One purpose of the study was to determine, for a sample of patients treated by the fenestration operation, the decibel levels which corresponded to varying degrees of social difficulty in communication due to hearing loss.

Subjects: A questionnaire was submitted to 161 patients on whom the fenestration operation had been performed. One hundred and twenty-three replies to this questionnaire were received (nearly 80 percent) and most of the replies were sufficiently complete to be used.

Procedure: In the questionnaire the patients indicated their degree of difficulty in hearing in a variety of social situations. From hearing tests which had been administered to the patients before and after the operations, calculations in decibels were made of each patient's hearing loss for speech. Comparisons were made between the patients' self-ratings and the objective hearing measure.

Results: The results indicate that a "threshold zone" of hearing extends from a hearing loss for speech of about 30 db, at which level patients began to have significant social difficulty, to a loss for speech of about 60 db, where most unaided social communication became virtually impossible. The middle of the threshold zone, about 45 db loss for speech, is taken as the "threshold of social adequacy of hearing."

Comment: More important in this review than the study's value as a means of evaluating the results of the fenestration operation, is its value as an attempt to attach psychological meaning to various categories of hearing loss. Such studies could be extended to other types of hearing loss and other age groups in order to provide meaningful classifications of the group now labeled homogeneously as hard of hearing.

In Review

Early definitions of hearing loss tended to consider the hard of hearing as a homogeneous group. More recent definitions tend to subclassify this group on the basis of the degree of hearing loss. Very few attempts have been made to formulate behavioral definitions based on the effects of a hearing loss on a person's behavior. The study cited above attempted to relate degree of hearing loss to social difficulty in communication. The need for further studies of this nature was emphasized. In such studies not only the degree of hearing loss needs to be considered but also the type of hearing loss and the age at onset of hearing loss.

IDENTIFICATION

The identification of individuals with impaired hearing is achieved primarily through otological and audiological diagnosis, although psychological and educational techniques may sometimes be used. The research literature in otology and audiology is so voluminous that information on the diagnostic procedures used by these professions in the identification and measurement of hearing impairment can best be obtained from textbooks.

The studies reviewed in this section concern the identification of hearing impaired children by the classroom teacher.

Curry, E. T. The Efficiency of Teacher Referrals in a School Hearing Testing Program. *Journal of Speech and Hearing Disorders*, 1950, 15, 211-214.

Purpose: A practice sometimes used in hearing surveys is to have the individual classroom teacher refer to the audiometric technician all students whom the teacher judges to have a hearing loss. One purpose of the study was to determine the efficiency of such teacher referrals.

160

Subjects: The study was part of a hearing survey of the schools in two rural counties in Illinois. All children in grades five, seven, and nine were given audiometric tests. Other children in the schools were tested only on teacher referral. Of the 6062 pupils in the two counties, 1217 were in the grades where audiometric testing was used throughout and 4845 were in all other grades where audiometric testing was used only on teacher referral.

Procedure: Standard audiometric procedures were used in testing seven frequencies from 256 to 11,584 cps. The definition of hearing loss used was failure to respond in individual testing to a stimulus of 30 db in one or more frequencies in one or both ears.

The teachers in the grades not scheduled for testing were informed of the testing program and of the great importance of early detection of hearing losses, and were urged to refer for testing all individuals they thought might have hearing losses.

Results: The incidence of hearing loss in the grades tested by audiometry was 12.8 percent. The incidence of teacher referrals from the other grades was only 3.8 percent. Furthermore, testing of the teacher referrals revealed that only 24.7 percent of them had a hearing loss as defined by the survey. The author concluded that the identification of hard of hearing children should be done by audiometric examination and not by a system of teacher referrals.

Comment: The design and scope of the study are adequate enough to justify the conclusion reached by the author that teacher referrals are a less reliable means of identifying hard of hearing children than audiometric testing.

Kodman, F. Jr. Identification of Hearing Loss by the Classroom Teacher. *Laryngoscope*, 1956, 66, 1346-1349.

Purpose: To compare audiometric findings with teacher identifications of hearing loss to determine the accuracy of the latter method.

Subjects: 665 elementary school children.

Procedure: The teachers of the children in the sample were asked to identify the children with hearing losses of 15 db or greater. All children then were given audiometric testing.

Results: Of the 125 children detected on audiometric tests to have hearing losses of 15 db or greater, only 20 were correctly identified by the teachers. Further, of the total of 53 teacher referrals, 33 did not have hearing losses.

Comment: The findings agree with those of Curry. It appears reasonable to conclude from the two studies that audiometric testing is a much better means of identifying hard of hearing students than is teacher judgment.

In Review

The otological and audiological information on the identification of persons with hearing loss is too voluminous to be included in this review. It can best be obtained from the many texts available on the subject. This section considered only the problem of teacher identification of school children with hearing losses. The two studies reviewed strongly indicated that audiometric testing is a more valid and reliable method for identification than is teacher judgment.

AURAL REHABILITATION

Aural rehabilitation for the hard of hearing is generally taken to include the use of hearing aids, auditory training, speechreading, and speech training to improve communication ability. Each of these is considered below in separate subsections.

Hearing Aids

It would be presumptuous to try to select a few major studies in this area because of the many studies available in the literature. There is, however, some doubt concerning the value of the amount of time usually spent in selecting hearing aids through detailed "fitting" procedures. The questions concerning this are pointed out in the following two studies.

Davis, H., Hudgins, C. V., Marquis, R. J., Nichols, R. H. Jr., Peterson, G. E., Ross, D. A., and Stevens, S. S. The Selection of Hearing Aids, Part II. *Laryngoscope,* 1946, 56, 85-115, 135-163.

Purpose: To investigate the transmission of speech by hearing aids, the limitations hearing aids impose upon intelligibility, and the quality of their transmission. The relation of these and other variables to the detailed "fitting" of hearing aids was studied.

Subjects: 25 hard of hearing subjects with moderate to severe hearing losses of the various clinical types.

162

Procedure: A "master hearing aid" was designed and constructed. This instrument offered the choice of five frequency characteristics clearly distinct from one another. Its basic frequency characteristic was flat from 100 to 7000 cps. Four "tilted" frequencies were provided: uniformly rising at 6 db per octave from 100 to 7000 cps; a similar rising characteristic at 12 db per octave; and two characteristics of low-tone emphasis of 6 and 12 db per octave, respectively. These frequency characteristics are similar to frequency settings available on individual hearing aids. A maximum acoustic output of 150 db was possible.

Each subject was tested with each frequency setting and with various acoustic outputs. Speech threshold and discrimination tests were used to evaluate the performance of the various frequency characteristics.

Results: For every subject the best performance could be obtained by using either the "flat" system or the 6 db per octave rising system. The subjects with severe losses that included the high tones tended as a group to do a little better with the rising 6 db characteristic. Those with "flat" losses did better with the flat characteristics.

Comment: The finding that most types of hearing loss can best be aided with the same type of frequency characteristic is at variance with clinical practice where much time is spent in detailed testing and "fitting" of hearing aids. Although many criticisms have been made of the experimental design of the study, the small number of subjects, and the treatment of the data, the findings at least indicate the need for more extensive investigation of this problem.

Shore, I., Bilger, R. C. and Hirsh, I. J. Hearing Aid Evaluation: Reliability of Repeated Measurements. *Journal of Speech and Hearing Disorders*, 1960, 25, 152-170.

Purpose: To determine if the reliability of three measures of speech audiometry commonly used in the evaluation of hearing aids is good enough to justify the investment of a large amount of clinical time with them in selecting among different hearing aids.

Subjects: 15 hard of hearing adults, 14 female and one male, between the ages of 28 and 69, with mild or moderate hearing losses in three diagnostic categories—conductive, mixed, and sensory-neural.

Procedure: The three diagnostic groups of subjects were given a battery of auditory tests to determine the amount and kind of loss. Each subject then was tested with two tone settings on each of four makes of hearing aids. The two tone settings were labeled *good* and *bad* and were

163

selected on the basis of specifications and information supplied by the manufacturers as being the most appropriate and the most inappropriate for each subject. Tests of hearing aid performance with all hearing aids and tone settings were repeated on four different days. Three auditory measures of hearing aid performance were used: gain or residual hearing level for speech, speech discrimination in quiet, and speech discrimination in noise.

Results: The results indicate that if there exists among hearing aids differences that make certain types of aids and/or tone settings within those aids more helpful for certain types of individuals than for others, the usual methods of speech audiometry are not reliable enough to detect the differences.

Comment: The study was well designed. The findings support those of Davis reviewed previously. Taken together, these two studies indicate a need for extensive research on the validity and reliability of present audiological practices in the selection of hearing aids.

Auditory Training

Hearing loss usually is not total. The hard of hearing person has residual hearing which it is believed can be improved by training. The procedures used are termed auditory training.

Silverman, S. R. Training for Optimum Use of Hearing Aids. *Laryngoscope,* 1944, 54, 29-36.

Purpose: To investigate the effects of auditory training in improving the speech perception of users of hearing aids.

Subjects: Seven users of hearing aids who had acquired understanding of speech prior to the onset of a hearing loss. They ranged in age from 24 to 65 years and all had worn hearing aids for more than two years.

Procedure: The subjects wearing their hearing aids were tested individually for perception of words and sentences before and after the training period. An adaptation of the word test developed by Thea and 25 sentences from the Fletcher-Steinberg articulation test were used.

The subjects received two one-hour training sessions per week for 10 weeks. Systematic auditory training was provided during these sessions.

Results: Six of the seven subjects showed appreciable improvement in the understanding of speech as a result of the auditory training.

Comment: This is one of the first research studies to demonstrate the value of auditory training in conjunction with a hearing aid. Although only seven subjects were used, thus prohibiting statistical treatment, it should be pointed out that the findings have been confirmed in later studies for both adults and children.

Hudgins, C. V. Auditory Training: Its Possibilities and Limitations. *Volta Review*, 1954, 56, 339-349.

Purpose: The report deals with part of a project sponsored by the National Research Council's Committee on Deafness to investigate the value of an experimental group hearing aid.

Subjects: Several classes of pupils were selected for intensive study under a program in which hearing aid equipment comparable in all essential features to the experimental aid was installed in a number of classrooms at the Clarke School for the Deaf. The progress of three groups of pupils is reported in the article. Group A consisted of four severely hard of hearing pupils with hearing losses ranging from 55 db to 86 db. Group B consisted of eight profoundly deaf children with hearing losses ranging from 90 to 98 db. Group C consisted of five profoundly deaf pupils who had hearing losses ranging from 90 to 98 db.

Procedure: Groups A and B were studied for a period of six years beginning at the fourth-grade level and Group C was studied for a period of four years beginning at the third-grade level. Each of the groups was given a number of tests periodically to measure progress with the use of a hearing aid and an auditory training program. The tests measured speech perception, speech intelligibility, and educational achievement (Stanford Achievement Test).

The progress of these classes in educational achievement was compared with the progress of classes in the same school during the years 1933 to 1945 when hearing aids were not generally available.

Results: The results indicate that the hearing aids and auditory training improved the speech perception and speech intelligibility of the groups studied. They indicate also that the progress in educational achievement for the three groups studied exceeded the average progress of the classes in school during the years 1933 to 1945 when hearing aids were not in general use.

Comment: It might be pointed out that this study, like Silverman's study reviewed above, had few subjects and little statistical analysis of the results, as well as poor control of other variables. It should be added, however, that the findings of both studies have been supported by other investigators.

DiCarlo, L. M. The Effect of Hearing One's Own Voice among Children with Impaired Hearing. *Volta Review*, 1958, 60, 306-314.

Purpose: To explore the extent to which children with impaired hearing rely on hearing to adjust their speech output.

Subjects: 23 hearing impaired subjects enrolled at the Syracuse University Summer Residence School and the Gordon D. Hoople Hearing and Speech Center, age seven to 18 years, with hearing losses ranging from moderate to severe (average loss 68.5 db. on the better ear). All the children attended public school; 12 wore hearing aids and had received auditory training; 11 had worn hearing aids but had had no auditory training prior to testing.

Procedure: Pure-tone and speech audiometry were administered to the children prior to recording their speech. Reading comprehension and word meaning sections of the Stanford Achievement Test were given. Thus, computation of the pure-tone loss for each ear, speech reception thresholds, discrimination, reading comprehension, and word meaning scores was possible. The subjects' speech was recorded with delayed feedback without amplification and with two levels of amplification.

Results: Among other striking phenomena, analysis of the data of the study showed that all children, regardless of hearing loss, exhibited: (a) change in rate of speech production, (b) disturbances of speech rhythm, (c) changes in voice quality, (d) increased intensity, and (e) prolongation and distortion of vowels and consonants. Children who depended upon auditory cues to correct their speech production exhibited greater disturbances when speaking under conditions which permitted them to hear their speech delayed.

Comment: This study suggests the possibility of the use of the delayed feedback technique to evaluate the results of auditory training and to detect other disturbances in hard of hearing children.

Speechreading

Although the literature on speechreading is quite extensive, not very much of it deals with research investigations. Of the research studies which have been conducted, many are attempts to determine through correlational techniques the variables associated with speechreading ability. This approach has not proven to be very productive. The following studies illustrate some of the approaches that have been used and some of the factors involved in research on speechreading.

166

Sumby, W. H., and Pollack, I. Visual Contribution to Speech Intelligibility in Noise. *Journal of the Acoustical Society of America*, 1954, 26, 212-215.

Purpose: One purpose of the study was to examine the contribution of visual factors to oral speech intelligibility as a function of the speech-to-noise ratio.

Subjects: 129 normally hearing subjects in groups of six.

Procedure: The subjects were presented with spoken word lists at different levels with respect to noise introduced into their earphones. The speech material was presented under two conditions: auditory presentation alone, and auditory and visual presentation combined, whereby the subject observed the words being spoken.

Results: Even though none of the subjects had formal speechreading training, visual perception was an important factor under the severe noise conditions. The subjects achieved better scores under auditory and visual presentation combined than under auditory presentation alone.

Comment: Although this study deals with normally hearing persons, it is presented here to illustrate the importance of the visual component in oral communication. The findings demonstrate rather conclusively that "listening and looking" are superior to listening alone. "Listening and looking" is a term sometimes applied to modern techniques of aural rehabilitation where speechreading and auditory training are used to supplement one another rather than substitute for one another.

O'Neill, J. J., and Stephens, Mary C. Relationships among Three Filmed Lipreading Tests. *Journal of Speech and Hearing Research*, 1959, 2, 61-65.

Purpose: To investigate (a) relationships among sets of scores obtained on three silent motion picture film tests designed to evaluate speechreading ability, and (b) relationships between teacher ratings of speechreading ability and scores achieved on each of the three tests.

Subjects: 26 hard of hearing adults enrolled in regularly scheduled speechreading classes at the Columbus (Ohio) Hearing Society. The age range of the subjects was from 20 to 60 years, with a mean age of 45.4 years. The length of enrollment in speech reading classes ranged from 12 weeks to 25 years.

Procedure: The three films used to assess speechreading ability were: the Mason Film 30; the Utley Lip-Reading Test Film, Form A, Part I

167

and Part III; and the Morkovin Life Situation Film Number 101. These were administered to the 26 subjects. In order to compensate for possible practice effects or fatigue, the films were shown in six counterbalanced orders. The experimental session required approximately 1.5 hours. The subjects also were rated by speechreading instructors in two ways: (a) by rating on a five-point scale of speechreading ability, and (b) by a rank-order listing of the subjects in terms of their speechreading ability. Correlations were obtained among the scores on the speechreading tests and between the two types of ratings and scores on the tests.

Results: The correlation coefficients of the Utley and the Morkovin tests with the Mason test ranged from 0.49 to 0.56 and were significant at or beyond the five percent level. The coefficients between the Utley and Morkovin tests were 0.26 and 0.27 and were not statistically significant. The coefficients obtained by correlating performance on the tests with ratings on a five-point scale were statistically significant for all four comparisons and ranged from 0.49 to 0.60. On the other hand, teacher rankings of the subjects with regard to speechreading proficiency correlated significantly with test scores in only five out of the 12 comparisons.

Comment: The study illustrates the problems of measuring speechreading performance, particularly the problem of determining the validity of measuring instruments.

Stone, L. *Facial Cues of Context in Lip Reading.* Los Angeles: John Tracy Clinic Research Papers V, 1957.

Purpose: To test three hypotheses: (a) success in lipreading is positively related to the amount of face exposed; (b) a speaker with a pleasant expression is more easily understood than a speaker with an unpleasant expression; and (c) a speaker with mobile lips is more easily understood that one with less than normal mobility.

Subjects: 256 college undergraduates of both sexes, none of whom reported a hearing disorder, visual defect, or previous experience in lipreading. There were more female than male subjects. However, random assignment of 16 subjects to each of 16 groups produced approximately equal proportions of male and female subjects in each group.

Procedure: Sound films were made of a single speaker uttering 20 short sentences taken from the *Film Test of Lip Reading.* The amount of face exposed, or the pleasantness of expression, or mobility of lips was varied while all other factors were held constant. There were 16 combinations of the various factors which provided 16 experimental conditions. Each ot the 16 groups of subjects was tested separately under one of the experimental conditions. The score for each subject was the number of words, he had correctly read from the 20 sentences of the test.

Results: Lip mobility had the most pronounced and most consistent effect of all the variables considered on success in lipreading. Next to lip mobility in order of importance was facial expression, and least important among these three variables was facial exposure. The only hypothesis substantiated was that speakers with mobile lips are more easily understood than those with less than normal mobility.

Comment: By definition in the hypotheses, the conditions expressed by the variables are limited to the extremes of the variables, i.e., mobile or non-mobile lips, pleasant or unpleasant expression, while many teachers of the deaf tend to think that moderate or normal mobility, and an expression neither "smiling" nor "grim" provide optimal conditions for successful lipreading. Thus conclusions from this study are necessarily limited to the defined conditions. However, it is clear that more research is needed before specific suggestions can be applied to teaching methods for the hearing handicapped.

Taafe, G., and Wong, W. *Studies of Variables in Lip Reading Stimulus Materials.* Los Angeles: John Tracy Clinic Research Papers III, 1957.

Purpose: The underlying assumption of this study was that certain characteristics of the lipreading stimulus material tend to make lipreading difficult while other characteristics tend to make it easier. Consequently, the basic objective of the study was to isolate variables descriptive of lipreading stimulus material which are related to the ease or difficulty with which such material can be read.

Subjects: Subjects selected for the study were normally hearing college students of both sexes. The data reported from the first part of the study were derived from the testing of 408 subjects enrolled in several colleges. Results in a later section are based on data obtained from 52 male and 121 female subjects. None of the subjects had any auditory or visual impairment or any previous experience in lipreading.

Procedure: The *Film Test of Lip Reading* was administered at the college or university where the subjects were in attendance. In the first part of the study the original form of the test was used. This consisted of 60 unrelated sentences and it was given to 168 male and 240 female subjects. Lipreading difficulty values for each sentence were computed for the males and females separately. In general these values were lower for the males than for the females. However, a product-moment correlation coefficient of .97 indicated that the relative ranking of each sentence according to difficulty was similar in each sex group. Therefore the data were combined.

In the latter part of the study the revised test was used; this consists of two forms, each including 30 of the original 60 sentences arranged in order of difficulty. The subjects were instructed to write what they thought had been said in the films and their score was the number of words correct.

Results: The factor contributing most to success in lipreading was a high vowel-to-consonant ratio. The pronoun "you" was found to be more easily lipread, on the average, than other parts of speech.

Factors related to difficulty in lipreading were sentence length measured by the number of words, syllables, vowels, consonants per sentence; and word length measured by the number of letters per word.

Factors having no relationship to success or difficulty of lipreading in this study were visibility indices, sentence order, and the number of pronouns per sentence. Inconclusive results were obtained in analysis of word position and difficulty and in a comparison of lipreading difficulty of questions and declarative sentences.

Comment: The experimenters point out that the results of this study must, of course, be restricted to the stimulus material used. However, there are other variables, semantic and syntactic, and many interrelationships which need to be studied with regard to their effect on success in lipreading. These filmed lipreading tests, together with the tests studied by O'Neill and Stephens, are the major ones which have been used in evaluating speechreading performance. None of them has proved to be very satisfactory. There is a need for a good instrument in this area.

In Review

Aural rehabilitation includes the use of hearing aids, auditory training, speechreading, and speech training to improve communication ability. Only a few selected studies in these areas were reviewed. Two studies on hearing aids (Davis, *et al.*; Shore, Bilger, and Hirsh) raised questions concerning the reliability and validity of present techniques used in the selection of hearing aids. Three studies of auditory training (Silverman, Hudgins, DiCarlo) demonstrated the value of auditory training in conjunction with the use of hearing aids. Research on speechreading with hard of hearing persons has produced few positive findings.

Research on a handicapped group often begins with studies to determine how the intelligence of that group compares on the average with non-handicapped persons. There have been few such studies with the hard of hearing.

> Madden, R. The School Status of the Hard-of-Hearing Child: An Analysis of the Intelligence, Achievement, and Certain Personality Traits of the Hard-of-Hearing School Child. *Teachers College, Columbia University Contributions to Education*, No. 499, 1931.

Purpose: To ascertain the school status of the hard of hearing child with respect to intelligence, educational achievement, and certain traits of personality. This abstract deals with the portion of the study devoted to the variable of intelligence. The chief question is: How does the hard of hearing child compare with the child of normal hearing with respect to intelligence?

Subjects: 46 hard of hearing children paired with 46 normally hearing children on race, sex, age, and parental occupational status. The children in both the experimental and control groups were selected from among the population of a public school in the city of New York.

Procedure: The entire population of a New York City school from the third to the sixth grades, inclusive, was tested by means of the 4-A audiometer. Standard testing procedures were used. From the total group of 892 students, 123 were selected who showed a loss of nine sensation units or more in the better ear. These 123 students were further examined by the 3-A audiometer one week after the 4-A test. Sixty-two of these students showed a loss of 15 sensation units or more in the better ear. These 62 were tested individually with the 2-A audiometer and 46 were selected as the experimental group of hard of hearing children. All 46 had a hearing loss of 15 sensation units or more in each ear. The experimental group of hard of hearing children and the matched control group of normally hearing children were given the Stanford-Binet Intelligence Scale. Comparisons of the two groups were made on the scores for the total test and on the scores of the various subtests.

Results: The mean IQ for the hard of hearing group was 77.04 and the mean IQ for the group with normal hearing was 83.46. The difference of 6.42 points in favor of the normal group is significant, being 4.93 times its P.E. Madden points out that this difference should be interpreted in view of the correlation found between intelligence and auditory loss. This correlation, although significant, was low, –1.23. This low relationship coupled with a great overlapping of the IQ scores of the two groups leads Madden to conclude that the intelligence of the hard of hearing child is of the same quality as that of the normal child. He states that the two differ only to a degree, which is significant when studying the hard of hearing as a group, but insignificant when studying the individual. As analysis of the individual test items, including the average vocabulary score, revealed no verbal handicap for the hard of hearing child.

Comment: Although the study is difficult to evaluate because of lack of some data in the publication, it should be noted that the IQs obtained for both groups (77.04 and 83.46) appear not to be typical of the general population. This casts doubt on the findings and does not permit any definite conclusions to be made.

Pintner, R., and Lev, J. The Intelligence of the Hard-of-Hearing School Child. *Journal of Genetic Psychology,* 1939, 55, 31-48.

Purpose: To compare the intelligence of normally hearing and hard of hearing children on two types of tests—verbal and nonverbal.

Subjects: A total of 1404 hard of hearing and 1556 normally hearing children in grades five to eight in the public schools of New York City.

Procedure: The hard of hearing children had been diagnosed as such on the basis of individual 2-A audiometer tests and otological examination. They were administered a verbal intelligence test (the Pintner Intelligence Test). A total of 315 hard of hearing and 372 normally hearing children were tested by means of a nonverbal test (the Pintner Non-Language Mental Test). The intelligence tests were administered by standard procedures.

Results: The mean verbal IQ for the normally hearing was 100.6; for the hard of hearing group 94.7. The difference is statistically significant. The mean nonverbal IQ for the normally hearing group was 102.2; for the hard of hearing group 99.3. The difference is not statistically significant. The author concluded that the results seem to indicate a slight handicap so far as the acquisition of language is concerned on the part of the hard of hearing school child.

Comment: Although average hearing loss for the hard of hearing group is not reported in the article, some of the data indicate that it might have been less than 15 db for the speech range. It appears somewhat surprising that this slight a hearing loss would have an effect on language acquisition. Nevertheless, the findings on the verbal intelligence test are in agreement with Madden's findings reviewed above, although Madden discounted the differences he found because of the great overlap between his two groups of subjects.

In Review

Very few studies have investigated the intelligence of hard of hearing children. The two reviewed indicate that hard of hearing children tend to score somewhat lower on intelligence tests than children with normal hearing. The Pintner and Lev study found this to be true on a verbal test but not true on a nonverbal test. Since the children in this study apparently had only a slight average hearing loss, the findings are somewhat surprising and should be treated with caution. The IQs obtained in the Madden study for the normally hearing group (83.46) and for the hard of hearing group (77.04) appear not to be typical of the general population.

EDUCATIONAL ACHIEVEMENT

It is reasonable to hypothesize that hearing loss would have an influence on educational achievement and to expect that this relationship would have been thoroughly investigated. There are, however, few research studies on educational achievement of the hard of hearing in the professional literature.

> Madden, R. The School Status of the Hard-of-Hearing Child: An Analysis of the Intelligence, Achievement, and Certain Personality Traits of the Hard-of-Hearing School Child. *Teachers College, Columbia University Contributions to Education,* No. 499, 1931.

Purpose: The purpose of this portion of the study was to compare the educational achievement of 46 hard of hearing children with that of a matched group of children with normal hearing.

Subjects: 46 hard of hearing children matched on age, race, sex, and parental occupational status with 46 normally hearing children.

Procedure: All children in the two matched groups were given the subtests in reading, spelling, and arithmetic of the Stanford Achievement Test.

173

Results: No differences were found between the two groups in any of the five subtests.

Comment: As pointed out in the review of this study in the section on intelligence, the mean IQs reported for the two matched groups were lower than the mean IQ for the general population. Thus, the absence of significant differences in educational achievement cannot be generalized to the total population of hard of hearing children.

Henry, S. Children's Audiograms in Relation to Reading Attainments. III. Discussion, Summary, and Conclusions. *Journal of Genetic Psychology,* 1947, 76, 49-63.

Purpose: To investigate the relation of reading attainment to auditory acuity.

Subjects and Procedure: Left- and right-ear audiograms were secured by a single person for 295 children on a Maico D-5 audiometer, and 262 of these were retested. The Progressive Achievement Test and the Gates Primary Reading Test were used to determine level of reading. The Progressive Achievement Test was given to grades two through six, and the Gates Primary Reading Test to the first grade. A total of 287 children, 143 males and 144 females, were given the reading tests. Durrell's Analysis of Reading Difficulty was then given to those children whose reading quotients were lower than 100. There were 98 such children.

Results: Reading attainment was studied in connection with low-, middle-, and high-tone loss. The mean difference in low-tone loss was negligible for the best and poorest readers. The mean differences in middle-tone loss, in favor of the best readers, was statistically significant, as was also the mean difference in high-tone loss. The results indicate that the poorest readers tended to have hearing losses for the middle and high frequencies.

Comment: This study appears to agree with the findings of others that difficulty in language acquisition is related to hearing loss. It should be noted, however, that data on the degree of loss, type of loss, and age at onset of loss, rarely are given in any of these studies. This makes it difficult to evaluate the applicability of the findings.

Young, C., and McConnell, F. Retardation of Vocabulary Development in Hard-of-Hearing Children. *Exceptional Children,* 1957, 23, 368-370.

Purpose: The purpose of the study was to determine if the vocabulary level of a group of hard of hearing children enrolled in regular classes differed significantly from that of normally hearing children.

Subjects: 20 hard of hearing children were matched with 20 normally hearing children on race, age, sex, socio-economic level, and nonverbal intelligence level as measured by the Raven's Progressive Matrices. The hard of hearing group had a mean hearing loss of 51 db averaged at 500-2000 cps. Individual levels ranged from 32 db to 75 db. Age at onset varied, but all the children had had sufficient hearing to learn speech in the normal manner during their preschool years.

Procedure: The Ammons Full-Range Picture Vocabulary Test was administered to each child. The words were presented both verbally and visually to both groups.

Results: There was a statistically significant difference between the two groups on the vocabulary test in favor of the normally hearing children. The difference was not only a group difference, for no hard of hearing child received a higher score on the vocabulary test than did his matched control subject. Furthermore, every hard of hearing child in the study was retarded verbally in comparison to his intellectual potential.

Comment: The study appears to be better controlled than the earlier studies on the hard of hearing. Because of the nature of the test used, the results could refer only to auditory and visual perception of words.

In Review

Madden's study of educational achievement found no difference between normal and hard of hearing children on five subtests of the Stanford Achievement Test. It was noted in the section on intelligence that the IQs for these groups were not typical of the general population. A study by Henry indicated that poor readers tend to have more hearing loss than good readers. Young and McConnell found that hard of hearing students made significantly lower scores on a picture test of vocabulary than a matched group of normally hearing students.

PERSONAL AND SOCIAL ADJUSTMENT

There appears to be a greater number of research studies in personal and social adjustment than in any other area with the exception of the areas relating to audiology. The findings of these studies, however, appear to be inconclusive.

175

Madden, R. The School Status of the Hard-of-Hearing Child: An Analysis of the Intelligence, Achievement, and Certain Personality Traits of the Hard-of-Hearing School Child. *Teachers College, Columbia University Contributions to Education*, No. 499, 1931.

Purpose: This abstract deals with the portion of the study devoted to how teachers rate hard of hearing children on certain personality traits.

Subjects and Procedure: 46 hard of hearing children in a New York City school matched with 46 normally hearing children on sex, age, and race. The teachers of these children were asked to rate each of them on a rating scale devised for the study. The five traits rated were attentiveness, obedience, leadership, attitudes toward their social treatment, aggressiveness. Each trait was rated on a five-point scale.

Results: The hard of hearing children never were rated as leaders and were rated as being more shy and withdrawn than the normally hearing children. No differences were found on the other traits.

Comment: Adequate description of the hard of hearing sample is not supplied. It will be recalled from the section on intelligence that the mean IQs of the two groups appeared to be lower than the mean for the general population and therefore the findings cannot be applied to the general population of hard of hearing children.

Habbe, S. Personality Adjustments of Adolescent Boys with Impaired Hearing. *Teachers College, Columbia University Contributions to Education*, No. 697, 1936.

Purpose: To determine how the personality of hard of hearing adolescent boys compares with the personality of normally hearing adolescent boys.

Subjects: 48 hard of hearing boys, age 12 to 16 years, were matched with 48 normally hearing boys on age, school, grade, intelligence (as measured by the Terman Group Test of Mental Ability), nationality, and socio-economic background (as measured by the Sims Scale of Socio-Economic Status). All the hard of hearing students had a minimum binaural hearing loss of 15 db as measured by the 2-A audiometer. The mean hearing loss was 27 and 29 db for the right and left ears, respectively.

Procedure: All of the subjects were given the Pintner Personality Outlines and the Symonds Adjustment Questionnaire. They also were rated by teachers on the Haggerty-Olson-Wickman Behavior Rating Schedules.

Using an outline prepared by the author, each subject wrote an autobiography. Items in these autobiographies were rated for adjustment-maladjustment by three psychologists. Finally, the 10 best and 10 poorest in the hard of hearing group, as determined by the personality tests, were interviewed.

Results: The two groups made almost equal scores on the two paper and pencil personality tests and on the teachers' ratings. Although five of the six scores derived from these measures favored the normally hearing group, none of the differences was statistically significant. There was a tendency for the hard of hearing boys to be slightly more submissive and introverted than the normally hearing boys.

Comment: Although this is a quite thorough study, it should be noted that the mean hearing loss in the better ear was only 27 db. Hearing loss is not generally considered to be socially handicapping until it exceeds 30 db. Thus, the average loss of the subjects in this study was only borderline. More severe loss of hearing might increase the obtained differences.

Pintner, R. Some Personality Traits of Hard-of-Hearing Children. *Journal of Genetic Psychology,* 1942, 60, 143-151.

Purpose: To compare the personality traits of hard of hearing and normally hearing children.

Subjects: 1171 hard of hearing and 1208 normally hearing children in grades five to eight inclusive of the New York City public schools.

Procedure: The hard of hearing children were selected on the basis of audiometric and otological examination. The Aspects of Personality Test was administered to all the children in the two groups. This test depends on oral and printed directions. It measures three phases of personality: ascendance-submission, extroversion-introversion, and emotionality.

Results: The results indicate that there is fundamentally no difference between normally hearing and hard of hearing children in such traits as ascendance-submission and extroversion-introversion so far as these traits can be measured by a group test of the inventory type. With regard to emotional stability, there appeared to be a tendency for the more extreme cases of hearing loss to score lower on this test. Such cases may on the average be slightly less emotionally stable than normally hearing children or than children whose loss of hearing does not exceed 30 db.

Comment: Complete data on hearing loss are not given in the report, and therefore it is not possible to draw any definite conclusions from the study.

Reynolds, L. G. The School Adjustment of Children with Minimal Hearing Loss. *Journal of Speech and Hearing Disorders,* 1955, 20, 380-384.

Purpose: To determine the effects upon school adjustment of a slight hearing loss.

Subjects: 36 hard of hearing children in the San Francisco City Schools matched with 36 normally hearing children on age, sex, attendance in the same school at the same grade level, nonlanguage mental age, race, and parental occupational status. For the hard of hearing group the average hearing loss in the better ear over the three speech frequencies was 21.26 db. The average period of time these children had a hearing impairment was 4.29 years. The hard of hearing group included only children who were enrolled in lipreading classes and did not use hearing aids.

Procedure: The criteria used to measure school adjustment were: (a) educational achievement as measured by the California Achievement Tests; (b) absences from school, with excused absences for medical reasons excluded; (c) personal and social adjustment as measured by the California Test of Personality; and (d) pupil ratings by teachers on behavior and personality traits along a five-point scale devised by the author.

Results: No statistically significant differences were found between the normally hearing and the hard of hearing groups on the variables measured. The author concludes that the failure to demonstrate statistical significance between the scores made by the two groups on the measures of school adjustment seems to indicate that the children with minimal hearing loss adjust to their school environment as favorably as their normally hearing partners.

Comment: Findings agree with Madden, Habbe, and Pintner that a slight hearing loss has no apparent effect on personality. This might be expected since hearing loss apparently does not become socially handicapping until it exceeds 30 db.

Kahn, H. Responses of Hard-of-Hearing and Normal-Hearing Children to Frustration. *Exceptional Children,* 1957, 24, 155-159.

Purpose: To investigate the relationship between hearing loss and response to frustration.

Subjects: Three groups, each consisting of 15 children, matched in terms of sex, age, grade in school, socio-economic status, and intelligence.

The three groups were designated as (a) the *normally hearing,* consisting of children whose audiograms indicated hearing loss no greater than one percent according to the American Medical Association system of evaluation, (b) the *moderately hypacusic,* consisting of children whose hearing losses were in the range from 3 to 25 percent, and (c) the *severely hypacusic,* consisting of children whose hearing losses were greater than 25 percent. The children were selected from a public school system and from a large public school for deaf children.

Procedure: The Children's Form of the Rosenzweig Picture Frustration Study was administered to each child individually. An additional technique was devised for the observation of response to frustration and was administered to each of the subjects between three and seven days after administration of the Rosenzweig. This device, designated the Block Design Frustration Technique, required the subject to reproduce with blocks a series of 35 dichromatic designs which were presented on 2-inch square cards. Ten of the designs could not be produced with the 24 blocks supplied to the subject. The test was continued until the subject had been frustrated in his attempts to produce these 10 designs.

The statistical techniques employed were concerned with (a) the relationship between degree of hearing loss and scores on the frustration response variables, (b) comparisons between the groups, and (c) comparisons of the three groups with the norms of the Children's Form of the Rosenzweig P-F Study.

Results: Few differences were found between the groups in terms of response to frustration. Differences which did appear tended to indicate a consistent tendency for the hard of hearing children to meet frustration more constructively than the nonhandicapped children.

Comment: It will be noted that this study attempted to subclassify hard of hearing subjects rather than consider them as a single, homogeneous group. The absence of differences in adjustment between the group with normal hearing and those with hearing losses is in agreement with the other studies in this section.

Elser, R. P. The Social Position of Hearing Handicapped Children in the Regular Grades. *Exceptional Children,* 1959, 25, 305-309.

Purpose: To determine to what extent hearing handicapped children were accepted, isolated, or rejected by their normally hearing classmates.

Subjects: 45 white children in rural Tennessee schools formed the experimental group of hard of hearing children. The sample was restricted to those children who had a hearing loss in excess of 35 db, best binaural average of the frequencies 500, 1000, and 2000 cps, who were between the ages of nine and 12, and had been members of their present class for at least seven and one-half months. The 45 children selected were in 45 classes in the third through seventh grade, and had mean hearing losses of 49.1 db. The control group consisted of the normally hearing classmates of the hard of hearing children.

Procedure: The hard of hearing children and their normally hearing classmates (a total of 1258 children) were given the Moreno sociometric questionnaire and a modified form of the Tryon "Reputation Test" or "Guess Who Test." The instruments used were designed to elicit the following information: (a) the friendship patterns of children, their intimate associates; (b) the reputation or social status a child enjoys among his peers; and (c) the child's awareness of his own status in a given group of which he is a member.

The Wilcoxon signed-ranks test was used for the statistical analysis.

Results: A comparison of the mean scores of the two groups on all questions having to do with status, friendship, and reputation showed that the hearing handicapped group was not as accepted as the average of their classmates. Most of the differences in favor of the control group were statistically significant. The author concludes that although the data reveal that the hearing handicapped as a group are not as well accepted as the average for their normally hearing classmates, there was considerable overlap between the groups. Some of the normally hearing children were more rejected by their classmates than some of the hard of hearing children.

Comment: The findings of this study with the hard of hearing are similar to the findings of others with mentally retarded and crippled children. Such research does not generally go far enough in finding out why a hearing loss affects adjustment and popularity.

In Review

All of the studies reviewed in this section used the same basic approach of comparing matched groups of normally hearing and hard of hearing subjects on various measures of personal and social adjustment. The findings were mostly negative, but there was a slight tendency for the hard of hearing subjects to be more submissive, introverted and emotionally unstable. One study which did result in statistically significant findings (Elser) indicated that hard of hearing children in regular classrooms were not as accepted in terms of status, friendship, and reputation as their normally hearing classmates.

SUMMARY

Educational research on the hard of hearing appears to be inadequate both in quantity and quality. The research which has been conducted often has produced conflicting and inconclusive results. This probably is partly due to the inadequacy of design and controls common to much behavioral research on handicapped groups. With the hard of hearing, however, there is the added important complication of inadequate definition of the group under study. Behavioral research in this area does not yet appear to have made adequate use of the findings of audiological research concerning the variables which are important in hearing loss. The audiological research suggests that behavioral studies might be more productive if the hard of hearing were subclassified into several categories rather than being considered as a single, homogeneous group. With this as a starting point, the following broad areas probably include many of the research needs with this group.

Adequate behavioral definitions of hearing impairment should be sought, utilizing the techniques of audiology, psychology, sociology, and education. Such research might result in the delineation of various categories of hearing impairment within the group now labeled as hard of hearing. Some of the variables to be considered here are degree of hearing loss, age at onset of hearing loss, and type of hearing loss.

Adequate definitions of hearing impairment should aid in the design of surveys to discover the extent of hearing loss in the population. There is great variability in the incidence of hearing impairment reported in surveys now in the literature. This variability appears to be due to differences in definition of hearing impairment; differences in techniques, apparatus, and conditions of testing; and differences in sampling procedures.

With adequate definition and classification of the hearing impaired and accurate information on the incidence of hearing impairment, it would be possible to study systematically the psycho-educational characteristics of the various groups of hard of hearing individuals. We need to know how the persons in various categories of hearing impairment compare with normally hearing persons in intelligence, educational achievement, and psychosocial adjustment.

There has been little research on the various types of educational environments and methods used with hard of hearing children. Yet it is likely that these would vary with the degree and type of hearing impairment and the psycho-educational characteristics of the individuals in question. Children with mild, conductive losses of recent origin might respond adequately to the use of a hearing aid without any other special provisions. Children with severe, sensory-neural losses of long standing might require highly specialized environments and techniques. Decisions on educational placement for hard of hearing children presently appear to be made almost completely on the basis of experienced judgment rather than on the basis of research findings.

There does not appear to be accurate information on the vocational adjustment, problems, and needs of the hard of hearing. There is a definite need for such information to aid in providing for the vocational rehabilitation of persons with hearing loss.

6

The Deaf

Kenneth R. Mangan

A deaf child is one who was born with little or no hearing, or who suffered the loss early in infancy before speech and language patterns were
acquired.

To provide a frame of reference, the material to be presented is organized under the following topics:

1. Intelligence.
2. Adjustment.
3. Education. -

INTELLIGENCE

Early research efforts were concerned with determining whether or not
certain tests were applicable to the deaf, comparing groups of deaf and
hearing subjects, and comparing groups of congenitally and adventitiously deaf children. Later investigations have shifted from the measurement of intelligence in a global manner to studies of more specific

Reviewed by Alice Streng, University of Wisconsin in Milwaukee.

aspects of intellectual functioning and the effect of deafness on mental development.

General studies of intelligence

Springer, N. N. A Comparative Study of the Intelligence of a Group of Deaf and Hearing Children. *American Annals of the Deaf*, 1938, 83, 138-152.

Purpose: To answer the question: Do deaf and hard of hearing children differ in mental ability when the language factor is eliminated and intelligence is measured by means of a non-language test?

Subjects: 330 deaf and 330 hearing children were tested in 1935. The deaf children attended public day and residential schools in New York City. The hearing children were from New York City public schools. On the whole, the deaf and hearing groups were similar in chronological age (six to 12), sex, nationality, and general social status.

Procedure: The Goodenough test was used since it requires no verbal responses. Teachers' ratings on seven intellectual traits were obtained by use of Division I, Intellectual Traits, of Haggerty-Olson-Wickman Behavior Rating Schedules.

Results: Analysis of results by age and sex revealed that, on the Goodenough test scale, at no age level did the deaf and hearing children differ significantly. There was a tendency for the hearing children, especially the hearing girls, to receive slightly better scores than the deaf. When all ages were combined, the mean IQ for hearing girls was significantly superior to that of the deaf girls. When the sexes were combined, the hearing children's mean IQ was significantly superior to that of the deaf children. The mean IQ of 96.24 indicated that the deaf children were of average intelligence. A tendency was indicated for children who became deaf at a later age to obtain better intelligence scores. Low negative correlations were found between the intelligence test scores and the teachers' ratings on the Haggerty-Olson-Wickman Behavior Rating Schedules, Intellectual Traits. Item analyses indicated that deaf and hearing children appeared equally successful.

Comment: This study is interesting educationally because the results indicated little difference in intellectual capacity or potential between deaf and hearing children when the handicaps of speech and language were minimized.

184

Burchard, E. M. L. and Myklebust, H. R. A Comparison of Congenital and Adventitious Deafness with Respect to its Effect on Intelligence, Personality, and Social Maturity—Part I: Intelligence. *American Annals of the Deaf*, 1942, 87, 140-154.

Purpose: To determine whether or not there are significant measurable differences in intelligence, social maturity, and personality between children who are congenitally deaf and those who have acquired deafness. This part of the report concerns *intelligence*.

Subjects: These were selected very carefully on the basis that congenital deafness means deafness which existed at birth, and adventitious deafness means that acquired after the child learned to talk. One hundred and eighty-nine pupils, seven to 19 years of age, were selected from the population at the New Jersey School for the Deaf. One hundred of these were male, 89 female; 121 were congenitally deaf, 68 had acquired deafness. One hundred and twenty-nine had resided at the school for more than four years.

Procedure: The Grace Arthur Point Scale of Performance tests were given to all subjects. The Haggerty-Olson-Wickman Behavior Rating Schedule was used for all possible subjects. One rating was made by a teacher, one by a vocational leader, one by a housemother. Information for the Vineland Social Maturity Scale was obtained from housemothers for 104 cases.

Results: Both congenitally deaf and adventitiously deaf groups were found to be of average intelligence with no significant statistical difference between groups. Although deaf boys tended to rate slightly superior in intelligence to deaf girls, the difference was not statistically significant.

Comment: Intelligence is not necessarily related to etiology of hearing loss, particularly when intelligence is considered a total entity. Since all of the subjects were enrolled in the same school, a selective factor may have been operating.

Kirk, S. A. and Perry, June. A Comparative Study of the Ontario and Nebraska Tests for the Deaf. *American Annals of the Deaf*, 1948, 93, 315-323.

Purpose: To determine the relative ratings when the Ontario School Ability Examination and the Nebraska Test of Learning Aptitude are

185

both administered to the same individual. Also, to compare these tests with the Stanford-Binet examination.

Subjects: 49 deaf and hard of hearing children were selected from the Paul Binner Day School for the Deaf in Milwaukee. Forty-nine hearing children were selected from the Milwaukee public schools. The children were from five to 11 years old, with from six to eight subjects at each age level.

Procedure: Within a period of not less than three days and not more than one week, the deaf and hard of hearing children were given the Ontario and Nebraska tests. One-half of the children had the Nebraska test first; the other half had the Ontario test first. The hearing children had been given the Terman-Merrill 1937 revision of the Stanford-Binet Scale. As with the deaf children, half were given the Ontario examination first; half, the Nebraska test first.

Results: The Ontario School Ability Examination yielded consistently higher scores than the Nebraska test with both deaf and hearing children. The difference between IQ and LQ was significant. When administered to hearing children, the results obtained from the Ontario examination were closer to the results from the Stanford-Binet Scale than were those from the Nebraska test. The Ontario examination was easier to use and seems superior to the Nebraska test if the Stanford-Binet Scale has any relation to learning ability. More work must be done in order to establish a real measure of validity of either the Ontario or Nebraska tests.

Comment: This study is helpful in interpreting differences in scores on the two tests. The similarity of the Ontario examination results to the Stanford-Binet results may indicate that the Ontario is a better predictor of language learning ability. Further study is needed on this point.

MacPherson, Jane G. and Lane, Helen S. A Comparison of Deaf and Hearing on the Hiskey Test and on Performance Scales. *American Annals of the Deaf,* 1948, 93, 178-184.

Purpose: To obtain information concerning the reliability and validity of Hiskey's Non-Verbal Test of Learning Aptitude; to compare deaf and hearing children on this scale; to analyze test items of increasing difficulty as related to increased chronological age and the comparative order of difficulty of test items for hearing and deaf subjects.

Subjects: 61 deaf children and 66 speech defective children with normal hearing and understanding. The age range was three to 13.

Procedure: The children were given Hiskey's Test of Learning Aptitude. Both groups were also given either the Advanced Performance Scale used at Central Institute for the Deaf or the Randall's Island series for younger children.

Results: There is some indication that the Hiskey test measures the same type of intelligence as the Performance Scale. LQs and IQs of deaf and hearing can be compared. First tests and retests compare favorably. Deaf and hearing children seem not to differ greatly in performance. Evidence involving increasing difficulty and its relation to increased CA and comparative order of difficulty is inconclusive.

Comment: This study indicates that the Hiskey test is a valid performance test of intelligence.

Hiskey, M. S. A Study of the Intelligence of Deaf and Hearing Children. *American Annals of the Deaf*, 1956, 101, 329-339.

Purpose: To compare the intelligence of deaf and hearing children by studying performances on the separate standardizations of the Nebraska Test of Learning Aptitude.

Subjects: The 466 deaf children and 380 selected hearing children on whom the Nebraska Test of Learning Aptitude was standardized.

Procedure: The individual test item responses of the deaf group were compared with those of the hearing group.

Results: The deaf, on the average, rated slightly lower than the hearing. The most common difference was one-half year (41.1 percent of the scores). The deaf rated as high as or higher than the hearing on 28.8 percent of the scores. The writer concludes that the hearing had an advantage on items in which vocalization aids immediate recall. The deaf excelled slightly on items demanding visual perception as the approach to analysis and performance.

Comment: The demonstration that deaf children are qualitatively deficient in some areas while excelling in others has implications for the instructional program. Further research is needed to indicate how superior abilities can be used most efficiently in learning and whether remedial instruction can strengthen other areas.

Studies of More Specific Abilities

Oléron, P. A Study of the Intelligence of the Deaf. *American Annals of the Deaf*, 1950, 95, 179-195.

Purpose: To determine whether the deaf show an inferiority in "abstract" intelligence.

Subjects: 246 subjects were selected from among the pupils of the Institution Nationale des Sourdes-Muets de Paris. They ranged in age from nine to 21.

Procedure: Raven's Progressive Matrices, 1938 Edition, was used. This test includes 60 items divided into five sets. The solution of the first problem of each set is self-evident and problems succeed each other in such a way that each is practice for the next. Directions can readily be given by pantomime. There is no time limit.

Results: There is confirmation of the idea that the deaf show inferiority in the sphere of abstract thought. Subjects who became deaf at age five or over were superior to the congenitally deaf or those who became deaf at a younger age. Residual hearing had no marked influence. Deafness seems to impair capacity to use abstract forms of intellectual activity.

Comment: Studies such as this are significant in appraising the effects of congenital deafness and in pointing the way for habilitative programs.

Myklebust, H. and Brutten, M. A Study of Visual Perception of Deaf Children. *Acta-Otolaryngolica Supplementum 105,* Stockholm, Sweden, 1953, 1-126.

Purpose: To investigate whether deaf children differ from hearing children in certain aspects of visual perception.

Subjects: The experimental group was made up of 55 deaf students in a combined school for the deaf. The CAs ranged from eight to 11 years. Intelligence and visual acuity were normal. The group averaged three years, seven months in school. The control group consisted of an equal number of children in an orphanage setting matched for sex, CA, and intelligence.

Procedure: The following tests were administered to both groups: the Marble Board Test, the Goodenough Draw-a-Man Test, a figure ground test, a pattern reproduction test, and a perseveration test. Comparisons were made between the deaf and hearing groups and between subgroups of the deaf labeled endogenous, exogenous, and undetermined.

Results: On the Goodenough test, the deaf group was not significantly inferior but it was less homogeneous. The difference in standard deviations was significant at the .01 level. The results of the tests of visual perception were all in favor of the hearing group except the test for reproduction of line patterns in which the difference was not significant.

The authors conclude that deafness may cause an alteration in the normal response modes of the organism, leading to a disruption in visual perception organization.

Comment: This study has generated other investigations on the perceptual abilities of deaf children and the possible effects of various types of therapy. A longitudinal study of the effects of therapy on visual perception might suggest ways of improving the instruction of deaf children.

Larr, A. L. Perceptual and Conceptual Abilities of Residential School Deaf Children. *Exceptional Children,* 1956, 23, 63-66.

Purpose: To duplicate in widely separated areas of the United States the methods and materials employed in the investigation performed by McKay* at the Rochester, New York School for the Deaf.

Subjects: 25 deaf students from the Missouri School for the Deaf at Fulton and 25 from the California School for the Deaf at Riverside were used. All experimental subjects were chosen from lower grades where oral methods are employed. They lived in dormitories located apart from the upper grades. Control groups were selected from schools at Springfield, Missouri. One group, 17 boys and eight girls, was composed of regular school children with IQs above 80; the other was comprised of children in classes for mentally retarded whose IQs were below 80.

Procedure: Perceptual ability was assessed by use of a number of tests: the Marble Board Tests I and II, the picture test, the tactual motor test I and II. Conceptual ability was measured by use of a color form sorting test, an object sorting test, and a picture object test.

Results: The deaf were equal to or superior to the hearing control groups in the area of visual perception. The deaf were deficient in the performance of conceptual tasks.

Comment: This study agrees with the work by McKay and disagrees with Myklebust's study on visual perception. All of the studies agree in the area of conceptualization. Further studies should be directed toward finding the reasons for the lack of agreement and assessing the results of various types of education on perceptual and conceptual functioning.

* Elizabeth B. McKay, An Exploratory Study of the Psychological Effects of a Severe Hearing Impairment. Unpublished doctoral dissertation. Syracuse University. 1952.

189

Hughes, R. B. A Comparison of Verbal Conceptualization in Deaf and Hearing Children. Unpublished doctoral dissertation, University of Illinois, 1959.

Purpose: To compare the verbal percept-concept sorting performance of three groups of deaf children with a group of children with normal hearing.

Subjects: 56 pupils in the oral, acoustic and manual departments of the Illinois School for the Deaf (CA 10-5 to 14-1 and MA 9-6 to 15-6), and 33 hearing children with CAs and MAs in the same range, residing in an Illinois children's institution.

Procedure: The pupils were tested on the meanings of 241 percept words, and were then asked to sort the words they knew into appropriate categories.

Results: The deaf knew the meanings of 163 of the 241 percept words but were able to sort only 46 of them correctly. The hearing recognized 230 of the 241 words and were significantly superior in their ability to sort them correctly. The verbal behavior of the deaf was more perceptual than conceptual.

Comment: The methods by which deaf children are taught may emphasize perception and knowledge of single meanings so that concept formation is inhibited. Concept refinement is lacking in the education of these pupils.

Doehring, D. G. and Rosenstein, J. Visual Word Recognition by Deaf and Hearing Children. *Journal of Speech and Hearing Research*, 1960, 3, 320-326.

Purpose: To specify the effect of retardation in the development of spoken language on the ability of deaf children to recognize visually presented verbal stimuli.

Subjects: 40 orally-trained deaf children and 40 hearing children. Half of the children in each group ranged in age from nine to 11 and the other half ranged from 12 to 16 years of age. Both the deaf and hearing groups were selected to be representative of the distribution of intelligence scores in their respective schools.

Procedure: Each child was tested individually by presenting the stimulus material (10 single letters, 20 trigrams—10 pronounceable, 10 unpronounceable, and 30 four-letter words—10 each of high, middle and low frequency) for .01 second in a darkened viewing box using a slide projector.

The Ammons Full-Range Picture Vocabulary Test (FRPV) was also administered to each subject.

Results: The range of total correct responses on the FRPV was 13 to 31 for the young deaf group, 35 to 57 for the young hearing children, 24 to 52 for the older deaf group, and 56 to 81 for the older hearing group.

The young deaf group was significantly less accurate than the hearing group in all three tests of visual recognition. The differences in accuracy of recognition between the older groups were not statistically significant. It was concluded that the accuracy of visual recognition of verbal material by the older deaf children was dependent upon an estimate of the probability of occurrence rather than upon the frequency of previous visual and auditory stimulation.

Blair, F. X. A Study of the Visual Memory of Deaf and Hearing Children. *American Annals of the Deaf,* 1957, 102, 254-263.

Purpose: To investigate the visual memory of deaf children as compared with the visual memory of hearing children.

Subjects: 53 deaf children ranging in age from 7-6 to 12-6 were matched with an equal number of hearing children in terms of intelligence, age, and sex.

Procedure: All of the subjects were tested individually on the following battery of visual memory tests: The Knox Cube Test, memory for designs, an object location test, and four memory span tests. Comparisons were made between the performance of the deaf and hearing and between three groups of the deaf, classified etiologically as endogenous, exogenous, and undetermined. A test of reading achievement was administered and the results correlated with the memory test results.

Results: The results of this study indicate that the visual memory of the deaf and the hearing differs depending upon the type of memory task involved. The deaf are inferior to the hearing in memory span tests. The differences on the other three tests (Knox Cube, memory for design, object location) were in favor of the deaf or nonsignificant. The author suggests that the tests involving sequence are relatively abstract tasks on which the deaf may be deficient, while the other tests involve only visual perception on which the deaf may be superior.

The differences between the three groups of the deaf were not significant.

All of the memory tests correlated to some degree with reading

191

achievement, but the four memory span tests correlated more significantly with reading achievement than did the others.

Comment: The relationship between language learning and memory merits further study with deaf children. The impact of specific learning experiences on memory is particularly important.

Templin, Mildred C. The Development of Reasoning in Children with Normal and Defective Hearing. *Institute of Child Welfare Monograph Series,* No. 24, Minneapolis; University of Minnesota Press, 1950.

Purpose: To determine the effects upon reasoning ability of a restricted environment due to reduced hearing and enrollment in a residential school.

Subjects: 177 children with defective hearing enrolled in a residential school, 108 children with defective hearing attending day schools, 293 children with normal hearing enrolled in a residential school, and 272 children with normal hearing attending day schools. All of the children were in grades five to 12. Sub-samples of these groups were paired on the bases of age, sex, intelligence, and grade placement. In addition, a group of 27 residential subjects were paired with 27 day school subjects on the basis of degree of hearing loss as well as on the other factors.

Procedure: All of the groups were given three tests of reasoning ability: the Deutsche Questions, the Long and Welch Test of Causal Reasoning, and the Brody Non-Verbal Abstract Reasoning Test.

Results: In the group studied, defective hearing appeared to have an effect on reasoning ability. Both residential and day school children with defective hearing showed lower reasoning ability at each age level on all tests except the classification subtest of the Brody Test.

The hypothesis that the extrinsic factor of institutional residence will affect reasoning scores was largely rejected by the test results. Degree of hearing loss, age at onset, and the length of time a child has been deaf appeared to be factors in reasoning ability. The relationship between reasoning and language was analyzed. Particular attention was directed to the fact that deaf children are deficient in reasoning by analogy even on the Brody Non-Verbal Reasoning Test.

Comment: This study is a significant contribution to the understanding of children with defective hearing since it analyzes some of the specific areas in which they have difficulty. Studies should be made of the relationship between instructional programs and reasoning ability to discover whether this ability can be developed.

Templin, M. C. A Qualitative Analysis of Explanations of Physical Causality. *American Annals of the Deaf*, 1954, 99, 252-269.

Purpose: To study the reasoning processes of deaf children by comparing their explanations of physical causality with explanations by hearing children.

Subjects: 293 children with defective hearing and 565 hearing children between the ages of 10 and 12.

Procedure: Explanations of the causes of 21 physical phenomena were written by both groups. These explanations were classified qualitatively according to methods developed by Deutsche and by Piaget. Comparisons were made between the two total groups and between three groups of 78 deaf, hard of hearing, and hearing, matched for age, sex, grade placement, and intelligence.

Results: Using the Piaget levels, the deaf were found to be five to eight years retarded in the kinds of explanation offered. The difference in the use of phenomenistic and logical deduction is significant at the .02 level. The hard of hearing respond more like the hearing than the deaf.

According to the Deutsche classifications, the deaf were retarded seven to eight years in levels of generalization used in the explanations. The deaf used the least generalized level more frequently than the hearing at the .001 level of significance.

Comment: Further studies of this nature may shed some light on which deaf children are most or least deficient in intellectual processes and whether prescribed instructional procedures, particularly in the early years, can raise their level of operation.

In Review

Many research studies on the intelligence of deaf children have been concerned with the kind of test needed: one which is standardized on hearing subjects or one which is standardized on the deaf. Other concerns relate to the testing of native and functioning ability and the relative emphasis placed on the abstract as opposed to the concrete. In recent years, Myklebust has been studying the selective effect of deafness on specific aspects of intellectual functioning.

There are indications that tests are needed which compare a deaf child with other deaf children as well as with the total population, and that a variety of measures must be used in order to predict what level of success a deaf pupil can achieve on abstract as well as concrete tasks. The study of the relationship between diagnostic and therapeutic programs for deaf children in which strengths are capitalized and weaknesses remedied as far as possible is the most challenging phase of the current research on the mental abilities of this group.

ADJUSTMENT

Attempts to obtain information on the personality and social adjustment of the deaf have included studies of general adjustment, emotional stability, fears and wishes, social maturity and group acceptance. Research efforts as well as the clinical management of deaf children have been hampered by the problem of communication and the lack of appropriate measuring instruments.

Personality

Brunschwig, Lily. A Study of Some Personality Aspects of Deaf Children. *Teachers College, Columbia University Contributions to Education, No. 687*, 1936.

Purpose: To attempt to answer the following questions: (a) What relationship may be found between the scores of deaf school children on a self-descriptive questionnaire and such variables as age, intelligence test results, amount of hearing, and age at hearing loss? (b) Are there any group differences, with respect to scores on a self-descriptive questionnaire, between samplings of deaf and hearing children? (c) How do the responses of deaf subjects to individual test items compare with those of hearing children?

Subjects: 159 deaf children, age nine to 18, chosen from three public residential schools, and 243 hearing children, age 10 to 16, drawn from grades six to 12 of public elementary schools. The hearing subjects, with an average IQ between 99 and 100, were representative of the school population.

Procedure: The Rogers Test of Personality Adjustment, with slightly modified vocabulary, was administered to deaf and hearing children during the spring term of 1933. All hearing children and about one-third of the deaf children were tested in groups, the others, individually. Hearing subjects were given supplementary explanations verbally, the deaf in writing. Sufficient time was allowed for each subject to complete the questionnaire.

The Personality Inventory for Deaf Children was designed. Form I of this test was administered to 114 deaf and 240 hearing children in their regular classrooms. Form II of the Personality Inventory for Deaf Children was given to 184 deaf pupils. Form III was administered to 183 deaf and 346 hearing children.

Results: Relationships between test results from personality inventories administered to deaf children and the variables of age, intelligence, amount of hearing, and age at becoming deaf were slight and in most cases unreliable. Differences between deaf and hearing groups on the Rogers Test of Personality Adjustment were, with but one exception, not statistically significant. The exception in favor of hearing children was in the measures of social adjustment. The tendencies of the deaf with respect to expressions of feelings of difference from other children and preferences in certain social situations deviated from the average of the hearing.

Comment: Practically applied, the Personality Inventory for Deaf Children which was developed in the course of this study may be of value in making surveys of pupil adjustment in intermediate and advanced grades of schools for the deaf and in supplementing information about pupils.

Springer, N. N. A Comparative Study of Psychoneurotic Responses of Deaf and Hearing Children. *Journal of Educational Psychology*, 1938, 29, 459-466.

Purpose: To determine whether there are group differences between deaf and hearing children in their manifestations of maladjusted behavior as measured by their psychoneurotic responses on a personality inventory.

Subjects: An experimental group of 397 deaf children, with a mean age of 16 years, attending three New York City public day and residential schools and a control group of 327 hearing children in grades four to nine (mean age 12) in the regular public schools.

Procedure: The Brown Personality Inventory for children was administered to both groups.

Results: All groups of deaf children received significantly higher neurotic scores than the hearing control children and the hearing norm group.

The relationship between intelligence and neurotic scores was not significant.

Comment: This study may be a measure of the lack of understanding of language by the deaf subjects rather than of their psychoneurotic tendencies. It is included here as an example of early research in the adjustment of the deaf.

Kirk, S. A. Behavior Problem Tendencies in Deaf and Hard-of Hearing Children. *American Annals of the Deaf,* 1938, 83, 131-137.

Purpose: To compare the behavior problem tendencies of deaf and hard of hearing children in an elementary day school for the deaf with norms for normally hearing children on the Haggerty-Olson-Wickman Behavior Rating Schedule.

Subjects: 112 deaf and hard of hearing children in the Paul Binner School for the Deaf in Milwaukee.

Procedure: The subjects were rated on the Haggerty-Olson-Wickman Behavior Rating Schedule, Schedule A and Schedule B, by trained teachers of the deaf.

Results: Deaf and hard of hearing groups showed greater behavior problem tendencies than did normally hearing children on this rating scale. Deaf and hard of hearing boys appear to be greater problems than deaf and hard of hearing girls, in the same way that normally hearing boys exceed girls on this scale. Results indicate that in emotional traits specifically, and for Schedule B generally, deaf and hard of hearing boys exceed normally hearing boys in problem tendencies. Results for girls are similar to those for boys. Combined scores of boys and girls show greater problem tendencies in the group with defective hearing.

Comment: Studies such as this furnish information regarding the problems of deaf children and are an indication of the applicability of this type of instrument to deaf children.

Burchard, E. M. L. and Myklebust, H. R. A Comparison of Congenital and Adventitious Deafness with Respect to its Effect on Intelligence, Personality and Social Maturity—Part III: Personality. *American Annals of the Deaf,* 1942, 87, 140-154.

Purpose: To determine whether there are significant measurable differences in intelligence, social maturity, and personality between children who are congenitally deaf and those who have acquired deafness. This part of the reporting concerns *personality*.

Subjects: These were selected very carefully on the basis that congenital deafness is deafness which existed at birth and adventitious deafness is that acquired after the child learned to talk. One hundred and eighty-nine pupils, age seven to 19 years, were selected from the population at the New Jersey School for the Deaf. One hundred of these were male, 89 female; 121 were congenitally deaf, 68 had acquired deafness; 129 had resided at the school for more than four years.

Procedure: The Grace Arthur Point Performance Scale was given to all subjects. The Haggerty-Olson-Wickman Behavior Rating Schedule was used for all possible subjects. One rating was made by a teacher, one by a vocational leader, one by a housemother. Information for the Vineland Social Maturity Scale was obtained from housemothers for 104 cases.

Results: It is indicated that the type of deafness is less important than the fact of deafness itself from the point of view of adjustment. Both the congenitally deaf and the adventitiously deaf were somewhat more unstable than the hearing. These data generally suggest that no significant difference exists between congenitally deaf and adventitiously deaf in intelligence, social maturity, or personality.

Comment: The handicap of deafness itself appears to be the cause of differences in the performance of the deaf group rather than other damage to the nervous system associated with the disease which caused deafness.

Levine, Edna S. *Youth In a Soundless World.* New York: New York University Press, 1956.

Purpose: To study the personality pictures of selected deaf subjects through the diagnostic testing of intelligence and personality.

Subjects: The experimental group included 31 deaf girls between 15 and 18 years of age who had begun school between the ages of five and seven. The group attended the Lexington School for the Deaf, had non-deaf parents, and were selected as "normal" by their teachers. The control group was 100 girls, age 16, from Wechsler's standardization population.

Procedure: The Rorschach was administered with emphasis on "imagination." The examiner communicated by speech and the subject responded through combined speech, signs, and gestures. There was an inquiry after each card instead of at the end of the test. The Wechsler

197

Performance Scale was given with no modifications. The Verbal Scale was administered with simplified language using the means of communication preferred by the subject.

Results: The Wechsler results showed the deaf to be significantly inferior to the hearing control group in all verbal subtests. In the performance tests the only difference between the two groups was obtained on the Object Assembly Test in which the deaf were superior.

The intra-group analysis of data for the deaf group showed that the difference between verbal and performance scores was significant.

In comparing mean standard subtest scores with the mean of all scores, the scores for the deaf on Digit Span and Arithmetic were significantly inferior and the scores on Block Design and Object Assembly were significantly superior.

The Wechsler data combined with the Rorschach material reveals a personality characterized by (a) underdevelopment in conceptual forms of mental activity, (b) emotional underdevelopment, (c) a lag in understanding the dynamics of inter-personal relationships, (d) egocentric life perspective, (e) a constricted life area and (f) a rigid adherence to a book of etiquette code rather than to inner sensibilities.

Comment: Since the group selected for this study were "normal" deaf people, the results obtained should furnish a yardstick for other studies of personality with deaf subjects. This study provided for excellent communication between examiner and subjects.

Myklebust, H. R. The Emotional Development of Deaf Children. *The Psychology of Deafness*, New York: Grune and Stratton, 1960, 58-177.

Purpose: To study the effects of early life deafness on self-perception, person-perception, and identification through the use of the Human Figure Test.

Subjects: 511 deaf pupils in residential schools, 319 deaf pupils in day schools and a control group of 274 hearing children.

Procedure: The test administered was an adaptation of the Goodenough Draw-a-Man Test and the scales devised by Witkin and by Machover. The drawings of a man, father, mother, and self were obtained for the 830 deaf subjects. The draw-a-man part of the test was given to the control group. Each of the 100 items on the test was scored separately and the chi-square technique was used to detect significant differences.

Results: The data indicate that the human figure test can be used to study the emotional development of deaf children and can be used to evaluate the effects of deafness on perceptual organization.

Comment: This study indicates that the test used has considerable merit in the study of deaf children. The test should be used in further investigations to validate the results found here and to measure the effectiveness of therapeutic procedures for improving the adjustment of deaf children.

Social Maturity

Bradway, Katherine P. The Social Competence of Deaf Children. *American Annals of the Deaf*, 1937, 82, 122-140.

Purpose: To determine the feasibility of using the Vineland Social Maturity Scale with deaf children.

Subjects: Group A was made up of 92 pupils in a residential school who had been deaf since before age two. The age range was five to 21 with a mean CA of 12.8. Group B consisted of 11 pupils who had lost their hearing after age five. This group had a CA range of 12 through 18 with a mean of 14.6.

Procedure: The Vineland Social Maturity Scale was administered for the pupils in both groups.

Results: The deaf in group A were 20 percent inferior to hearing subjects. No sex differences were found. When the results obtained with group B were compared with those of group A, there was no significant difference in social competence, but there was a significantly greater variability in group B. The author concludes that the Vineland Scale is useful with deaf children.

Comment: This study opened a significant field of research with deaf children and stimulated a number of additional investigations. The question of whether deaf children are irreversibly handicapped in social competence is still unanswered. Attention should be directed toward discovering the types of programs that develop social maturity.

Streng, Alice and Kirk, S. A. The Social Competence of Deaf and Hard-of-Hearing Children in a Public Day-School. *American Annals of the Deaf*, 1938, 83, 244-254.

Purpose: To study the social competence of deaf and hard of hearing children in a day school environment.

Subjects: 97 deaf and hard of hearing children, (ages six to 18) at the Paul Binner Day School in Milwaukee, Wisconsin, were used. All but three children lived in English-speaking homes and had social contacts with hearing children in their homes and neighborhood. Three children (siblings) had deaf parents but these parents communicated by means of speech.

Procedure: Scores on the Vineland Social Maturity Scale were obtained through interviews with mothers or guardians. All children were given the Grace Arthur Point Scale of Performance. Eighty-seven children were given the Chicago Non-Verbal Examination.

Results: The group was within average limits in Social Quotient (96.2 with an SD of 12.8). There was a low positive correlation between the IQs and the SQs. No differences were found in SQ or IQ between the deaf and hard of hearing or between boys and girls. There was no significant age difference in SQs, and age at onset seemed to have no effect on SQ.

Comment: This is an interesting sequel to Bradway's study. The fact that pupils in this study were normal in social maturity while those studied by Bradway were inferior is deserving of more comprehensive study.

Avery, Charlotte. Social Competence of Pre-School, Acoustically Handicapped Children. *Journal of Exceptional Children,* 1948, 15, 71-73.

Purpose: To attempt to answer the following question: Are preschool acoustically handicapped children retarded in social maturity when compared with children who do not have an aural handicap?

Subjects: 50 auditorily defective children, from 10 months to six years of age, living in or attending school in two large metropolitan areas. The parents were slightly above average in educational status.

Procedure: The Vineland Social Maturity Scale was used. Mothers, teachers, and dormitory matrons were interviewed. The scale was scored as directed by the author, and also by a modified method.

Results: The results of this study indicate that there is no reason to believe that preschool hearing handicapped children should be socially inadequate when compared with hearing children. Aurally handicapped children appear to develop social maturity at a constant rate, as do hearing children.

Comment: This study is in partial agreement with the Bradway study and confirms the results of Streng and Kirk. It is possible that deaf children mature socially at the preschool age because language is less important at this time than in later periods.

Burchard, E. M. L. and Myklebust, H. R. A Comparison of Congenital and Adventitious Deafness with Respect to its Effect on Intelligence, Personality, and Social Maturity—Part II: Social Maturity. *American Annals of the Deaf*, 1942, 87, 140-154.

Purpose: To determine whether there are significant measurable differences in intelligence, social maturity, and personality between children who are congenitally deaf and those who have acquired deafness. This part of the reporting concerns *social maturity*.

Subjects: These were selected very carefully on the basis that congenital deafness is deafness which existed at birth and adventitious deafness is that acquired after the child learned to talk. One hundred and eighty-nine pupils, age seven to 19 years, were selected from the population at the New Jersey School for the Deaf. One-hundred of these were male; 89 female; 121 were congenitally deaf; 68 had acquired deafness. One hundred and twenty-nine had resided at the school for more than four years.

Procedure: The Grace Arthur Point Scale of Performance was given to all subjects. The Haggerty-Olson-Wickman Behavior Rating Schedule was used for all possible subjects. One rating was made by a teacher, one by a vocational leader, one by a housemother. Information for the Vineland Social Maturity Scale was obtained from housemothers for 104 cases.

Results: The congenitally deaf are somewhat more variable in social maturity than the adventitiously deaf. It is indicated that there is a social maturity retardation of from 15 to 20 points. Deaf children in residence less than four years have a higher mean SQ than those in residence more than four years.

The data support the view that residential schools are not training deaf children adequately in social competence.

Comment: The deafness itself rather than factors associated with etiology imposes the limitations on the individual. The effects of the residential school environment should be studied further.

Heider, F. K., and Heider, Grace M. Studies in the Psychology of the Deaf. *Psychological Monographs*, 1941, 53, No. 5, 1-56.

Purpose: To observe the effect of the young deaf child's communication handicap on his social behavior.

Subjects: Two groups of seven deaf children, group 1 with an average

201

CA of 4-9 and group 2 with an average CA of 5-11; and two nursery school groups of hearing children, group 1 made up of 18 children with an average CA of 4-3, and group 2 consisting of 16 children with an average CA of 3-10.

Procedure: Seventy-five observations averaging 27 minutes each were made. Of these, 53 were with deaf children and 22 with hearing children. The observations were made of free play situations. The method was to follow one child, recording by minutes what he did and said. A series of nine short motion pictures made up the second part of the study. The material was not treated quantitatively.

Results: While the deaf child can carry out many kinds of social behavior in their basic forms, he is limited in important respects. For example, the young deaf child calls attention only to things in the present environment and has difficulty in verbalizing size, quantity, and quality. His demands are less specific and he must be near the helper. His questions are limited to asking permission. The deaf child can protest against restrictions or compulsions but he lacks the ability to give reasons.

Comment: Deaf children are limited in social behavior, but a considerable amount of interchange occurs. Teachers who can readily provide the language which the interchange requires can capitalize on the interests of the child.

In Review

The serious limitations of the tools of investigation are apparent in this area of research. Instruments that were constructed for hearing people are not appropriate for the deaf because of language complexities and problems in communication. The use of norms for the hearing population presents an exaggerated picture of the lack of adjustment of the deaf.

In studies of the adjustment of the deaf, attention should be directed toward the development and use of diagnostic instruments and adequate communication between the investigator and subjects.

EDUCATION

The major research studies in the education of deaf children are presented in the following categories: (a) oral communication—speechreading and speech, (b) auditory training, (c) language, (d) reading, (e) general educational achievement, and (f) school placement.

Pintner, R. Speech and Speech Reading Tests for the Deaf. *American Annals of the Deaf,* 1929, 74, 480-486.

Purpose: To study the relationship between speech and speechreading tests and tests of intelligence and educational achievement given by Day, Fusfeld, and Pintner* in the survey of American schools for the deaf.

Subjects: Test results were tabulated for 400 cases, about equally divided among day school and residential pupils. The children were in the three most advanced classes in each school, making this a highly select group.

Procedure: Sets of sentences were prepared. One set of speech tests was read by the child to his teacher; a similar set was read by the child to an outside examiner. A set of speechreading tests was read by the teacher to the child; a similar test was read by an examiner to the child. Therefore, there were two measures of speechreading and two measures of intelligibility of speech for each pupil examined.

Results: Within this select group of advanced students there was no correlation between intelligence and intelligibility of speech. There was also no correlation for this group between speechreading and intelligence. Day school pupils showed markedly higher average scores for speech and speechreading than residential school pupils, while their intelligence rating was slightly below that of residential school pupils. It would seem that beyond a certain level, intelligence of the nonverbal type is not a factor in speech and speechreading. Educational achievement is related to speech and speechreading to some extent. There are indications that amount of hearing and age at onset of deafness are important for speech intelligibility.

Comment: This study is an early attempt to discover the factors related to success in speech and speechreading. Because of the limitations of the measuring instruments, the results can be considered only as tentative indications of relationships.

Heider, F. and Heider, Grace M. An Experimental Investigation of Lip-Reading. *Psychological Monographs,* 1940, 52, No. 1, 125-153.

Purpose: To measure and define some of the problems and relationships in lipreading.

---

* H. E. Day, I. S. Fusfeld, and R. Pintner, *A Survey of American Schools for the Deaf.* Washington, D. C.: National Research Council, 1928.

Subjects: Test I was given to 86 children, ages seven to 17, in the lower and middle schools; Test II was given to 93 children, ages nine to 19, and Test III to 68 children, ages nine to 19, in the middle and upper schools of the Clarke School for the Deaf, Northampton, Massachusetts.

Procedure: Results from three motion picture tests of lipreading given over a five-year period were analyzed to measure achievement and to show the relationship of achievement to other factors.

Eight pupils from among the poorest lipreaders were given 20 minutes of lipreading training each day for 14 weeks with emphasis on recognition of vowels.

Results: (a) The motion picture tests of lipreading were found highly reliable. (b) The rank order of children in lipreading achievement remained constant to a high degree over a period of years. (c) Great individual differences were found. (d) Yearly progress was small. (e) Individual differences were not due to differences in length of training. (f) The *r* between lipreading and educational achievement was .54. (g) Ability to recognize vowels was found to be more highly correlated with general lipreading ability than was ability to recognize consonants. (h) A positive correlation was found between ability to follow a rhythm and lipreading. (i) The lipreading of nonsense syllables and general lipreading were found to be unrelated.

In the experimental teaching program, the experimental teaching group placed 2.8 rank places better than the control group on the post-test.

Comment: An attempt to analyze lipreading ability in an objective manner was facilitated by the use of film tests. The remedial teaching experiment is an example of a therapeutic program to overcome a specific deficiency in a group of children. This type of research offers promise for the improvement of teaching methods.

Johnson, Elizabeth H. The Ability of Pupils in a School for the Deaf to Understand Various Methods of Communication —I. *American Annals of the Deaf*, 1948, 93, 194-213.

Purpose: To compare the ability of pupils in the Manual, Oral and Acoustic departments of the Illinois School for the Deaf to understand language by means of the particular methods of communication used in their classrooms, and to evaluate the ability of these pupils to understand language through any of the various means of communication employed by pupils in a school for the deaf.

Subjects: 253 pupils from the Illinois School for the Deaf, Jacksonville, Illinois. There were 141 boys and 112 girls, ranging in age from 11 to 24 years. Seventy-seven pupils were from the Manual Department, 96 from the Oral, and 80 from the Acoustic Department. The Chicago Non-Verbal Examination results were available for 188 pupils, indicating an IQ range of 47 to 134 with a mean of 97.

Procedure: The Gates Reading Survey Form I was administered and scored by the reading supervisor of the Oral and Manual departments. A 10-sentence intelligibility test was administered separately to each department, to the Manual students through signs and finger spelling, to Oral pupils through lipreading, to Acoustic pupils through a combination of hearing and lipreading.

All 253 pupils were given tests of speech-hearing ability, lipreading ability, hearing plus lipreading, finger spelling only, and signs plus finger spelling.

Results: Only the Acoustic group had a classroom method of communication which could be called satisfactory. The more restricted the speech-hearing experience for whatever reason, the greater was the retardation in reading. Even large amounts of residual hearing appeared to be of no practical value for interpreting speech sounds if meaningful experience in hearing such sounds was lacking.

Finger spelling was the most satisfactory means of communication for the group as a whole and for the Manual and Oral groups. There was an indication that, given equal experience with finger spelling, the pupils whose language patterns had been learned at least partly through hearing would show greater ability to understand finger-spelled language than would those who had learned language through the visual channel only. It was suggested that replacing combined signs and finger spelling with finger spelling alone would probably improve the Manual pupils' ability to understand language. It was also suggested that certain oral pupils, in addition to being given extensive and intensive auditory training, could probably be helped by the use of varying amounts of finger spelling.

The author suggests that the provision of hearing experience through auditory training would probably significantly increase the academic, reading and general communication abilities of many pupils.

Comment: The process of establishing a functional language pattern is the basis of the education of deaf children. The effective use of residual hearing is an important aspect of developing this pattern. More research is needed on methods for establishing language with children who have little usable hearing.

Quick, Marian. A Test for Measuring Achievement in Speech Perception for Young Deaf Children. *Volta Review*, 1953, 55, 28-31.

Purpose: To develop a test which would measure the ability of young deaf children to perceive speech through lipreading, hearing, and a combination of lipreading and hearing.

Subjects: 46 pupils at the Clarke School for the Deaf, varying widely in age, school experience, hearing loss, and response to acoustic training.

Procedure: A test of speech perception made up of two lists of 25 monosyllabic words representing all of the English speech sounds was developed. Eighteen scrambled versions with multiple choice answer sheets were prepared for each list. Average scores, in terms of correct responses, were determined for each of the three testing conditions (lipreading, hearing, and lipreading-hearing).

Results: The two lists were found to be of equal difficulty by item analysis. The reliability of the test was measured by correlating the average scores for the two lists in the two testing conditions—lipreading only and lipreading-hearing. The reliability coefficients obtained were high.

Comment: This test is a practical method for evaluating the young child's ability and growth in speech perception and should prove helpful in the evaluation programs in schools for the deaf.

Hudgins, C. V., and Numbers, F. C. An Investigation of the Intelligibility of the Speech of the Deaf. *Genetic Psychology Monographs*, 1942, 25, 289-392.

Purpose: To identify the speech errors of deaf children, to classify these errors and determine their frequencies; and to determine the relative effects of each type of error on the intelligibility of speech samples.

Subjects: 192 deaf pupils between the ages of eight and 20 in two oral schools for the deaf.

Procedure: The speech of each pupil reading a set of 10 simple, unrelated sentences was recorded. The records were audited by an average of seven persons familiar with the speech of deaf children. The speech samples were also transcribed phonetically. The data were analyzed for speech intelligibility, consonant and vowel errors, errors of rhythm, errors of articulation, according to age and degree of hearing loss, and the relationship of types of error to intelligibility.

Results: Two general types of errors appeared—errors in articulation and errors in rhythm. Consonant errors were classified into seven categories and vowel errors into five categories. Twenty-one percent of all consonants and 12 percent of all vowels were malarticulated. Errors involving surd-sonant distinction, compound consonants, and the failure of releasing consonants were most frequent and most important for speech intelligibility. Sentences spoken with correct rhythm had a four to one chance of being understood over those with incorrect rhythm.

Comment: This study was one of the first major studies of speech intelligibility of the deaf. The methodology, particularly the vowel and consonant classification, has served as a model for other studies. The results furnish evidence for changing from an elements method of teaching speech to a method emphasizing whole syllables spoken in correct rhythm.

Hudgins, C. V. A Method of Appraising the Speech of the Deaf. *Volta Review,* 1949, 51, 597-601.

Purpose: To develop a method for testing the intelligibility of the speech of deaf children.

Subjects: 83 pupils in the Clarke School for the Deaf. Five college juniors served as listeners.

Procedure: Four equated 50 word PBF (phonetically balanced familiar) lists were developed. A tape recording of each pupil reading a list of words was obtained. After a training period to familiarize them with deaf speech, the listeners audited the recorded tests. The median score for the five listeners was taken as the intelligibility score for the pupil. The pupils' scores for the word lists were tabulated and compared with scores on a sentence test.

Results: The average score on the word list was 42± 2.6 percent. The scores ranged from 9 to 86 and were distributed normally about the mean. The sentence list test for the same group of pupils resulted in a mean of 71± 2.8 and a range of 35 to 100. The correlation between the tests was .81± .03.

Comment: This test is a practical method for evaluating the speech of deaf children.

Carr, Josephine. An Investigation of the Spontaneous Speech Sounds of Five-year-old Deaf-born Children. *Journal of Speech and Hearing Disorders,* 1953, 18, 22-29.

Purpose: To investigate the number of speech sounds and their relative frequency in the spontaneous vocalizations of five-year-old deaf children and to discover the relationship of the spontaneous speech sounds of five-year-old deaf children to the speech sounds of hearing infants at various ages.

Subjects: The speech of 27 boys and 21 girls from the Iowa School for the Deaf was studied for more than two years. The subjects selected were required to be five years of age sometime during the period of investigation, to have a hearing loss severe enough and acquired early enough to have prevented development of connected, functional speech, and to have received no formal speech instruction previous to entrance in the Iowa School for the Deaf.

Procedure: Three to five subjects at a time were taken to a kindergarten classroom and allowed to engage in undirected activity. Such sounds as were carried on the exhalation phase of a single respiration were transcribed phonetically. A sample of 30 such breaths was taken three times, at intervals of two weeks, for each subject. During the period of the investigation, the subjects were not given classroom speech instruction. Reliability of the observer was established by percentage of agreement with another rater who made separate observations.

Results: This investigation indicated that the subjects used many spontaneous speech sounds. The deaf children studied did not develop spontaneous speech sounds much beyond the level of 12- to 13-month-old hearing infants. Deaf children use a higher percentage of front consonants than hearing children do. Both deaf and hearing children use more front vowels than back vowels.

Comment: This study suggests an approach to teaching speech using the sounds which occur spontaneously with individual children. Further study should be made of procedures for utilizing spontaneous vocalizations in developing meaningful words.

Numbers, Mary E. and Hudgins, C. V. Speech Perception in Present Day Education for Deaf Children. *Volta Review,* 1948, 50, 449-456.

Purpose: To determine to what degree hearing supplements lipreading in speech perception by deaf children.

Subjects: A class of eight sixth grade deaf children. Six of these pupils had been wearing hearing aids throughout their school lives. The range in age was from 11-6 to 15 years. The degree of hearing loss for speech covered a range of from 60 to 103 decibels.

Procedure: The test material consisted of equated 50-word lists containing a representative number of consonants and vowels. The tests were given under two conditions: (a) the pupils were allowed to look at the speaker as well as to listen over their earphones, and (b) the pupils listened only. In the first condition, the intensity of the speech was reduced to obtain a measure of pure lipreading.

Results: Speech perception by lipreading alone was high for the group regardless of hearing loss. Pupils who obtained high scores in hearing alone were just as good or better in lipreading than those who did not hear speech at all. Speech perception invariably increases as hearing supplements vision.

Comment: In the education of even the most profoundly deaf children, auditory training should be considered an important supplement to lipreading.

Auditory Training

Hudgins, C. V. The Response of Profoundly Deaf Children to Auditory Training. *Journal of Speech and Hearing Disorders,* 1953, 18, 273-288.

Purpose: To compare the progress of matched groups of profoundly deaf children; an experimental class using a special group hearing aid, and a control group using a group aid of the type in use prior to 1948.

Subjects: The experimental group was composed of eight pupils in the Clarke School for the Deaf with an average CA of 11 years 11 months (range 9-6 to 12-10), and an average educational age of 9-1. The control group was made up of 12 pupils in the same school for whom comparative data were available.

Procedure: The experimental hearing aid had a wide frequency range, powerful amplification, a minimum of distortion, compression amplification, and a filter which attenuated sounds below 500 cps. The experimental group was taught while wearing the special hearing aid in an acoustically treated room, and the control group was instructed with similar teaching techniques but using the standard group aid in a regular classroom.

The experimental and control groups were given the following tests at the beginning of the period and periodically during the two-year experiment: (a) speech perception; lipreading, hearing, and the two combined; (b) speech intelligibility and speech production; and (c) educational achievement.

Results: The experimental group showed significantly greater gains in speech perception, general educational achievement and, to a lesser

209

extent, speech intelligibility. In a second experiment with younger children (two years younger on the average), the experimental group made significantly greater gains in speech perception and speech intelligibility although differences in educational achievement were not significant.

Comment: This study seems to indicate conclusively the benefit to profoundly deaf children of using high-quality auditory training equipment. The desirability of beginning this training early is also demonstrated. ,

Hopkins, Louise A. and Hudgins, C. V. The Relationship between Degree of Deafness and Response to Acoustic Training. *Volta Review*, 1953, 55, 32-35.

Purpose: To investigate the relationship between severity of hearing loss and response to acoustic training.

Subjects: 79 pupils in the Upper and Middle Schools of the Clarke School for the Deaf.

Procedure: The pupils were given pure-tone audiometric tests and speech perception tests to measure lipreading ability alone and lipreading and hearing ability combined. The difference scores (representing the differences between speech perception by lipreading alone and speech perception by lipreading and hearing) are considered to be a measure of the contribution of the ear in the speech perception process. These difference scores for the 79 pupils were plotted against their average pure-tone losses.

Pupils in the profoundly deaf category were divided into three groups depending upon the extent of the frequency range of their residual hearing. The difference scores for these groups were then compared.

Results: The data of this study indicate that the variation in response to acoustic training is not dependent upon the relative severity of the hearing losses nor on the frequency range of the ear.

Comment: Further research should be done to investigate the relationship of other variables to success in using residual hearing. The success in acoustic training of profoundly deaf children as demonstrated in this study has important implications for the training programs in schools for the deaf.

Strizver, G. L. Frequency Discrimination. *Volta Review—Proceedings Issue*, 1958, 60, 304-306.

Purpose: To attempt to find means of evaluating the hearing remnant, in terms other than magnitude, with the hope of discovering the reason why pupils with similar degrees of hearing loss respond differently to similar auditory training programs.

Subjects: 20 advanced pupils at Clarke School for the Deaf. Seventeen were classified as profoundly deaf, three as partially deaf.

Procedure: Pure tones were used as stimuli for both the measurement of absolute thresholds for intensity and difference limens for frequency. Threshold measurements were made for seven standard frequencies. Measurements of difference limens for frequency were made for 500, 1000, 2000 cps. The data were analyzed statistically to determine relationships between (a) hearing loss and frequency discrimination, (b) hearing loss and speech perception, (c) speech perception and frequency discrimination.

Results: Variability noted in achievement in auditory training may be due to the ability to discriminate pitch at low frequencies as well as to the degree of hearing available in the high frequency range.

Comment: This study is part of a more intensive program which may provide a more complete understanding of this problem.

Language

Pintner, R. The Measurement of Language Ability and Language Progress of Deaf Children. *Volta Review,* 1918, 20, 755-764.

Purpose: To contribute to the attempt to arrive at objective standards in the measurement of the language ability of deaf children.

Subjects: Over 1000 children in four state schools for the deaf in Ohio, Indiana, Texas, and Kentucky.

Procedure: The Trabue Language Completion Tests were used. Scale B was given to some children, Scale C to others, and a third group was given both B and C. Comparative studies were made. The Trabue Scales were used because it was felt that they were well graded and had a number of scales to use for retesting.

Results: Comparison of norms for deaf and hearing children showed much greater difficulty encountered by the deaf in the acquisition of language. Progress in language ability among the deaf during a six-month period was too slow to show changes in score. Whatever progress was made by the deaf was much less than that made by hearing children. Further study must be done.

Comment: It is unfortunate that the studies begun by Pintner were not followed by more extensive projects aimed at improving the instruction of deaf children. The Trabue Language Scale which Pintner used may still have possibilities for studying language acquisition by deaf children.

Heider, F. K. and Heider, Grace M. A Comparison of Sentence Structure of Deaf and Hearing Children. *Psychological Monographs*, 1940, 52, No. 1, 52-103.

Purpose: To describe some of the differences between the sentence structure of the deaf and hearing by comparing a large number of compositions on the same subject under similar conditions.

Subjects: 301 pupils in the North Carolina School for the Deaf, the Pennsylvania School for the Deaf (Mt. Airy), and the Clarke School. The CAs ranged from 11 to 17. The hearing group was 817 pupils, CA eight to 14, from public schools in Massachusetts. The age group in both cases represented the youngest group that could write the story successfully.

Procedure: Each child in the study wrote a composition describing what had taken place in a simple film which had been prepared for this study. The compositions were analyzed quantitatively and with respect to the use of subordinate clauses.

Results: The sentences of the deaf were shorter and simpler in language structure than those of the hearing. The deaf children used the more difficult forms of subordination less frequently than the hearing. The performance of the deaf resembled that of less mature hearing children.

Comment: This is one of the most comprehensive studies of the language of the deaf. Further research should be directed toward discovering the factors which cause some deaf pupils to be more competent than others in using language.

Kline, T. K. A Study of the Free Association Test with Deaf Children. *American Annals of the Deaf*, 1945. 90, 237-257.

Purpose: To investigate the responses of deaf children in a free association test and compare them with responses of hearing children and hearing adults.

Subjects: 50 children from the Clarke School for the Deaf, and 157 from the Illinois School for the Deaf, Jacksonville. They were from 11 to 17 years of age and all had become deaf before age five. No mentally retarded children were included in the study.

Procedure: Fifty stimulus words were chosen from Woodrow and Lowell's list of 100. Five preliminary words were added to the beginning of the chosen list and were used as a check on the children's responses. In addition, 10 words were used for a practice period. The written method was used for both stimuli and responses. Instructions were given orally by the respective class teachers.

Results: Responses of deaf children differ from those of hearing children. Deaf children show more failures of response. The deaf have a greater percentage of commonest responses than the hearing. Age trend results appear generally to agree.

Comment: The free association method may be a useful technique for evaluating the extent and depth of vocabulary of deaf children.

Brill, R. G., and Orman, J. N. An Experiment in the Training of Deaf Children in Memory for Sentences. *American Annals of the Deaf,* 1953, 98, 270-279.

Purpose: To determine if visual memory for sentences can be improved by training, to measure the effects of training after an interval of time, and to compare deaf and hearing children in visual memory.

Subjects: An experimental and a control group, each of 10 deaf children, matched for CA (14.0 and 13.9), number of years in school (8.7 and 8.5), Stanford Achievement Test Reading Score (2.85 and 2.42) and score on the initial test of visual memory (90.7 and 88.9). The hearing group consisted of 24 seventh graders, CA range 12 to 14, average IQ 103.4, and an average reading grade of 7-4 years.

Procedure: Four groups of test sentences were constructed. Tests A and C had sentences four or five words in length. Tests B and D had sentences eight to 10 words in length. Tests A and B were given to the two deaf groups at the beginning of the period. Tests C and D were given to these groups at the end of the training period. All four tests were given to the hearing group at the beginning of the period and to the two deaf groups 10 weeks after the training had stopped. The training consisted of finger spelling drill and recall for sentences similar to the test sentences.

Results: There were no significant differences in the scores for the hearing group on the four tests. This is used as evidence that the tests are parallel. The hearing group was superior to the deaf group at the

213

.01 level of confidence on initial Test B. After seven weeks of training the deaf experimental group was superior to the deaf control group at the .05 level of confidence. After the training of the deaf group there were no significant differences between the deaf and hearing on Tests C and D. Ten weeks after the training was stopped there were no significant differences between the two deaf groups.

Comment: A deficiency in visual memory for sentences may be a part of the overall language handicap. This study was not carried on for a long enough period for the special training to have a lasting effect. However, it is an example of a remedial program aimed at one of the areas in which the deaf have been found to be lacking.

Goda, S. Language Skills of Profoundly Deaf Adolescent Children. *Journal of Speech and Hearing Research*, 1959, 2, 369-376.

Purpose: To study the oral and written, receptive and expressive language abilities of a group of deaf children.

Subjects: 56 congenitally deaf students in the Michigan School for the Deaf, CA 12 to 18, with a hearing loss greater than 75 decibels in the range of 512 through 2048 cps.

Procedure: The following data were gathered on each of the subjects: oral compositions in response to picture stimuli, written compositions in response to pictures, scores on a test of lipreading proficiency, a reading grade level on the Stanford Achievement Tests, and intelligence scores on the Chicago Non-Verbal Test and the Revised Beta Test. The material was analyzed by means of correlation and factor analysis techniques.

Results: All of the measures (oral composition, written composition, lipreading, reading, and intelligence) correlated positively with each other except the measure of length of spoken sentence and length of written composition. By means of factor analysis, the author identified a general language factor and language confidence factor. When the data were studied by age group the differences between chronological age groups were significant for the written measures but non-significant for oral measures.

Comment: The measures of language ability used in this study appear to be a logical test of language proficiency. Tests such as these should be used in the achievement testing programs in schools for the deaf and in longitudinal studies of language development.

Myklebust, H. R. Language and Language Development. In *The Psychology of Deafness,* New York: Grune and Stratton, 1960, 246-318.

Purpose: To study the language of the deaf by observing the inter-relationships of measures of language ability and other factors and by comparing the read and written language of the deaf and the hearing.

Subjects: Groups of day and residential school deaf pupils selected at CA 7, 9, 11, 13 and 15. The number of deaf children studied was over 600. Control groups of hearing children were used in appropriate parts of the study.

Procedure: The following information was gathered: (a) teachers' ratings of lipreading ability, (b) scores on the Draw-a-Man Test, (c) the Columbia Vocabulary Test, (d) the Picture Story Language Test, and (e) teachers' ratings on pupils' ability to use spoken language. Comparisons on all measures were made between the deaf and the hearing on the vocabulary and language tests and between the deaf in residential and in day schools. The results of the various tests for the deaf were studied for inter-relationships.

Results: (a) Children rated as excellent—good—average in lipreading were also the more intelligent. More females than males were considered to have excellent—good—average lipreading ability. (b) The results indicate a definite correlation between lipreading ability, as rated by teachers, and reading, as well as between lipreading and ability to use written language. (c) Females were rated higher than males and day-school students higher than residential students in spoken language. (d) Ratings in spoken language were found to be unrelated to intelligence. (e) The deaf group was significantly inferior to the hearing group (at the one percent level of confidence) in reading, and the degree of retardation increased with age. (f) The differences between day and residential school pupils on reading vocabulary were not significant for males and may be due to differences in intelligence in the case of the females. (g) The deaf group was significantly inferior to the hearing on sentence length and syntax, the two measures of language productivity considered most valid. (h) On comparisons between the deaf and hearing in the use of Abstract-Concrete Concepts in a written story, the deaf were inferior at all age levels. The retardation is least at upper levels, and, in contrast to measures of verbal facility, a plateau has not been reached.

Comment: This comprehensive study furnishes a wealth of information on the level of language achievement and the interrelationships of language abilities. It suggests a number of avenues for further study to improve the instruction of deaf children. The finding of continued growth in the use of abstraction up to the age of 17 may be an indication that language teaching methods are not keeping pace with the intellectual potential of the students. Research should be directed toward discovering the specific teaching techniques and environmental conditions that foster optimum growth in language.

Reading

Thompson, Helen. An Experimental Study of the Beginning Reading of Deaf-Mutes. *Teachers College, Columbia University Contributions to Education,* No. 254, 1927.

Purpose: To determine whether, by utilizing the deaf child's visual sense to a maximum, it might be possible to plan a method of reading instruction which would increase his comprehension of written language.

Subjects: 20 children in the first two grades of a school for the deaf, divided into two matched groups. In the control group the CA ranged from 5-3 to 8-3, the MA from 5-0 to 8-11. In the experimental group the CA was 5-1 to 8-3, the MA from 5-0 to 8-6. It was determined from records that these children were from average homes.

Procedure: Experimental teaching was done daily from 10:30 to 11:30, October 1, 1925 to June 1, 1926. An observer recorded events and responses. It was the conscious aim of the experiment to teach the comprehension of connected language involving a small vocabulary.

Results: (a) In one hour per day for one school year, deaf-mutes of an average age of 6-10 achieved five-sixths of the achievement of a normal hearing class in one year of beginning reading. (b) In one year of beginning reading, two and one-half times as much reading ability was developed as was developed under the system used with the control group. (c) Under the proposed method there was only a slight loss in other abilities taught. (d) Under the proposed method it was possible to develop better attitudes than under the system in use. (e) It was possible to overcome many of the difficulties of teaching reading to the deaf.

Comment: This is one of the few experimental studies in teaching deaf children to read. The investigation was not conducted long enough to indicate whether the gains of the experimental group were a result of the methods used or the enthusiastic teaching of the experimenter, or whether the deaf pupils could achieve as readily on the more advanced levels of reading.

Pugh, Gladys S. Summaries from "Appraisal of the Silent Reading Abilities of Acoustically Handicapped Children." *American Annals of the Deaf,* 1946, 91, 331-349.

Purpose: To set up tentative norms for the silent reading abilities of deaf children and to reveal the relative retardation of deaf pupils in various phases of reading according to the norms for hearing children.

Subjects: 344 pupils selected from 56 American schools for the deaf. The pupils had attended school for seven and 13 years.

Procedure: The Iowa Silent Reading Test and the Durrell-Sullivan Reading Achievement Test were administered to all of the subjects. The Otis Mental Ability test was also given to the group to obtain an estimate of verbal ability.

Results: (a) Tentative norms for deaf children on the various parts of the Iowa Silent Reading Test were established. (b) On the Iowa Silent Reading Test the medians were lower for deaf children than for hearing children who had been in school the same number of years, although some deaf children exceeded the medians for hearing children on every part of the test. (c) The medians for all the deaf in the study on the Durrell-Sullivan Test were slightly below the sixth grade equivalent for hearing pupils. (d) The reading achievement of deaf pupils for certain reading skills was below their verbal ability as measured by the Otis Test. (e) A comparison of an unselected group of pupils with a very superior group indicated the importance for success in reading of intelligence, age at becoming deaf, percent of hearing loss, interest in reading, social adjustment, attendance in a regular school, and encouragement of language usage in the home.

Comment: Normative surveys such as this are important in that an estimate is obtained of the present status of teaching deaf children to read. The conditions that favor good school achievement are indicated. Further studies of a more definitive nature may reveal more clearly why some children learn so much better than others, and whether low achievers can be helped through remedial instruction.

Falconer, G. A. Teaching Machines for the Deaf. *Volta Review,* 1960, 62, 59-63.

Purpose: To explore the possibility of deaf children learning to recog-

217

nize nouns through training on a multiple-choice teaching machine.

Subjects: Eight profoundly deaf primary children at the Illinois School for the Deaf. The age range was 6-2 to 7-6 years.

Procedure: An electrically motivated, multiple choice, immediate reinforcement machine was constructed. The eight subjects spent five minutes a day for 10 days drilling on 15 unfamiliar nouns.

Results: The eight subjects learned to recognize 13.75 nouns in 50 minutes at the machine. Retention after two weeks was nearly perfect.

Comment: This is the first reported application of a teaching machine to a group of deaf children. Teaching machines should be particularly useful in teaching the deaf because repetition can be provided in an interesting manner, the teacher is relieved of part of the group so that she can do individual teaching with the others, and pupils learn at their individual rates without teacher help.

General Educational Achievement

Day, H. E., Fusfeld, I. S., and Pintner, R. *A Survey of American Schools for the Deaf.* Washington, D.C.: National Research Council, 1928.

Purpose: To gather information regarding the administration, equipment, curriculum, and pupils in representative American schools for the deaf.

Subjects: 4689 pupils, 4006 in residential schools and 683 in day schools, ranging in CA from 12 to 24.

Procedure: 29 residential and 14 day schools were studied by the two field agents through visits to the schools. Individual audiometric tests, speech and speechreading tests, the Pintner Non-Language Mental Test and the Pintner Educational Survey Test were administered.

Results: The median of the degree of hearing loss of the children in the survey was 75 to 80 percent. Only three percent of the total number tested were found to be totally deaf. The day-school children had more residual hearing than the residential school children.

The speech and lipreading tests used pointed to the possibility of developing a standard method of evaluation.

A marked divergence between the deaf and hearing was found in regard to educational achievement, a divergence much greater than the intellectual differences between the two groups.

Comment: This was one of the first large-scale studies of the education of the deaf in this country and was significant in that it raised some

218

questions regarding the reasons for the educational retardation of the deaf and pointed the way toward later investigations.

Schick, Helen F. A Five-Year Testing Program to Measure the Educational Achievement of the Deaf Child. *Oralism and Auralism,* June 1936, 5-16.

Purpose: To attempt to answer the following questions acknowledging the existence of educational retardation in deaf children: (a) Is this retardation the same at all age levels or does it become greater with older deaf children? (b) In which subjects of the school curriculum is the retardation most marked? (c) Are equivalent test forms for the hearing also equivalent in difficulty for the deaf?

Subjects: 237 students at Central Institute for the Deaf, St. Louis, ranging in age from 7-1 to over 18.

Procedure: The Stanford Achievement Test, Advanced Form V, was administered in November, 1930. Form W was given March, 1932. Subsequently Forms X, Y, Z were given in successive years. In March, 1933, the Primary Form V was given to second and third grades. Three forms of the primary test were given up to the time of this reporting.

Results: There is a gradual decrease in the educational quotient with an increase in CA. The curve flattens at the 16-year age level. Retardation is greater for tests involving language, with Paragraph Meaning most difficult and Arithmetic Computation least difficult. The deaf children in this study were educationally retarded about two years.

Comment: This study showing educational retardation of approximately two years is in contradiction with other studies which showed retardation of from three to five years. There may be some indication that under ideal conditions, including careful grouping of pupils, the deaf child may more nearly approach his educational potential.

Fusfeld, I. S. The Academic Program of Schools for the Deaf. *Volta Review,* 1955, 57, 63-70.

Purpose: To attempt to evaluate the immediate outcomes of the programs offered by American schools for the deaf in terms of standard academic achievement measurement for two successive annual testing programs, in the spring of 1953 and again in the spring of 1954.

Subjects: 134 candidates in 33 residential schools in 25 states plus the District of Columbia and one province of Canada were tested in 1953. In 1954 a total of 145 candidates were tested at 33 residential schools, one private school for the deaf, and one public high school for hearing children. Most of the candidates were in graduating classes. Some were post-graduate pupils; a few were in classes immediately preliminary to the final year in school. In general these groups may be considered samplings of the finished academic product of their schools. The average age was about 19 years. The average length of time spent in school was about 13 years.

Procedure: The Stanford Achievement Test, Advanced Battery Form J was administered in 1953 and Form L in 1954.

Results: The gross median school level in 1953 was 9.2 with a range of achievement from grade 12 at one end and grade four at the other. In 1954, the grade level was 8.9 with a range from grade 12 to grade five. In language and spelling the candidates displayed relatively high ability, while showing pronounced weakness in paragraph and word meaning. The written work of the subjects showed marked discrepancy in competence between *apparent* command of language and *practice*. The deaf pupils used a tangled-web type of expression.

Comment: This study indicates the need for the development and effective use of a better language teaching program. Helping the capable deaf child express his thinking ability in an acceptable pattern of expression is one of the great challenges to education of the deaf.

Goetzinger, C. P. and Rousey, C. L. Educational Achievement of Deaf Children. *American Annals of the Deaf,* 1959, 104, 221-231.

Purpose: To discover the achievement level of congenitally deaf children and children with early acquired severe deafness who had no preschool training, little or no auditory training, and who were taught in classes of 10 or more; to observe differences in educational achievement of the congenitally deaf and those who acquired deafness from disease other than meningitis; between the congenitally deaf and the meningitic deaf, and between two groups of pupils with acquired deafness when the subjects are matched according to age, sex, IQ and years spent in school.

Subjects: 101 deaf students between the ages of 14 and 21 in a state residential school for the deaf. Sixty-one of the total were congenitally deaf. Of the 40 with acquired deafness, 18 were deaf as a result of meningitis.

Procedure: Each subject was given the Wechsler Adult Performance

Scale (Form II), the Binet Vocabulary Test, a pure-tone audiometric test, and an educational achievement test. Only the subtests, paragraph meaning, vocabulary, arithmetic reasoning and arithmetic computation were used in this study.

Results: The 61 congenitally deaf students (average IQ 103.5, average CA 17-2, average years in school 10-5) had the following average educational achievement scores: Paragraph Meaning 4.4, Vocabulary 4.2, Arithmetic Reasoning 6.0, Arithmetic Computation 6.5. The achievement of the group with acquired deafness was not significantly different.

No significant differences in educational achievement were found between the sub-groups.

The correlations between the Binet Vocabulary Test and the achievement subtests indicate that the Binet Vocabulary Test affords an abbreviated measure of an adolescent's educational level.

No differences in educational achievement were found between children whose parents were deaf and children whose parents were hearing except in Arithmetic Computation, in which the former excelled.

Comment: This study suggests an approach to measuring the efficiency of educational programs for deaf children. It should be replicated under more desirable educational conditions.

Fiedler, Miriam F. A Comparison of Good and Poor Learners among Young Children in an Oral School. *Proceedings of the 37th Meeting, American Instructors of the Deaf,* 1955, 140-148.

Purpose: To discover factors related to the school achievement of deaf pupils.

Subjects: 49 pupils, ranging in age from 5-4 to 9-9 years in the fall of 1952, classified as follows: 12 very good learners, 12 very poor learners, and 25 average learners.

Procedure: The following types of information were gathered and analyzed over a three year period: developmental data, mental tests and personality assessments, hearing and vision tests, teacher reports on school progress, and observational data.

Results: Good learners as a group come from families of higher socioeconomic status and better education, have had more preschool training, are physically superior, have had fewer emotionally disturbing experiences, scored higher on the Goodenough Draw-a-Man Test, appeared superior on a test of visual perception and on a projective test of personality functioning.

Comment: This study suggests the multiple causation of high or low achievement and points toward procedures for relating clinical evaluation methods to the instructional program.

Rutledge, L. Aspiration Levels of Deaf Children as Compared with Hearing Children. *Journal of Speech and Hearing Disorders,* 1954, 19, 375-380.

Purpose: To determine whether deaf children differ from hearing children in level of aspiration behavior; whether goal-setting differences exist only on tasks in which the deaf children are handicapped; and whether there is a consistent level of aspiration for a child.

Subjects: 52 deaf pupils, 26 male, 26 female, CA 14 to 15, enrolled in the Minnesota School for the Deaf, and a control group of 52 residents of Mooseheart, Illinois, matched with the deaf on CA, sex, and paternal occupation.

Procedure: The two groups completed a series of 10 goal settings on two motor tasks (the Heath Railwalking Test and the Rotter Aspiration Board). Aspiration scores and goal discrepancy scores were obtained.

Results: Significant and consistent differences were found only on the task (Railwalking) in which the deaf were presumed to be handicapped.

Comment: The goal-setting behavior of a person is presumed to be important for educational and vocational success. Yet little research has been conducted in this area with the deaf. Investigations should be made of the deaf child's level of aspiration in such areas as lipreading and speech.

School Placement

Justman, J. *et al.* The Integration of Deaf Children in a Hearing Class. *Bureau of Educational Research Publication* No. 36, New York City Board of Education, 1956.

Purpose: To study the transition of acoustically handicapped children from a special school to a school enrolling hearing children.

Subjects and Procedure: 10 fourth-grade acoustically handicapped children, selected on the basis of intelligence, academic achievement, and communication ability, were enrolled as a group with 25 hearing children in Public School 40, Manhattan. The class was taught jointly by a teacher from P. S. 40 and a teacher from the School for the Deaf. Tests of intelligence and achievement were administered; children, parents and teachers were interviewed; and social relationships were studied using observational and sociometric techniques.

Results: Both the deaf and the hearing children showed somewhat better than expected gains in academic achievement. The deaf improved in self confidence, independence, and lipreading, but there were inadequacies in social adjustment between the two groups.

Justman, J. and Moskowitz, Sue. The Integration of Deaf Children in a Hearing Class: The Second Year. *Bureau of Educational Research Publication* No. 38, New York City Board of Education, 1957.

Purpose: To study the adjustment of deaf children to a class of hearing children when only two deaf children are enrolled in a regular class.

Subjects and Procedure: 10 deaf children from grades four, five, and six were assigned in pairs to classes at P. S. 40, Manhattan. Six of the pupils were enrolled for a second year and four were enrolled there for the first time. A teacher from the School for the Deaf was assigned to P. S. 40 for consultation with teachers and for coaching deaf pupils, but she did not work in the regular classroom as in the previous year.

The second-year study focused on social adjustment in the classroom. The appraisal was conducted by direct observation, sociometric measures, and interviews with teachers.

Results: The entire second-year group of deaf children made a higher proportion of contacts with hearing children than did the previous year's group. The six children spending a second year in a hearing class made three times as many contacts with the hearing as the four "new" children.

The sociometric data indicated that the deaf children were not truly accepted by the hearing. The teachers of the five classes containing deaf children felt that the deaf and hearing children had adapted to each other very well. Classroom discussion offered the most difficulty.

Comment: Deaf children have been integrated into classes for the hearing for some time. This study is one of the few efforts to evaluate this educational procedure. Further studies should be conducted on the adjustment of deaf graduates and on the types of education and guidance programs that lead to the best adjustment.

In Review

The instructional procedures in use in schools for the deaf today are

223

largely the result of the accumulated experience of outstanding teachers. Relatively few of these methods have been developed or modified as a result of scientific study. Notable exceptions are the shift from an "elements" approach to the "rhythmical-syllables" method of teaching speech and the emphasis on auditory training even with profoundly deaf children. Both of these developments were, to some extent at least, a result of the work of Hudgins.

The studies in the other areas of the education of the deaf have indicated where the deaf stand as a group, but with a few exceptions have shed little light on the reasons for the educational deficiencies of the deaf or on the educational programs and procedures that offer promise for better results.

SUMMARY

Little research has been carried on in the area of instruction. There is a need for a more objective evaluation of methods now being used, as well as for the development of improved teaching techniques.

Teacher Recruitment: The most pressing problem in the education of the deaf is to recruit and retain a well-trained staff of teachers. A research study identifying some of the reasons why more young people do not enter this profession and why many teachers do not remain in the classroom might help alleviate the teacher shortage.

Prescribing Teaching Methods for Specific Pupils: The education of the deaf has been characterized by a variety of teaching methods. The proponents of the various methods have indicated that their procedures have been successful with large numbers of deaf children. There are indications that some of these methods work with certain children but not with others. An interesting question for research would be whether it is possible to describe and analyze the characteristics of children who would learn optimally with a given teaching method, to prescribe the teaching methods to be used, and finally to measure the results of this program.

The Linguistic Method: Streng* has pointed out that the linguistic method may have possibilities for the teaching of language to deaf children. A research project which would develop teaching materials using linguistic teaching procedures is needed in order to be able to compare this method with those currently in use.

Communication Methods Used by Adults: A recent study conducted

* Alice Streng. On Improving the Teaching of Language. *American Annals of the Deaf,* 1958, 103, 553-563.

by investigators at the Clarke School for the Deaf indicated that Clarke School graduates were making good use of their speech and lipreading skills. Similar studies for other schools for the deaf would provide information regarding the effectiveness of teaching programs.

Automated Learning: Recent developments in the use of learning machines for teaching various skills to children with normal hearing hold promise for improving the teaching of deaf children. One of the problems in teaching the deaf is concerned with providing sufficient repetition. It is also necessary to individualize the learning program to provide for the needs of each pupil. Another classroom problem results from the need for providing meaningful materials for part of the class while the teacher works with the others. Learning machines which are properly designed and programmed can be employed to help solve all three of these problems. Pupils may work individually on learning programs planned for specific children with as much repetition as is necessary, without direct help from the teacher.

Auditory Training: Wedenberg* has indicated that many children now classified as deaf could be considered hard of hearing if a hearing education program were begun early enough and carried on in a systematic fashion. A research program should be designed to test this premise.

School Placement: The research carried on by the New York City Board of Education suggests that some deaf children can be integrated satisfactorily into a regular school program. This study provided information regarding the characteristics of children who can be integrated most easily. In addition, some guidelines for the process of integration were presented. For example, integration seems to work better when only two deaf pupils are enrolled in a regular class than when as many as ten pupils are placed in the same regular class.

A study should be made of the progress and adjustment of children enrolled in the various school programs which are presently available. The advantages and disadvantages of different school organizations are being discussed with very little research evidence.

Coordination between research centers and among the various disciplines that can contribute to the understanding of deafness is a prime requisite for further progress. Bringing the results of research to the clinician and classroom teacher in order that procedures may be modified in line with new knowledge is another important phase of the research program.

* E. Wedenberg. Auditory Training of Severely Hard-of-Hearing Pre School Children. *Acta Atalaryngalica Supplementum.* 1954, 110.

7

Children with Cerebral Dysfunction

L. Leon Reid

A child with cerebral dysfunction is one whose intellectual, motor, behavioral, or sense functioning has been impaired or altered as a result of improper functioning of the central nervous system. As pointed out by Laufer,* "This impaired or altered function may be, and often is, due to developmental anomalies, delayed maturation, and possible non-structural alteration, as well as to specific brain injury." Denhoff, Laufer, and Holdent have urged that we replace the terms brain injured and brain damaged with "syndromes of cerebral dysfunction."

The content of this chapter has been organized under the following topics:

1. General surveys.
2. Education.
3. Psychology.
4. Teachers.
5. Vocational rehabilitation.

* M. W. Laufer. A Psychiatrist's View. In *The Child with Brain Damage*—Proceedings of the 1959 Annual Meeting of the Association for the Aid of Crippled Children. New York: Association for the Aid of Crippled Children, 1959. p. 11.

† E. Denhoff, M. W. Laufer, and R. H. Holden. The Syndromes of Cerebral Dysfunction. *Journal of the Oklahoma Medical Asociation*. 1959 (June), 52, 360-366.

Reviewed by Boyd Sheets, United Cerebral Palsy Research and Educational Foundation.

The importance of studying all aspects (medical, psychological, educational, social, and economic) of the problems of cerebral palsy has been particularly emphasized in the last two decades. The major surveys have been the Schenectady County, New York Survey in 1948,* the Connecticut Study in 1950,† the New Jersey Study and the Texas Survey (both reviewed below).

Wolfe, W. G. and Reid, L. L. *A Survey of Cerebral Palsy in Texas.* Austin: United Cerebral Palsy of Texas, Inc., 1958.

Purpose: To ascertain, insofar as possible: (a) the incidence and prevalence of cerebral palsy in Texas; (b) the prevalence of the types of cerebral palsy and the severity of involvement for each case; (c) the frequency of certain possible etiological factors and other associated medical factors; (d) the developmental patterns of the cerebral palsied; (e) the educational background and experiences; (f) the nature of treatment and care; (g) the occupations of the cerebral palsied; (h) the social status and index of value orientations of the cerebral palsied persons' families; and (i) parents' opinions concerning their cerebral palsied children.

Subjects: Cases referred by medical authorities and agencies concerned with the cerebral palsied in Texas. A central registry of 8074 cases was established. Of this number, 5901 were surveyed, with 2408 cases being studied comprehensively.

Procedure: The entire number of cases reported were requested to complete and return by mail a one-page questionnaire. The questionnaire was returned by 65.7 percent. Of these, 2408 cases were intensively studied through personal interviews and case study techniques. The parents of these subjects were requested to complete a 77-item questionnaire relating to their feelings about being parents of a cerebral palsied child. Of these parents, 72.8 percent cooperated.

Results: This study revealed important findings on many aspects of the problems of the cerebral palsied, including the following:

1. The prevalence rate was determined to be 308 cerebral palsied persons of all ages per 100,000 population.

* W. J. Butler (Chairman). *Report of the New York State Joint Legislative Committee to Study the Problem of Cerebral Palsy.* Albany: Legislative Document N. 55., 1949.

† S. H. Osburn (Commissioner). *The Study of Cerebral Palsy in Connecticut, 1951.* Hartford: Connecticut State Department of Health, 1951.

2. The incidence rate was estimated to be 2.34 cerebral palsied per 1000 live births.

3. 58.8 percent of the cerebral palsied were quadriplegic, 14.3 percent right hemiplegic, 11.3 percent left hemiplegic, 9.3 percent paraplegic, 3.2 percent monoplegic, 2.5 percent triplegic, and 0.5 percent diplegic.

4. 90.4 percent were cerebral palsied at birth.

5. In 80.7 percent, symptoms of neuromuscular involvements were noted by the parents before the child was one year of age.

6. 70.3 percent of the mothers of the cerebral palsied studied had some condition during pregnancy that might have been a contributing factor to the etiology of cerebral palsy in the child. Miscarriages prior to the birth of the cerebral palsied child were reported by 18.9 percent of the mothers. Rh incompatibility was reported by 14.2 percent of the parents. 76.1 percent of the mothers had inadequate diets according to United States Public Health Standards.

7. 27.6 percent of the children were born prematurely. Precipitant labor was reported in 39.8 percent of the cases. The condition of anoxia at the time of birth was reported in 23.7 percent of the children.

8. The condition of jaundice was present in 34.7 percent within six days after birth. The condition of cyanosis was reported in 51.4 percent within six days after birth. 48.3 percent of the children were reported as poor nursers. 42.7 percent of the group at one time had convulsions.

9. 10.5 percent of the cases had auditory impairments. 37.9 percent of the cases had visual impairments.

10. The cerebral palsied children in this study had a mean delay of from 4.1 months to 27 months in developing skills such as sitting, standing, walking, and talking, when compared with the Gesell norms.

11. Of the children over six years of age, only 63.6 percent had attended school. The average grade completed by those who had attended school was 4.9 grades. 59.4 percent of the cerebral palsied individuals seven years or older could not read or write.

12. 74.5 percent of the children three years of age and older had a significant speech problem.

13. It was reported that 16.5 percent had had some type of orthopedic surgery. 80.5 percent at one time needed crutches, 37.4 percent at one time needed braces, and 15.7 percent at one time used a wheel chair. Hearing aids were being used by 2.0 percent, and glasses by 14.9 percent. The average annual cost of medical care was $386.33. It was determined that this amount increased 5.7 times per year for the first four years the individual had cerebral palsy.

14. Of the cerebral palsied who were employed: 25.5 percent were engaged in professional, semi-professional, and managerial occupations; 19.1 in skilled and semiskilled occupations; 18.1 in agricultural and kindred occupations; 17.0 in clerical, sales and kindred occupations; 11.7 in service occupations; and 8.5 in unskilled occupations. The salary range for those employed ranged from $50 per year to $6200 per year with a median salary of $1500 per year. The average age for beginning work was 20.9 years.

15. The social classes were represented as follows: 1.9 percent upper, 12.1 percent upper middle, 26.1 percent lower middle, 39.2 percent upper lower, and 20.7 percent lower lower.

16. There was no greater prevalence of divorce or separation among the parents in this group than would be found in the general population of the United States.

Hopkins, T. W., Bice, H. V., and Colton, Kathryn C. *Evaluation and Education of the Cerebral Palsied Child—New Jersey Study*. Washington: Council for Exceptional Children, 1954.

Purpose: To summarize medical, psychological, and educational information about the cerebral palsied.

Subjects: The records were summarized of 1505 active cases known to the Crippled Children's Commission in the State of New Jersey during the period 1936 to 1951. The 1505 cases were divided into the state group (1406 cases), and the A. Harry Moore School group (99 cases).

Procedure: The records of the state group were analyzed according to sex, type of cerebral palsy, etiology, vision, hearing, speech problems, dominance, seizures, hand function, and the like. The records of the 99 pupils attending the A. Harry Moore School were investigated in similar manner. These 99 children, however, were given psychological examinations and more detailed analysis, particularly in the area of intelligence and in planning for education.

Results: This study revealed many important findings, some of which follow:

1. An analysis of records of the state group revealed that: birth injury as a causal factor was present in 38.9 percent of 1105 cases; unquestionable visual defects were noted in 21.4 percent, defective hearing in 5.3 percent, and defective speech in 68 percent of the children studied; 29.2 percent revealed a history of seizures.

2. An analysis of the A. Harry Moore School group revealed the chil-

dren to be one to two years retarded in their age-grade level because of the physical impairments present and the delay on the part of parents or school officials in arranging admission. The median IQ was 79, with 35.4 percent below 70 IQ, and 4.0 percent with a 110 IQ or above. Unquestionable visual defects were noted in 44.5 percent, defective hearing in 16.2 percent, and defective speech in 36.4 percent.

3. Individual psychological findings for almost 1000 children revealed a median IQ of 73.9 for the spastic type, 80.0 for the athetoid type, 53.8 for the ataxic type and 53.9 for the rigidity type. In addition, it was concluded that no one emotion is characteristic of a particular type of cerebral palsy—the similarity of emotion of the group studied to the emotions of normal children was marked.

4. The counseling sessions with parents revealed the parents to believe that much of the behavior of their children was a necessary result of the physical condition. However, some were more aware of similarities in behavior to non-handicapped children. Some embarrassment was evidenced by parents for having a crippled child.

5. Certain aspects of the educational program at the A. Harry Moore School were discussed, including philosophy, program, grouping, teaching methods, handedness, testing, consultation, and guidance conferences.

Comment: This study is a general survey of several factors relating to cerebral palsy. Perhaps the aspect of the study that should be most emphasized is that of the psychological factors, factors in the counseling of parents, and the educational therapy and training program.

EDUCATION

The need for the reference on educational methods in the education of the child with cerebral dysfunctions has not been met. This has been due, among other things, to our inability to draw adequately from the findings of associated disciplines (e.g., experimental psychology, developmental psychology, and neurology), to obtain proper experimental populations, to find expert teacher-researchers, and to acquire adequate funds for such an involved proposal. The following are presented as research-oriented references on teaching methods, theory, and practice with the child who reveals symptoms of cerebral dysfunction. In addition to these references, the reader is referred also to the works of Wolfe and Reid, Hopkins, Bice, and Colton cited above. The reader is also referred to *A Teaching Method for Brain-injured and Hyperactive Children* by Cruickshank, Bentzen, Ratzeberg, and Tannhauser, which is reviewed in Chapter 10 of this Monograph.

Strauss, A. A., and Lehtinen, Laura E. *Psychopathology and Education of the Brain-Injured Child.* Vol 1: *Fundamentals and Treatment of Brain-Injured Children.* New York: Grune and Stratton, 1947.

Purpose: To develop special education methods through clinical observations and psychological experimentation for children with cerebral dysfunction whose primary manifestations are intellectual retardation or abnormal behavioral patterns.

Subjects: Children studied and taught in institutions, private schools, clinics and similar settings by the authors and their colleagues during a period of approximately 20 years.

Procedure: An analysis was made of pertinent background information such as prenatal events, developmental history, psychological and educational evaluations, in an effort to better understand children with cerebral dysfunction. In addition, individual and group experiments were conducted in thinking and in perceptual and behavioral processes related to educational methods.

Results: Some of the results of the clinical and experimental work with these children revealed: (a) certain foreground-background visual perceptual disturbances which hindered the learning process. (b) a characteristic perceptual-motor syndrome concerned with the auditory, tactual and visual fields. (c) perseveration and rigidity in discriminative tasks. (d) uncommon and peculiar responses to common tasks, i.e., sorting objects and placing pictures in a logical sequence. (e) performance on the Strauss and Kephart behavior rating scale was " . . . erratic, uncoordinated, uncontrolled, uninhibited, and socially unaccepted" (p. 86). (f) Catastrophic reaction was prevalent in many children. (g) "With few exceptions there does not exist at this moment a pattern or type of response characteristic and specific for the brain-injured defective child on standardized tests of intelligences, academic achievement, and visuomotor performance" (p. 104). (h) A training program for the endogenous child is not adequate for the exogenous child. (i) Twelve children with syndromes of cerebral dysfunction are the maximum number that can be taught in one class. (j) The efforts of the teacher must be directed at manipulating and controlling the external environment, and helping the child to gain voluntary control. (k) These children may often have an excellent verbal memory. (l) There is a need for specialized techniques and devices for teaching arithmetic, reading, and writing.

Comment: This is an important compendium of theories and techniques for teaching the child with syndromes of cerebral dysfunction. It is based upon clinical and experimental work by the authors and their associates. The teacher and researcher must bear in mind the type of diagnostic framework within which this work has been done in making comparisons with other groups and planning research in this area.

Schonell, F. Eleanor. *Educating Spastic Children: the Education and Guidance of the Cerebral Palsied.* New York: Philosophical Library, 1956.

Purpose: To study causation, incidence, and intelligence levels among cerebral palsied children. To study selected programs for the cerebral palsied and suggest guidelines in planning an educational program.

Subjects: 354 children between the ages of three and 15 years, who were referred by physicians, health agencies, and educational sources in five counties in England.

Procedures: The procedure was to evaluate case history data, examine all children, and obtain evaluations of intelligence through the Stanford-Binet Scale on 340 of the 354 children. Comparisons were also made of levels of intelligence with physical aspects such as incoordination of the hands, speech impairments, multiple handicaps, sensory impairments, and types of cerebral palsy. In addition, every child capable of reading was given a Schonell Graded Work Reading Test to ascertain his level of reading attainment. The economic status of the parents was also ascertained.

Results: An analysis of the results of this study revealed the following:

1. The probable incidence of cerebral palsy was approximately one per 1000.

2. A mean estimated IQ of 67.5 was found with spastics, 67.5 with athetoids, 62.3 with ataxics, and 62.4 with the mixed type of cerebral palsy. The mean estimated IQ tended to decrease as the degree of physical involvement increased.

3. Data from the Schonell Graded Work Reading Test suggested that the normally intelligent and very bright child tended to read at a lower level than his intellectual potential would suggest, because of insufficient opportunity and stimulus to develop his potential.

Suggestions were made concerning educational provisions for children with varying degrees of physical involvement and levels of intelligence. Various aspects of the curriculum at the Carlson House School were discussed. Counseling of parents was explained in this report.

Comment: This particular study was primarily concerned with intelligence level and various aspects of physical involvement. It provides some valuable clues for the educational program for the cerebral palsied, especially in methods and organization. In addition, it provides suggestions concerning parent counseling.

Dunsdon, Marjorie I. *The Educability of Cerebral Palsied Children*. National Foundation for Educational Research in England and Wales, Publication No. 4. London: Newnes Educational Publishing Company, 1952.

Purpose: To study the various aspects of cerebral palsy which affect the education of children with cerebral palsy.

Subjects: 3700 cerebral palsied children ranging in age from newborn through 16. A central registry of 3700 cerebral palsied children was established, from which 1044 were studied. The registry was established from referrals by parents, physicians, schools, hospitals, and social agencies concerned with the cerebral palsied in selected major cities and areas of England.

Procedure: Investigation of case records and psychological evaluations were made with each child.

Results: The pertinent results of this study are as follows:

1. Only one out of every 10 cerebral palsied children could sit by the age of one year, and only four in 10 had accomplished this by the age of two years. In general, the higher the level of intelligence, the earlier the child could sit.

2. Verbal abilities of the children with cerebral palsy are far below the non-handicapped, with 79 percent defective in speech.

3. Visual impairments were found in one-third of the cases; 85 percent of the children had a hearing loss of more than 10 percent, and 18 percent a loss of more than 20 percent.

4. 50 percent of the children studied were considered emotionally unstable.

5. The level of progress in school was related to the child's mental capacity; however, in many instances the contrary was observed.

6. Notations were made concerning the selection of children for classes, parent counseling, and types of educational programs.

Comment: This is a comprehensive study of a large number of cerebral palsied children with emphasis on comparing the intellectual ability with physical involvement as it relates to educational planning. The size of the sample makes this study of particular significance.

Gallagher, J. J. *The Tutoring of Brain-Injured Mentally Retarded Children: An Experimental Study.* Springfield, Illinois: Charles C Thomas, 1960.

Purpose: To determine the effects of one hour a day of individual tutoring sessions with brain injured, mentally retarded children.

Subjects: 42 brain injured, mentally retarded children residing in Dixon State School, Dixon, Illinois. The children ranged from 7-4 to 13-9, with Stanford-Binet IQs from 33 to 63. They were divided at the beginning of the experiment into two groups according to mental development.

Procedure: Each child was subjected to a series of tests prior to the beginning of the experiment to determine his verbal intelligence, non-verbal intelligence, perceptual skills, language development, quantitative conceptualization, and perceptual memory. Soon after the study was begun, personality ratings were also obtained on each child. These same tests were readministered after nine months, 21 months, and 33 months.

The children were divided into two groups. One group of 21 members was given individual tutoring for two years and no tutoring in the third year. The other 22 children received no tutoring for two years and were given tutoring during the third year.

No rigid plan was followed by the four tutors in this particular experiment. The readiness of the particular child and his level of ability were considered, and the teacher's own techniques were elicited. Essentially, the tutoring was in the area of instruction in perceptual skills, language skills, memory skills, conceptualization and reasoning, and quantitative conceptualization. One year of tutoring consisted of approximately one hour per day of individual tutoring for approximately 120 to 150 days.

Results: It was discovered that improvement in the intellectual functioning of the brain-injured mentally retarded child was obtained through the methods of this study. It was also indicated that when the tutoring methods were eliminated from the life of the child, the tendency was to regress regardless of the treatment group. Children who revealed unusual growth in one area of development revealed similar growth in other areas of development. It was rare to find a child who showed unusual improvement in just one area and not in another. It

234

was also found that the younger the child, the greater the beneficial improvements in the tutoring program.

Comment: This study should be considered a contribution to educational practice. The results indicated that, for many brain-injured mentally retarded children, an individual approach is productive of intellectual progress. It pointed out that, through individual tutoring by a trained person in the proper setting, accelerated mental development can be attained by many of these children.

Psychology

The role of the psychologist in evaluating the intelligence, personality, aptitudes, interests, and achievements of the child with cerebral dysfunction is invaluable. The importance of the attitude of the child and his parents in the treatment and education has been emphasized by many authorities. The salient nature of psychological factors as they affect the teaching process has been recognized. The researcher is referred to the significant studies which follow. Attention is again directed to the works previously cited.

Cruickshank, W. M., Bice, H. V., and Wallen, N. E. *Perception and Cerebral Palsy: A Study in Figure-Background Relationship.* Syracuse: Syracuse University Press, 1957.

Purpose: To compare the performance of non-mentally retarded cerebral palsied children with that of non-mentally retarded, physically normal children, on certain visual and tactual tasks which are designed to investigate figure-ground aspects of perception.

Subjects: 325 cerebral palsied children, ages six to 16 years. Of these, 211 were diagnosed as spastic and 114 as athetoid. These children were compared with 110 non-mentally retarded, physically normal children. The cerebral palsied had at least one usable upper extremity, intelligible speech, and a minimum mental age of six years. The physically normal children were of the same age and level of mental functioning as the cerebral palsied group.

Procedure: Both the cerebral palsied and the physically normal group were administered the following tests: Binet Vocabulary, Tactual Motor Test, Disc I Test, Syracuse Visual Figure-Grounds Test, Marble Board Test, Disc II Test, and Maze Test.

Results: The cerebral palsied group appeared to perform at a lower

235

level than the non-physically handicapped group, and the spastic group performed at a lower level than the athetoid group. It was further discovered that although the three diagnostic groups (athetoid, spastic and physically normal) differed considerably in the level of performance on the tests, within each of the diagnostic groups there was little evidence of overall general perceptual impairment such as might have been expected from some reports in the professional literature. A tendency for less drawing of background with increasing chronological age was noted in the cerebral palsied group. This observation was not noted in the physically normal group. Low relationships were discovered between the various perceptual tests used in this particular study.

Comment: This is a most significant investigation of the performance of cerebral palsied persons on the perceptual tests mentioned. Despite the weaknesses of sampling, this study should be regarded as the most reliable study currently available. Some theoretical questions as to figure-ground relationship, perceptual ability versus inability of the cerebral palsied persons to organize on a given task have been posited. This particular study points out the importance of considering other variables than the perceptual ones in understanding the learning problems of the cerebral palsied. These data are of particular importance to the educational psychologist as he relates to the teacher in terms of learning problems of cerebral palsied children.

Taylor, Edith M. *Psychological Appraisal of Children With Cerebral Defects.* Cambridge: Harvard University Press, 1959.

Purpose: To bring together data concerning the intelligence of different types of cerebral palsied persons and the techniques for evaluating the intelligence of persons with cerebral dysfunctions.

Subjects: A large number of children with sensory-motor and neurological impairments who had been examined by Dr. Taylor and her associates at Children's Hospital in Boston since 1943.

Procedure: A review was made of approximately 1800 children seen at Children's Hospital. In addition, as a result of follow-up inquiries, 615 children were re-examined for re-evaluation purposes during the years 1951-1955. Pertinent developmental and medical information were related to intellectual functioning through the analysis of case history data and performance on verbal and nonverbal items.

Results: The results of this study can be grouped into two broad areas:

236

1. Selected case portraits revealed the multiplicity of psychological problems which might be presented to a psychological examiner by the child with cerebral dysfunctions.

2. The techniques for evaluating children with cerebral dysfunctions were explained through the use of blocks, pictures, selected paper and pencil tests, fitting and assembly of objects, following of directions, matching, sorting, grouping, design problems, learning and memory exercises, judgment and reasoning problems, common knowledge and comprehension questions, and selected academic content examinations.

Comment: This is a useful compendium for the psychologist on the evaluation of intelligence of the person with cerebral dysfunctions. It is an invaluable manual for the educational psychologist concerned with this group of children.

TEACHERS

The most important person in the educational setting, other than the child, is the teacher. The following study is related to what the teachers of cerebral palsied children think and something of their training.

Geer, W. C., and Wolfe, W. G. *Education of the Cerebral Palsied in the South.* Atlanta: Southern Regional Education Board, 1960.

Purpose: To estimate the educational needs of children with cerebral palsy in 15 southern states, and to determine the levels of training professional persons have had who are concerned with the cerebral palsied in both educational and therapeutic settings in the South.

Subjects: School administrators in the South were asked to submit names of physical therapists, teachers, occupational therapists, and speech therapists working with the cerebral palsied. The data in this study were obtained from 215 teachers, 59 physical therapists, 30 occupational therapists, and 42 speech therapists. In addition, data were obtained from four schools of occupational therapy, seven schools of physical therapy, and 20 schools training speech therapists.

Procedure: Personal interviews were obtained with all the 215 teachers. Data from the physical therapists, occupational therapists, and speech therapists, as well as from teaching institutions, were obtained through questionnaires.

237

Results: The pertinent findings of this study are as follows:

1. 37.2 percent of the teachers of the cerebral palsied were in ungraded or multi-graded special classes, 15.8 percent in hospital settings, and 14.0 percent in special day schools for children with various types of handicapping conditions.

2. 47.5 percent of the teachers possessed a bachelor's degree, and 40.9 percent held a master's degree. Of the 215 teachers interviewed, only 22.8 percent had majored in special education during their degree programs.

3. A section on teacher's competencies was included.

4. Survey of Exceptional Children, Speech Correction, Methods and Materials for Teaching Exceptional Children, Tests and Measurements, Methods and Materials for Teaching the Mentally Retarded, and Cerebral Palsy Workshops were the courses most frequently named as the most valuable to the teacher.

5. The majority of the teachers interviewed listed the following types of courses as needed: Methods and Materials, Practice Teaching with the Cerebral Palsied, Psychological Testing of the Cerebral Palsied, and Parent Counseling.

6. The characteristics and traits of teachers listed as most important for work with the cerebral palsied were: patience, understanding of limits imposed by cerebral palsy, empathy, sense of humor, objective attitude, strictness but not rigidity, acceptance, emotional stability, interest in the individual child, and flexibility.

7. 48.7 percent of the teachers reported they had been adequately trained to interpret medical, social, and psychological records.

8. The major problems presented by the children, as listed by the majority of the teachers, were speech difficulty and lack of hand, arm, and eye coordination.

9. One-fourth or more of the teachers interviewed indicated that the educational program for the children could be improved if better facilities were provided, special teaching materials and equipment were available, and proper screening programs for admission were established.

10. In addition, important information was obtained concerning the formal preparation of physical therapists, occupational therapists, and speech therapists for the understanding of cerebral palsy.

Comment: This is a useful study of the competencies of teachers of the cerebral palsied, their work situation and training programs. This research should be of value to colleges and universities in planning training programs for teachers in this particular area.

Since the enactment of the first civilian vocational rehabilitation act in 1920, the importance of the school in the vocational rehabilitation process has been evolving. The educational planners in our schools are concerned with providing the proper kinds of programs for the exceptional child. This implies several curricula designed both for the pre-vocational and the vocational level. The following are presented as examples of studies of individuals with cerebral dysfunction in gainful employment.

Brinn, Carolyn, and Smith, Esther Elder. *Opportunities Limited—a Study of Employment Problems of the Cerebral Palsied and Epileptic.* San Francisco: California Society for Crippled Children, 1951.

Purpose: To study the occupational and placement potentials of 100 epileptic and 100 cerebral palsied persons in Los Angeles, California.

Subjects: 100 cerebral palsied and 100 epileptic individuals who were referred from the Bureau of Vocational Rehabilitation, Veterans Administration, or the Crippled Children's Society of Los Angeles County.

Procedure: The records of 100 cerebral palsied and 100 epileptic persons were studied and evaluated at various levels in the rehabilitation process. All of these individuals were currently receiving rehabilitation services.

Results: Some of the results of this study follow:

1. 57 percent of the cerebral palsied had been disabled since birth, whereas 47 percent of the epileptics developed convulsions between ages 16 and 30 years.

2. Of the 100 cerebral palsied studied, 71 were unmarried; and of the 100 epileptics studied, 47 were unmarried.

3. 41 percent of the cerebral palsied were hemiplegic, 33 percent were quadriplegic, and 17 percent paraplegic.

4. The employed cerebral palsy cases were known to a rehabilitation agency from one to 63 months, with an average of 20.9 months. The employed epileptics were known to a rehabilitation agency from two to 46 months, with an average of 16.6 months. The average cost for each case for rehabilitation, exclusive of administration costs, was $132.01 for the cerebral palsied and $150.33 for the epileptics. Vocational training courses were provided for 26 percent of the cerebral palsied and 13 percent of the epileptics.

Comment: The importance of the team approach and the training of vocational counselors was emphasized. This study pointed out the need for early vocational guidance and training for these two groups of individuals in order for them to be more successful in an area of employment, whether it be in a competitive situation or a sheltered or home employment situation.

Glick, Selma J. *Vocational, Educational, and Recreational Needs of the Cerebral Palsied Adult.* New York: United Cerebral Palsy of New York City, Inc., 1953.

Purpose: To learn the vocational, educational, and recreational needs of the adult cerebral palsied.

Subjects: 200 ambulatory cerebral palsied adults between the ages of 18 and 45 years who had applied to United Cerebral Palsy of New York City or the Federation for the Handicapped for help with their vocational problems.

Procedure: The procedure was to interview each of the cerebral palsied in his home through the method of a formal questionnaire. In addition, 50 of these adults were seen on several occasions by research workers for the purposes of psychological investigation and obtaining complete social history and other pertinent information such as data on emotional stability and parental attitudes.

Results: Some of the pertinent findings were as follows:

1. 15 percent were mildly disabled, 25 percent were moderately disabled, and 60 percent were seriously disabled.

2. Almost three-fourths of the cases studied were found to be emotionally maladjusted by factors such as unfavorable parental attitudes, lack of motivation to achieve, and the presence of excessive fears.

3. The average age at which formal education was started was 7.5 years, with 23 percent completing grades two to seven. Twenty percent were elementary school graduates, seven percent were graduates of technical high schools, 34 percent were high school graduates, and 16 percent were college graduates. Of the college graduates, 10 had master's degrees, two had degrees in law, and two had doctoral degrees. It was further noted that 24 of the 33 college graduates majored in fields in which they would find it difficult to function as a result of their physical limitations. Of the 33 college graduates, only nine were employed.

4. It was found that 22 percent of the moderately disabled and 24 percent of the severely disabled group were employed, whereas only seven

percent of the mildly disabled group were employed. It was felt that persons in the mildly disabled group were unable to hold a job because of their inability to get along with fellow employees.

5. It was found that only 25 percent of the group were members of some social club or group, and that only 30 percent of those interviewed had a hobby which occupied a good portion of their time.

Comment: This study pointed out the importance of total planning for the vocational rehabilitation of the individual with cerebral dysfunction. The important problems in his work adjustment are concerned with more than just training on the job, as personality factors and what the individual can do with leisure time are very important and must be planned for in the rehabilitation process.

Curtis, Linn W. *Vocational Placement of the Cerebral Palsied: A Brief Experience in Dealing with the Vocational Problems of 200 Cerebral Palsied Adults.* New York: United Cerebral Palsy of New York City, Inc., 1953.

Purpose: To summarize the findings on 56 cerebral palsied adults who were placed in jobs during the period July 1951 through April 1953.

Subjects: 56 cerebral palsied adults placed in employment by the Vocational Rehabilitation Service of United Cerebral Palsy Associations of New York City during the period of July 1951 through April 1953.

Procedure: The records of the 56 subjects were studied to find out the length of training for a position, type of position entered, cost of rehabilitation, weekly salary, and other significant information relating to vocational rehabilitation.

Results: It took 7.9 months of intensive service from the Vocational Rehabilitation Agency to place these individuals in a successful position. Thirty-four clients were placed in semi-skilled jobs, 11 in skilled work, and 11 in unskilled work. The lowest salary earned was $25 per week for an individual placed in a part-time job; $44 was the average weekly salary for those individuals in a full-time job, with the highest salary being $75 per week. The average age was 28.3 years, with a range of 18 to 48 years. Additional information was included as to degree of involvement, follow-up on those who had been retained on the job or dropped from the job, and those who had received promotions.

Comment: This is one of the early studies of vocational rehabilitation of the cerebral palsied by an agency specializing in the placement of such clients. This study pointed out the need for such agencies and the cooperation of many professionals in helping the cerebral palsied individual, regardless of his degree of involvement, to attain an adequate vocational adjustment.

SUMMARY

It must be pointed out that a very large number of children reveal syndromes of cerebral dysfunction. The exact number is difficult to estimate. The cerebral palsied constitute only a small portion of the total group. The term *cerebral dysfunction* includes all neuromuscular disorders resulting from brain damage, and many other associated difficulties, such as disorders in language and thought processes, learning disabilities, and certain personality deviations.

Research on the education of the child with cerebral dysfunctions must take into account the professional contributions of the educator (both special and general), psychologist, social worker, and physician. It is mandatory that the findings of the experimental psychologist, neuropsychiatrist, neuropharmacologist, clinical psychologist, neurologist, internist, and others be communicated to the members of the teaching profession who are responsible for their application through instruction, and that they be followed by the necessary application of procedures and experimentation in the school setting.

It must be pointed out that the non-educational specialists mentioned above, and others, should not be expected to deliver pat answers to the educator. The teacher is concerned with the behavior set patterns of a given child, and these behavior set patterns must be modified or expanded, depending upon the objectives of the educational institution. The educator is interested in devising techniques and modifying existing techniques for the education of children with cerebral dysfunctioning. The programming of instruction, therefore, must consider course content and the techniques for teaching the prescribed content to the child who reveals syndromes of cerebral dysfunction. The talents of the non-educational specialists should be used to the extent that they can contribute to the educational process. Research from the behavioral sciences must be finally checked out in the teaching-learning environment. The one must follow the other. However, in our present state of professional development, what a teacher does in the classroom often has very little reference to research methodology.

Several publications have been cited as examples of programs of research in education and training. Much further research is needed on educational techniques, devices (i. e., teaching machines), and environments (i. e., room decorations, cubicles, sound levels). The effect of teacher personality should be studied. What influence does the teacher's personality patterns have on the learning of a given child in a specific instance? What are the conditions for optimal teaching of a child with cerebral dysfunctions in a regular classroom? What are the possible vocational choices of these children, and what implications does this have for curricula? The role of the parents and the importance of parent conferences and/or organizations for this group should be ascertained.

The above recommendations imply the importance of appropriate facilities and faculties of universities, school systems, institutions, and private agencies cooperating in research. In final analysis, the paramount role of the education specialist in research must be observed.

8

Children with Orthopedic Handicaps and Special Health Problems

Laura J. Jordan

Children with orthopedic handicaps or special health problems such as diabetes or heart disease, especially those whose mobility is curtailed by the handicap, are easily recognized as an exceptional group for whom the schools must make special provision if they are to receive the education best suited to their needs. Traditionally, provision for them has taken the direction of the establishment of special classrooms with easy access, increased space for maneuvering wheel chairs or braces, and such aids to locomotion as sturdy handrails. These classrooms have amply justified their existence through allowing children who would otherwise be isolated in their homes or in hospital schools to participate in at least some of the contacts and activities of the normal school world.

In reviewing the research related to the education of these exceptional children, it is striking how few studies relate directly to their learning characteristics or to the best ways to accommodate their needs through the use of special teaching methods. Research has instead been directed primarily toward study of the incidence and causes of crippling, or toward the psychology of its after-effects. Why should there not be more research truly educational in nature, when special programs for this group have for so long a time been an accepted and respected part of the educational scene?

The most probable answer is hinted in the conclusion drawn almost universally from studies of the orthopedically handicapped—namely, the extreme educational heterogeneity of the children of this classification, a heterogeneity which discourages generalization. Furthermore, physical handicap which does not extend to damage to the visual or auditory channel of learning is not an essentially educational handicap. There is little reason to expect a close relationship between a child's intelligence or learning characteristics and some physical condition which affects his mobility, dexterity, or vigor, unless that condition includes neurological damage. Recent research in this area has tended to focus on cerebral palsy, a type of crippling which unquestionably promotes educational problems. These studies are treated in another chapter of this monograph. Where the palsied are included in the research presented here, it is only as a subgroup within a large sample. When the cerebral palsied are subtracted from their ranks, there is little reason to expect the physically handicapped to differ consistently or extensively from the non-handicapped in the way or in the amount that they will learn, given the opportunity to learn.

Many studies have tried to measure the intelligence of the physically handicapped as a group, or the effect on intelligence of a specific disease such as poliomyelitis. Again, the educational usefulness of a large part of this research is limited. Many of the studies were made with tests now obsolete. Frequently no allowance was made for a possible limitation of experiential background in the handicapped, or for the effect of lessened dexterity on test performance. Even more rarely has there been an attempt to measure the degree of such experiential or physical limitation. Finally, the ever-present heterogeneity of the research samples attenuates the usefulness of the findings. When the pupils enrolled in a single class may range in ability from retardation to superiority, knowing a hypothetical average IQ score does little to help the teacher's planning.

There are concomitants of crippling conditions which do have educational significance. Restriction of mobility may mean restriction of background experiences, or prolonged hospitalization may adversely affect language development. However, not all orthopedically handicapped or ill children experience these restrictions, nor do they always occur at the crucial periods in the child's development. The heterogeneity of the group seriously limits the predictability of educational disruption from such causes. Also, there are strong indications, as in the

245

case of children hospitalized or placed in institutional settings at early ages, that such after-effects as disruption of language or learning difficulties may be symptoms of problems primarily psychological in nature, while their educational importance is secondary.

The educational management of the physically handicapped requires school plant changes and alterations in physical arrangements, rather than special teaching techniques. The need for a special program will exist as long as many public school classrooms are not physically equipped to accommodate the handicapped. It is, however, neither necessary nor reasonable to try to justify continuance of the program by a search for ways in which the educational characteristics of these children set them apart from the average.

The studies presented here were chosen on the basis of their design, their pertinence to educational problems, and the generalizability of their conclusions. They are grouped under the following headings:

1. Studies of incidence.
2. Psycho-social characteristics.
3. Special programs for children with orthopedic and health handicaps.

The categories are necessarily broad, as a number of researchers in this field have attempted to investigate a broad spectrum of problems in a single study.

STUDIES OF INCIDENCE

The essential characteristics of an adequate study of incidence are a sufficiently large and representative sample and a clear definition for all referral sources of the kinds of disabilities for which the search is being made. The studies reported here, while very different in nature, meet both of these criteria.

Mackie, Romaine P. Crippled Children in American Education. *Teachers College, Columbia University Contributions to Education*, No. 913, 1945.

Purpose: To obtain data on certain characteristics of crippled children and on special educational provisions for the crippled throughout the United States.

Subjects: A sample of 16,696 crippled children who were reported from 40 states of continental United States and from Hawaii.

Method: Questionnaires were sent to directors of educational programs for the crippled or for children with special types of handicaps within this broad category, asking information concerning the children enrolled. These programs included day and residential classes, special schools, and hospital and homebound programs. The data from the completed questionnaires were compiled and reported.

Results: The term "crippled children" designates a group of children extremely heterogeneous as to type and degree of physical disability. The following characteristics of this group were reported: (a) Infections, cerebral palsy, cardiac, and undiagnosed conditions were the categories most often reported. (b) The cerebral palsied were rated the most difficult to care for and the most likely to show secondary handicaps. (c) The children tended to be over-age in the age-grade data. (d) The major program modification in certain disabilities, as cardiac and tubercular conditions, was a shortening of the daily program, with provision for extra rest. (e) Intelligence test data suggested a median tested IQ for the crippled lower than that of normal children. (f) As the majority of the programs did not extend beyond the ninth grade, only seven percent of the children were enrolled in secondary programs.

The following characteristics of the programs were reported: (a) The median classroom enrollment was approximately 22 children. (b) There was little vocational guidance reported for the crippled, possibly as a correlate of the small number of secondary programs. (c) Day schools were found to emphasize educational provisions, while other programs emphasized health care.

Comment: Although this study was made approximately 20 years ago, no comparably comprehensive research has superceded it. While medical advances can be expected to have altered the incidence with which certain conditions appear, and there have been changes in psychological testing, many of the characteristics noted would still be found in present-day programs. The data suggest a continuing need for extreme flexibility in educational planning for crippled children, and the fallacy of regarding them as a group homogeneous as to educational needs.

Barker, Louise S., Schoggen, Maxine, Schoggen, P., and Barker, R. G. The Frequency of Physical Disability in Children: A Comparison of Three Sources of Information. *Child Development,* 1952, 23, 215-226.

Problem: To compare laymen, teachers, and physicians on their adequacy as sources of information on the incidence of physical disability in children, and to take a census of physically disabled children in a rural county without special education services.

Subjects: Interviewed for this study were 133, or 90 percent, of the county's teachers, the six county physicians, and 425 laymen from women's study club groups.

Method: A physically disabled child was defined as any individual under the age of 21 "who is generally perceived in his cultural group to have a physique that prevents him from participating in important activities on terms of equality with normal individuals of his own age" (p. 217). A local publicity campaign preceded interviews of teachers, physicians, and laymen, to inquire as to how many physically disabled children they could identify. Both group and individual interviews were used. Disability categories were specified and interviewees were questioned on each, to aid recall and to insure consistent interpretation of "physical disability."

Results: Interviewees reported 226 children as disabled, or 5.9 percent of the children of the area. More boys than girls were perceived as handicapped, and more school-age than non school-age children. Of those of school age, 90 percent attended regular schools. The few children attending special schools were in residential schools outside of the county. Teachers reported 76.5 percent of the total number of children identified as disabled; 41.5 percent of the teachers' nominees were not named by the other two groups. Laymen reported 48.2 percent, 13.4 percent exclusively. Physicians reported 17.7 percent, 7.5 percent exclusively. Types of disability in order of descending frequency were: speech defects, visual impairment, orthopedic disabilities, central nervous system disorders, cardiac defects, auditory impairment, anomalies of physique, diabetes, and miscellaneous conditions. It was concluded that contact with a large proportion of the children, rather than special training, was a major factor in awareness of disability cases.

Comment: Although the teachers proved relatively effective in naming disabled children, that they missed one in four and that they named predominantly school-age children argues for the employment of as many referral sources as possible. This study was concerned with "perceived" disability, which put a premium on the visibility of the defect. The findings emphasize the importance of school-community cooperation for intelligent educational planning for all of the physically disabled.

STUDIES OF PSYCHO-SOCIAL CHARACTERISTICS

This area is a difficult one in which to work, both because of the lack of adequate measuring instruments standardized on this atypical population, and because of the difficulty in distinguishing correlation from causation where the number of uncontrolled variables is necessarily large. The following studies demonstrate various types of investigation and illustrate some of the factors which force extreme caution in the generalization of results.

Fernald, Mabel R. and Arlitt, Ada H. A Psychological Study of a Group of Crippled Children of Various Types: A Preliminary Report. *School and Society,* 1925, 21, 449-452.

Purpose: To discover the reasons why crippled children tend to earn somewhat inferior scores on intelligence tests. Three sets of test-influencing factors were outlined for study: (a) factors other than intelligence (e.g. lack of schooling); (b) factors resulting directly from the type, age at onset, or severity of the disease; and (c) factors which would have predisposed the children to inferior scores had they never been crippled.

Subjects: 194 children with orthopedic problems examined for admission to a school for the crippled. Many types of handicapping conditions were represented, poliomyelitis being the most common diagnosis. Application for admission to a special school for the crippled was seen as an indication that the children were probably handicapped to a relatively serious degree and probably came from homes predominantly of the lower socio-economic level. These factors limit generalization to the entire population of children with orthopedic handicaps.

Method: Data were gathered from medical records, school records, and administration of the Stanford Revision of the Binet-Simon Scale, and subjected to analysis.

Results: The mean tested intelligence of the group was IQ 82.35, with a range from IQ 30 to IQ 138. When the sample was divided according to diagnosis of disability, the only outstanding variations from the total group mean were found in the significantly lower scores of the small groups which had suffered from spastic birth paralysis (mean IQ 69.11) or central nervous system involvement (mean IQ 75.93). There was no clear evidence of a relationship between intelligence and age at onset of the crippling condition, and only a slight trend toward a decrease in level of tested intelligence with increasing degree of handicap. When intelligence tests were given to siblings of a portion of the sample, there was a trend toward lower scores for the handicapped children than for the non-handicapped children from the same families, although the

249

mean score of the non-handicapped was a rather low IQ of 89.2. This relatively low mean intelligence supported the contention that the study sample may not have come from home environments representative of those of crippled children in general.

Comment: This early study served for many years as the reference point for further research on the intelligence of crippled children. The test scores are not directly comparable to those obtained on studies using present-day measuring instruments, but the comparisons between subgroups, all tested on the same instrument, retain their interest. A large share of this study's present significance lies in its early delineation of variables other than level of cognitive functioning which may, in the case of the handicapped, be reflected in the intelligence test score.

Donofrio, A. F. A Study of Crippled Children in an Orthopedic Hospital School. *Exceptional Children,* 1951, 18, 33-38.

Problem: To compare the physically handicapped with the nonhandicapped in intelligence, in school achievement, and in emotional adjustment; to investigate whether the type, severity, or duration of a crippling condition, or length of hospitalization, affects these factors.

Subjects: 270 physically handicapped children, age five through 16 years, attending an orthopedic hospital school. In the study, 32 different kinds of diseases or crippling conditions were represented, poliomyelitis being the most common diagnosis. The children were classified into five subgroups according to the degree of severity of the handicap.

Method: The Stanford-Binet or the Kuhlmann-Anderson Test was administered to assess intelligence, and the Brown Personality Inventory and a teacher rating scale were completed on each child. Information was gathered on grade placement and on academic achievement.

Results: The mean IQ of the group as a whole was within the normal range. When intelligence was correlated with diagnosis of the crippling condition, children with central nervous system involvement earned the lowest scores. Correlations of IQ with chronological age, duration of crippling condition, or length of hospitalization were low.

Educational achievement showed no relation to type or duration of disability, or to length of hospitalization. On the average, the children were found to be working up to their estimated capacity.

Emotional adjustment of the group appeared to fall within a normal range, with a trend toward decrease of maladjustment with increasing chronological age and some indication that the less severely handicapped showed less maladjustment.

Comment: This study emphasizes the heterogeneity of the children classified simply as "crippled." This and similar research reporting low correlations between the physical characteristics and the educational characteristics of these children suggest relatively low interaction between the two areas.

Copellman, Fay S. Follow-up of One Hundred Children with Poliomyelitis. *The Family,* 1944, 25, 289-297.

Purpose: To study school and home problems that arose subsequent to hospital discharge of children who had contracted poliomyelitis, and to study the role of the medical social worker in the solution of such problems.

Subjects: 100 children, representing all of the children recovering from epidemic polio who were seen between two specified dates at a clinic to which all such cases were referred upon hospital discharge. The children ranged in age from one to 15 years. None of them had suffered paralysis as a result of the disease.

Method: Coordinated medical, therapeutic, and educational recommendations were made for each child by a team conference technique in which case studies were reviewed jointly by medical and social workers, an occupational therapist, a psychologist, and a psychiatrist. At two months after the initial contact, and again at six months, visits were made to each child's school and home. Parents and school personnel were interviewed as to problems involving the child. Where problems were reported, help was offered.

Results: In 38 percent of the cases, there were problems serious enough to be discussed with the social worker. They commonly included a statement that the child was difficult to manage. While these problems could be interpreted as sequelae of the disease, evidence is presented to suggest that illness can also intensify already existing problems, or precipitate a crisis whose basis lies elsewhere. Problems regarded as the direct result of the illness or of its accompanying emotional trauma commonly centered around increased irritability in the child. The gradual decrease in severity of the symptoms suggests that convalescence may extend over a period of months after the child appears to have recovered from all clinical symptoms. It is suggested that the social worker may

251

make an important contribution by helping the home and school determine the true basis of problems occurring after a serious illness.

Comment: These findings urge caution in assuming behavior problems to be the result of an illness because they follow an illness. When such an assumption masks underlying irritants only aggravated by the illness, the mis-diagnosis can delay effective treatment. Other diseases to which behavioral concomitants are often ascribed should be subjected to similar review. The unexpected length of the convalescent period urges the sensitization of regular class teachers to the possibility that a child who looks well may still be suffering the after-effects of an illness.

Meyer, Edith, Psychological Considerations in a Group of Children with Poliomyelitis. *Journal of Pediatrics,* 1947, 31, 34-40.

Purpose: To investigate certain disturbances in behavior and in mental functioning believed to persist after apparent recovery from poliomyelitis.

Subjects: 52 children ranging in age from 18 months to 14 years, all recovering from poliomyelitis. The cases were a largely unselected group of hospital admissions during a polio epidemic. Children obviously retarded or having a history of previous nervous disorder were not included in the study.

Method: The children were followed, by observations and by home and school interviews, for three years after onset of the disease. The Gesell Developmental Schedule, Stanford-Binet, Wechsler-Bellevue, and Merrill-Palmer tests, along with tests of specific functions, supplemented the interviews. Illustrative case reports are offered.

Results: Children discharged as recovered from motor effects of the disease commonly showed behavioral problems centered around irritability and restlessness. These were accompanied by difficulties on tasks requiring form discrimination and comprehension, although the level of tested intelligence was normal. Of those with more lasting and serious motor impairment, the children under five years of age experienced a lag in speech development, and difficulty in the comprehension of form and object relationships. Those children five years of age and older had difficulty in sustaining attention, in comprehension of forms, and in concentration. Both behavioral and psychological problems tended to diminish with the passage of time.

Comment: This study urges recognition of the possibly extended length of the readjustment period following disappearance of the clinical symptoms of illness, and the importance of a qualitative assessment of the nature, as well as the level, of a child's intellectual functioning during that period.

Reed, M. K. The Intelligence, Social Maturity, Personal Adjustment, Physical Development, and Parent-Child Relationships of Children with Congenital Heart Disease. Unpublished doctoral dissertation, University of Minnesota, 1959.

Purpose: To examine certain aspects of the intelligence, social maturity, adjustment, and physical development of children with congenital heart disease, and the attitudes of their mothers.

Subjects: 23 boys and 27 girls, age three to eight years, randomly selected from the out-patients of a cardiac clinic. Each child was matched with a non-disabled control on age, sex, socio-economic status, and number of siblings. Control subjects were obtained from the enrollment of day nurseries.

Method: Each cardiac subject was given standardized intelligence, manipulative, and social maturity tests, and a physical examination. The medical history was taken, and a clinical judgment made of personal adjustment. A physician rated each child as to the severity of the cardiac condition. Mothers of all subjects completed the Parent Attitude Research Instrument and supplied opinions of their children's adjustment.

Results: Among the clinical subjects, neither intelligence quotient nor social maturity was significantly related to severity of cardiac disability. The cardiac children were significantly slower and more variable than their paired controls on tests of manipulative skill. The clinical impressions of adjustment suggested that the cardiac group showed greater social anxiety and social responsiveness, while the control children appeared both more relaxed and less responsive to social interaction cues. Responses to the Parent Attitude Response Inventory showed no significant differences between mothers of boys of the clinical and control groups, while mothers of clinical girls did score significantly higher on scales labeled "Intrusiveness" and "Fostering Dependency." Control children tended to be taller and heavier, the difference reaching significance only for the girls.

Comment: The findings indicate that large differences from the norms in the areas tested need not be expected among young cardiac patients.

253

That the differences encountered were differences of physique and speed in manipulative tasks has significance for setting expectations in the teaching of such primary-grade skills as writing.

Force, D. G. Jr. Social Status of Physically Handicapped Children. *Exceptional Children,* 1956, 23, 104-107, 132-133.

Purpose: To compare the social position of physically handicapped children with that of their non-handicapped classmates in integrated elementary school classes.

Subjects: 63 physically handicapped and 361 non-handicapped children in 14 elementary classes from the first through the sixth grades. The handicapped included small numbers of children with defective vision and hearing, and six with cerebral palsy. All of the handicapped were of normal intelligence.

Method: A near-sociometric instrument was administered to determine the children's choices of friends, playmates, and workmates, the three choices in each of the 14 classes making a total of 42 comparisons. Educational and medical records furnished information on the handicapped group, and the teachers of all subjects were asked to indicate outstanding behavioral traits of the children.

Results: The physically handicapped were chosen significantly less often on 15 of the 42 comparisons. They were significantly under-chosen as friends in four classes, as playmates in seven classes, and as workmates in seven classes. In three classes they were significantly under-chosen in all three of the categories. There was a tendency for both handicapped and non-handicapped children to choose within their own groups, indicating a low degree of social integration. Those among the handicapped who were chosen by the non-handicapped tended to be those with disabilities less obvious to their peers. The cerebral palsied were chosen least often and this lack of preferment was judged related to the obvious nature of the handicap. It was concluded that physical handicap readily perceptible to other children can significantly handicap a child socially.

Comment: The low degree of social integration reported here is the general finding of studies of the handicapped in regular classes, regardless of the type of handicap under investigation. Several other related questions are raised pertaining to why this should be so, whether the attitudes can be changed, and whether the social isolation of many of these children outweighs for them the apparent advantages of regular class stimulation.

The three studies reviewed here were conducted in the New York public school system and are broad-spectrum investigations. While there are many similarities, each study makes its own point, and each has something different to contribute to the knowledge of special program characteristics or to methodology. Applicability of many of the findings extends far beyond the system in which the studies were made, as the large number of handicapped children enrolled in those schools allows for greater generalization than would be true of self-studies in almost any other city.

> McCormick, H. W. (Director). The Committee for the Study of the Care and Education of Physically Handicapped Children in the Public Schools of the City of New York. *Orthopedically Handicapped Children*. New York City: Board of Education, 1941.

Purpose: To study a public school program for the orthopedically handicapped.

Subjects: Children enrolled in the 111 classes for the orthopedically handicapped in the city's elementary public schools. Chronological age range was from six to 20 years. Intelligence was described as ranging widely and negatively skewed.

Method: School records were searched, questionnaires were completed by teachers of the orthopedically handicapped, and classroom programs were observed. The information gathered was analyzed, and extensive recommendations for the improvement of the program were formulated.

Results: It was concluded that the special classes were educationally inferior to regular classes in meeting the needs of their respective pupils. This appeared to be the result of the extremely wide age and grade spans in the classes for the handicapped, the heterogeneous ability groupings, and the resultant skeletonizing of the curriculum to little more than the academic fundamentals. Many special facilities and program modifications highly desirable for the handicapped were lacking. A large proportion of the special class enrollees were judged able to function in the regular grades, while others who should have been included in the classes remained in the homebound program. Few of the handicapped received vocational counseling or were enrolled in the available vocational courses taught in the system's schools.

Comment: This work is representative of self-study by a school system of an existing program. Only by the study of specific, on-going programs can educators establish such factors as the response of the children to special programs, the usefulness of special provisions, and ways to improve the offerings.

Wrightstone, J. W., Justman J., and Moskowitz, Sue. Studies of Children with Physical Handicaps: I. The Child with Cardiac Limitations. *Bureau of Educational Research, Publication,* No. 32. New York City Board of Education, 1953.

Purpose: To study certain intellectual and behavioral characteristics of children with cardiac limitations enrolled in the special classes of a large public school system, and the effectiveness of such classes in meeting the needs of these children.

Subjects: Children at the sixth through eighth grade levels enrolled in special classes for the physically handicapped as having cardiac limitations. From 74 to 301 children participated in each phase of the study; the subgroups for the various phases were not mutually exclusive.

Method: Intensive medical examinations were given 74 eighth-grade children to determine the nature and extent of cardiac damage. Ability and achievement were estimated through group tests administered to 301 children enrolled as cardiac cases in the special classes of 65 schools in the system. Intensive psychological studies were made of 80 children from the eighth grade, and the social work department interviewed the parents of 76 of the latter group, all but two of whom had received physical examinations. To establish classroom practices, 38 classes representative of the 268 classes enrolling children with cardiac limitations were rated on observable characteristics according to a checklist.

Results: The medical survey of 74 children revealed only possible or potential cardiac disease in 21 cases, misdiagnosis in three cases, and 50 cases with organic heart disease. Very few required restriction of ordinary activities, raising a question as to why they were in a special program. The children enrolled as cardiac cases tended to be over-age for their grade, usually because of excessive absences. Ability tended toward "low average" on group tests, and achievement tended to be slightly below the expectation. Individual tests showed a mean IQ of 94, with a wide range negatively skewed. Eleven percent scored in the range of educable mental retardation. Emotionally the children showed immaturity and a need for greater stimulation, while their parents displayed ambivalent attitudes of simultaneous acceptance and rejection. Study of the classes showed a generally adequate program marred by wide mental age spans within classes and static and traditional teaching.

Comment: This comprehensive study provides a detailed plan by which other systems may evaluate their own programs. The findings indicate a tendency on the part of the school to overprotect children who might well have joined regular classes, and a retention in the special rooms of outdated teaching methods. The findings indicate fewer differences from the average than might have been expected in the children.

Wrightstone, J. W., Justman, J., and Moskowitz, Sue. Studies of Children with Physical Handicaps: II. The Child with Orthopedic Limitations. *Bureau of Educational Research, Publication,* No. 33, New York City Board of Education, 1954.

Purpose: To determine whether the program of a large public school system was meeting the needs of children with orthopedic limitations. The intelligence, achievement, adjustment, and families of the children were investigated.

Subjects: Two groups of orthopedically handicapped pupils, 49 enrolled in the eighth grade and 20 in the fifth, with similar physical handicaps, served as subjects.

Method: The fifth and eighth grade children were examined and compared as groups as to their physical status, intelligence, achievement, behavior, and adjustment. Individual clinical studies were also made of the same areas in most of the children; their families were studied; and classroom practices were surveyed.

Results: No unusual findings resulted from the comparison by groups. Physical status was similar, both groups showing a wide range of orthopedic handicaps, predominantly static in character. Both tended to be somewhat over-age for their grade placements, and to have achieved slightly less than the age-grade or mental-age expectancy would have predicted. Intelligence for the groups was rated as "low average." When clinical studies were made of the children, the cerebral palsied pupils were found to differ sufficiently from the rest of the group that their findings were reported separately. The results of the clinical investigations stress the range of abilities and disabilities masked by measures of central tendency and emphasize the heterogeneous nature of the orthopedically handicapped. It was concluded that certain patterns of response on individual intelligence tests, presence or absence of neurological involvement, motivation, and previous atypical school experience were stronger factors than level of intelligence in determining the level

257

of achievement reached by individual pupils. Individual differences in adjustment and their probable causes were illustrated.

Comment: This study, contrasting the group and clinical approaches, points up the questionable usefulness of continuing to report measures of central tendency for a classification so admittedly heterogeneous as the orthopedically handicapped. Where wide spans of age, grade, and ability are found within single educational units, and where the etiology of handicap is so diverse, clinical study of the individual would appear to be the only way of meeting his educational needs.

SUMMARY

Necessary research remains to be done in the area of the orthopedically handicapped, and on the major crippling conditions. The existing studies of incidence are becoming out-dated by such medical advances as the development of the Salk vaccine and surgical correction in infancy of congenital defects. These studies should be brought up to date, both to aid the schools in their planning and to see if there are regions or socio-economic groups which are not benefitting maximally from new medical knowledge. A second type of needed research, which has until now been confined largely to the area of social work, is the intensive, clinical study of the individual. This might be expected to shed light on some of the factors making prediction possible in the case of the individual, the factors which determine why one child will be educationally or psychologically hurt by experiences which leave another child apparently unscathed.

Finally, education is changing rapidly today, both in curriculum and in architectural planning. The program for ill or orthopedically handicapped children was conceived before most of these changes came about; it is time for re-evaluation. Has the wide age and achievement span found in most such classes bound this exceptional group to a traditional, academic curriculum without the enrichment provided for their non-handicapped peers? Have one-story buildings and improved school planning made it possible for more of the crippled to attend regular classes? If their needs have not been taken into account, how can this be remedied? Have educators retained enough flexibility in their thinking concerning special health problems to insure such individual planning that every child able to attend the regular grades is so placed, and no child able to get to school is left to the lesser stimulation of a homebound program? These questions demand answers.

9

Children with Speech and Language Impairments

Richard L. Schiefelbusch

A *speech impairment* refers to a deviation which is sufficiently extreme to attract attention to the process of speech, to interfere with communication, or to affect adversely either the speaker, the listener, or both. A *language impairment*, in this report, refers to difficulty in comprehending speech of others or in projecting one's own ideas through the medium of speech. Together, *speech impairment* and *language impairment* include four broad categories of impairment: (a) articulation—the way sounds are formed; (b) rhythm—the time relationship between sounds in a word and words in a sentence; (c) voice—the sounds produced by the vibrating vocal folds and modified by the resonators; and (d) language usage—difficulties in comprehending the speech of others or in projecting one's own ideas through the medium of speech.* Each of the categories can be further subdivided into the following topics:

1. Articulation disorders.
2. Stuttering disorders.
3. Voice disorders.
4. Cleft palate disorders.
5. Aphasia (adults).
6. Aphasia (children).
7. Cerebral palsy.
8. Mental retardation and delayed language development.

* R. Milisen. Chapter 7, in L. Travis (Ed.), *Handbook of Speech Pathology*. New York: Appleton-Century-Crofts. 1957. p. 248.

Reviewed by John J. O'Neill, University of Illinois.

Articulation has recently been defined as " . . . the audible and visible phonetic aspects of the oral communication process."* Disorders of articulation are associated with "faulty placement, timing, direction, pressure, speed, or integration of lip, tongue, velum, or pharyngeal movements resulting in absent or incorrect speech sounds.† Very often the term "functional" is used as a prefix to the general term to indicate that the problem is non-organically determined. In this report the distinction is not highlighted, however, since the review of the research literature fails to show data to support the dichotomy (functional and organic). The incidence of articulation defects ranges from 15 percent for the first grade to an average of two to four percent for fourth grade children. Apparently after the age of nine or 10, misarticulated sounds tend to remain defective unless therapy is provided. Prior to this time articulation tends to improve discernably with each succeeding grade level.‡ Estimates by speech correctionists in public school settings usually place articulation problems at 75 to 80 percent of the entire case load.

Articulation disorders, then, may be regarded as the major problem in the field of speech correction. The following reviews are concerned with recent contributions to the study of articulation difficulties.

Jordan, E. P. Articulation Test Measures and Listener Ratings of Articulation Defectiveness. *Journal of Speech and Hearing Research*, 1960, 3, 303-319.

Purpose: To analyze the relationships between certain factors associated with defective articulation and listener reaction as indicated by listener ratings of the severity of defective articulation in short samples of children's speech.

Subjects: 150 children with mild to severe articulation deviations. They were selected from speech and hearing clinics of three universities and colleges and five public schools.

Procedure: Primarily two types of data were obtained: (a) scale values of articulation defectiveness derived from responses of listeners to samples of continuous speech, and (b) measures of various aspects of mis-

* Research Needs in Speech Pathology and Audiology. *Journal of Speech and Hearing Disorders,* Monograph Supplement 5, Sept., 1959.
† Margaret H. Powers. Chapter 23. in L. Travis (Ed.), *Handbook of Speech Pathology.* New York: Appleton-Century-Crofts. 1957, p. 207.
‡ Milisen. *Op. cit.* p. 253.

articulation derived from results of articulation testing. Tape recorded 30-second speech samples were rated on a 9-point equal-appearing interval scale by 36 listeners. The major method of statistical treatment was a multiple regression analysis designed to identify those relatively few variables which relate highly to judged severity.

Results: Pertinent findings include the following: (a) Articulation test responses provided valid information on articulatory behavior in connected speech. (b) Reactions of listeners to articulation defectiveness are primarily dependent upon two factors—frequency with which articulatory deviations occur and degree of articulatory deviations. (c) To the listener, omissions are more deviant than substitutions, and substitutions are more deviant than distortions. (d) Articulation test measures of number of defective items and number of defective single sounds are both highly related to measures of defectiveness of articulation derived from listener responses to connected speech.

Comment: This study attempts to identify the characteristics of defective articulation which most distract the listener and make the speech seem defective. The comprehensive results provide interesting guidelines and suggest new directions for further research. The study is outstanding both conceptually and methodologically.

Steer, M. D., and Drexler, Hazel G. Predicting Later Articulation from Kindergarten Tests. *Journal of Speech and Hearing Disorders,* 1960, 25, 391-397.

Purpose: To determine the effectiveness of certain variables measured at the kindergarten level in predicting the articulation ability of the same children five years later.

Subjects: 93 school children selected from a larger group of subjects who participated in a study conducted by Wilson.* The children were divided into two groups: a group of 54 subjects who participated originally in the speech improvement program, conducted by Wilson, and a control group of 39 subjects who followed regular kindergarten classroom procedures.

Procedure: Articulation tests were administered to the children individually at the kindergarten level and again five years later. Two examiners evaluated each child's responses independently. In addition to the articulation tests, data were derived from the Goodenough Draw-

* B. A. Wilson. The Development and Evaluation of a Speech Improvement Program. *Journal of Speech and Hearing Disorders,* 1954. 19, 4-13.

a-Man Test and the Vineland Social Maturity Scale. The Wherry-Doolittle test selection method was used to find the best combination of tests for prognosis.

Results: The results of the study indicate that certain variables measured at the kindergarten level do have predictive value. The most effective and reliable predictive variables appear to be: (a) the total number of errors in all positions within words, (b) errors in the final position, (c) errors of omission in the final position, and (d) errors on the "f" and "l" sounds of the consonant group. In addition, the amount of improvement in articulation ability shown by a child during a 12-week period in kindergarten, independent of the number of errors preceding that period, appears to be highly significant.

Comment: The study attempts to answer one of the persistent questions facing speech correctionists: What measures will best predict how a child with articulation deviations will fare in the years ahead? The reported information should aid therapists in determining which children are the most urgent candidates for speech therapy.

Weaver, C. H., Furbee, Catherine, and Everhart, R. W. Articulatory Competency and Reading Readiness. *Journal of Speech and Hearing Research,* 1960, 3, 174-180.

Purpose: To determine the relationship between articulatory competency and reading readiness as measured by the Gates Reading Readiness Test. It was hypothesized that the skills and capacities measured by this test are related to the early acquisition of adequate speech.

Subjects: 638 first-grade children selected carefully with regard to chronological age, intelligence, race and socio-economic level. Pupils possessing articulatory defects stemming from organic etiologies, stutterers, and mental defectives were excluded from the sample.

Procedure: The Gates Reading Readiness Test was administered by the regular classroom teacher during the first four weeks of school. Percentile scores were obtained for the subtests: word-matching, picture directions, word-card matching, rhyming, and letters and numbers. Average percentiles were determined from these percentile scores and were calculated and used as the total Reading Readiness scores.

Results: Of the 638 children, 163 were judged to have normal speech. The remaining 475 exhibited from one to 78 out of a possible 98 articulation errors. Data derived from the Reading Readiness tests showed an almost steady decrease in reading readiness as the number of articulation errors increased. A product-moment correlation coefficient was computed to be −.20, significant at the one percent level. The strength of the relationship between reading readiness and articulatory skill in grade one seems to be about the same for each of the Gates subtests.

Comment: Articulatory competency and reading readiness suggest a possible relationship that challenges both teachers and speech therapists. The research reports a low negative correlation between these two measurable features of language functioning at the first grade level. The results, however, do not indicate what common factors may operate to produce the correlation.

Everhart, R. W. The Relationship Between Articulation and Other Developmental Factors in Children. *Journal of Speech and Hearing Disorders,* 1953, 18, 332-338.

Purpose: To study the importance of various factors of maturation of speech articulation for children in grades one through six. Specifically, the research was concerned with the relationship of physical, mental, and environmental variables for children with and without defective articulation.

Subjects: 110 children with articulatory defects were compared with a like number of children with normal speech.

Procedure: Each child was given a series of achievement and motor tests, and additional data were derived from the use of a mimeographed questionnaire which was sent to each home. The difference between means was computed and a chi-square statistical technique was used to compare the relationships of the several growth and developmental factors.

Results: There were no significant differences between groups in respect to the onset of each of the following: holding head up, crawling, sitting alone, walking, talking, voluntary bladder control, eruption of the first tooth, grip, height, weight, and handedness. However, there was positive correlation between the factor of low intelligence and the incidence of articulatory disorders. The factor of parental occupation was found not to be related to the occurrence of articulatory deviations.

Comment: The author acknowledges that the size of his sample, the limitations of sampling, the use of group test data, and the cross-sectional method of the survey limit the usefulness of the study. Neverthe-

263

less, the approach provides tentative results which may be compared with other analyses of the relation between articulation and other developmental factors.

Mange, C. V. Relationships Between Selected Auditory Perceptual Factors and Articulation Ability. *Journal of Speech and Hearing Research*, 1960, 3, 67-73.

Purpose: To examine the hypothesis that one of the principal causative factors in certain functional articulatory defects is the presence of some auditory deficiency or immaturity which prevents normal development.

Subjects: 35 children with functional misarticulation of "r" and 35 matched, normal-speaking children served as the experimental and control groups. It was required that each of the children in the experimental group exhibit functional misarticulations involving the "r" sound but not the "s" sound. The school records revealed that none of the subjects had an organic or structural condition which might produce the articulatory problem. None of the children selected had received previous speech therapy. The children with articulatory problems were matched with those having normal speech on the following factors: intelligence, age, and sex.

Procedure: All of the children were administered the Seashore measures of pitch, loudness, and timbre; a test of auditory flutter-fusion rate; and a test of word synthesis. Pearson *r* correlations were obtained for the measures.

Results: There was a significant but low partial correlation between phonetic word synthesis ability and number of articulation errors. There were no significant relationships between other auditory abilities tested and number of articulation errors. The control group achieved significantly higher scores than the experimental group in discrimination of pitch. There were no significant differences between mean scores of control and experimental groups in other auditory abilities tested. In all cases the control group achieved numerically higher mean scores.

Comment: The study focuses upon five auditory perceptual abilities: discrimination of loudness, discrimination of quality, rate of auditory perception (flutter-fusion), pitch and phonetic word synthesis. These abilities had not previously been studied in relation to articulatory problems. The study, therefore, provides a meaningful supplement to previous studies of sound discrimination.

Sommers, R. K. *et al.* Training Parents of Children with Functional Misarticulation. *Journal of Speech and Hearing Research,* 1959, 2, 258-265.

Purpose: To evaluate the results of a program for training parents to help children with functional articulation defects.

Subjects: 36 children (10 girls and 26 boys) in the experimental group, and 36 children (nine girls and 27 boys) in the control group. All children in both groups had functional articulation problems. The groups were matched on the basis of four factors: chronological age, mental age, sex, and number of misarticulated sounds.

Procedure: Parents of children in the experimental group received intensive training in techniques of helping their children at home. Parents of children in the control group received no training. Articulation tests were administered prior to the three and one-half week clinical program, immediately following it, and again nine weeks later. Mean differences were evaluated by the *t* test for related measures.

Results: The two groups showed about the same improvement in increasing the mean number of correct sounds. The experimental group showed more improvement by reduction of the number of substitutions and distortions than did the control group. The control group showed a post-clinic period reduction of omissions significantly greater than that of the experimental group. Parental attitudes toward the clinic program and their children's improvement, as indicated in questionnaire answers, were not significantly different for the two groups.

Comment: The time allotted to the parent-child program seems unfortunately brief for purposes of answering so important a question. The value of the study is primarily its attempt to answer a question which is basic to the operation of a speech clinic. The tentative answers provided should serve to encourage clinicians and research workers to seek more comprehensive results.

In Review

The studies selected for the *Articulation Disorders* section fulfilled three essential criteria: They investigated an important area, they were competently done, and they are recent. The last criterion was deemed important because other research commentaries have examined the literature of an earlier vintage. Recent studies are more likely to reflect the farthest advances made in the area, since they build upon earlier studies.

Thus a composite of recent research provides a relatively accurate impression of the current frontiers of knowledge in the field.

The studies reviewed in this section also may be regarded as descriptive in nature. The term *descriptive* is in contrast to *manipulative*. A review of the literature reveals few studies of the therapeutic process of speech correction. There appears to be a great need for such investigations.

There is also a need for normative data and a better description of conditions under which articulation is learned (or not learned); a need for better methods of measurement; and a need for better methods of diagnosis and treatment. Each of these broad areas has many challenging sub-areas which call for resourceful efforts by workers equipped with the means to conduct both long range descriptive studies and rigorous manipulative studies. The field seems literally to be waiting for research studies which apply the principles of modern learning theory to the study of a number of the independent variables which pertain to articulation training.

STUTTERING DISORDERS

There is no one generally accepted definition of stuttering. However, Van Riper's* description of stuttering has achieved popular acceptance. According to Van Riper, stuttering is a disorder characterized by blockings, prolongations, or repetitions of words, syllables, sounds, or mouth postures, all of which (together with the contortions or devices used to avoid, postpone, disguise, start, or release the speech abnormality) produce interruptions and breaks in the rhythmic flow of speech.

Obviously the description points primarily to the symptomatic and behavioral aspects of the problem. A more briefly stated definition by Johnson describes stuttering as "an anticipatory, apprehensive, hypertonic avoidance reaction." This description focuses primarily upon the presumed feelings and reactions of the stutterer as he experiences stuttering events.

Surveys usually reveal that stuttering is a communication problem for slightly less than one percent of the general population. The following brief research accounts have been selected from among the numerous studies available. The five presented are all recent studies which draw upon research conducted primarily during the past thirty years.

* C. Van Riper. *Speech Correction Principles and Methods.* (3rd Ed.) New York: Prentice Hall. 1954. p. 342.

266

Johnson, W. *et al.* Effects of Hyperventilation and Tetany on the Speech Fluency of Stutterers and Non-Stutterers. *Journal of Speech and Hearing Research,* 1959, 3, 203-215.

Purpose: To test the hypothesis that stuttering is associated with latent tetany. If stutterers hover on the brink of some critical imbalance, then they could be expected to show a deterioration of speech performance under hyperventilation.

Subjects and Procedure: 20 stutterers and 20 non-stutterers read a 150-word passage three times and were hyperventilated between the second and third readings until signs of tetany appeared. The five measures of alveolar CO_2 pressure were obtained from each subject during each of two experimental sessions. An analysis of variance design was used to determine changes in speech fluency and carbon dioxide tension.

Results: It was concluded that the stutterers and non-stutterers did not differ significantly with respect to alveolar air-carbon dioxide tension and that there were no significant changes in the speech fluency of the stutterers as the result of hyperventilation and tetany. There was, however, a slight decrease in the speech fluency of the non-stutterers following induction of tetany through hyperventilation. The findings imply that the problem called stuttering is to be differentiated from the problem of speech non-fluency as such.

Comment: This study is one of the latest and best of a series of studies investigating possible chemical imbalance conditions of stutterers. It is a study of unusual sophistication, combining knowledgeability of previous research and a tight experimental design. Interpretations of the results suggest that stuttering can be distinguished from non-fluency, per se, and that fluency, as such, may be altered under certain conditions by hyperventilation as shown by the speech patterns of both normal speakers and stutterers.

Rousey, C. L. Stuttering Severity During Prolonged Spontaneous Speech. *Journal of Speech and Hearing Research,* 1958, 1, 40-47.

Purpose: To investigate possible decrement of stuttering during prolonged periods of spontaneous speech. The hypothesis evaluated was that stuttering severity would decrease during spontaneous speech continued over a period of five consecutive days with 10 consecutive hours of spontaneous speech each day.

Subjects: 18 stutterers—five girls and 13 boys of high school age—were used as the experimental group. Intelligence quotients obtained on the Henmon Nelson Test of Mental Ability, Form A, ranged from 67 to 133.

Procedure: The basic task of each subject was to talk continuously and spontaneously for 10 hours a day during five consecutive days. Four-minute taped recordings and visual observations of overt stuttering symptoms were made each day when the stutterer began talking, at the succeeding two-hour intervals, and at the end of the experimental day. A trend analysis of the number of words spoken, the number of secondary symptoms, and the rated severity of stuttering, both on an intra-day and an inter-day basis, was computed.

Results: The obtained results apparently support the hypothesis that a significant decrement in the severity of stuttering during spontaneous speech occurred on the average on all three measures both on an intra-day and an inter-day basis with one exception—the rated severity of stuttering on an intra-day basis failed to show the significant decrement. None of the stutterers completely stopped observable stuttering as the result of the experimental technique.

Comment: The study represents an elaborate attempt to determine the effects of prolonged, spontaneous speech upon the severity of stuttering symptoms. The methods employed and the quality of the work were excellent. Nevertheless the reader is inclined to wonder what the results mean since the study does not go beyond the empirical level and seems to be almost completely lacking in theoretical constructs or other basis for interpretation.

Glasner, P. J., and Rosenthal, D. Parental Diagnosis of Stuttering in Young Children. *Journal of Speech and Hearing Disorders,* 1957, 22, 288-295.

Purpose: To learn something of the general thoughts and attitudes of parents regarding the occurrence of non-fluency in their young children and to examine how these thoughts and attitudes are related to the conclusion that the child has stuttered or has continued to stutter.

Subjects: 996 parents of first-grade children were interviewed by speech correctionists.

Procedure: Each parent was interviewed by a speech correctionist who filled out a questionnaire as a feature of the interview. The data were expressed in percentages and chi-square relationships.

Results: 153 parents said that their children had stuttered at some time. This represents 15.4 percent of the total sample. The percentage was the same irrespective of the investigator or the locale. Of the 153 diagnosed stutterers, 83 were said to have stopped stuttering, 48 to still be stuttering, and 22 to be stuttering only occasionally. Thus, of the total sample, 4.8 percent were still diagnosed unqualifiedly as stutterers. Approximately 70 percent of the parents who had made the diagnosis actively sought to correct the disturbance. The 30 percent who minimized the disorder were concerned, but to a lesser degree. There was a relationship between active correction of the non-fluency and the perpetuation of the stuttering; however, almost half of the children treated incorrectly were said to have stopped stuttering..

Comment: The authors of this study have accepted the formidable challenge of describing the "thinking" and "attitudes" of parents relative to their child's "stuttering" (or not stuttering). The data seem to elicit additional questions and, as such, increase the speculations about the parents' likelihood of adding to or decreasing the stuttering problem. The study should not stand alone, but should desirably be the first of a series. If additional studies should follow, they might profit from several careful operational definitions.

Santostefano, S. Anxiety and Hostility in Stuttering. *Journal of Speech and Hearing Research*, 1960, 3, 337-347.

Purpose: To investigate whether stutterers and non-stutterers can be differentiated on the basis of anxiety and hostility, and whether this anxiety and hostility add a relatively more disrupted influence to the functioning of stutterers than of non-stutterers.

Subjects: 26 stutterers and 26 non-stutterers, each group consisting of 20 males and six females. The groups were matched in regard to sex, mean age, and mean IQ. The mean age of both groups was approximately 20 years; the mean IQ of both groups was approximately 121.

Procedure: The Rorschach test was administered to each subject and was rated with the validated scale for anxiety and hostility. In addition, all subjects were asked to recall previously learned material in neutral conditions (that is, following their free associations to neutral words spoken by the investigator) and in stressful conditions (that is, following their free associations to emotionally toned words).

Results: The results showed that the stutterers projected on the Rorschach significantly more content indicative of anxiety and hostility than did non-stutterers. In the laboratory situation all subjects showed a significant decrement in performance under stress conditions as compared to neutral ones, but stutterers showed a significantly greater decrement than non-stutterers.

Comment: The study itself was carefully designed. In interpreting his results, however, the author seems to go somewhat beyond his data in theorizing that by the time a stutterer reaches adulthood, he has developed an enduring, emotional disposition characterized by general anxiety and hostility which interfere with his personal adjustment and efficiency of functioning. On the basis of results derived from 26 stuttering adults, the author may also be a bit incautious to suggest that "workers doing either speech therapy or psychotherapy with stutterers should take into account, directly, this emotional disposition [anxiety and hostility] in understanding and treating the particular stutterer." Nevertheless, the study provides fresh fuel to a live controversy and should stimulate a variety of companion studies which utilize the Rorschach and other techniques.

Sheehan, J. G., and Voas, R. B. Stuttering as Conflict: Comparison of Therapy Techniques Involving Approach and Avoidance. *Journal of Speech and Hearing Disorders,* 1957, 22, 714-723.

Purpose: To test the effect on stuttering adaptation of three different techniques of negative practice currently used in speech therapy for stutterers. These techniques are (a) imitation of the actual stuttering pattern, (b) bounce (voluntary syllable repetition), and (c) slide (voluntary prolongation).

Subjects: 21 male and three female stutterers, ranging in age from 15 to 40 years.

Procedure: The materials used were four 200-word reading passages roughly equated for word difficulty and verbal content. Each experimental subject read the four different passages a total of six times in a comparison of the effect of negative practice. Eight subjects used each of the three different techniques. An analysis of variance design was used in drawing comparisons between methods.

Results: None of the three groups proved superior to a control adaptation reading during a final test trial under control conditions. The Dunlap technique (strengthening avoidance behavior by the practice of secondary stuttering responses) significantly retarded the course of adaptation. Of the methods studied, *slide* produced the greatest percentage of improvement. However, both *bounce* and *slide* seem to strengthen approach behavior in the stutterer and seem safe for clinical use.

Comment: The significance of this research is that it subjects four techniques of stuttering "therapy" to research scrutiny. The value of the commonly used procedures can, in this way, be objectively considered apart from the individual clinician's biases and "success-failure" defensiveness. The author, unfortunately, tended to generalize incautiously from data that "approached significance" or simply showed some numerical gains for one or more of the methods studied. Perhaps this research should best be used as a pilot study for generating questions to be answered in more complete studies yet to be formulated.

In Review

These research reports deal generally with behavioral characteristics of stuttering. The first of the studies, though, assesses behavior resulting from a modification of the physiology (tetany) of the individual. Additional studies of the chemical and physical factors are likely to be forthcoming. Refinements of the methods of studying stuttering as behavior is also likely to abound in the immediate future. The pioneer work by Johnson at the University of Iowa has established much of the groundwork for careful manipulative studies. Perhaps each of these loci of interest will soon contribute fundamentally to an increasing understanding of the nature and causes of stuttering. The means for prevention and treatment will then likewise be advanced.

Voice Disorders

In Chapter II of *Research Needs in Speech Pathology and Audiology* the Subcommittee states that ". . . the category of voice problems encompasses a complex group of disorders, which cannot be defined precisely or classified wholly systematically at this time." The Subcommittee called for fundamental research to provide a satisfactory classification. One way to simplify classification has been to divide the problem into *organic* and *functional* categories. Moore* defines the organic group of problems as "those defects of pitch, loudness, and quality which are related to abnormalities in size, shape, tonicity, surface conditions, and muscular control of the phonating and resonating mechanisms. These differences result from such causes as heredity, disease, injury, abuse, and surgery." Presumably then, functional disorders of voice are "those defects of pitch, loudness and quality" which are not related to structural or physiological factors. Three studies of *voice* are presented in this report.

* P. Moore. Chapter 22. in L. Travis (Ed.), *Handbook of Speech Pathology*, New York: Appleton-Century-Crofts, 1957, p. 653.

271

Diehl, C. F., White, R., and Burk, K. W. Voice Quality and Anxiety. *Journal of Speech and Hearing Research,* 1959, 2, 282-286.

Purpose: To examine the relationship of voice quality to anxiety as measured by the Taylor Anxiety Scale.

Subjects: 179 seminary students, 169 males and 10 females, with a mean age of 25 years.

Procedure: Each subject read orally a passage from the Bible. They were instructed to read as if in the pulpit Sunday morning. The voices were judged and classified by the authors under the following voice quality headings: normal, harsh, nasal, and hoarse-breathy. The four groups were compared on the basis of scores on the Taylor Anxiety Scale.

Results: Analysis of variance for testing differences was computed and found to be significant beyond the .01 level. The results indicated also, as shown by *t* tests of mean anxiety scores, that persons with hoarse-breathy voices are more anxious than: (a) persons with normal voices, and (b) persons with harsh voices.

Comment: The principal criticism of this study is supplied by the authors themselves. ". . . the lack of appropriate instruments with which to isolate and measure both voice and personality variables under realistic conditions, make definitive research in this area difficult." This seems reason to quote their concluding statement: "There seems evidence to justify further research into the relationship between voice quality and personality."

Diehl, C. F., and McDonald, E. T. Effect of Voice Quality on Communication. *Journal of Speech and Hearing Disorders,* 1956, 21, 233-237.

Purpose: To learn the extent to which the quality of a speaker's voice interferes with his ability to communicate information; and the extent to which the speaker's voice quality affects an audience's rating of his voice.

Subjects and Procedure: A trained speaker was used to simulate four voice quality defects: hoarseness, harshness, breathiness, and nasality—and a fifth, normal voice. One-minute recordings of the speaker's productions of the five voice quality types were rated by five trained listeners on a five point scale. The ratings were used to determine suitability of the voice quality types developed by the speaker. The speaker then recorded a 14-minute informative lecture. Two samples of the 14-minute recording were then rated by eight speech specialists for similarity of quality, consistency of the voice, and the remaining voice variables. Six experimental groups of 35 each were then asked to listen to the final recordings, following instructions which were designed to elicit listener responses pertinent to several research questions.

Results: On the basis of data derived from these listening sessions, the following conclusions were drawn: (a) Simulated breathy and nasal voice quality appeared to interfere with the speaker's ability to communicate information. (b) Neither simulated harsh nor hoarse voice quality appeared to have any negative effect on the ability of the speaker to communicate information. (c) Voices free from hoarse, harsh, nasal and breathy characteristics were rated very good, a hoarse voice "poor," a harsh voice only average, and a nasal voice only average. (d) The relationship between an audience's judgment of the goodness of a voice and the ability of that voice to communicate information appears to warrant further study.

Comment: The rationale provided by the authors seems adequate and the workmanship first rate. Nevertheless, an essential question should be raised: Does a *simulated* voice disorder have the same impact on listeners as a *real* disorder? The authors are careful to refer to the recorded samples as "simulated breathy and simulated harsh, etc., voices." The implications drawn from the study, however, are essentially those of *voice disorders.* This minor criticism does not negate the value of the study with its suggestions for further inquiry.

Hollien, H. Some Laryngeal Correlates of Vocal Pitch. *Journal of Speech and Hearing Research,* 1960, 3, 52-58.

Purpose: To present data showing the relationship between certain measures which may be considered indices of laryngeal size and vocal pitch level. Comparisons were made both between the two sexes and among individuals of the same sex.

Subjects: 254 volunteers were screened in order to select four groups of subjects of six each. The subjects were chosen primarily on the basis of pitch range, age, absence of speech or voice problems, and ability to produce specified vocal tones easily. The groups were composed of six males with very low voices, six males with very high voices, six females with very low voices, and six females with very high voices.

273

Procedure: A lateral Xray procedure was used to make four measurements of laryngeal dimensions (two anteroposterior, one vertical, and one area) to establish indices of laryngeal size. An analysis of variance design was used for testing differences among group means for each of the four measures.

Results: Significant differences in laryngeal size were found both between the sexes and between the pitch groups within sexes. Therefore, it can be concluded that individuals with low-pitch levels exhibit generally larger laryngeal structures than do individuals with higher pitch levels.

Comment: The study is a good example of the many ways that Xray film techniques can be utilized in the precise study of speech production. We can expect that through such studies many long held beliefs about speech processes will in time be upheld or disproved and that a precise science of speech will gradually unfold. The author has provided a remarkable conciseness of method which may well serve for other studies of its kind.

In Review

A brief description of three research studies does not provide a representative look at the range and complexity of voice disorders, nor does it suggest the scope and rigor of research in voice science laboratories that seek answers to many critical questions of voice production. The research needs in this area are especially apparent. Leaders in the field call especially for substantial interdisciplinary cooperation among otolaryngologists, social case workers, psychologists, audiologists and speech pathologists who diagnose voice problems.

CLEFT PALATE DISORDERS

Cleft lip and palate are described by Koepp-Baker* as "deformities of tissue disposition, specifically of disjunction and inadequacy . . . of the tissues of the lip, nose, jaw, hard palate, velum, pharynx, and cranial base." The varieties of cleft lip and palate may be grouped into four general categories: (a) those involving the lip alone; (b) those involving the lip, palate, and velum; (c) those in which the palate and/or velum only are affected; and (d) those in which the palate is congenitally insufficient.

* H. Koepp-Baker, Chapter 19, in L. Travis (Ed.), *Handbook of Speech Pathology*, New York: Appleton-Century-Crofts, 1957. p. 570.

The speech deviations of the person with cleft palate involve disturbances of intelligibility and alterations of voice quality. The most obvious features often are excessive "nasality" and distorted or omitted consonant sounds.

Fink, B. R. and Kirschner, F. The Incidence of Nasal and Lateral Defects of Articulation in Cleft Palate. *Folia Phoniatrica,* 1959, 11, 208-215.

Purpose: To analyze and compare the incidence of nasal and lateral articulatory defects in different types of cleft palate.

Subjects: Examinations were conducted on 263 cases of cleft palate. These were divided into three classifications: post-alveolar clefts—midline clefts of the soft palate and part or whole of the hard palate; alveolar clefts—unilateral cleft of the lip and alveolus extending through the whole palate; and alveolar clefts—bilateral cleft of the lip and alveolus extending into mid-line cleft of the palate.

Procedure: Each subject received a speech assessment before and after speech therapy, further surgery or orthodontic treatment. The assessment provided information about the degree of nasal escape, a description of articulation (normal, nasal or lateral) and the degree of nasal resonance.

Results: The study revealed that nasal escape and nasal articulation are the chief problems in cleft palate cases when the primary repair of the palate is unsuccessful. However it also found that problems of incompetent palate-pharyngeal sphincter are usually corrected by present-day surgery techniques. Consequently, the problem of nasal speech seems to be diminishing in importance but the problem of the alveolar cleft gains in significance as increasing numbers of cleft palate individuals use the oral cavity in articulation and develop lateral articulatory defects.

Comment: Although the authors acknowledge difficulties in precise assessment of nasal escape, nasal tone, and lateral articulation, they have conducted a careful study of these variables and have provided results which challenge speech pathologists who plan clinical programs for youngsters who have had surgery or other restorative treatments in cleft palate centers. The study would be difficult to replicate but it nevertheless suggests a direction which other studies of greater precision might well take.

275

Hagerty, R. F., and Hill, M. J. Pharyngeal Wall and Palatal Movement in Postoperative Cleft Palates and Normal Palates. *Journal of Speech and Hearing Disorders,* 1960, 3, 59-66.

Purpose: To investigate palate and posterior pharyngeal wall mobility in a group of young subjects with cleft palates and in a group with normal palates.

Subjects: 50 white, postoperative cleft palate subjects, ranging in age from seven to 25 years; and 50 white normal subjects, ranging in age from seven to 22 years. The groups were equated as to age, sex, and race.

Procedures and Equipment: Lateral laminagraphic skull films were made of each of the subjects. The laminagraphs were taken under three conditions: (a) with the soft structures at rest, (b) during phonation of the vowel "a", and (c) during production of the continuant consonant "s", or while blowing a toy horn. The subjects were carefully prepared for maintaining the desired conditions during the time the laminagraphs were being taken. Trained personnel were present to listen and judge whether the sounds produced were the desired phonemes. The actual measurements employed in the study were made from tracings which were derived from the Xray photographs of the structures.

Results: The results indicated a tendency for more forward movement of the posterior wall in the postoperative cleft group than in the normal group. A distinct limitation of activity was noted in the postoperative palates in all important functions: upward movement from rest to vowel "a" was less than two-thirds that of the normals, and from rest to the consonant "s" about one-third. Contact with the posterior pharyngeal wall during production of "s" was seen in all of the 50 normals, but in only 17 of the 50 postoperative subjects. Posterior movement of the postoperative cleft palates was one half of the normals for "a" and only one-third that of normals for "s".

Comment: Informaton about velar and pharyngeal wall mobility of cleft palate subjects is crucial for clinicians who provide speech training. The importance of this study, then, is that it provides reliable data regarding a critical area of the cleft palate problem. The competence and precision of the study are evident.

Spriestersbach, D. C., and Powers, G. R. Articulation Skills, Velopharyngeal Closure, and Oral Breath Pressure of Children with Cleft Palates. *Journal of Speech and Hearing Research,* 1959, 2, 318-325.

Purpose: To investigate the relationships among articulation skill, oral breath pressure, and velopharyngeal closure of children with cleft lips and palates, as revealed by lateral head Xrays.

Subjects: 103 subjects, consisting of 38 girls and 65 boys, ranging from five through 15 years of age. Eight of the group had clefts of the lip only, 23 had clefts of the palate only, and 72 had clefts of both lip and palate.

Procedure: Articulation skill was measured by the Templin Diagnostic Picture Articulation Test. Two measures of oral pressure also were obtained. One was a measure of vital capacity obtained by the use of a spirometer which had been modified to require a minimal amount of oral pressure to activate the equipment. Another set of pressure scores was obtained by using an oral manometer designed to measure air pressure in ounces per square inch. Xray data were obtained for each subject phonating the vowel "u" and also sustaining the fricative sound "s". Measurements were made of the degree of velopharyngeal opening under both of these conditions only for those subjects who had cleft lips only or cleft palates that had been surgically repaired.

Results: The main findings were as follows: (a) Measures of intraoral breath pressure were related to velopharyngeal competency and articulation scores. (b) All of the subjects with cleft lips only had, in general, normal oral pressure and articulation scores. (c) Subjects with good articulation scores almost invariably had high pressure scores; subjects with high pressure scores occasionally had relatively poor articulation scores. (d) Individuals with cleft lips and palates, in general, achieve better articulation scores and higher breath pressure than do individuals with cleft palates only. (e) Measurement of oral breath pressure of speakers with cleft lips and palates can be of major diagnostic value in establishing the basis for the articulation problems.

Comment: The importance of adequate velopharyngeal closure and adequate breath pressure are demonstrated in this study. The two measures provide a basis for predicting articulation adequacy and also for planning the future physical and therapeutic management of the child.

In Review

As demonstrated by these three studies, research in the field of cleft palate disorders is achieving both increased precision and functional realism. It is now possible to see as well as hear the bases of the speech disorder and to make relatively accurate judgments and predictions about speech performance.

Berry and Eisenson* write, "An aphasic patient manifests an inability to deal with symbols; consequently all functions involving language, a symbolic process, are disturbed. These functions include reading, writing, speaking, and the comprehension of speech . . . the aphasic individual has difficulty with language because he cannot associate experience with representative symbols as normal persons do." Aphasia is a behavioral complex determined to an extent by a physiological disorder. That is, a disorder aphasia is described in terms of the behavioral responses, but the causative features are assumed to be organic.

Two examples of research in adult aphasia disorders are presented in the following reviews.

Karlin, I. W., Eisenson, J., Hirschenfang, S. and Miller, M. H. A Multi-evaluational Study of Aphasic and Non-Aphasic Right Hemiplegic Patients. *Journal of Speech and Hearing Disorders,* 1959, 24, 369-379.

Purpose: To study the symptom complex of aphasia as it presents itself in brain-damaged patients with right hemiplegia.

Subjects and Procedure: 26 patients who sustained a cerebrovascular stroke involving the left cerebral hemisphere resulting in right hemiplegia were given neurologic, psychologic, audiologic and electroencephalographic assessments. Results of these examinations were analyzed to determine whether or not significant differences exist between right hemiplegic patients with aphasia as compared to right hemiplegic patients without aphasia.

Results: The following observations were made: (a) 20 out of 26 right hemiplegic patients were found to have aphasic involvements. (b) Aphasic patients with an illness of intermittent onset show greater disturbance in both receptive and expressive areas than do those having a disease of sudden onset. (c) Patients with aphasia due to thrombosis were found to have language disturbance predominantly of the receptive type in contrast to patients whose aphasia was due to embolism. (d) On the performance scale of the Wechsler Adult Intelligence Scale, patients with aphasia showed significantly lower scores than patients without aphasia. Both groups showed comparatively good scores on subtests requiring abstract reasoning ability. (e) Electroencephalographic

---

* Mildred Berry and J. Eisenson. *Speech Disorders: Principles and Practices of Therapy,* New York: Appleton-Century-Crofts, 1956, p. 387.

studies showed that patients with predominantly expressive language involvement may show either frontal and posterior accentuation, or posterior accentuation only. No cases were found of frontal accentuation only. (f) Hearing loss seems to be present in the same proportion for aphasic and non-aphasic patients.

Comment: This study is the first in a series of interdisciplinary studies planned by the authors. It reflects the experience and insight of the authors who seek to provide reliable information in an area that has long challenged clinicians from a number of disciplines.

Siegel, G. M. Dysphasic Speech Responses to Visual Word Stimuli. *Journal of Speech and Hearing Research,* 1959, 2, 152-160.

Purpose: To determine whether dysphasic individuals show consistent patterns of speech error in response to word stimuli classified according to: (a) part of speech, (b) level of abstraction, and (c) word length.

Subjects: 31 patients diagnosed as dysphasic ranging in age from 20 to 66 years.

Procedure: The stimulus material for the study consisted of a set of 90 words typed in upper case letters on individual four- by six-inch white cards. The subjects were required to utter each of the 90 stimulus words as the cards were presented in a random order. The subjects' responses were later replayed and evaluated by the investigator as being either right or wrong. An analysis of variance design was used to analyze errors made on nouns, verbs, adjectives and on words of low, medium and high levels of abstraction.

Results: The obtained results indicate that dysphasics make more errors on adjectives than on either verbs or nouns (no evidence of anomia was found); more on long words than on short; more on words of both high and low abstraction level than on those of medium level; and more on words occurring infrequently in the language than on those occurring frequently.

Comment: The author defines the study as an ". . . analysis of speech behavior of dysphasic subjects in terms of certain operationally defined aspects of words." This approach enables the author to avoid a number of assumptions about neurological functioning and to proceed directly to the study of *behavior* related to the word parameters.

Aphasia (Children)

The aphasic child is often designated as the *congenitally* aphasic child.

He is assumed to be brain damaged and to have sustained the injury before, during or shortly after birth. The language impairment apparently exists because the brain damage occurred before language usage had become firmly established. Berry and Eisenson explain that some brain damaged children do not show linguistic disability. They also point out "that failure to develop speech, in and of itself, is not presumptive of congenital aphasia . . . No child should be diagnosed as congenitally aphasic unless brain damage can be demonstrated directly or indirectly in either motor or perceptual involvement."* The studies which follow relate to the perceptual dimension.

Wilson, Lillian F., Doehring, D. G., and Hirsch, I. J. Auditory Discrimination Learning by Aphasic and Non-Aphasic Children. *Journal of Speech and Hearing Research,* 1960, 3, 130-137.

Purpose: To assess the ability of aphasic and non-aphasic children to discriminate among four sounds which differ with respect to two acoustic dimensions and to associate each of these sounds with a different visual stimulus.

Subjects: 14 children with sensory aphasia and a control group of 13 children, selected from lipreading and auditory-training classes and a speech clinic. The two groups were comparable with respect to mean and range of age, IQ, and hearing loss.

Procedure: The study included two acoustic dimensions: duration and quality. Four tone units were employed: short tone, long tone, short noise, and long noise. Children were asked to distinguish among these four sounds by learning to associate each with one of four randomly selected letters of the alphabet.

Results: Eight of the aphasic children learned the task in about the same number of trials as the non-aphasic children. The remaining six aphasic children failed to learn the task within the alloted number of trials. This difference in learning ability within the aphasic group was unrelated to age, IQ, or amount of hearing loss. Informal observations on further training of the children who had failed to learn the task indicated that they were able to make the required discriminations among auditory stimuli and that their poor performance was the result of a specific difficulty in learning to associate four visual stimuli with four auditory stimuli.

* *Op. cit.,* p. 420.

Comment: This study, together with the following study by Doehring, provides intriguing information about the functional performance of aphasic children in sensory perceptual dimensions. The information derived is especially useful for clinicians who are faced with the daily problem of contriving learning tasks for these children.

Doehring, D. G. Visual Spatial Memory in Aphasic Children. *Journal of Speech and Hearing Research,* 1960, 3, 138-149.

Purpose: To compare the performance of aphasic children with that of deaf children and normal children on a test in which memory for spatial location was determined as a function of: (a) duration of exposure of the visual stimulus, (b) delay of recall, and (c) interference with fixation of the visual field.

Subjects: 20 children classified as aphasic, 20 normal children, and 20 deaf children.

Procedure: Each subject was asked to indicate the position of a spot of light which had been briefly flashed on a piece of paper. Importance of immediate recall for accurate localization of the visual stimulus was determined by requiring the subject to wait eight seconds before responding on certain trials. Each of the three groups of subjects was subdivided into two age groups. Four exposure durations, two delay conditions, and two interference conditions, were presented to each subject. Each subject was given one trial with each of the 16 experimental conditions. An analysis of variance of the effects of age, delay, interference, and exposure time on visual spatial memory in the groups was computed.

Results: Results showed that the accuracy of performance of all three groups was unaffected by variations in duration of exposure. Accuracy was decreased by about the same amount for each group by delay of recall and interference of fixation, and changed as a function of chronological age in about the same way for all three groups. The aphasic group was, however, significantly less accurate than the deaf group and the normal group in terms of total amount of error. These results suggest that children classified as aphasic are retarded in some, but not all, aspects of visual perceptual ability.

Comment: The unevenness of performance of these children on aspects of visual perceptual ability, together with the difficulties of associating visual and auditory stimuli (previous study), suggests that perception should be more widely explored as a vital area in the assessment of childhood aphasia.

281

The relatively modern emphasis upon *behavior* provides a means for broadening the approach to the study of aphasia. Each of the studies reported derived data from the measured or observed responses of the subjects. In addition, the first (Karlin *et al.*) utilized physiological data as part of the description. It is possible that excessive reliance in the past upon physiological constructs and assumptions has limited the progress of knowledge in the field.

CEREBRAL PALSY

Cerebral palsy may be grossly defined as a motor disability resulting from damage or deficit in the upper central nervous system located within the cranium.* Along with motor involvement, there are likely to be other symptoms of upper neural damage: problems in channeling sensation, perceptual problems, reduced or distorted conceptual functioning, difficulties with symbolization, and emotional problems. The ever-present motor disability is only part of the clinical problem.

The disability of cerebral palsy is most apparent in the comparative lack of motor control. The symptoms of motor incoordination usually involve the speech musculature producing severe distortions of phonation and articulation. Both of the studies reported in this section pertain to a phase of this latter problem.

Flores, Pura M., and Irwin, O. C. Status of Five Front Consonants in the Speech of Cerebral Palsied Children. *Journal of Speech and Hearing Disorders*, 1956, 21, 238-244.

Purpose: This study is concerned with the articulation by cerebral palsied children of five front consonants (p, b, m, d and t) as elicited by pictorial and verbal stimulations.

Subjects: The subjects were 96 cerebral palsied children ranging in age from 3-7 to 15-11 years.

Procedure: The test procedure consisted of 15 pictures and 15 words so that the five consonant sounds could each be tested in the initial, medial and final position of the word. An analysis of variance design consisting of two Latin square factors was utilized.

---

* Research Needs in Speech Pathology and Audiology. *Journal of Speech and Hearing Disorders*, Monograph Supplement 5, 1959, p. 44.

Results: (a) The pictorial and verbal stimulations had the same effect in the initial and final positions of consonants in word patterns. (b) The verbal stimulation elicited more correct responses in the medial position than did the pictorial stimulation in the same position. (c) Order of the presentation of the stimuli did not affect the number of correct articulations. (d) There were significant differences between the initial and medial positions, initial and final positions, and medial and final positions. (e) None of the lower order interactions which involved schools, group and order were significant. (f) None of the higher order interactions which involved schools, group and order were significant.

Comment: This careful descriptive study provides important data relative to the methods of assessing articulatory behavior. However, as a descriptive study of children with "cerebral palsy" it has limited generalized usefulness since it covers a wide range of age and undescribed etiological classifications.

Irwin, O. C. Difficulties of Consonant and Vowel Sounds in the Speech of Children with Cerebral Palsy. *Cerebral Palsy Review*, 1961, 22, 14-15.

Purpose: To learn which sounds are the most difficult for the cerebral palsied child to pronounce, and whether the order of difficulty of phonemes for them was similar in the initial, medial and final positions in words.

Subjects: 265 cerebral palsied children from three to 16 years of age.

Procedure: An articulation test consisting of 87 word items including 35 phonemes was administered individually to each child.

Results: Most consonant sounds varied widely in order of difficulty in the initial, medial, and final positions. There was no order of difficulty even among the most difficult of consonants. The order of difficulty of vowels likewise varied between initial and medial positions, but the percentages of any given vowel nevertheless were quite close.

Comment: The findings of this study on the difficulty of sounds (presented in six tables) are important for a program of therapy for children with cerebral palsy. It is good educational practice to begin teaching first with easy materials which enable the learner to gain confidence in his ability, and to motivate him by means of initial success. A difficult learning task attempted too soon may frustrate the child and weaken or overwhelm his self-confidence.

Burgi, E. J., and Matthews, J. Predicting Intelligibility of Cerebral Palsied Speech. *Journal of Speech and Hearing Research,* 1958, 1, 331-343.

Purpose: To evaluate the means of predicting the intelligibility of the speech of young adult cerebral palsied subjects from measures of their consonant articulation.

Subjects: Speech samples were obtained from 17 male and 12 female cerebral palsied subjects, ranging in age from 17 to 49 years.

Procedure: Tape-recorded speech samples were obtained from 29 subjects and were then audited by five speech clinicians who evaluated each subject's articulation ability. In addition, nine listeners wrote down what they understood of each subject's intelligibility recordings. Prediction of intelligibility by each of the eight articulation measures was evaluated by correlating each set of predictor or articulation measures with each set of criterion or intelligibility measures.

Results: Each of the three short articulation tests and each of the two longer, simple articulation test measures predicted the two intelligibility measures as well as did the two more complex weighted indexes. Word intelligibility and sentence intelligibility were predicted about equally well by any one of the several articulation measures.

Comment: This study should provide reassurance for clinicians who may hesitate to rely on simple tests and yet who may not have time to apply the complex weighted indexes.

In Review

Although speech pathologists share with other specialists the need to become better acquainted with the neurology, physiology and psychology of cerebral palsy disorders, their principal problem is to improve speech production. Intelligibility is only one of a variety of research areas which bear upon this function. Others pertain to the imbalances and weaknesses of the facial, masticatory and lingual muscles which interfere with sound formation. Studies of these and other secondary problems may lead to better ways of alleviating them and thus to improvements in communication effectiveness.

MENTAL RETARDATION AND DELAYED LANGUAGE DEVELOPMENT

Mental retardation refers to that group of conditions which is characterized by: (a) slow rate of maturation; (b) reduced learning capacity; (c) inadequate social adjustment related to below average intellectual functioning. The term *mentally retarded* should not be applied to children who have "delayed language" but who do not conform to these general conditions.

The mentally retarded are slower than the normal in acquiring speech and show marked deficiencies in language development. In addition to frequent deviations in articulation and phonation, the mental retardate seems also to have difficulties in social interaction, symbolic functioning, and vocabulary development.

Studies of speech and language behavior of retardates have been few in number. The five studies presented here contribute substantially to knowledge in the field and may also serve as facilitators to new studies. The first two are descriptive or assessment studies, and the last three are treatment or therapy studies.

Lerea, L. Assessing Language Development. *Journal of Speech and Hearing Research*, 1958, 1, 75-85.

Purpose: To construct a set of clinical inventories which would yield quantitative data concerning the vocabulary and language structure of children between the ages of three and nine.

Subjects: Subjects used in the preliminary phases of the testing were 245 children representing seven age levels, ranging from three to nine years. In addition, 65 males and 75 females were used in the reliability and validity testing phases of the experiment. For purposes of determining validity of the inventories, two groups of 16 language-retarded children and two groups of children who were normal with regard to language development served as additional subjects for the study.

Procedure: The author constructed a four-choice picture vocabulary test of 49 key pictures. In addition, he developed a picture language structure inventory of 75 key items. Test data were also derived from the Columbia Mental Maturity Scale.

Results: The computed reliability and validity measures suggest that these picture language inventories possess sufficient sensitivity eventually to become effective supplementary tools in the diagnosis of language retardation. However, the inventories remain in an experimental stage and, as yet, have no accompanying normative data.

Comment: The study represents one of the best approaches to test construction found in the speech and language literature. Nevertheless, it is incomplete as it stands and should have further item analysis and a larger test sample for normative purposes.

Winitz, H. Relationships Between Language and Non-Language Measures of Kindergarten Children. *Journal of Speech and Hearing Research,* 1959, 2, 387-391.

Purpose: To examine the relationships among the major language and non-language variables for kindergarten children.

Subjects: 75 girls and 75 boys randomly selected.

Procedure: Non-language variables studied were socio-economic status and three IQs as measured by the Wechsler Intelligence Scale for Children: Verbal Scale IQ, Performance Scale IQ, and Full Scale IQ. The language variables employed were verbalization measures (mean length of response, number of one word responses, mean of the five longest responses, number of different words, structural complexity score, and mean standard deviation), Templin Screening Test of Articulation score, size of vocabulary as measured by the Ammons Full-Range Picture Vocabulary Test, and four fluency measures (rhymes, child names, adult names, and object names).

Pearson product-moment correlations among the major language and non-language variables were computed for boys and girls separately and for the sexes combined.

Results: Comparison of the correlations for boys and girls indicated that few of the differences were statistically significant. Very high correlations were found between the WISC Performance Scale and Verbal Scale IQs and the Full Scale IQ. Moderately high correlations were found between the WISC Performance Scale IQ and the WISC Verbal Scale IQ; between the Ammons Test scores and the WISC Full Scale IQ; and among the various verbalization measures. Low correlations were found for many of the remaining comparisons.

Comment: The author states that the relative independence of these variables (as shown by the preponderance of moderate and low correlations) suggests that until investigation indicates which measures best indicate language retardation, they should all be included as diagnostic tools of language development.

Schlanger, B. B. A Longitudinal Study of Speech and Language Development of Brain-Damaged, Retarded Children. *Journal of Speech and Hearing Disorders,* 1959, 24, 354-360.

Purpose: To determine the results of a three- to four-year program of speech therapy with a selected group of mentally retarded children.

Subjects: The subjects were 12 brain-damaged, institutionalized children who were mentally retarded and whose speech and language development was severely delayed. No gross motor crippling defects or dysarthria were present.

Procedure: Evaluations were made of the children's oral communication abilities at their entrance examination, 18 to 24 months later, and finally 36 to 42 months after their initial examination. Measurements and observations were made of their abilities in word imitation, intelligibility of spontaneous speech, sentence length, and communication attidutes.

Results: After three to four years of therapy, varying improvement was seen in all measures. Compared to normal maturation gains, the improvements were meager, but it was suggested that these children would not be mute in later development as were older institutionalized children and adults with similar symptoms.

Comment: The study suffers from lack of a control group and from lack of operational descriptions of "speech therapy." It would be an impossible study to replicate, but results might be derived from a companion study conducted under more carefully controlled conditions. The reported results are certainly provocative and suggest that speech therapy activities have a valuable part to play in the training program for institutionalized mentally retarded children.

Johnson, G. O., Capobianco, R. J., and Miller, D. Y., Speech and Language Development of a Group of Mentally Deficient Children Enrolled in Training Programs. *Exceptional Children,* 1960, 27, 72-77.

Purpose: The study was designed to measure the development of trainable mentally deficient children in a number of areas over a two-year period.

Subjects: 32 mentally deficient children attending public schools and 80 severely retarded children residing in institutions.

Procedure: An articulation test was administered in January 1955, with retests in the spring and fall of 1955 and in the spring of 1956. Eleven sounds were tested in the initial, medial, and final position of a word represented by a picture. The Illinois Test of Language Abilities was administered to two groups of individually matched pairs of children at the beginning of the second year of the study. The experimental group was given an intensive language development program. The other group received no training.

Results: Test analysis showed a trend toward fewer committed errors as IQ increases. The institution and public school group made approximately the same progress between the initial and final testing. The public school group had slightly fewer errors and made slightly more improvement than did the institution group.

During the year of training the non-therapy group made more progress than the therapy group, but the difference was non-significant. The measured language growth was only 0.13 and 0.02 for the two groups during the year.

Comments: This is a good descriptive study of the speech and language of the severely retarded. However, the meager description of the therapy method, the reliance on one therapist, the small Ns for both the experimental and control groups, and the short period of therapy combine to limit the extent to which generalizations may be drawn from it.

Kolstoe, O. P. Language Training of Low Grade Mongoloid Children. *American Journal of Mental Deficiency,* 1958, 63, 17-30.

Purpose: The problem was to determine whether or not low-grade mongoloid children could improve in language functions when given intensive individual training.

Subjects: 30 mongoloid children between 5-6 and 14-6 years with a mental age above 1-6 years, who were free from crippling defects. Fifteen were randomly placed in each group (control and experimental). Intelligence scores on the Kuhlman Test ranged from 16 to 36.

Procedure: Language behavior was measured by the Illinois Language Test, an Observational Rating Scale, and a Composite Scale made up from selected items taken from the Kuhlman Tests and the Revised Stanford-Binet, Form L.

Three instructors were each randomly given five children and taught them individually in periods of 45 minutes duration, five days per week for five-and-one half months. An attempt was made to tailor instruction to the individual child. In general a procedure was used which included: (a) attracting the child's attention through movement or the initiation of activities; (b) the interjection of verbalization commensurate with activities; and (c) reward or reinforcement when the child used the desired word or symbol.

Results: The experimental group improved significantly in IQ scores and on tests involving labelling objects and pictures, word associations, and gestural conversation (especially noted among children with higher

MAs). Scores on the Observational Rating Scales and on the Rating Scale were not significantly different.

Comment: This is an impressive study of mentally retarded children in the lower IQ range. It supports an earlier study by Goldstein which found children under 25 IQ to provide poor aptitudes for learning activities. On a more positive note, Kolstoe found that mongoloid children above that IQ range did make some improvement. Additional research with mongoloid children of higher mental levels is needed to determine the degree to which these children can be expected to profit from language training.

In Review

Two of the five studies reported in this section deal with the task of assessing language, and the other three with the long-range task of speech training. It is interesting to note that the studies were carried on at about the same time, and that each author developed or adapted tests which sampled a variety of performance variables with very little similarity to the other studies.

SUMMARY

A careful reading of recent surveys of research and research needs in speech and language disorders suggests that all areas are in need of additional study. The most recent statement of needs* points to a special urgency in the following areas:

1. A compilation of comprehensive bibliographical information (a step has already been taken to meet this need through the DSH Abstracts—Deafness, Speech and Hearing Publications).

2. A more substantial research underpinning of diagnostic and remedial procedures.

3. The degree to which each of the different types of impairment contributes to social maladjustment.

4. The specification of language in terms of its semantic and code properties.

Another recent summary† adds encouragement for (a) more collaboration in research among universities, (b) greater effort to define neu-

---

* Research Needs in Speech Pathology and Audiology. *Journal of Speech and Hearing Disorders,* Monograph Supplement 5, 1959.

† The Education of Exceptional Children. *Review of Educational Research,* 1959. 29, 550-561.

289

rological and psychological substrates of linguistic structures and communicative disruptions, and (c) greater acceptance of the worth of case studies and the necessity of longitudinal research.

The author would like also to add that there is the exciting possibility for a variety of studies within a learning theory framework. The procedures of operant and instrumental conditioning should be applied to a variety of therapeutic objectives. Manipulative studies, in general, have an exciting future in laboratories where speech and language studies are conducted.

10

The Emotionally Disturbed

Norris G. Haring

The emotionally disturbed child is one who, because of organic and/or environmental influences, chronically displays: (a) inability to learn at a rate commensurate with his intellectual, sensory-motor and physical development; (b) inability to establish and maintain adequate social relationships; (c) inability to respond appropriately in day-to-day life situations, and (d) a variety of excessive behavior ranging from hyperactive, impulsive responses to depression and withdrawal. Although there are varying degrees of the above behavioral deviations in emotionally disturbed children, the key to the eventual diagnosis of this condition is the chronicity of these symptoms.

The research selected and reviewed for this chapter has been organized under the following headings:

1. Etiology.
2. Therapy.
3. Evaluation of Psychotherapy.
4. Education.

ETIOLOGY

The investigations reported in this section have been divided into two general categories. One group of investigators assumes that the cause of

Reviewed by James J. Moss, University of Illinois.

emotional disturbances is psychogenic factors. This group explores conditions in the psychological environment for the major source of causation. The second group searches for a biogenic relationship between the individual and his disturbed behavior.

Psychogenic Factors

Kanner, L. Problems of Nosology and Psychodynamics of Early Infantile Autism. *American Journal of Orthopsychiatry*, 1949, 19, 416-426.

Purpose: The frequency with which parents of psychotic children display abnormal personality patterns has been impressively great. This paper points out a number of these patterns of the parents of autistic children.

Subjects: 55 autistic children and their parents.

Procedure: Data were obtained from case histories and observations of the children and their parents. Some of these observations were made in clinics, some in the homes of these families.

Results: All 55 autistic children had "sophisticated" parents. Besides very high level of intelligence, the vast majority of parents had the following features in common: (a) they were not comfortable with people, they preferred reading, writing, or just "thinking"; (b) their matrimonial life was a rather cold and formal affair; (c) there was a conspicuous lack of genuine warmth from the mother; (d) fathers hardly knew their autistic children. They were outwardly friendly but rarely stepped down from the pedestal of somber adulthood to indulge in childish play. The fathers were also devoted to duty. (e) They often surrendered unconditionally to standards of perfection. (f) They acted like transmitters despite their very high intellectual level. (g) They were extremely obsessive and observed their children with minute precision. The child was essentially the object of an interesting experiment and would be put aside when he was not needed for this purpose. (h) The mother lacked warmth and carried out rules and regulations mechanically.

Comment: The investigator explored the characteristics of parents of autistic children, implying a relationship between the attitudes and patterns of the child-rearing practices and the child's disorders. His lucid approach to the classification of the disease was presented in the beginning of the study. Although Kanner observed common characteristics among the parents of autistic children in this study, it is significant to note that many parents with normal children have attitudes comparable to the parents in this study.

Goldfarb, W. Effects of Early Institutional Care on Adolescent Personality: Rorschach Data. *American Journal of Orthopsychiatry,* 1944. 14, 441-447.

Purpose: To attempt to confirm previous findings on the effects of institutional care of infants and to study how these characteristics are revealed through a projective test.

Subjects: Subjects consisted of two groups: experimental and comparison. Experimental groups were eight boys and seven girls between 10 and 14 years of age. They were institutionalized at the mean age of 4.5 months and remained there for an average of three years and three months. At the age of about three years, seven months, they were transferred to foster homes where they were reared to the time of this study.

The comparison group consisted of children reared in foster homes beginning at a mean age of 14 months. They were equated with the experimental group with respect to age and sex.

Little was known about the fathers. The mothers in both groups did not differ in regard to national derivation and educational status. However, the vocational status of the mothers of the institutionalized group was superior to those of the foster-home group.

Procedure: Children in both groups were given the Rorschach test and compared on the basis of the quality of their responses.

Results: There was a marked difference in quality of responses. The institution group was inferior on the accuracy of perception. They were described as less controlled and less capable of developing logical constructs. Their behavior could be expected to be thoughtless and not goal-directed. The institutionalized group had a higher incidence of inaccurate perception of original responses which would indicate deviation from the normal in behavior and general adjustment.

Comment: This study offers support to the hypothesis that children institutionalized during childhood suffer in areas of control, perception, and goal-directed behavior as compared to children placed in foster homes. Since institutionalization will be necessary in many cases for some time to come, it seems reasonable to suggest exploration of accounting for and correcting this apparent deficiency. The implications raised by the results of this study with respect to the effect of the environment upon the psychological development of the child are obvious.

Eisenberg, L. The Fathers of Autistic Children. *American Journal of Orthopsychiatry*, 1957. 27, 715-724.

Purpose: To explore the family dynamics of homes with autistic children with particular reference to the father and his relationship to the personality development of the child.

Subjects and Procedure: This is a clinical investigation of the fathers of 100 children. Emphasis was placed on the parent-child relationship. The diagnostic criteria for infantile autism as used in this study were: (a) extreme self-isolation, (b) obsessive demand for routine, (c) rhythmic repetitive patterns of motor behavior, (d) language disturbances, (e) detachment from interpersonal contacts, (f) preoccupation with objects and details, and (g) peculiarities of thought.

Results: The author presented convincing descriptive data suggestive of common personality characteristics among the fathers of autistic children. Eighty-five out of 100 fathers of autistic children demonstrated the following traits: perfectionistic, detached and humorless, intellectual, preoccupied, ineffective as fathers and husbands.

It was pointed out that the 100 autistic children in this study had 131 siblings. Only three of the 131 siblings revealed any evidence of emotional disorder. This gives evidence that the fathers of the autistic children were capable of rearing normal children.

Comment: One would not question the presence of the undesirable traits in the experimental population of fathers. It would be interesting to have information upon the extent to which these same characteristics are present in an equal number of fathers without autistic children, drawn randomly from a comparable population.

Klebanoff, L. B. Parental Attitudes of Mothers of Schizophrenic, Brain-Injured, Retarded and Normal Children. *American Journal of Orthopsychiatry,* 1959, 29, 445-454.

Purpose: To investigate the relationship between maternal attitudes toward child rearing and the family, and childhood schizophrenia.

Subjects: 15 mothers of hospitalized schizophrenic children without mental retardation or gross known organic signs, and 15 mothers of hospitalized mentally retarded and brain damaged children who exhibited behavioral symptoms similar to those of the schizophrenic children. In a third group were mothers whose children had no history or symptoms of neurologic, psychiatric, or chronic physical illness.

Procedure: The groups of mothers were compared according to age, religion, socio-economic status and education. The Parental Attitude Research Instrument was used in the assessment of attitudes. The attitudes which were defined as pathological were compared between the mothers of schizophrenic children and the mothers of similarly-behaving retarded and brain damaged children.

Results: The results showed that the mothers of schizophrenic children had fewer pathological attitudes than the mothers of brain damaged and retarded children. This finding would cast doubt upon the idea that maternal attitudes cause schizophrenia.

The attitudes of the mothers of the two groups of ill children—schizophrenic, and retarded and brain damaged—were compared with the attitudes of mothers of normal children. The results showed that the mothers of both the schizophrenic and organic groups had more pathological attitudes than did the mothers of normal children. The evidence would support the notion that mothers with children who have serious behavior disorders, with or without organicity, were influenced by their relationships with their children toward more pathological attitudes than were mothers of normal children.

Comment: This study raises strong question about the idea that the mothers' attitudes are the cause of schizophrenia in their children. The evidence does support the hypothesis that the reaction of mothers toward their children's disordered behavior is influential upon their expressed attitudes.

Biogenic Factors

Kallman, F. J., and Roth, B. Genetic Aspects of Preadolescent Schizophrenia. *American Journal of Psychiatry*, 1956, 112, 599-606.

Purpose: To investigate important factors of disturbed parent-child relationship and the home milieu throughout childhood which may lead the individual to disturbance at an early age.

Subjects: 52 twin and 50 singleton patients of both sexes under age 15. A marked change in the behavior of a child who previously seemed to develop normally was a crucial diagnostic feature. Diagnosis for selection was made only on the basis of the clinical history of the child without knowledge of family background, and all diagnoses were made by one investigator. Symptoms observed were loss of interest in the environment, blunted or inappropriate affect, peculiar motor activity, diffuse anxiety with phobias and vague somatic complaints, tendency toward exaggerated fantasies, and hallucinations.

Procedure: Children were observed from the onset of symptoms. The period of observation varied from 5.5 years in single-born cases to 9.9 years in twins.

The monozygotic and dizygotic pairs were differentiated with respect to schizophrenia and schizoid personality and were compared with previous data on schizophrenia in adult twins. Single-borns were compared with their siblings in mental and emotional status.

The parents of the groups were investigated with respect to their emotional and intellectual status as well as the adequacy or inadequacy of the homes. The homes were analyzed in a simplified scheme, combining socio-economic and psychological criteria. Those homes which (a) appeared good or fair from a socio-economic standpoint, (b) were not broken due to desertion, divorce or death of a parent, and (c) were maintained by two well-adjusted parents, were all classified as adequate. The presence of one emotionally or socially inadequate parent was sufficient to place the home in the "poor" category even if there was no economic distress.

Results: When family backgrounds of pre-adolescent schizophrenics were compared with those of comparable adult ones, there were no significant differences between the groups. In other words, the same genotypic factors seemed to have been responsible for both childhood and adult schizophrenia.

There was an increase in the number of early schizophrenia cases among the co-twins and siblings. A marked excess of males over females was found in the pre-adolescent group. This was probably connected with various secondary factors lowering constitutional resistance.

It was found to be difficult to evaluate the role of poor home and/or disturbed intra-family relationships in the etiology of childhood schizophrenia as compared with that of adult cases. There seems to be a complex relationship, not a single correlation. In the present study, 71.4 percent of all the homes of all siblings and dizygotic co-twins, and 82 percent of the homes of co-twins and siblings, diagnosed schizoid or schizophrenic were inadequate. However, of all the normal co-twins and siblings, nearly two-thirds (64.8 percent) came from an inadequate home.

Comment: There does not seem to be a remarkable difference in the adequacy of homes between the schizophrenic co-twins and siblings and the normal co-twins and siblings. The author of this study points out that the causes of schizophrenia are complex as opposed to a cause and effect relationship.

Cohn, R., and Nardini, J. E. The Correlation of Bilateral Occipital Slow Activity in the Human E.E.G. with Certain Disorders of Behavior. *American Journal of Psychiatry*, 1958, 115, 44-54.

Purpose: To determine if there is a developmental history of abnormal electrical activity, and to show, by means of categories of patients, that the bi-occipital slow-wave output observed by EEG in certain disorders of behavior may be a continuous development of the abnormal bi-occipital slow wave activity observed in the records obtained from children.

Subjects: Data were collected and organized into two groups which were designated Series A and Series B. Eighteen hundred patients referred consecutively to the National Naval Medical Center, Bethesda, Maryland were used in the study.

Procedure: EEG's were given to the experimental population. The patients were divided into two groups for study by age. One group (Series A) ranged in age from 6.5 years to 25 years. The other group (Series B) had an age range of 17 to 50 years. The bi-occipital activity of one group was compared to the other. A comparison of the patients in each group who revealed bi-occipital slow waves was made with their behavior patterns.

Results: Bi-occipital slow wave activity was observed in approximately 14 percent of the 1800 patients between the age of six and one-half and 25 years. In the older group (Series B), bi-occipital slow activity was observed in seven percent of the patients. Seventy-five percent of the first group (ages six and one-half to 25 years) with bi-occipital slow activity showed varying intensities of aggressive clinical behavior. The individuals in this group between the ages of six and one-half and 17 years were having difficulty in their school adjustment, play and other social relationships. The primary problems consisted of "unruliness, hyperactive play, strong sense of acquisitiveness, failure to be considerate of their associates, and inability to respond appropriately to their supervisors" (p. 53).

The patients between the ages of 17 and 25 were even more overtly aggressive. The behavior patterns consisted of more than usual truancy,

297

unauthorized liberty from naval duty, need for excessive stimulation such as drag racing and highway speeding, sexual hyperactivity, and a rebellious attitude toward authority figures.

Comment: The presence of the occipital dysrhythmia in individuals with behavior disorders seemed apparent. Does this mean that abnormality of brain-wave patterns is a causative influence on behavior or could it be said that behavior disorders may affect brain-wave rhythm or that neurological disorders, as assessed by the EEG, may also be reflected in behavior disorders? Clarifications as to the meaning of this study could be increased by describing the behavior of children with other types of EEG patterns.

Kennard, Margaret. The Characteristics of Thought Disturbances as Related to Electroencephalographic Findings in Children and Adolescents. *American Journal of Psychiatry,* 1959. 115, 911-921.

Purpose: To compare disorders in thinking with findings on the electroencephalogram, with emphasis on exploring differences, if any, between the thinking disorders due to psychogenic factors and those resulting from the cortical defects of brain injuries.

Subjects: 200 children and adolescents, seven to 16 years of age, consecutively admitted to a mental hospital, grouped according to maturational and behavioral patterns. The groups were: 48 subjects, ages seven to 12; 52, ages 13 to 14; and 100, ages 15 to 16.

Procedure: The status of each of the 200 children was evaluated with reference to thought disturbance and organic brain disorder according to the four following diagnostic categories: (a) thought disturbance, (b) thought disturbance with organic component, (c) non-thought disturbance, and (d) non-thought disturbance with organic component. The criteria for the above diagnostic categories were as follows: (a) past history, (b) clinical behavior and psychiatric appraisal, and (c) psychological appraisal. The data from EEG or neurophysiological examinations were used in categorizing the children. The findings on the EEG for each of the groups were compared according to thought categories and organicity and to duration of illness and the frequency pattern of the EEG and thought disturbances.

Results: A diagnosis of organic brain disorder was obtained from the clinical history, and behavior pattern had a significant, positive correlation with abnormal EEG results.

Thought disturbance was found to be related to abnormal EEG findings. There was evidence that thought disturbance in younger ages is related to abnormal EEG patterns. There was evidence to support the conclusion that abnormal EEG patterns are present to a greater degree in children who have behavior disorders than in adults.

Thought disturbance, either non-organically or organically related, was positively correlated with pattern disturbances on the EEG when compared with non-thought disturbance categories.

In the younger age group particularly, organic brain injury and autistic or schizoid thinking patterns are strongly related not only as gathered from the history but also from the EEG.

Comment: Although a significant relationship appears between behavior disorders and positive EEG findings, it is not as strongly predictive as in the preceding study. More abnormal EEG records were found in autistic and brain-injured children. At the same time, a positive relationship exists between both non-organic and organic children with behavior disorders and the EEG.

In Review

The studies reviewed above represent only a few of the many investigations that have been conducted in an effort to learn more about the causes of emotional disturbances. No evidence has been reported which completely supports single factors as being causative in any area of emotional disturbances.

Defining causes of emotional disturbances in terms of single factors seems to yield fruitless returns. The interaction between functional and organic contributions in disorders of emotions seems to be integral to the nature of disorders. Further clarification of causes may come from more refined methods of studying this interaction.

THERAPY

There are few carefully controlled studies of psychotherapy with children and youth. The majority of studies describe the therapeutic procedures and outcome used by the therapist without due attention to controls. In this section on therapy, studies from four typical therapeutic media are included. These are: camp therapy, group therapy, play therapy, and child psychotherapy. Drug therapy was necessarily omitted even though this area of therapy has been reported generously in the literature.

299

Morse, W. C., and Small, Edna R. Group Life Space Interviewing in a Therapeutic Camp: The Life Space Interview Workshop 1957. *American Journal of Orthopsychiatry*, 1959, 29, 27-44.

Purpose: Social interaction is thought to reflect children's basic problems, and therefore provides a channel for therapy. This study presents a pilot analysis of dealing with children's behavioral disturbances during group interactions through "reality-focused life space interviews".

Subjects: Children from the University of Michigan Fresh Air Camp which serves about 90 emotionally disturbed boys ranging from eight to 15 years of age.

Procedure: The method used was "interviewing" conducted by experienced clinical staff members. The size of the group varied from three to nine, all coming from the same cabin group. Length of interviews averaged about an hour. When possible, the interviews were held soon after a minor problem or a serious incident in the group had occurred, such as fighting, stealing, and excessive swearing. Following group sessions, individual interviews were held to go over the child's specific problems. Material from the group sessions was incorporated into individual interview sessions.

Results: During the seven weeks, 88 group sessions were held, 19 of which were taped and eight dictated in interpretive summary. Some of the conclusions drawn by the experimenters as a result of the interviews were:

The group interviews provided an opportunity for concrete planning to meet the difficulties.

"The leader-therapist must be sensitive to the interaction going on in the group and the motives for particular children's statements and questions, and he must be able to express himself rapidly and well" (p. 30).

The leader should impose structure if the group does not produce it.

The emphasis in interviews should not be to establish facts of what happened, but to learn the children's perception of an incident and the significance they attach to it.

The authors established five categories to study differential processes in group life space interviews:

1. Systematized antisocial behavior: This group illustrated a contentment with its way of life and resisted any arousal of anxiety.

2. Symptomatic compliance: This group's reactions were essentially ambivalent. There was considerable defensiveness combined with the recognition of legitimate social values.

3. Interpretive acceptance: There seemed to be a more positive relationship to the adult leader. Often this group was composed of members who had had productive individual therapy.

4. Spontaneous therapeutic interaction: This group moved into spontaneous production of significant life experiences. The interview was characterized by mutual discussion and sympathetic concern over one another. Different camp behaviors were discussed in the same manner.

5. Unclassified type of group interviews: These were group interviews which did not seem to fit into any of the above categories.

Comment: The notion of reality-focused interpretation of actual social situations seems to have merit. Certainly if we assume that behavior modifications result from increased learning and understanding, actual social interaction with immediate follow-up interviews provides concrete, meaningful experiences.

Hewitt, Helen and Gildea, Margaret. An Experiment in Group Psychotherapy. *American Journal of Orthopsychiatry,* 1945. 15, 112-127.

Purpose: Group work as a psychotherapeutic technique with children has gained an increasing acceptance in the last decade. With the increasing demand and popularity of day camps, nursery schools, and after-school playgrounds, the problem of socially maladjusted children is a tremendously urgent and significant issue. This study is an attempt to find a solution to the problem of effects of therapeutic techniques on the social adjustment of children.

Subjects: Five girls, ages seven to nine, drawn into a small unit within the program of a large day camp of 100 children, ranging in age from five to 14. The selection of the small group was made on the basis of the child's problems of social adjustment in the large group, and on past history as a social misfit.

Procedure: The activities of this small experimental group were so arranged that none of the children thought there was anything special about the set-up. In the mornings the group met in their cabin headquarters, and later in the day the children returned to participate in the large group activities. There were 18 meetings altogether. The activities were unstructured and were based more or less on the group's interest. The therapist confined her role, in the special groups, to "that of a passive observer, but responded with positive friendliness and reassurance to the emotional demands of the children so that they could never doubt her real acceptance of them as individuals" (p. 113).

301

Results: In the last 16 meetings it was observed that the children "gradually became freed emotionally to a point where they could openly express their feelings and face some of their personal conflicts and the dangerous consequences, since they felt reassured by the consistent accepting attitude of the therapist" (p. 118).

It is concluded that it is easier for socially maladjusted children to learn the fundamentals of social adjustment in small groups. "To such children the permissive outlet of a small unit, offering a chance to work off hostilities, fears, and guilt, is of inestimable value in relieving them of almost unbearable inner pressures" (p. 126). The small group served as a learning process in developing close interpersonal relationships, which the children practiced within the large group. The small group provided a far more adequate basis to study the psychodynamics of individuals, and their different problems.

The personality and experience of the therapist did have great importance in the character of the group and the speed with which situations and developments occurred.

Comment: This study, like all other descriptive studies, offers no empirical support for the outcome of therapy. The reader must take at face value the criteria for judgments such as "freed emotionally" and "could openly express their feelings and face their personal conflicts." Of more concern than this, it would seem, is the strong role that the personality of the therapist played in this therapy program. Perhaps this means that we cannot separate the role of the therapeutic technique from the therapists and possibly even the patient when evaluating the therapy.

Conn, J. H. The Child Reveals Himself Through Play. *Mental Hygiene,* 1949, 33, 49-70.

Purpose: To show that the child needs to express his dissatisfaction, his fears, and his hopes in his own natural fashion, through play, and that this can be a valuable source of information in understanding a child.

Subjects and Procedure: This study consists of a series of case studies from the Children's Psychiatric Clinic of Johns Hopkins Hospital. With the presentation of each case study in play therapy, the author gives an analysis of the factors involved and his own interpretation of the data he presents.

Results: The author stresses his belief that no one theory can account for all of the factors in any one case. There is the factor of original endowment as well as the situational, physical, and developmental factors to be evaluated. The attitudes of the parents, of the school teachers, of the child's associates at home and in the playground or neighborhood must be studied to determine their effect on the child in his daily living. As the child is allowed to express himself in his own natural fashion through the medium of play, he can begin to understand what he has contributed to the total situation and thus to accept his share of the responsibility for what is happening.

Comment: This study describes the value of a play situation which allows the child to express his conflicts and thereby helps him to understand more fully his responsibility and perform more effectively. An additional observation which is important to consider is the effect that the attitudes of the child's parents, teachers, and associates have upon his performance.

Moustakas, C. E. The Frequency and Intensity of Negative Attitudes Expressed in Play Therapy: A Comparison of Well-adjusted and Disturbed Young Children. *Journal of Genetic Psychology.* 1955, 86-87, 309-325.

Purpose: To determine the frequency and intensity of negative expressions among well-adjusted children as compared to disturbed children.

Subjects: Nine well-adjusted and nine disturbed children, all four years of age, who were matched on various other characteristics.

Procedure: Each child had four play therapy interviews. Verbatim tape recordings of the children's statements and stenographic notes of movements and actions provided the data.

Results: The nine disturbed children expressed a total of 150 negative attitudes in their play as compared to 91 negative attitudes expressed by well-adjusted children.

The disturbed children had a range from 11 to 22 negative attitudes expressed in two 40-minute play sessions. The well-adjusted expressed from 4 to 16 negative attitudes. The mean of the disturbed group was 16.7; of the well-adjusted group, 10.1. The types of negative attitudes expressed by well-adjusted and disturbed children were similar.

Each disturbed child expressed moderate to severe intensity of feeling. In the well-adjusted group, only one child showed more than moderate intensity of feeling. The remaining well-adjusted children showed essentially mild negative feelings.

The disturbed children expressed considerably more intense anxiety and hostility than did the well-adjusted children. The strongest negative attitude of the well-adjusted group was hostility toward siblings.

The disturbed children more often expressed negative attitudes in a diffuse and generalized way, while the well-adjusted expressed their feelings more directly.

Comment: This study was more explorative than definitive, since the results were drawn from only four individual play therapy sessions with each child. It would be interesting to see the results of a study which included more subjects, extended over a longer period of time, and provided periodic evaluations on all subjects after leaving therapy.

Phillips, E. L. Parent-Child Psychotherapy: A Follow-up Study Comparing Two Techniques. *Journal of Psychology.* 1960, 49, 195-202.

Purpose: This study includes the process, technique, and outcome of child psychotherapy. Specifically, this investigation was done to compare results of short-term, non-depth therapy with the traditional depth therapy commonly practiced in child guidance clinics. (The author of this study uses the term "depth" to describe the concept of a "deep seated" psychological conflict which requires an extended period of expression in some therapeutic media to uncover and subsequently resolve the conflict.)

Subjects: 59 subjects drawn from a suburban child-guidance clinic. One group of children received therapy using a non-depth therapy technique, the other received the more traditional depth technique. There were 29 cases who received non-depth therapy and 30 cases in the control group who received depth therapy. Age range of the non-depth therapy group was 3-5 to 11-4 years with a mean of 8-2 years. Age range of the depth group was 3-5 to 11-4 years with a mean of 8-1 years. The IQ range of the non-depth group was 100 to 135 with a mean IQ of 109.1. The IQ range of the depth group was 95 to 140 with a mean IQ of 110. Parents of both the experimental and control group were seen at the guidance clinic.

Procedure: A six-item questionnaire was completed by the parents of children who had been seen over a five-year period. The questionnaire requested the parents to rate the child on: improvement since the original complaint, parent's ability to handle child better, child's behavior at home, child's behavior in formal groups, child's behavior in informal play groups, and behavior specifically at school. The non-depth therapy group was compared statistically to the depth therapy group by use of the *t* test.

The non-depth method of therapy placed emphasis upon the following procedures:

Therapy began with the first interview.

The therapy hours were divided equally between parent and child.

After the first two or three interviews, meetings were decreased to two a month. After the initial period of structuring with the parents, parents were encouraged to be on their own for longer periods.

The therapist worked with the teacher in an information giving and taking role. Continuity of method and outlook was established between the therapist and teacher.

The parents were given "common sense" explanations of what the child's behavior means.

Stress was placed on "keeping structure," that is, on setting limits on behavior and specific aims for achievement.

Homework, household chores, and a fairly set routine were stressed. The structure was firmed up in sensibility, fairness, and consistency.

The interview period of 45 to 50 minutes was divided between the parent and child. The non-depth therapist spent one-half as much time as the depth therapist.

Results: The non-depth therapy yielded significantly better results on all six of the items as judged by the parents.

The results indicated that the outcome success ratio was 25 out of 27 (92 percent) in the children seen in the non-depth setting and 18 out of 30 (60 percent) for the depth therapy cases.

Comment: The most encouraging signs reflected by this study are the real concerns which personnel in child guidance clinics have with reference to shortening of the waiting lists and offering more efficient treatment programming. The inclusion of parents and teachers in the treatment program is one of the few progressive developments in psychotherapy in the past ten years. Continued exploration into the treatment process, as exemplified by this study, should yield more efficient psychotherapy programs for children.

In Review

Some therapists are reluctant to do research dealing with the outcome of psychotherapy. They assert that proof of the effect of psychotherapy is no longer needed. This assertion is more fantasy than fact. There is a great need for well-controlled investigation comparing various approaches, length of therapy, therapy setting and process. Psychotherapy as a single influence on the adjustment of children may not prove to be the most efficient or effective approach to modifying the behavior of children. It is possible that milieu therapy or the so-called non-depth therapy with parents and teachers as a part of the team may be the most practical and also the most effective method.

EVALUATION OF PSYCHOTHERAPY

The development of child study and psychotherapy with children in the past 35 to 40 years has led to a substantial number of evaluation studies. Three typical evaluation studies have been included in this section.

> Lehrman, L. J., Sirluck, Hilda, Black, B. J., Glick, Selma J., *et al.* Success and Failure of Treatment of Children in the Child Guidance Clinics of the Jewish Board of Guardians, New York City: Analysis and Follow-ups of Cases Closed Between April 1, 1941 and March 31, 1942. *Jewish Board of Guardians Research Monograph,* 1949, 1.

Purpose: To investigate the success and failure of treatment of children in the JBG clinics, through the comparison of adjustments of a group of treated children at follow-up with those of a control group of similar but untreated children.

Subjects: 366 cases seen by a child guidance clinic in New York City.

Procedure: The total group was divided into three categories: the treatment group (N-196, 53.5 percent), the control group (N-110, 30.1 percent), and the rejected group (N-60, 16.4 percent) who had entered treatment but had been referred to more appropriate treatment sources or had voluntarily withdrawn from Jewish Board of Guardians Child Guidance Clinics and secured treatment elsewhere. The rejected group was excluded from the study. The status of each child in the treatment group at closing and at follow-up was evaluated by a special agency committee on the basis of information supplied by specially employed research personnel; information was structured so as to make it impossible for the committee to know whether the case being evaluated belonged to the treatment, control, or rejected group. The status of children in the control group was evaluated in a like manner by the same committee. Two kinds of evaluations—one sociological and the other clinical—were used. Criterion for the first was the present acceptability of the child's behavior in the community; the clinical evaluation was a relative one, based on comparison of the child's past and present subjective and objective performance, if problems, symptoms, and the subjective pressures associated with them were favorably modified without lessening of subjective discomfort.

Results: Successful community adjustment was much greater among the treatment group than among the control group (TG-50.5 percent; CG-31.8 percent). The positive effect of treatment on community adjustment was much greater for younger than for older children. Treatment appeared to be much more effective with girls than with boys, and slightly more effective among children with primary behavior disorders than with psychoneurotics. Treatment effects were far more favorable with children who had two adequate parents, although there was some evidence to indicate that children with two inadequate parents benefitted somewhat more than those with one adequate and one inadequate parent.

Comment: The study appears to be about as complete as any available. The only point in question, as with all similar studies, lies in the selection and use of a control group. There is some question as to whether or not the evaluation, in itself, did not constitute some form of treatment in the course of the intensive diagnostic and study process. It was difficult, as is usually the case, to determine with any degree of accuracy the reasons behind children becoming control group members, indicating a possible unknown bias in the findings of the control/treatment relationship.

Levitt, E. E., Beiser, Helen R. and Robertson, R. E. A Follow-Up Evaluation of Cases Treated at a Community Child Guidance Clinic. *American Journal of Orthopsychiatry,* 1959, 29, 337-349.

Purpose: To evaluate the effect of psychotherapy at the Institute for Juvenile Research, Illinois State Department of Public Welfare.

Subjects: A random sample of 1006 cases defined as treated and untreated made the original sampling population. After omitting cases that had received past clinical treatment and cases who could not be located, the number consisted of 237 experimental and 93 comparison cases. The comparison group was made up of cases who applied for treatment but defected before treatment began.

Sixty-nine percent of the 330 cases were males. The mean age at the time of follow-up was 15.87 years with a standard deviation of 4.20 years. An average of 5.4 years intervened between termination of treatment and the follow-up interview. The standard deviation was 3.3 years.

Procedure: The treatment (experimental) group was compared with the non-treatment (comparison) group. The following types of data were collected: (a) objective psychological tests; (b) objective facts, such as marriage, armed forces service, institutionalization, or completion of schooling; (c) parents' opinions and evaluations of the child and his symptoms; (d) statements about himself and his feelings by the child; and (e) clinical judgments of the child by the interviews in the data collection situation.

The data were analyzed, using at least five one-hour therapy sessions as criteria for treatment for the first analysis. The analysis was repeated using at least 10 one-hour sessions as the criteria for treatment.

Results: Using five one-hour therapy sessions as criteria, the results were analyzed by means of chi square and t tests. The differences between the experimental and control groups were analyzed for 26 outcome variables. Two of the 26 probability values were significant. For all practical purposes, there were no real differences between the two groups.

In the second analysis, treatment was re-defined as 10 therapy sessions. Increasing the number of treatment sessions resulted in losing 45 experimental subjects. No significant differences were found to exist between the experimental and control group on the 18 variables used in the second analysis.

Comment: Again this study can be criticized on the basis that defectors as a control group are not comparable to the treatment group. Even though the criticism is essentially a valid one, a good number of arguments can be presented to support the defector group as a control.

In order to obtain an acceptable control, it would be necessary to assign individuals randomly to a treatment and a control group. In this case, of course, it would be necessary to withhold treatment from the patients assigned to the control group. The difficulty with this is that it would be virtually impossible to keep the control individuals from getting therapy. A far less complicated design would be to compare several psychotherapeutic approaches, thus providing treatment for all individuals in the study. Of course, it could be argued that this approach would not yield evidence to support treatment; however, it does seem impractical to assume that an adequate study could be designed that would assure a comparable non-treatment control.

In Review

In evaluating the various studies and approaches to research on psychotherapy with children, several major factors require consideration. In addition to the need for a more adequate system of statistical control, more rigidly defined terminology must be used. Studies have been equated and conclusions drawn on essentially dissimilar data. Added to these problems are the differing philosophies and approaches to treatment, differences of training and background among those designated as therapists, variable measurement criteria, the lack of an appropriate baseline, and a general lack of validated definitions.

The critique of the design and results of the existing evaluation studies could continue *ad infinitum,* but the fact remains that the results of psychotherapy in affecting major adjustment changes among disturbed children are discouraging. Considering the relatively high incidence of emotional disturbances as reported in epidemiologic studies, it is obvious that additional facilities must be provided for children with emotional problems.

EDUCATION

Until recent years, wide gaps have existed in the services for emotionally disturbed children. There have been very limited facilities available for children who needed more help than could be provided by the supportive services of private psychologists, psychiatrists, or public agencies and child guidance clinics, but who did not require residential placement or institutionalization. This, plus the great need for additional facilities for emotionally disturbed children, has prompted a few public school systems to provide psychological services, guidance services, school social workers and special classes. The present trend is toward establishing special classes in regular elementary and secondary school buildings of large public school systems.

The review of studies in education included in this chapter has focused largely upon school facilities for emotionally disturbed children within public school systems. Particular emphasis has been placed upon demonstration and controlled investigations concerned with special classes.

Birch, J. W. Special Classes and Schools for Maladjusted Children. *Exceptional Children,* 1956. 22, 332-337.

Purpose: To gain information concerning current educational practices for children presenting behavior and/or personality problems.

Subjects: 10 major school systems with special classes and schools were used in this survey. These were: Baltimore, Chicago, Cincinnati, Dade County (Miami), Detroit, Los Angeles, New York, Philadelphia, Rochester and Seattle.

Procedure: A questionnaire and follow-up correspondence was carried on with the school officials of the above school systems. The results were tabulated.

Results: The majority of the cities studied have more than one type of special school or class for maladjusted children. The tendency is to have three or four different school facilities. The most frequent facility is the special school in a detention home operated by the court. Next in order are special classes in regular schools and special residential schools. Some indications are pointing toward an increase in special classes for emotionally disturbed children.

Comment: The trend toward providing special classes for emotionally disturbed children, as pointed out by Birch, has been strengthened in recent years.

Bower, E. M. The Emotionally Handicapped Child and the School. *Exceptional Children,* 1959. 26, 182-188.

Purpose: To determine the prevailing facilities and trends with regard to the education of emotionally disturbed children.

Subjects: The investigator visited 15 facilities and/or projects. These are listed as follows: (a) Quincy, Illinois Youth Development Project; (b) Illinois State Department of Education; (c) the program on mental health consultation to schools, Harvard School of Public Health; (d) Massachusetts State Department of Education; (e) Wellesley, Massachusetts Public School Project; (f) Juvenile Delinquency Evaluation Research Project of the City of New York; (g) New York City Public Schools; (h) New York State Department of Education; (i) New York City Community Welfare Council; (j) Pennsylvania State Department of Education; (k) Education Testing Service, Princeton; (l) Child Research Branch of the National Institute of Mental Health; (m) Community Services Branch of the National Institute of Mental Health; (n) Syracuse University-Montgomery County Research Study on Hyperactive Children with Learning Disabilities; and (o) the Juvenile Delinquency Project of the National Education Association, Washington, D.C.

Procedure: The investigator spent from less than half a day to two days visiting the programs. The selection of the projects and programs visited was based on travel accessibility, time, and nature of project. Prior to the visitation, correspondence directed to those in charge of each program stated the nature and purpose of the survey. In almost every case the key person in the project was interviewed.

Results: The following conclusions are drawn from the programs seen on this trip and other visits: (a) The problem of educating emotionally disturbed children and youth has become a critical one for the majority of school systems. (b) In school systems where no planning or programming has been accomplished, the problem of the emotionally disturbed child in the systems has become more acute. (c) For some children the program needs to include therapeutic activities to achieve successful learning. (d) A planned program of mental health is considered to be an essential part of school preventive measures. (e) The nature and quality of the school program has a positive effect upon the educational and social growth of the child.

Comment: Although the investigator made little attempt to evaluate the practices used in his survey, this seems to represent a reliable summary of current trends in the management of emotionally disturbed children. Apparently the role of the schools in the total program for these children is receiving more recognition.

Eisenberg, L. School Phobia: A Study in the Communication of Anxiety. *American Journal of Psychiatry,* 1958, 114, 712-718.

Purpose: To determine the cause of school phobia and to report the effects of treatment. The hypothesis was that successful treatment lies in insistence on an early return to school for older children or the introduction to a therapeutic nursery school for the younger.

Subjects and Procedure: The preschool-age children were placed in a specialized nursery school for emotionally disturbed children. The elementary and secondary school-age children were studied in an outpatient clinic. A thorough psychiatric evaluation was performed on each subject. The children in the nursery were observed carefully and the behavior of the child and the mother during the initial and transitional period was recorded.

Results: School phobia was shown to be a variant of separation anxiety. Encouraging positive results were gained from insistence on an

311

early return to school accompanied with treatment for the older children and a therapeutic nursery school for the younger ones.

Comment: The absence of a control group places the researcher in a difficult position when asked to determine whether early return to school or the therapeutic aspects of the nursery program yielded the observed positive results. It seems reasonable, however, to assume that insisting upon the separation from the mother supported with a therapeutic environment does provide an effective treatment program to overcome fear of school.

Hay, L. A New School Channel for Helping the Troubled Child. *American Journal of Orthopsychiatry,* 1953, 23, 676-683.

Purpose: To describe the effectiveness of "guidance classes" for troubled children conducted in the New York City school system.

Subjects: 60 of the most poorly adjusted children from the third, fourth and fifth grades in an elementary school with an enrollment of approximately 1600 children. The children were withdrawn, submissive, of low vitality, hyperactive, or aggressive; had a school phobia or a marked speech defect; or had notable physical disabilities such as asthma and epilepsy, or were academically retarded. All children had at least average intellectual ability.

Procedure: The children were placed in special classes with 15 to 20 children in each class. The curriculum of the classes was determined by the needs of the children. Non-academic units of experience were designed to give the child success and develop self-confidence. Academic work was not ignored. Much special attention was given to make the academic work interesting. Large classrooms were assigned to the group to provide enough space for a variety of activities, tools and supplies. The parents were seen by social workers on the staff and were offered guidance in their relationships with their children. Achievement and adjustment scores of the classes were used for evaluation measures.

Results: The greatest improvement was in the area of "self-confidence." Marked improvements were noted in leadership and social adjustment. In addition, satisfactory academic progress was noted.

Comment: This descriptive study of special classes for emotionally disturbed children represents one of the first practical approaches to the task of providing appropriate educational placement and programming. Since this study, important refinements have developed in the selection criterion, methods of teaching and curriculum.

Newman, Ruth G. The Assessment of Progress in the Treatment of Hyperaggressive Children with Learning Disturbances Within a School Setting. *American Journal of Orthopsychiatry,* 1959, 29, 633-643.

Purpose: To assess the progress of adjustment and learning of emotionally disturbed, hyperaggressive boys in treatment at the Clinical Center, Child Research Branch of the National Institute of Mental Health.

Subjects: Six boys of normal intelligence, ranging in age from eight to 10, without known organic damage, who displayed an extreme degree of hyperaggressiveness.

Procedure: From the beginning of the study, descriptive comments were recorded on every incident of behavior of the boys in both group school and individual tutoring situations. These descriptive incidents were used to formulate descriptive characterizations and three broad classifications were made. Under each general classification of descriptive behavior or incident, seven subcategories were formed. This was a modification of the Critical Incident Technique.

The three major classifications were Self, Relationships, and School. Under the Self category, the following sub-categories were created: Self-Picture, Inner Drives and Forces, and Infantile Needs Frustration Tolerance. Under Relationships were Relations to Adults and Relations to Peers. The sub-categories under School were School Methods, Materials, Subject Matter, and Teacher Personality. The ratings of the incidents were judged by one judge in terms of the above categories and these ratings were subjected to four objective judges to be rated independently.

Results: Based upon the above categorization of incidents, the author formed the following conclusions: (a) Hyperaggressive, emotionally disturbed boys require explicit, limited, concrete, carefully defined, brief assignments. (b) Subject matter which is emotionally loaded with happy family life or charming naughty pranks and tender material is too threatening. (c) Programs with activity and manual emphasis are more likely to succeed than heavy doses of desk work. (d) Clear communication between the child and the teacher with reference to behavior that is acceptable and that which is only tolerated and must eventually be prohibited should be continuous. (e) Very rigid, unimaginative, highly structured methods are more acceptable than open-ended, creative, fantasy-arousing tasks. (f) A close interpersonal relationship between the teacher and child seems to be very threatening. (g) Conscious or unconscious desires of the teacher for the child's achievement when detected by the child are an extremely disruptive influence on the child's achievement.

Comment: This was an elaborate demonstration study concerned with hyperaggressive boys. A great deal of descriptive data was collected on the boys' responses to various educational and treatment procedures.

This is one of the first studies which actually refines and defines specific teaching techniques. The use of structured methods and instructional materials is an important new development in the education of emotionally disturbed children. Although this report has included only a portion of the data that were collected during the five-year period of research, several more reports on the project may be anticipated.

Cruickshank, W. M., Bentzen, F., Ratzeberg, F., and Tann-hauser. M. A. *Teaching Method for Brain Injured and Hyperactive Children: A Demonstration Pilot Study.* Special Education and Rehabilitation Monograph Series, Syracuse University, 1961.

Purpose: To investigate and evaluate the effectiveness and instructional usefulness of teaching methods and techniques developed for brain injured children when used with hyperactive emotionally disturbed children with or without evidence of brain injury.

Subjects: 40 hyperactive, emotionally disturbed children ranging in age from 6-11 to 10-11 years. Two groups were designated experimental and two control. The groups were in special classes in three elementary schools in Montgomery County, Maryland. The children were intellectually within the normal range.

Procedure: Each child in the study received a complete pediatric, neurological, electroencephalographic recording, psychiatric, psychological and educational evaluation. Based upon these data, the children were divided into two groups: children diagnosed neurologically and medically as brain injured, and children with psychological behavior and learning disabilities typical of that displayed by brain injured children, but without evidence of brain injury. Five in each of the four groups of children were classified as brain injured and five were classified as emotionally disturbed.

The two experimental classrooms had several modifications including: removal of all extraneous stimuli, the walls and woodwork the same color, individual work cubicles, enclosed supply cabinets and frosted windows. The two control classrooms received no environmental changes.

The instructional methods and materials in the experimental classes used the auditory, kinesthetic and tactile sensory processes in the learning experience. The school day was scheduled rigidly with respect to both time and activity. No deviation from this type of programming was permitted. The instructional methods and materials for the two control groups were traditional in most cases. The control teachers were permitted to use any of the experimental methods in which they found an interest.

Results: The children were in this instructional program for a maximum of 10 months. They received a thorough psychological and psychiatric evaluation at the beginning and the end of the school year.

A significant improvement in social growth and development and in academic achievement was seen for both the experimental and control group, but there was no difference between the groups. Apparently no significant differences were noted between the brain injured and the emotionally disturbed. The authors inferred that evidence with hyperactivity and emotional disturbances shows gains from the experimental program regardless of the causes of the behavior.

Comment: The original statement of the problem was centered on determining the usefulness of teaching methods developed for brain injured children when applied to emotionally disturbed children without demonstrable brain injury. The experiment, however, was not so designed as to yield an answer to this very important question. The controlled variables were the uniform color of the classroom and individual work cubicles.

In spite of these weaknesses in experimental design and statistical analysis, this is thus far one of the best attempts to investigate and control instructional techniques for hyperactive emotionally disturbed children.

Haring, N. G. and Phillips, E. L. *Educating Emotionally Disturbed Children.* New York: McGraw-Hill, 1962.

Purpose: To compare the results of three educational settings for emotionally disturbed children.

Subjects: Three groups of 15 emotionally disturbed children ranging in age from seven to 12 years.

Procedure: The children were selected and diagnosed as having emotional disturbances by a team consisting of a special educator, psycholo-

315

gist, physician, and school social worker. The team used a list of four specific criteria.

Forty-five children were randomly assigned to three groups of 15 each. The groups were varied in size, educational placement and educational approach. Group I was divided into two groups. The classroom environment was structured, each child was programmed in terms of his ability. Emphasis was placed upon completion of tasks. The children in group II were assigned to 15 regular classrooms. Every possible assistance was given the regular classroom teacher from the psychologist and school social worker in a traditional relationship. Group III consisted of 15 children in a special class. A traditional educational approach was used in this class. Curriculum was based upon the child's interests and much less structure was imposed.

Achievement testing was done with the children in the three groups at the beginning of the study, at the end of the first academic year and again at the end of the school year. A behavior rating scale was administered in the same way. An analysis of variance was applied to the achievement scores and the scores on the behavior rating scale.

Results: The children in Group I (structured special class) showed significantly more gain in academic achievement and social adjustment when compared with groups II and III. The children in group II (regular class) displayed significantly more gains in academic achievement than group III. The gain in social adjustment for group III (loosely structured special class) was significantly greater than that of group II.

Comment: The results of this study were strikingly in favor of the structured educational experience with firm expectations from the children and small special classes. Although positive programming with constant follow-through seemed to provide efficient and effective conditions for educating emotionally disturbed children, this approach should be subjected to considerably more investigation before conclusive statements are made about the superiority of this approach.

In Review

A trend toward establishing special classes for emotionally disturbed children in public school systems of metropolitan areas has been observed. Attention has been given to the specific learning and psychological characteristics of disturbed children in organizing and programming special classes. Some evidence is available to support the use of special classes for the education and treatment of emotionally disturbed children when these classes are appropriately organized and supervised.

SUMMARY

The studies reviewed in this chapter were concerned with the causes, therapy, evaluation, and education of emotionally disturbed children. Although a substantial amount of research is reported in these areas, descriptive studies seemed to predominate. The lack of controlled investigation, particularly among the studies involving therapy and education, presents serious limitations to the conclusions that can be drawn at this point.

Among the most serious of the difficulties which complicate the research with emotionally disturbed children are: (a) the lack of information about the specific causes of emotional disturbances; (b) the lack of uniformity of terminology; (c) the varying personality theories and philosophies used as frames of reference influencing treatment methods; and (d) the difficulty encountered in establishing adequate controls.

The assumption that conventional methods of psychotherapy are effective in modifying behavior and emotional adjustment is based largely on faith. It is reasonable that psychotherapy with children and parents would produce significant changes. However, controlled studies on the outcome of therapy, by and large, have not supported this assumption.

Relatively few changes have been made in the status of psychotherapy for at least a decade. The research on psychotherapy which appears in the literature does not reveal answers to important questions. The assumptions that have been made about personality theories and treatment methods have precluded scientific investigations. The variations in theoretical constructs which underlie psychotherapy are great. Each therapist makes convincing claims for the particular personality theory of his subscription. Does the quality of therapy vary with the personality theory or do all of the therapeutic approaches have equal effectiveness? If one method of treatment is more efficient and effective than the others, this should be known.

The role of education is becoming increasingly more dominant in providing programs for emotionally disturbed children. Since this development is evident, serious consideration must be given to a series of investigations. To begin with, it is important to study several methods of teaching, curricula, class size and classroom conditions. Once the most effective combination of techniques and conditions has been determined, it would then be worthwhile to compare results from special classes (including medical and psychological consultation) with other treatment facilities, such as community child guidance clinics and private therapists.

11

The Delinquent

Herbert C. Quay

It is customary to begin a review of research literature with a commonly accepted definition of the topic to be reviewed. When considering the delinquent child, it is apparent that the diversity of definitions and the conceptual unclarity as to how delinquency should be defined have been major hindrances to research and its interpretation.

By far the most popular definition of the delinquent child has been the legal one: a child who has appeared before a juvenile judge for an official hearing and disposition. While this definition is operational in that the researcher has a well defined criterion for selection of subjects, it is far from ideal for a number of reasons. First of all, laws pertaining to juvenile behavior vary from locality to locality. What is delinquent behavior in one community may not be in another. Curfew laws are an outstanding example. In the second place, and perhaps even more important, enforcement of laws and disposition of apprehended offenders can be seen to be much less than uniform, even for different areas of the same municipality. This lack of uniformity introduces biases. Studies have shown, for example, that children from families of lower socio-economic status are more likely to be arrested, convicted, and institutionalized for a given offense than are children of middle- or upper-class families. The use of a legally defined population also eliminates from

Reviewed by William C. Kvaraceus, Boston University.

research scrutiny the population of "hidden" delinquents, those who have committed some offense for which legal action could have been taken but who have not been apprehended. It has been estimated that there is one hidden delinquent for each official case.

Other definitions have been proposed for research purposes. Some investigators have studied delinquent behavior by contrasting groups differentiated on the basis of their admitted commission of delinquent acts. This approach, while eliminating many of the problems inherent in using official or institutional samples, has the disadvantage of depending upon self-report of the subjects and of eliminating from study individuals who have committed serious offenses repeatedly and are thus not at large in the population. Other researchers have used as their experimental population adolescents who had been characterized by school personnel as "aggressive." This definition has the advantage of eliminating all of the vicissitudes of judges and police officials but requires the sometimes questionable judgment of school personnel as a replacement. Recidivism, or repeated official contact, has been used. This criterion tends to eliminate many of the less serious delinquents by assuring that those defined for research as delinquents have a history of difficulties with the authorities. However, the socio-economic bias may be even greater here. These definitions covered are by no means exhaustive.

Obviously, the definition used to define the sample of delinquents to be studied will influence the results obtained. Since there is no readily apparent, completely satisfactory solution to this question of definition of delinquency for research purposes, the student of delinquency simply has to live with the problem for the time being.

For purposes of trying to bring some organization to the research reviewed, studies will be reviewed under six major headings:

1. Descriptive and definitional studies.
2. Psychological correlates of delinquent behavior.
3. Causes of delinquency.
4. Educational aspects of delinquency.
5. Treatment of delinquents.
6. Prevention.

A word about the selection of studies seems in order. This reviewer has selected for presentation only those major studies which presume to meet the criteria of scientific acceptability as contributions to knowledge. In this regard the reviewer has explicitly considered two prime criteria: (a) the use of control groups where necessary, and (b) statistical, rather than impressionistic, analysis of the data used. These criteria seem not to be prejudicial toward any effort of an empirical nature but will eliminate most of the "observational," "clinical," or "intuitional" types of studies. In addition, since the emphasis of this entire monograph is on research studies, theoretical papers have not been reviewed unless they included research data in support of the theoretical propositions.

DESCRIPTIVE AND DEFINITIONAL STUDIES

A number of studies have attempted, by various methods, to subdivide the delinquent population into more homogeneous categories. There appears to be a considerable amount of basic agreement in the results of these studies despite methodological and semantic differences. While delinquents themselves have been the object of research designed to develop subcategories, delinquent acts have also come under scrutiny. Studies have questioned the unidimensionality of delinquent behavior and have presented evidence for the existence of different kinds of delinquency. It is obvious that future research should continue to explore both of these questions and should seek links between the two.

Murphy, F. J., Shirley, Mary M., and Witmer, Helen L. The Incidence of Hidden Delinquency. *American Journal of Orthopsychiatry*, 1946, 16, 686-696.

Purpose: To estimate the occurrence of delinquency in boys who had never been apprehended and to determine if personality factors played a major role in whether or not an offender was "caught."

Subjects: 114 boys, age 11 to 16, who were participating in the Cambridge-Somerville Youth Study.

Procedure: Interviews were conducted by caseworkers of the Cambridge-Somerville Youth Group and extensive case histories were studied. Offenses were classified under (a) violations of city ordinances, (b) minor offenses, and (c) more serious offenses. A range of rarely (one to three per year), occasionally (four to nine), and frequently (10 or over) was used to classify the number of offenses. IQs from the 1937 revision of the Stanford-Binet were compared for unofficial and official delinquents. Case histories were reviewed for personality factors that might have been influential.

Results: Of the 114 subjects, 13 had no violations, 40 were official delinquents, and 61 were unofficial. Over the five-year period, official action had been taken in less than 1.5 percent of the infractions. However, the transgressions of the official group were more frequent and more serious than the unofficial group. The median number of violations for official delinquency was 79 as compared with 30 for unofficial delinquency.

No IQ difference was found. Both groups had well-adjusted boys and boys with neurotic disturbances. Personality factors, as assessed here, were therefore not related to apprehension.

Comment: This study is often quoted in support of the proposition that legally defined delinquents are only a limited portion of actual delinquents. The results obtained here certainly are conclusive as regards the high incidence of unapprehended delinquency. The only methodological problem lies in the question of the veracity of the replies of the children who served as subjects. No estimate of the reliability of the data is provided.

Short, J. F., and Nye, F. I. Extent of Unrecorded Juvenile Delinquency: Tentative Conclusions. *Journal of Criminal Law, Criminology and Police Science,* 1958, 49, 296-302.

Purpose: To study the extent of unrecorded delinquency among both males and females.

Subjects: 570 boys from western and midwestern high schools, 125 boys in a western training school, 512 girls from western and midwestern high schools, and 48 girls in a western institution.

Procedure: All subjects were asked to indicate anonymously whether or not they had ever committed any of 23 acts of delinquency presented in a checklist.

Results: The major finding of this study was the strikingly high incidence of reported delinquent acts among the legally nondelinquent subjects. While the institutionalized groups commit virtually all the offenses, commit them more often, and can be differentiated from the normals on the basic scales derived from the list of delinquent acts, the nondelinquents admit commission of delinquencies in numbers ranging from 18 percent who admit having driven a car without a license to one percent who admit using narcotic drugs. Skipping school, fighting with one person, taking things worth less than two dollars, buying or drinking beer, wine or liquor, deliberate property damage, and violating game laws were admitted by more than 50 percent of the high school boys.

321

Comment: This study is a recent demonstration of the high incidence of unrecorded delinquency. It is, of course, open to those criticisms employed against self-report technique. Further, the only reliability data offered is a comparison between the two high school samples (western and midwestern) which indicated few statistically significant differences. While their questionnaire technique contained items to trap the over-conformer, the possibility of bias in the other direction remains uncontrolled.

Reiss, A. J., Jr. Social Correlates of Psychological Types of Delinquency. *American Sociological Review,* 1952, 17, 710-718.

Purpose: To attempt to isolate social correlates of psychological types of delinquents.

Subjects: 1110 white male juvenile probationers from a metropolitan juvenile court.

Procedure: From an analysis of case-history material, psychiatrists and social workers classified subjects into: (a) the relatively integrated delinquent; (b) the delinquent with markedly weak ego controls; and (c) the delinquent with relatively defective superego controls. The relatively integrated delinquent is described as "an adolescent with relatively integrated personal controls who in all probability will become a mature adult." Delinquents with relatively weak ego controls "are generally viewed as highly insecure persons with low self-esteem or as highly aggressive or hostile persons. They usually experience a great deal of internal conflict and exhibit marked anxiety." Defective superego delinquents have not "internalized the social-conforming controls of middle-class society and experience little sense of guilt over their delinquent acts. Typically they identify with an adolescent delinquent peer culture which rejects these norms." Following the classification of subjects, various social indices were examined for their differential relationships with the three psychological types.

Results: Over 100 comparisons were made. Space permits only a selected few to be reported in this review. Weak ego delinquents were found significantly less often to reside in high delinquency areas when compared with the other two types. The defective superego delinquent was found least often in settled residential areas.

A significantly larger portion of both the relatively integrated and defective superego types had left school. A significantly higher proportion of the relatively integrated group had achieved the level of a high school

322

education. Of those delinquents still in school, the weak ego group was more often academically retarded. Of those who had left school, fewer of the weak ego group were employed.

A significantly higher proportion of the defective ego and the defective superego types had foreign-born fathers as compared to the relatively integrated group. Various indices of socio-economic status were not statistically different for the three groups.

In regard to family structure variables, delinquents with defective superego controls significantly more often came from families where the father was absent but other siblings present. Further, they more often came from families broken by separation, desertion, and divorce than did the integrated type. More parental conflict appeared in the homes of both the defective ego and superego groups. The delinquent with defective superego controls more often had delinquent siblings than did the other two types. In respect to participation in a delinquency peer culture, the defective superego type was more frequently a gang member than was the weak ego delinquent. The weak ego group was significantly more withdrawn from social participation; members were significantly more often lone offenders.

In summary, the relatively well integrated delinquent appeared to be from a poor neighborhood but to come from a less mobile family which was more apt to be structurally intact and more apt to have harmonious relations and to maintain effective control over the children. The defective superego type also came from a poor neighborhood but emanated from disorganized families with other delinquent children. This type participated in a delinquent peer culture and had the highest recidivism rate. The weak ego delinquent came from a better neighborhood but from a rather mobile family. For him, family relationships were more apt to be in conflict and the children victims of neurotic conflicts. There was much less participation in a delinquent peer culture.

Comment: As the author points out, the interpretation of the relationships between the psychological types and the social factors cannot be interpreted as causative since the social factors may well have influenced the classification of a boy as one of the three types. In this study, as in others based on case history material, the reliability of the data is open to question. This research has the additional problem of the reliability of the classification of subjects into the three categories. In general, the reliability of clinical "diagnosis" of this type has been disappointingly low. Unfortunately, no estimate of the reliability of subject classification is provided by the author.

323

Peterson, D. R., Quay, H. C., and Tiffany, T. L. Personality Factors Related to Juvenile Delinquency. *Child Development,* 1961, 32, 355-372.

Purpose: To generate a set of unitary, independent, and meaningful personality constructs related to delinquent behavior in order to offer a rigorously defined frame of reference for further research.

Subjects: 186 institutionalized delinquents and 220 high school students. All were white males in the age range of 10 to 18. The delinquents and nondelinquents were roughly equated for type of neighborhood of residence.

Procedure: A battery of four questionnaires, all previously shown to differentiate delinquents from normals, was administered to the subjects in groups. The items of each questionnaire were intercorrelated and 10 centroid factors extracted. Three to four factors, accounting for a major of the variance, were rotated for each test to an analytic approximation to orthogonal simple structure. The resulting factors were independently interpreted. A second-order factor analysis was then performed on the matrix of correlations obtained between the factors obtained in the first analysis.

Results: The most important results are those of the second-order analysis. Each test contained a factor reflecting neuroticism or emotional disturbance, and each of these first-order factors appeared in the same second-order factor. The same was true for factors reflecting an aggressive antisocial attitude. The third second-order factor contained those first-order factors which seemed to reflect a delinquent background and the participation in a delinquent subculture.

Comment: This study strongly suggests that there are at least three independent personality dimensions which are related to delinquent behavior. Research on the relationship of these dimensions to social factors and to the dimensions of delinquent activities is needed.

Scott, J. F. Two Dimensions of Delinquent Behavior. *American Sociological Review,* 1959, 24, 240-243.

Purpose: To investigate the possibility that, rather than delinquency being a unidimensional attribute, there might be different kinds of delinquency.

Subjects: 120 male college students enrolled in undergraduate courses in criminology.

Procedure: A questionnaire covering a wide range of delinquent behavior was administered to the subjects, who were asked to indicate, anonymously, whether or not they had ever committed the offense. Scalogram analysis was then used in order to isolate items that might comprise unidimensional scales.

Results: Two dimensions of delinquent activity emerged. The first dimension was composed of eight items which were interpreted as reflecting delinquent activity directed against impersonal entities. The second dimension was composed of four offenses which were interpreted as commissions against known individuals who had some relationship to the actor's personal affairs. A correlation of only .16 was found between the two scales, indicating the distinctness of the two dimensions.

Comment: This study is important in that it indicates that there may be different types of delinquency which can be discovered by empirical means. This work, of course, needs to be extended both in the number of delinquent acts dealt with and in the type of population utilized. Additional dimensions may appear if a wider variety of acts are studied in a group in which delinquent activity is both more serious and more prevalent.

PSYCHOLOGICAL CORRELATES OF DELINQUENT BEHAVIOR

The personality and intellectual characteristics of delinquents have traditionally been the major focus for delinquency research by psychologists and psychiatrists. Many earlier studies applied assessment devices (of varying degrees of validity and reliability) to groups of delinquents and groups of controls supposedly similar except for the delinquency. A review of these studies lead two sociologists to conclude, justifiably, that there is little evidence for the association of personality characteristics with delinquency. It is obvious that the behavioral heterogeneity of delinquents is a severe handicap to this type of research. Encouraging results in this area have generally been obtained only when the delinquent group is subdivided in some way in order to make it more homogeneous and when a really comparable control sample is used.

Jones, D. S., Livson, N. H., and Sarbin, T. R. Perceptual Completion Behavior in Juvenile Delinquents. *Perceptual and Motor Skills,* 1955, 5, 141-146.

Purpose: The authors suggest that the class of delinquent behavior that is impulsive, unpremeditated and repetitive has its origin in part in a retardation of perceptual-cognitive development. The purpose of this study was to obtain measures of a perceptual function which would differentiate the delinquent boy from his nondelinquent peers.

Subjects: The delinquent group was made up of 41 boys, ages 14 to 18 (mean of 16.1 years), who had committed at least three acts of legal delinquency and who were incarcerated at the time of the study. The controls were 49 boys of the same age range and mean who had been selected on the criteria of lack of behavioral problems, no record of school or other misdemeanors, and freedom from obvious physical or psychological abnormalities. All subjects were Caucasian. The delinquent group consisted of boys who had been convicted of a serious offense. Truants, school delinquents, and narcotics violations were not included. The means for school grade placements and delinquency incidence in the boys' home neighborhoods were the same for both groups.

Procedure: 12 pictures from the Street Gestalt tests were used: two for practice and 10 in the test series. Pictures were chosen for their high interest value to adolescent boys. Each card was exposed a maximum of 60 seconds or until the correct recognition response was given. Data recorded were time of first response, time of correct response, and all of the verbal responses made by the subjects.

Results: The delinquents showed significantly fewer solutions during the full 60-second period. When numbers of correct solutions during the first 10 seconds were compared, the delinquents performed even less well. The biserial coefficient for the 60-second measure was .33; for the 10-second measure it was .36.

Comment: As the authors point out, no measures of intelligence were obtained on either sample and the relationship between test performance and intelligence is open to question. However, previous studies have failed to indicate any correlation between intelligence and the Street Gestalt. Since the authors interpret their results as providing support for their perceptual functioning hypothesis in regard to "psychopathic" delinquency, it seems that a somewhat more stringent criterion of "psychopathy" than multiple delinquent offenses might have been used. Multiple offenses, even of a serious nature, are not the exclusive property of the "psychopathic" delinquent but will be found also among subcultural and neurotic groups. This is not to minimize, however, the importance of the perceptual differences found in this study. Better selection of the "psychopathic" delinquent might well have served to maximize the differences found here.

Porteus, S. D. Q Scores, Temperament, and Delinquency. *Journal of Social Psychology*, 1945, 21, 81-103.

Purpose: To check the validity of qualitative scores on the Porteus Mazes as a method of discriminating delinquent traits of temperament.

Subjects: 100 delinquent boys, 100 delinquent girls, 100 nondelinquent boys, 100 nondelinquent girls, 100 adult criminals, and 100 bus drivers.

Procedure: The maze test was given to each subject with special care to provide clear initial instructions, and, with a demonstration, included a warning against crossing lines and lifting the pencil after beginning the test. Such qualitative test errors were totaled, given the Q score.

Results: The mean of the group of 100 delinquent girls was 28 points above the mean of an equal number of nondelinquent girls; a similar mean difference of 27.5 points separated delinquent and nondelinquent boys; bus drivers scored a mean of 39 points lower than that of adult criminals. The correlation between Stanford-Binet IQ and Q score was –.35 with 100 delinquent girls and –.34 with delinquent boys.

Comment: This study provides some evidence in support of the notion of greater carelessness and impulsiveness on the part of delinquents. These findings have been replicated in later studies such as that cited below.

Docter, R. F. and Winder, C. L. Delinquent vs. Nondelinquent Performance on the Porteus Qualitative Maze Test. *Journal of Consulting Psychology,* 1954, 18, 71-73.

Purpose: To provide additional nondelinquent normative data on the Porteus Mazes, and to provide an independent study of "matched" groups of delinquents and nondelinquents.

Subjects: 60 institutionalized delinquent and 60 nondelinquent boys matched for age, mental ability, and socio-economic level.

Procedure: Subjects were given the Porteus Maze test and qualitative scores were computed based on their regard for instructions, carefulness, impulsivity, etc.

Results: The qualitative performance of delinquents and nondelinquents corresponded almost exactly with results previously reported for these two groups. The qualitative (Q) score for delinquents was 47 and for nondelinquents 25, a difference significant at the .0001 level. This difference suggested possible predictive value: with a 29 Q score cutoff,

327

70 percent of the delinquents scored above this figure while only 30 percent of the nondelinquents did so. The Q score correlated −.27 with the Wechsler-Bellevue and −.16 with the California Test of Mental Maturity.

Comment: While there remains some uncertainty as to just what the Q score reflects, the separation of the groups obtained in this study is impressive. Further research into the psychological functions which are manifest in the Q score is certainly indicated.

Wattenberg, W. W. Factors Associated With Repeating Among Pre-adolescent "Delinquents." *Journal of Genetic Psychology,* 1954, 84, 189-195.

Purpose: To ascertain whether or not there was any distinctive group of factors associated with repeated "delinquency" among pre-adolescent boys as contrasted with those previously reported for youngsters in the adolescent age range.

Subjects: 334 boys, age 11, with records in the Youth Bureau of the Detroit Police Department. Of these, 99 were boys who had had more than one contact. Fewer than 10 percent had been referred to a juvenile court.

Procedure: Repeaters and non-repeaters were compared on 44 items which had been collected by specially trained officers.

Results: Of the 44 items compared, five were reported statistically significant at the .02 level or better. The repeaters were found more often to have poor or failing grades in school, to be judged by the police as being below average in intelligence, to belong to a gang classed as "rambunctious," to be classified by police as a "Peck's Bad Boy," and to be considered by police as dishonest in their dealings with others. None of the items relating to family conditions, boys' attitudes toward their homes, and socio-economic status were significantly different at the .02 level of confidence chosen as the criterion by the author. However, when the .05 level was accepted, the repeaters more often expressed unfavorable attitudes about home and came from neighborhoods rated below average. The association between school achievement and repeating is emphasized, and it is suggested that schools having visiting teachers or clinics might give priority to boys known to be in trouble with police.

Comment: In any study of this type there is always the question of the reliability of the data. In such items as those regarding the attitude of the police toward the boy there seems to be ample opportunity for biased ratings unless the ratings were obtained at the time of the first contact. As the author pointed out, the school failure can be seen as a product of repeated delinquency rather than as a precipitating stress.

CAUSES OF DELINQUENCY

Theories about the etiology of delinquency have generally been of two major types. Sociologists have argued for the primacy of social factors, such as social disorganization and the deviant subculture; while psychiatrists and psychologists have maintained that intrapsychic factors and interpersonal relationships are the primary determinants. In view of the mounting evidence that there are different kinds of delinquencies and different kinds of delinquents, this dichotomy is obviously a false one. Recent research has demonstrated that an interaction of personal and social factors can account for more of the variance of delinquent behavior than can either alone. A study of research bearing on both types of theories appears to lead to the conclusion that certain delinquents and their delinquencies are probably primarily products of social factors while intrapsychic forces better explain other facets of the problem.

Shaw, C. R., and McKay, H. D. *Juvenile Delinquency and Urban Areas; A Study of Rates of Delinquency in American Cities.* Chicago: University of Chicago Press, 1942.

Purpose: To explore the ecology of delinquency and crime in American cities.

Subjects: The unit of study in this research was an arbitrary geographic unit which was studied with regard to delinquency rate and socio-economic variables.

Procedure: Five zones were set up at two-mile intervals, with the heart of the central business district as the focal point. Male juvenile delinquents were defined in terms of contact with either the juvenile court or other court with jurisdiction, or official contact with an officer of the law which did not result in a court appearance. Three series of delinquents for three different time periods were obtained. Delinquency rates were calculated on the basis of the number of delinquents compared to the total male population of ages 10 to 16 in each zone.

Results: The highest rates were found in the inner zones—the business area, the slum area, and the area of working men's homes, while the lowest rates were found in the outer zones—the residential zone and the outer commuters' zone. In general, the rates declined regularly with progression from the inner to outer zones. The data from the three time periods were remarkably similiar, with correlations generally in the .70's, and perfect similarity appeared to be mitigated only by changes in the nature of the zones themselves as a function of time. Further analysis of the socio-economic characteristics of various city plots (census tracts) indicated that the delinquency rate was substantially correlated with decrease or increase of population, high percentage of families on relief, low median rentals, low percentage of home ownership, high percentage of foreign-born and Negro heads of families. The authors interpret all of these relationships as reflecting the nature of delinquency as a manifestation of social disorganization and social disadvantage found in the high delinquency areas.

Comment: This is the classic study in the demonstration of the relationship between urban delinquency and socio-economic variables. Its major weakness as an explanation for all delinquency lies in its inability to account for the phenomenon of the nondelinquent living under the same condition of social disadvantage as the delinquent. Too, there is the point that the delinquent may grow up in an immediate world rather highly organized, but around values and norms in opposition to the rest of the society. That is, there may actually be less social disorganization than the variables used here seem to warrant. Further, there is the consideration that correlations which indicate relationships between variables when taken over geographic areas do not necessarily mean that such relationships obtain for the individuals within those areas. For example, within a given census tract those individuals with the lowest income may not be most likely to be delinquent.

Lander, B. *Towards an Understanding of Juvenile Delinquency: A Study of 8464 Cases of Juvenile Delinquency in Baltimore.* New York: Columbia University Press, 1954.

Purpose: To clarify a number of problems in juvenile delinquency having to do with varying delinquency rates in different census tracts of a city; to provide a test of the Burgess concentric-zone and gradient hypothesis; to study the relationship of delinquency rate to certain social and economic indices; and to investigate the use of these variables in understanding differential delinquency rates.

Subjects: "Subjects" for this study were 155 census tracts in the city of Baltimore for which delinquency rates were computed on the basis of 8464 official court hearings over a four year period (1939-42).

Procedure: For each census tract the following data were obtained from the 1948 census: (a) median years of school completed by all persons 25 years of age or over; (b) contract or estimated monthly rent; (c) percentage of persons living in homes where there were 1.51 or more persons per room; (d) substandard housing; (e) percentage of nonwhites; (f) percentage of foreign born; and (g) percentage of homes owner-occupied. All of these variables were related to one another and to the delinquency rates by various correlational methods. Further, a factor analysis was performed on the intercorrelation matrix of these seven variables and delinquency rate.

Results: Delinquency rate was found to correlate significantly with all of the variables studied; coefficients ranged from a high of +.80 with the percentage of homes not owner-occupied to the inverse relationship of −.16 with percentage of foreign born. Further analysis indicated some of these relationships to be less straightforward than they appeared. The relationship of delinquency rate to proportion of Negroes was found to increase as the proportion of Negroes in an area increased from zero to 50 percent, but to decrease as the percentage of Negroes increased from 50 to 100 percent. There were also indications that some of the other relationships were nonlinear.

When partial correlations between the delinquency rate and each variable were computed holding the other variables constant, the relationships dropped to zero magnitude except for home ownership and Negro population concentration. The index of multiple correlation between all the predictor variables and the delinquency rate was .89, indicating a high degree of predictability of the delinquency rate from the social and economic variables studied.

Perhaps the most interesting result was that of the factor analysis. Two centroid factors were extracted which accounted for almost 95 percent of the commonality. From inspection of the plot of these two orthogonal factors, Lander hypothesized that the correlations could be best represented by an oblique rotation which was then performed visually. This resulted in a first factor with sizeable loadings on delinquency rate, many Negroes, many renters, and few foreign-born; and a second factor with loadings on low education, low rent, overcrowding, substandard housing, and many foreign-born, but with a very low loading on delinquency rate. The first factor, with which the delinquency rate was positively associated, was felt to represent social disorganization and was named *anomie*. The second factor was interpreted as reflecting poor economic conditions. The results were interpreted as indicating the importance of the social disorganization factor in contributing to the delinquency rate. In general, the Burgess hypothesis was not confirmed, due both to a failure of the city of Baltimore to conform to the zonal hypothesis and the failure of the delinquency rate to conform to the gradient hypothesis.

Comment: This study certainly represents a major contribution to the analysis of official juvenile delinquency from the standpoint of social and economic factors. Lander is very straightforward in pointing out the shortcomings of correlational design in investigating causation as well as the danger in inferring relationships about individuals from relationships in ecological units. The reviewer is most concerned, methodologically, with the arbitrary rotation procedure used in the factor analytic portion of the study. Hypothesizing a structure among a known set of variables and rotating visually to that point arbitrarily eliminates other factor solutions which might bring much different interpretation to bear on the data. In addition, Lander's argument that delinquency is related primarily to *anomie* and not to economic factors seems a failure to take adequate cognizance of the correlation of .68 found between these two factors.

Maccoby, Eleanor E., Johnson, J. P., and Church, R. M. Community Integration and the Social Control of Juvenile Delinquency. *Journal of Social Issues,* 1958, 14, No. 3, 38-51.

Purpose: To investigate the manner in which social disorganization might have its effect in producing juvenile delinquency. The basic hypothesis was that in disorganized neighborhoods an individual adult would feel less responsibility for guiding other peoples' children into "good" behavior and would tend to ignore deviant behavior unless personally involved, with the result that children "trying-out" deviant behavior would be less apt to suffer painful consequences.

Subjects: 129 adults living in a high delinquency area and 107 adults living in a low delinquency area.

Procedure: Two areas of Cambridge, Massachusetts were chosen as being as similar as possible in regard to socio-economic status of residents but as different as possible in delinquency rates. Good matching resulted for education and occupation but median income showed considerable differences. Dwelling units were chosen by sampling, and from these units 50 percent of the adults were selected for the interview. Interviews were conducted by means of a standard list of open-end questions, plus the recording by the interviewer of incidents in which the respondent reported having observed juvenile misconduct.

Results: The results indicated the high delinquency area to be less integrated in terms of less homogeneity of religious beliefs, less ethnic homogeneity, greater tendencies for respondents not to know their neighbors by name, not know them well enough to borrow things, not to feel common interests with their neighbors, and not to like the neighborhood. In attitudes toward the seriousness of various deviant behaviors, no differences were found. In actual reaction to deviant behavior, those living in the high delinquency areas were somewhat less likely to take any action against the child than respondents living in the low delinquency area. (Due to the nature of the data collection method, comparisons for statistical significance were difficult and indeterminate.) The authors concluded that the fact that the high delinquency area is less well integrated appears well substantiated but that the hypothesis in regard to social control is not so well substantiated.

Comment: Of interest is the similarity in standards in regard to deviant behavior of those living in high delinquency areas with the control subjects, which seems to provide some evidence against the notion of the delinquent subculture. In studies based on interviews there is always the problem of the frankness and veracity of the respondents. In addition, no evidence for the reliability of the interview techniques or content is provided.

Wattenberg, W. W., and Balistrieri, J. J. Gang Membership and Juvenile Misconduct. *American Sociological Review,* 1950, 15, 744-752.

Purpose: To study the effects a home (characterized by weak supervision or discipline plus the surrounding neighborhood) would have on the personality structure of adolescent boys who are delinquent and who participate in "gangs."

Subjects: 5878 Detroit boys, ages 10 to 16, who were contacted by the Detroit police in 1946 and 1947.

Procedure: Crime prevention bureau officers interviewed the boys and each home was visited. A history sheet obtained by the officers contained some 50 items on home conditions, neighborhood situations, gang membership, etc. The boys were divided into groups: gang participants (2737) and nongang participants (3141); those with records only in 1946 (1462); those with records only in 1947 (3746); and those with records in both years (670).

Personal data were compared statistically in three ways: (a) gang members with the nongang group; (b) 1946 nonrepeaters, 1946 repeaters, and new offenders of 1947; and (c) 1946 repeaters and nonrepeaters paired for gang members and nongang members. A gang was defined as a group of four or more boys who spent their spare time regularly with each other.

Results: Gang boys differed from nongang boys in evidence of coming from easy-going homes and living in socio-economically low neighborhoods. The nongang group more frequently showed disturbed family relationships. The gang members were more likely to come from substandard homes and racially mixed neighborhoods.

In predicting repeating, socio-economic indices were more indicative for gang members, while family conditions were more indicative for non-gang members.

Comment: This study points up the fact that both broad social and interpersonal factors may be related to delinquency in two different groups of boys. Unfortunately, this study is quite vulnerable to criticism in regard to the reliability of the data. In the collection of data from official records there is always the problem of subjective bias in the data gathering which may be further compounded when investigators make judgments from such data as the presence or absence of social and psychological factors.

Wattenberg, W. W., and Balistrieri, J. J. Automobile Theft: A "Favored Group" Delinquency. *American Journal of Sociology,* 1952, 57, 575-579.

Purpose: To explore some of the implications of "white collar" criminality or the theory that it is not the fact of crime which is associated with socio-economic disadvantage but only the form of crime.

Subjects: 230 white males who had been charged by police with some form of automobile theft and 2544 white males charged with other offenses.

Procedure: From information contained in police records, the two groups were compared on 50 variables. Statistically significant differences were found for 14 of the variables.

Results: The automobile thieves were more likely to come from better socio-economic situations as indicated by a number of specific variables. Since the auto theft group was largely confined to older boys, a number of variables related to age were significantly different for the two groups. In addition, more adequate relations with their peers were found for the experimental group.

The authors interpreted their results as being indicative of the importance of personality structure in delinquency since a significant proportion of those guilty of auto theft were free from the inimical influence of social disorganization. They proposed that delinquency for this group may be the result of a personality structure which is easily susceptible to the influence of factors immediately present but has limited susceptibility to the more abstract social controls.

Comment: This study, which indicated the existence of delinquency and the prominence of a specific type of offense in a group which is socioeconomically not seriously disfavored, provides ammunition against the too-ready acceptance of the social disorganization theory of causation for *all* delinquency. It is an example of results which may emerge when delinquent behavior is not treated as a unitary class. As in all studies based on police files, probation histories, etc., the question of the reliability of the data is open.

Reckless, W. C., Dinitz, S., and Kay, Barbara. The Self-component in Potential Delinquency and Potential Nondelinquency. *American Sociological Review*, 1957, 22, 566-570.

Purpose: To compare boys who, although living in adverse social circumstances in a high delinquency area, were potentially insulated against delinquency, with boys from the same area who were potential delinquents.

Subjects: 101 white boys thought to be potential delinquents and 125 white boys thought not likely to become delinquents.

Procedure: Sixth-grade teachers in high delinquency areas were asked to nominate boys whom they felt would experience future police and juvenile court contact. All subjects and their mothers were interviewed with a structured schedule. The boys were administered the Socialization (So) and Responsibility (Re) scales from the California Psychological Inventory. In addition, four items from an occupational preference scale previously shown to differentiate delinquents and a scale designed to measure self-concept were administered. The self-concept scale was also administered to the mothers. Background characteristics and questionnaire responses of these boys were compared to those of a group of boys selected in an earlier study by the same teachers as being insulated against delinquency.

Results: In general, social background characteristics were no different, due in part, of course, to the method of selection. However, fewer of the "insulated" boys came from broken homes. On the So scale the potential delinquents scored significantly lower than did the "good" boys. At the same time, the "good" boys scored significantly higher on the Re scale than did the potential delinquents. The results of the 18-item self-concept scale indicated that a more socialized self-image had been developed in the insulated group. The mothers of the potential delinquency group more frequently reported that their sons could have chosen better friends, that they were often unaware of the whereabouts of their sons, and that the family situation was more characterized by conflict.

Comment: This study demonstrates that differential personality characteristics are related to potential delinquency when social background factors are held constant. Of course, the question remains of the predictive validity of the teachers' judgments; i.e., do the "insulated" boys continue to stay out of trouble. Of further interest is the question as to what differential experiences with family and peers leads to the development of those personal characteristics insulating against delinquency.

Dinitz, S., Reckless, W. C., and Kay, Barbara. A Self-Gradient Among Potential Delinquents. *Journal of Criminal Law, Criminology, and Police Science.* 1958, 49, 230-233.

Purpose: A further exploration of the differences in self-concept found between potential delinquents and a group of "good" boys.

Subjects: 101 white boys, all living in a high delinquency area, who had been nominated by their teachers as being potentially delinquent. Twenty-four of these boys were already on police records as having committed some act of delinquency.

Procedure: The 24 boys with previous histories of delinquency were compared to the remaining 77 boys, who had not had any official contact, on a measure of self-concept and on scales measuring Socialization (So) and Responsibility (Re). Responses of the mothers to items regarding their sons' behavior were also obtained.

Results: More of the boys with previous court contact perceived themselves as likely to have future court contacts, less likely to stay out of trouble, and less likely to finish high school. In addition, the boys in this group more frequently neglected to inform their parents of their whereabouts and activities, more frequently relied on friends rather than parents for advice, and more frequently had older friends. The group with previous court contact history also scored significantly lower on the So and Re scales. The mothers of the previous contact group more frequently expected their sons to have future troubles.

Comment: The fact that differences in self-concept and personality structure emerge in these two groups despite the built-in homogeneity is striking. Of course, the problem of whether these differences are the cause of delinquency or the result of delinquency remains. A follow-up of the "predicted delinquency" group might aid in answering this question.

> Healy, W., and Bronner, Augusta F. *New Light on Delinquency and Its Treatment: Results of a Research Study Conducted for the Institute of Human Relations, Yale University.* New Haven: Yale University Press, 1936.

Purpose: To investigate the origins of delinquent behavior in the family situation with the family as the unit for study.

Subjects: 133 families with a total of 461 children old enough to be potential delinquents. Of these children, 194 were legally delinquent. In 103 cases it was possible to contrast a delinquent with a nondelinquent sibling.

Procedure: A great deal of information was collected from the delinquent and his family, including both demographic and dynamic material. For the most part, data were collected by the case study method. Personality attributes, for example, were clinically assessed by two or more members of the staff.

Results: In comparing families of delinquents with data on normal families, and in comparing delinquents with nondelinquents, a large number of contrasts were drawn. The assessments of the families of the delinquents lead the authors to conclude that " . . . in very many of our families the opportunities ordinarily regarded as necessary for the absorption of good ideals from parental examples or for the development of respectful attitudes toward parental personality and authority were decidedly lacking" (p. 28). For a group of 153 delinquents first studied, in only 22 cases were reasonably good home conditions, family attitudes, and neighborhood influences present. In only 30 percent of the families was there judged to be harmony between the mother and the father about the discipline of the children. In regard to the delinquents themselves, the modal age was between 12 and 14 years, the first known delinquency occurred at eight years or earlier in 48 percent, and after 12 years in only 22 percent. These findings, like similar ones from other studies, point up the early age at which delinquent trends appear in children.

The most interesting and meaningful results are those obtained from a comparison of the delinquents with a nondelinquent sibling. In physical status and in measured mental abilities both groups were similar.

337

For the 100 pairs for whom satisfactory information in regard to developmental history was obtained, it was found that deviations, e.g., mother sick and worried during pregnancy, cross or fussy babyhood, many illnesses and injuries, occurred twice as frequently among the delinquents. In diagnosable personality deviations, the delinquents-controls contrast was quite significant; the same was true for peculiar physical habits thought to be indicators of inner tension. In personality traits, the delinquents were more frequently hyperactive, aggressive, impulsive, and gregarious. Further, the delinquents were more often characterized as having feelings of inferiority. Of interest is the fact that not more than half a dozen of the delinquents were characterizable as being without conscience while fewer than 25 percent were felt to be without guilt or remorse over the wrongfulness of their behaviors. In a comparison of emotional experiences, the authors indicated that in no less than 91 percent of the delinquents there was clear evidence of past or present unhappiness, discontent, or extreme disturbance because of emotion-provoking life situations, while such was true for the nondelinquent siblings in only 13 percent of the cases.

The authors' theoretical explanation for delinquency, based on their findings, is essentially that of delinquent behavior as a substitute satisfaction for frustration endured in their relationships with their parents.

Comment: This research represents a pioneering effort in the study of parent-child relationships. Methodologically, it has the obvious faults of an almost complete lack of definition of terms and lack of any information in regard to the reliability of data-gathering procedures.

Glueck, S., and Glueck, Eleanor. *Unraveling Juvenile Delinquency.* New York: Commonwealth Fund, 1950.

Purpose: To assess a wide variety of factors of potential importance to delinquency.

Subjects: 500 delinquents and 500 nondelinquents matched for age, general intelligence, ethnic-racial origin, and residence in underprivileged neighborhoods.

Procedure: The delinquent group was selected from boys committed to state training schools who, for the most part, had court records reflecting persistent delinquency. The nondelinquent group was chosen from the general public school population. All control subjects were free from any official delinquency, while about three-fourths seemed free of even minor misconduct. After these criteria were met, subjects were then selected so as to match the two groups on the factors noted above. Extensive data in several areas were then collected for the two groups. Social histories were obtained from various official records and from home interviews. Somatotyping and medical examinations were done by medical personnel. Intelligence was measured by the use of the Wechsler-Bellevue Scale and academic achievement assessed by the Stanford Achievement tests. The Rorschach test and psychiatric interviews were chosen as the major devices for assessing personality dynamics.

Results: The multitude of comparisons made in this study yielded many significant differences between the delinquents and the nondelinquents. Space limitations permit only a summary here. In home conditions, the delinquents were more mobile and their homes were more crowded and less sanitary. Their families were more often recipients of public aid. Fewer were living with their own parents. As regards the setting of family life, the groups were similar in size of families and in economic circumstances. However, the paternal and maternal families of the delinquents were more frequently characterized by mental retardation, emotional disturbances, drunkenness, and criminality. There were more forced marriages among the parents of the delinquents. More frequently the principal breadwinner of the family was unwilling to assume proper responsibility for family support. The poorer quality of the home life for the delinquents was reflected in a less planned routine, poorer standards of conduct, and greater lack of supervision. The delinquents were more frequently the victims of indifference or actual hostility and less frequently were seen to be identified with their father. Discipline, for the delinquent, was less frequently either kindly or consistent. Educational retardation was more prevalent among the delinquents, despite the original matching for intelligence. The delinquents more often expressed a dislike of school, resentment at its restrictions, and a lack of interest in academic work. A higher proportion of delinquents expressed the desire to stop school at once, and fewer expressed mature vocational ambitions. Poor school conduct, as might be expected, characterized the delinquents. In their leisure time, the delinquents were more inclined to adventuresome activities and less likely to seek supervised recreation. A striking difference in gang membership was found: 56 percent of the delinquents were gang members as opposed to less than one percent of the controls. In physical health there were few differences. In physique the mesomorphic build was found more often among the delinquents, and the delinquents were found to have fewer bodily disproportions. In personality characteristics, the delinquents were to a greater degree socially assertive, defiant, ambivalent to authority, resentful of others, impulsive, and vivacious.

The final result of the study was the construction of tables designed to predict delinquency, of which the social factors table has received the most interest. In this table a prediction is arrived at by means of ratings of discipline of boy by father, supervision of boy by mother, affection of father for boy, affection of mother for boy, and cohesiveness of family.

Comment: Rubin has criticized this study on a number of grounds, including what he feels was the Gluecks' attempt to exclude residence in an underprivileged neighborhood as a causative source for delinquency by holding this variable constant. Further, he has also criticized the use of institutionalized offenders as the sample of delinquents and the results of matching of the two groups on certain factors such as home conditions and mobility. He has also pointed out that while the data on the delinquents were collected when a majority of them were 14 to 15 years of age, the factors included in the prediction tables are, theoretically at least, to be employed with much younger children.

Reiss has levelled a number of criticisms at the methodology. He cites the lack of reliability for the methods of data collection and the evaluation of the relationships which emerged, the poor matching in some instances, and considerations in regard to the use of the social prediction table in a population in which the base rate for delinquency is not 50 percent.

This study certainly represents a contribution to the understanding of delinquency through the discovery of many factors correlated with delinquency. Whether the study has actually produced a law of crime causation is highly problematical. The predictive validity of the five factors of social background as yet remains unestablished.

Hewitt, L. E., and Jenkins, R. L. *Fundamental Patterns of Maladjustment: The Dynamics of their Origin—A Statistical Analysis Based Upon Five Hundred Case Records of Children Examined at the Michigan Child Guidance Institute.* Springfield, Illinois: State of Illinois, 1946.

Purpose: To attempt to distinguish different types of juvenile maladjustment from behavior syndromes which might also be differentiated in terms of particular environment patterns to which the juvenile was exposed.

Subjects: 500 case record files of the Michigan Child Guidance Institute were used as the data source in this study. Information had been obtained from statements by parents, relatives, teachers, other persons in the community, and family physicians. Most of the cases were from five counties and had a racial homogeneity (97 percent) of white parentage. Seventy-eight percent were boys with a mean age of 11.7 years, and 22 percent were girls with 11.2 years mean age. The mean IQ of the cases was 93.5.

Procedure: A code schedule was devised for transcribing the case record material. The tetrachoric correlation coefficient was then used to find the statistical correlations between the different behavior traits and situational items of the code schedule. Behavior syndromes were then constructed on the criteria that: (a) each trait should have positive tetrachoric correlation of not less than .30 with the other traits and all traits included should be logically consistent; (b) the number of items in a syndrome should not be excessive; and (c) the number of selected traits required to be present in any case in order to classify that case should not be too high or too low (three out of six).

Situational patterns were constructed by selecting items which were moderately positively correlated with one of the behavior syndromes and which related conceptually by logical implications. Intercorrelations of behavior syndromes and situational patterns were then calculated. A follow-up study was made of three groups to see how they responded to suggested treatment.

Results: Three behavior syndromes were constructed: (a) the unsocialized aggressive behavior syndrome with the following traits: assaultive tendencies, initiatory fighting, cruelty, open defiance of authority, malicious mischief, and inadequate guilt feelings; (b) the socialized delinquency behavior syndrome composed of the variables of association with undesirable companions, gang activities, cooperative stealing, furtive stealing, habitual school truancy, running away from home overnight, and staying out late at nights; (c) the overinhibited behavior syndrome consisting of the traits of seclusiveness, shyness, apathy, worrying, sensitiveness, and submissiveness.

Four situational patterns were also constructed: (a) parental rejection; (b) parental negligence and exposure to delinquent behavior; (c) family repression; and (d) physical deficiency.

Relating the behavior syndromes to the situational pattern, it was found that the unsocialized aggressive behavior syndrome correlated .48 with the parental rejection situational pattern but insignificantly with other situational patterns. The socialized delinquent behavior syndrome correlated .63 with the negligence and exposure situational pattern but

341

insignificantly with others. The overinhibited behavior syndrome correlated .52 with the family repression and physical deficiency situational
syndromes but negatively with the others.

A follow-up study revealed that unsocialized aggressives showed the
least tendency to change. The socialized delinquent showed more of a
tendency to change than did unsocialized aggressives, but change went
in both directions; i.e., it either improved or the problem became
greater. The overinhibited problem child showed greatest improvement.

The theory was proposed that effective therapy of these "problem"
children must involve transference, a condition in which the child trans-
fers his feelings toward parent or parents or to the therapist and then
releases tension, anxiety, hostility, etc., surrounding these feelings.

Comment: This study is an extremely important one in that it produced a classification scheme for children's adjustment problems and
related that scheme to patterns of family interaction. Its method can be
criticized on two major grounds: the unknown but always questionable
reliability of case history material and the rather subjective method of
arriving at the behavioral and situational syndromes. Factor analysis
without respect to any criterion of clinical appropriateness would have
been a more preferable method of clustering the behavior and situational variables.

Bandura, A. and Walters, R. H. *Adolescent Aggression: A
Study of Influences of Child-Training Practices and Family
Interrelationships.* New York: Ronald Press, 1959.

Purpose: To find the child-training factors and family interrelationships that cause development of antisocial aggressive behavior in
adolescent boys.

Subjects: 52 adolescent boys of whom 26 had histories of aggressive
antisocial behavior. All subjects were of average or above average intelligence, came from legally intact homes, had parents who were steadily
employed, and did not live in high delinquency neighborhoods. The
median age was approximately 16.5 years. Aggressive boys were selected
from the county probation service and from those who had come in contact with the law or school authorities. Control boys were selected from
two large high schools. The subjects were matched in age and in occupational status of their fathers.

Procedure: Three members of each family (father, mother, adolescent)
were interviewed separately by a different interviewer of the same sex as
the interviewee. Interviews were semi-structured with open-end ques-

tions to elicit material in a number of areas. Parent interviews were rated on 61 five-point rating scales. The boys in the study were also given a thematic projective test. Reliabilities of interview ratings were found to be adequate. Adequate reliability was also demonstrated for scores on the projective list.

Results: The data were analyzed in regard to specific areas of interest as indicated below. All results presented here were statistically significant.

1. Dependency: Aggressive boys exhibited less emotional dependency on their parents than did the control boys and manifested more anxiety about relating to their parents in a dependent manner. Parents of aggressive boys more often stressed a need for the boy to be independent, thus showing a rejection of their son's dependency behavior. During the early childhood of the aggressive boys, their fathers had spent little time in affectionate interaction. Aggressive boys also showed little dependency on their teachers or peers.

2. Aggression: Mothers of aggressive boys were significantly more permissive of aggression toward themselves. While the two groups of fathers did not differ significantly, all fathers were nonpermissive toward such aggression. However, fathers of aggressive boys actually encouraged their sons to show aggression outside the home. Many times the mothers encouraged this also. Aggressive boys displayed more physical, verbal, and indirect aggression and more hostility toward their fathers than did the control boys. Aggressive boys reported more physical aggression toward peers and expressed this aggression more directly than did the control boys. Aggressive boys gave significantly more responses indicating hostility toward the father than did the control boys.

3. Sex: The handling of early forms of sex behavior by the parents of the aggressive boys did not differ significantly from that of the control parents. Both were nonpermissive but nonpunitive. Control parents were slightly more permissive toward masturbation during adolescence but less permissive toward heterosexual behavior. Differences between fathers and mothers were greater than between aggressive and control groups. Aggressive boys associated aggression with sex and had engaged more freely in sexual relations than control boys. Aggressive boys showed significantly less anxiety about sex than did the control boys.

4. Restrictions, demands, and disciplinary techniques: Parents of aggressive boys expected less of them in school achievement and in assuming responsibility than control parents. Aggressive mothers placed fewer restrictions on their sons' behavior in the home than the control mothers and were less demanding of obedience and less consistent in this de-

343

mand. Restrictions on aggressive boys were less extensive than control boys, but aggressive boys resisted and resented them more. Control parents used disciplinary methods that developed internal controls, i.e., reasoning, etc., while aggressive parents used coercive physical methods.

5. Identification and the internalization of controls: In the families of aggressive boys, the affectionate relationship was weak between husband and wife as well as between parents and boy. Control parents expressed close attachment for each other and for their sons. The control boys identified significantly more with their fathers than did the aggressive boys. Aggressive boys showed little or no guilt about their antisocial behavior. For the control boys guilt feelings acted as a strong control over their behavior.

Comment: This study is exceptionally well done methodologically and attacks the problems of delinquency by attacking a single behavioral variable of considerable importance. It is an excellent example of an approach toward understanding "delinquency" through the analysis of a carefully chosen group of boys who may only incidentally be legally delinquent. The rigor with which this study was carried out should serve as a model for attacking other facets of personality which contribute to a behavioral pattern of "delinquency."

McCord, W., and McCord, Joan. *Origins of Crime: A New Evaluation of the Cambridge-Somerville Youth Study.* New York: Columbia University Press, 1959.

Purpose: A follow-up of the subjects in the Cambridge-Somerville Youth Study and a study of factors in the histories of those boys who were later convicted of a criminal offense.

Subjects: The experimental and control boys who had been subjects for the Cambridge-Somerville Youth Study. The analysis of causation factors was based primarily on data obtained from 253 boys who were in the treatment group due to the lack of complete information on many of the control cases.

Procedure: Court records of the boys were searched for information in regard to criminal offenses. For study of the relevance of certain variables in the causation of criminality, judgments were made on the basis of history material recorded during the course of the original study. These judgments were reported to have generally satisfactory reliability and to be independent of the knowledge of the later delinquencies of the subjects.

Results: Results of the follow-up study are presented first. A number of analyses were made in comparing the treated group with the control group. These results indicated that ". . . the Cambridge-Somerville Youth Study, on the whole, failed to prevent either delinquency or adult criminality. Neither in the number of crimes committed nor in the number of boys who became criminals did the 253 treated boys differ significantly from the 253 untreated boys" (p. 40). Further, ". . . the treated boys failed to evidence an advantage over the control group, even when a variety of important variables was held constant. The Cambridge-Somerville treatment was, in general, as ineffective with the intelligent child as with the dull child, the loved child as with the unloved, the brutally disciplined as with the undisciplined, the child from the slums as with the child from the non-slum area" (p. 40).

Results obtained in regard to causative factors from the analysis of the multitude of data collected on both groups were extensive, both in negative and positive findings. Intelligence, general physical health, glandular abnormalities, and bodily abnormalities were not significantly related to later criminality. Boys with neurological handicaps, however, had a statistically significant greater tendency to commit crimes.

When neighborhoods were rated on a four-point scale, there was no significant tendency for the later criminality to be associated with type of neighborhood. It should be noted, however, that all subjects came from generally lower or lower-middle class circumstances. There was a highly significant association between participation in a delinquent gang and the development of a criminal record; this association was interpreted by the authors as evidence in support of the delinquent subculture as a causative factor in crime. In an attempt to answer the question of why some boys join gangs and others not, a number of other cultural variables were examined. The only significant relationship which emerged was that of the failure of the gang-member boy to accept the culture of the parents.

The control of the child by his parents was studied because previous research had related delinquency to disciplinary practices in the home, and research in a wider context had related conscience development to types of discipline administered. Six types of discipline were defined by the authors and 250 cases were categorized according to one of the methods; good reliability was indicated by the fact that three judges agreed on 88 percent of these categorizations of a series of cases selected at random. Results indicated that lax discipline or erratic discipline involving punitiveness was related to criminality; over one-half of the boys so disciplined were later convicted of crimes. Consistency of discipline, irrespective of whether it was punitive or love-oriented, was productive of noncriminality.

Many additional aspects of home life and parent-child interaction were also studied. Later criminality was found to be related to a quarrelsome and neglecting home atmosphere. Interaction between this type of home atmosphere and other variables was also found, e.g., all 10 boys whose homes were rated as quarrelsome and for whom discipline was judged to be lax later became criminals. When the relationships of the father to the son were classified, it was found that passive and warm fathers had the smallest number of criminal sons while fathers who had died and who had been characterized as neglecting had significantly more criminal sons. The father as a role model was also related to criminality; the criminal father had more criminal sons, especially if he had been cruel or neglecting in his relationship to his son and if he had been lax in discipline. The relationship of the mother to the boy was also related to outcome. Neglecting, passive, and absent mothers produced criminality, while loving, even though overprotective or neurotic, mothers produced less. There was also a pronounced tendency for the mother who provided a deviant role model to produce later criminality. The most likely prospect for criminality was a boy whose mother was rejecting, provided a deviant role model and was erratically primitive in her disciplinary practices. In considering the interaction of maternal and paternal characteristics, a number of rather complex relationships occurred, indicating that the interaction of the parents' characteristics was important. For example, rejection by only one parent did not produce more criminality than acceptance by both, but rejection by both produced criminality in 70 percent of the cases. The effect of the characteristics of the father was largely dependent upon the mother; if she was loving, crime remained low. Much the same was true for the mother so that opposite parents may have a counteracting effect except for the case of the frankly neglecting mother.

The relationship of a number of the factors considered above to the type of criminal act was also studied. A number of significant relationships emerged, e.g., passivity of mother positively associated with sex crimes but negatively associated with crimes against the person, indicating that the "choice" of the criminal act itself is differentially related to those factors which are etiologic of crime in general.

Comment: This study provides what may be the most thorough investigation of social and interpersonal factors associated with delinquent and criminal behavior now available. It is much more careful in method than many earlier studies, and its assessment of the interaction of social and familial factors with one another is especially interesting.

Wirt, R. D., and Briggs, P. F. Personality and Environmental Factors in the Development of Delinquency. *Psychological Monographs*, 1959, 73 (Whole No. 485).

Purpose: To study factors producing delinquency in boys whose character structure appeared antithetical to delinquency, and to study factors mitigating against delinquency in a group whose personalities appeared to be delinquent-prone.

Subjects: Four groups were formed from a pool of almost 2000 children who had been given the MMPI seven to eight years earlier and for whom follow-up data for official court contacts had been collected. Group I was composed of 71 boys with nondelinquent personality dispositions who had not become delinquents; Group II was made up of 71 boys with nondelinquent personality dispositions who had in fact become delinquents; Group III contained 71 boys with delinquent-prone personalities who never became delinquents; and Group IV was composed of 73 boys with delinquent-prone personalities who had become delinquents.

Procedure: The subjects were interviewed with special reference to history since ninth grade, family attitudes demonstrated during adolescence, general adjustment in social, occupational and educational relations, and present personality dynamics. Ratings were made on 157 items. The subjects also completed a self-administered history record containing 138 items. Additional data relating to 42 items were obtained from the records of social service agencies. A large number of cross-sample comparisons were made.

Results: Findings were extensive and can only be summarized here. The delinquency of the subjects was found related to social agency contact of family members and could be combined with the personality pattern to predict delinquency more accurately than either taken singly.

Those subjects who had delinquency-resistant personalities but became delinquents were different from those with the same personality dispositions who did not become delinquents in their coming from economically poorer homes, having parents with poor social adjustment, and suffering from poor relationships within the family.

The delinquents, irrespective of personality disposition, more often had parents who were poorer role models and less stable. Educationally they were less successful, received lower grades, remained in school a shorter time, disliked school intensely, and were more often in trouble. The personalities of the group were also described differently in respect to a large number of items.

Comment: This study demonstrates well the value of the integration of personality assessment and the study of social factors in the prediction and understanding of delinquency. It should serve as a model for further research in the interrelationship of these factors.

Educational Aspects of Delinquency

Controlled research in the educational aspects of delinquency is practically nonexistent. While the educational retardation of the delinquent group has been demonstrated in the context of numerous studies investigating the delinquent in broad perspective, the question of whether delinquents should be placed in special classes, whether the curriculum should be modified, and whether remedial education is of benefit remain essentially unanswered. Practices in this area are based mainly on impressions and opinions rather than on definitive investigation.

Kvaraceus, W. C. *Juvenile Delinquency and the School.* Yonkers-on-Hudson, New York: World Book Co., 1945.

Purpose: To provide a contribution to the subject of the role of the school in relation to the prevention and control of juvenile delinquency.

Subjects: Approximately 750 delinquent children who had received the services of a children's bureau attached to a school system.

Procedure: A wide variety of information was collected from case records, school records, official records, etc., concerning children who had had contact with the agency. It should be noted that these data had a broader base than is usually obtained when only adjudicated delinquents are studied.

Results: A complex set of findings is presented in regard to the descriptive nature of the cases studied, background variables, outcome variables, etc. Of concern here are those findings centering on delinquency and the educational process. More than half the delinquents came from grades six to 10, inclusive. A significant difference was noted in grade repetition; almost all delinquents repeated one or more grades and girls repeated more grades than boys. Delinquents overwhelmingly received very "low marks." A third of the delinquents were known to have been truant prior to their referral for some misdemeanor and the delinquents were significantly more truant than the general population. Two-thirds of the delinquents expressed a dislike for school or some person associated with the school. Nearly three-fourths of the group had transferred schools on at least one occasion. The junior high was found to be the terminal school for most of the delinquents. The school situation for the delinquent was characterized as a generally unhappy and frustrating one.

Comment: This study points up the fact that school is generally an unrewarding experience for the delinquent and the frustrations he encounters there may even serve to intensify his deviant behavior.

> Kvaraceus, W. C., and Ulrich, W. E. (with the collaboration of McCormick, J. H., Jr. and Keily, Helen J.). *Delinquent Behavior: Principles and Practices.* Washington, D. C.: National Education Association, 1959.

Purpose: "To provide general principles and specific guidelines for school action based on research-oriented theory and to illustrate how many of these operational principles have been implemented in different school systems throughout the United States."

Procedure: The authors of this volume surveyed the programs of school systems throughout the United States which were concerned with the problems of norm-violating children.

Results: Information was presented as to the ways in which various school systems were meeting problems of the norm-violating child and guidelines were suggested as to the ways in which problems may be dealt with by the teacher and the administrator. The areas dealt with were: (a) identifying the youngster needing help in the classroom; (b) providing help within the classroom; (c) providing help through curricular adjustments; (d) providing help through special classes; (e) working with the family; (f) working with law-enforcement and court personnel; and (g) working with community agencies.

Comment: This volume represents the most complete survey of actual practices in the schools that has ever been available. While the practices reported have rarely been subject to critical evaluation, the survey is a valuable source of information for educational personnel.

> Bowman, P. H. Effects of a Revised School Program on Potential Delinquents. *Annals of the American Academy of Political and Social Science,* 1959, 322, 53-61.

Purpose: Accomplished in the context of a much wider effort to influence the growth and development of youth, this study sought to provide data on the effect of special classes on variables related to delinquency.

349

Subjects: Children of below average ability who were doing poorly in the eighth grade. The majority were discipline problems in school and 41 percent had police or court records. The number of subjects used was not stated.

Procedure: The subjects were divided randomly into three equal groups. Subjects in one of the groups continued in regular classes as a control group, while the children in the other two were placed in special classes. Teachers selected for the two special classes were chosen on the basis of their interest rather than for any special training. In the mornings the program was academic for the first two hours, with the third hour spent in discussion and films on civics, general problems, and social problems. In the afternoon there were study periods, small discussion groups, handwork, and special projects. Some of the children also worked outside the school during the afternoons. Psychologically, the program provided the children with a sympathetic teacher who knew them well, a variety of experiences in which success was possible, and a relief from pressure for success in competition with more able students.

Results: The result of primary interest here was that in regard to delinquency rate. The control group tripled while the delinquency rate of the experimental subjects declined by one-third, and there were fewer serious offenses than in the group of control children.

Comment: While, as the author points out, ". . . the numbers are too small for generalizations, and the data are incomplete . . ." the preliminary findings of this study certainly indicate the need for additional research in the effects of curriculum revision in the prevention of delinquency.

TREATMENT OF DELINQUENTS

The treatment of delinquents has been based primarily upon methods evolving from philosophical and moral considerations rather than empirical ones. Institutional treatment in the traditional correctional school is oriented more toward custody and punishment than toward rehabilitation. Criticism of treatment procedures must be tempered, however, by the consideration that very little controlled research in the evaluation of various treatment procedures has been done. Impressionistic evaluations made by those administering the treatment are obviously inadequate. More research is needed in which the treatment variables are adequately defined, control procedures are used, and some criterion other than subjective evaluation is employed.

Weeks, H. A. *Youthful Offenders at Highfields: An Evaluation of the Effects of the Short-Term Treatment of Delinquent Boys.* Ann Arbor: University of Michigan Press, 1958.

Purpose: This study proposed to provide answers relative to: (a) a differential recidivist rate between a short-term treatment program and other kinds of treatment programs; (b) changes in expressed attitudes, values, and opinions as a function of the treatment program; and (c) changes in basic personality structure as a result of participation in the treatment program.

Subjects: 229 boys who participated in short term residential treatment and 116 who had been committed to a more traditional type of correctional institution. Unfortunately for research purposes, the boys of the group sent to the short term treatment facility were apparently considerably less serious delinquents. They were significantly younger, had had more schooling, and were predominantly white rather than Negro.

Procedure: The general approach of this research was to compare delinquents who had participated in a short term treatment program which stressed group interaction in as free an atmosphere as possible with delinquents who had had the more traditional reformatory experience. Recidivism rates for the two groups were compared before and after administration of a number of attitude and personality scales was completed.

Results: Of the 229 boys sent to the short term treatment facility, 145, or 63 percent, completed their treatment and, after having been released for at least one year, were in no further difficulty great enough to send them to another custodial facility. Of the 116 boys sent to the reformatory, 47 percent completed their treatment and, after having been released for at least eight months or more, were in no further difficulty severe enough to send them back to a custodial facility. A breakdown between whites and Negroes indicated that the success rate was not significantly different for the white boys but that there was a 50 percent vs. 33 percent difference in the case of Negro boys. The Negro boys sent to the short term facility were found to have had a more favorable social background, but this finding was unrelated to outcome. It should be noted that about 20 percent of the boys sent to the short term facility were returned to the court as unsuitable for the program; these boys were not counted as treatment failures.

In regard to the attitude measures, the authors concluded that ". . .

351

there is very little evidence that Highfield's boys, over the length of their treatment, change their attitudes toward family and toward law and order, and their outlook toward life, so far as the eight scales used to measure these attitudes show" (p. 122). This was also generally true for boys who had been sent to the more traditional facility. There was also little evidence of significant change on measures of personality structure. Of considerable significance, however, was the differential in per capita cost for the two institutions; the short term facility cost about one-third as much as the traditional program. This, of course, does not consider the gain accruing from the differential success rate.

Comment: This study represents a major contribution to the institutional treatment of delinquents. It is unfortunate, from a scientific point of view, that the actual "treatment" remained essentially unspecified. The differential success rate may have been due to a variety of factors: the physical setting, group counseling, factors associated with the personnel themselves, unmeasured factors associated with the boys, etc. There certainly needs to be further research in this area with an attempt to specify treatment conditions more fully. However, these comments are not intended to detract from the merit of this research.

Gersten, C. An Experimental Evaluation of Group Therapy with Juvenile Delinquents. *International Journal of Group Psychotherapy,* 1951, 1, 311-318.

Purpose: To evaluate behavioral changes resulting from participation in group psychotherapy by a group of institutionalized male delinquents.

Subjects: 44 boys at the New York State Training School for Boys, with a mean age of 15-7, and a mean IQ of 85.6.

Procedure: The subjects were divided into two groups of 22 each. The experimental group participated in 20 sessions, one hour a week, of group therapy; the control group did not. A battery of tests was administered to all 44 subjects before and at the close of the experimental period.

Results: A small (three points) but statistically significant rise in the Wechsler-Bellevue IQ was demonstrated for the experimental group. School achievement, as measured by Stanford Achievement Tests, indicated a gain of three months in grade level for the control group as compared to a gain of 18 months for the experimental group. The results of the Haggerty-Olson-Wickman Schedules showed a trend (apparently not statistically significant) for the experimental group to progress more in emotional security and emotional maturity. The Rorschach results also suggested better personality integration in the therapy group. Case studies and verbal reports of the staff failed to reveal any differential progress.

Comment: This study suggests that somewhat improved personality integration may be achieved in the delinquent by group therapy. A more crucial problem, however, may be that of comparing the results of group therapy, precisely defined, with the results obtained by other treatment alternatives.

Caditz, S. B. Effect of a Training School Experience on the Personality of Delinquent Boys. *Journal of Consulting Psychology,* 1959, 23, 501-509.

Purpose: To determine whether, as a result of training school experience, delinquents become more like the nondelinquent population.

Subjects: 94 boys committed to a state training school and 97 unselected high school sophomore boys.

Procedure: The delinquent boys took the MMPI and the Edwards Personal Preference Schedule prior to entry and again after an average institutional experience of approximately six months. The nondelinquent boys took the same tests and were retested approximately six months later.

The results of the first testing of both groups were compared for significant differences on 12 MMPI scales and 16 EPPS scales, and the second test results for the two groups were similarly compared. The differences between the first and second test results for each group were also compared. Each of the subgroups of the delinquents, based on broken or unbroken family background and severe or moderate delinquent history, was independently compared with the nondelinquents on the MMPI.

Results: The training school experience was not effective in modifying the significant differences between the delinquents taken as a group and nondelinquents which were found before the delinquents entered the training school. Delinquents and nondelinquents do not differ in their basic personality needs as measured by the EPPS. Both groups showed improvement in terms of lower MMPI mean scores when their second test results were compared with the results of their first testing. In the case of the delinquent subgroup comparisons, the boys from broken homes were more different from the nondelinquents than were boys from intact families. However, the delinquents from broken homes

353

benefited more from the training school experience—mainly in terms of better personality organization and stability. Evidence is limited that subgroupings of delinquents, based on severity of offenses, responded differentially to the institutionalization. The variable considered as the most appropriate measure of specifically delinquent traits, the Pd scale of the MMPI, was not materially affected by the delinquents' training school experience, a finding most pronounced in the case of boys from unbroken home backgrounds.

Comment: This study indicates that the traditional correctional school did little to modify the attitudes of the delinquent group. If the differences between the two groups are in fact important determinants of delinquent behavior, then the school experience was obviously not a corrective one.

Prevention

As in the case with treatment, delinquency prevention programs are not based on a firm empirical foundation. The most effective treatment of delinquency is prevention, but, in order to prevent delinquency, a fuller understanding of its nature is needed. The major research effort in assessing a program of delinquency prevention produced results which were not encouraging. Other efforts in prevention have been undertaken and some are in progress at this writing. Only those which employed control procedures and objective evaluations can hope to produce research evidence as to their merit.

Powers, E., and Witmer, Helen. *An Experiment in the Prevention of Delinquency. The Cambridge-Somerville Youth Study.* New York: Columbia University Press, 1951.

Purpose: To test the hypothesis that aid from a resourceful counselor can forestall delinquency in a group of "problem boys" or predelinquents."

Subjects: Originally, 325 boys were assigned to counselors, while a like number, matched with the experimental group on a variety of factors, served as controls. The median age was about 11 years. About 50 percent in each group were judged to have high delinquency potentials.

Procedure: The original plan of this study was to provide the treatment group with 10 years of counseling by a single counselor while the control group was to be left to its own devices. However, due to practical difficulties encountered during the war, only one-third of the 325 boys were carried by their original counselor without transfer to a second worker, and only 75 boys were carried through the entire treatment program. The treatment itself was apparently in the nature of maintaining a friendly and supportive relationship but without environmental manipulation. After a period of about four years the treatment plan was reorganized somewhat, with a trend toward working with the boys in small groups. Tutorial services were also expanded at this point. As war conditions made continuation of the project impossible, all cases were closed by the end of 1945.

Results: This study produced a number of research results of interest in the study of delinquency. The major result was one bearing most directly on the hypothesis tested: the prevention of delinquency by the treatment employed. The measurement of this variable was accomplished in a number of ways: a count of boys with single court appearances, a count of boys with multiple court appearances, and an analysis of the seriousness of offenses, etc. Results, taken as a whole, were seen not to indicate the treatment group to be less delinquent than the controls. This inability to demonstrate differences lead the authors to conclude that ". . . the special work of the counselors was no more effective than the usual forces in the community in preventing boys from committing delinquent acts" (p. 337).

Comment: As Gordon W. Allport pointed out in the introduction to this book, it was difficult to decide whether or not the hypothesis had a fair test. Certainly the length of treatment and the nature of treatment were unavoidably altered during the course of the research. There was, of course, the obvious point that the control group itself did not go "untreated"; it was subject to many influences mitigating against the development of delinquency. An additional follow-up study of the subjects for this study has been provided by McCord and McCord in a paper discussed in the section on etiology. As noted there, the treatment was not effective in preventing adult criminality.

SUMMARY

One cannot help but be impressed by the complexity of the phenomena referred to as juvenile delinquency. Research effort has suffered from the heterogeneity of behavior considered delinquent and the heterogeneity of individuals classified as delinquents. With such variability it is small wonder that each study of etiology seems to explain some delinquency but not all, and that the studies of prevention and treatment, involving only a single experimental approach, provide results which are suggestive at best.

At this point it seems most likely that future research will be more fruitful if it seeks to understand the relationships of empirically demonstrable dimensions of delinquent acts to equally demonstrable dimensions of personality characteristics as these may in turn be related to clusters of social and family background variables. The discovery and demonstration of treatment and prevention methods can then more logically follow.

12

Administration

Clifford E. Howe

Although behavioral research studies in the separate fields of exceptional children are extensive, few such studies exist in the area of administration and supervision of special education. Published materials are devoted largely to statements of opinion and reports of practices followed throughout the country. This situation is no different from that which existed until recently in the whole field of administration. Current developments in educational administration are being directed more toward explanatory theory and testable hypotheses. It is hoped that in the future, investigations in the administration of special education will contribute research-based observations and conclusions.

Administration of special education defines the role occupied by the person or persons in direct charge of a program for exceptional children. The school organization could be a district, county, or state. The material in this chapter is organized as follows:

1. Surveys and exploratory studies in administration of special education.
2. Inclusive prevalence studies.

Reviewed by Morvin A. Wirtz, St. Louis County Schools.

Mackie, Romaine P., and Engel, Anna M. *Directors and Supervisors of Special Education in Local School Systems.* U. S. Department of Health, Education and Welfare Bulletin, 1955, No. 13.

Purpose: To collect information on competency, experiences, professional preparation, and personal characteristics which contribute to the success of directors and supervisors of special education in local school systems.

Subjects: 1625 special educators from various parts of the country.

Procedure: Information was secured by two techniques. The first was the use of a series of inquiry forms completed by the following four groups: 153 directors and supervisors of special education in local school systems; 102 directors and supervisors of special education in state departments of education; 279 instructors in colleges and universities preparing teachers of handicapped and gifted children; and 1079 superior teachers in every area of exceptionality. A committee of 12 experts also prepared a statement in which they identified and described the unique competencies needed by local directors and supervisors of special education.

Results: The functions of administration and supervision each consumed approximately one-third of the time of these local directors and supervisors. The remaining third was divided almost evenly among the functions of inservice education, professional study and research, public relations, and direct services to exceptional children.

It was felt that distinctive abilities and skills are needed by any person giving leadership to a local special education program, whether that person is designated as a director or a supervisor. He must be cognizant of: (a) the physical, mental and emotional deviations of handicapped and gifted children; (b) the effects of handicaps on the family; (c) the specific agencies and community services available; (d) current trends in educational programs for exceptional children; and (e) major studies about each group of exceptional children. The majority of persons contacted in this study want directors of special education to come from the teaching ranks and to have had experience in teaching exceptional children.

Comment: This was an important first step in attempting to analyze the position of director or supervisor of special education. Although general and based upon opinion, such a study does help to describe the existing situation and provide leads for additional research.

Los Angeles City School Districts. *Major Report, Special Education Study: Definition, Function, Organization, and Administration of the Special Education Program.* Los Angeles: Office of the Superintendent, 1960.

Purpose: To make a critical analysis of recommendations for special education as indicated by data from a questionnaire survey of selected special education specialists, a random sampling of professors of school administration, and personnel in state departments of education in the United States.

Subjects: Questionnaires were sent to 48 state departments of education; 26 universities which had a department of special education headed by a director or coordinator; and 117 professors of school administration in colleges and universities throughout the United States.

Procedure: A comprehensive questionnaire was developed with forced-choice responses. A space was also provided for comments if the stated categories did not fit the respondent's answer. The total percentage of usable replies from each group received was as follows: (a) 82 percent from state departments of education; (b) 69 percent from special education experts; and (c) 50 percent from professors of school administration. Statistical treatment of the data was limited to classification tabulation and computation of percentages. In addition, data indicating the line and staff relationship of the special education program were solicited from superintendents of city school districts with 200,000 or more population.

Results: 1. Respondents were agreed that the following special education categories should be the direct responsibility of a department of special education: blind, partially seeing, deaf, hard of hearing, lip reading, speech correction, cerebral palsied, orthopedically handicapped, mentally retarded, chronic medical problems, emotionally and/or socially disturbed, hospital and home teaching. The following categories were thought not to be the responsibility of a department of special education: remedial reading and arithmetic, foreign adjustment classes, and corrective physical education. An interesting result was that while special educators tended to recommend that the mentally deficient and the gifted should be a part of special education, a majority of professors of school administration indicated that these two areas should not be included.

2. Special education experts and state department of education respondents indicated clearly that school districts should be responsible for providing preschool educational opportunity for the blind, deaf, and cerebral palsied. Professors of school administration were opposed to school districts providing any type of preschool educational opportunities for exceptional children. Experts in special education felt that the current per-pupil load was too high for the emotionally disturbed and for the preschool deaf. Professors of school administration stated that the suggested (Los Angeles) pupil norm for each category of special education was satisfactory.

3. All three groups agreed that final authority for pupil placement should be the responsibility of an educator, rather than medical or psychiatric personnel.

4. A centralized pupil placement plan should be used, rather than a decentralized plan in which each school or sub-district places pupils.

5. There was agreement that exceptional children, with the exception of the mentally retarded and the mentally deficient, should be included in the "regular" elementary school age promotion policy.

6. State department respondents indicated by a two-to-one majority that the mentally retarded group should not be included in a "regular" high school age graduation policy. Specialists were evenly divided in response to the item. A majority of the professors of school administration would include the retarded in the "regular" high school age graduation policy.

7. Principals of special education schools should possess a special education credential. Principals of regular schools containing special education classes should have from four to six hours of basic course work in special education.

8. Specialists and state department respondents failed to give any one administrative framework plan a majority response. They seemed to favor a plan where the department of special education has the entire or at least shared control for special education schools. Professors of school administration recommended that the authority be vested with the district assistant superintendent. For regular schools containing special education classes, the specialists preferred an administrative framework plan in which the principal would be dually responsible (a) to the local district assistant superintendent and (b) to the head of the department or division of special education. Professors of school administration and state department of education personnel favored "regular" administrative control by the assistant superintendent.

Comment: This comprehensive study is outstanding in that it calls

360

attention to many of the major unsolved problems in the administration of special education. For this reason it has been reviewed in some detail. It is interesting to note the frequent cleavage of opinion between the professors of school administration and the special education respondents. In essence, the professors of school administration reflected a "status quo" point of view by approving present class sizes; wanting programs for the gifted and mentally deficient excluded from special education; vesting authority for administration of special education with the assistant superintendent; and opposing preschool education for the deaf, blind, and cerebral palsied. This divergence of views points up the need for better communication between the two groups if special education is really going to function as an integral part of the total school program.

Howe, C. E. *Roles of the Local Special Education Director.* Urbana: University of Illinois, Institute for Research on Exceptional Children, 1960. Mimeographed.

Purpose: To develop a job description for directors of special education and to study the functions presently performed by 10 directors in a midwestern state. As with any pilot study, the purpose was to generate notions which could be followed by more precisely designed research.

Subjects: A sample of 10 directors of special education selected from systems in cities ranging in total population from 20,000 to 80,000.

Procedure: This descriptive pilot study was based on three-hour tape-recorded responses of these directors to an open-end questionnaire.

Results: There were wide differences among the directors studied, both as to how they perceived their jobs and as to the duties they performed. They could be classified roughly into two groups, according to their conceptions of their positions. The first group of directors felt that there was nothing unique which would differentiate their functions from those of a regular administrator. The second group believed that the unique requirement was something which could probably best be labeled "content competency in various areas of special education." In general those individuals with the most comprehensive background in special education, both by virtue of training and experience, were the ones who geared their work as directors to staff development and improvement of the quality of instruction within their system. Others, who had minimal training, seemed to confine themselves primarily to administrative details and to quantitative expansion of services. A few directors with minimal training in special education admitted that they avoided staff development and program evaluation because they felt too insecure in their own knowledge of special education to attempt such an emphasis.

Comment: This was an exploratory study of a small group of directors of special education. It revealed that the roles actually performed by directors of special education vary widely, a fact which may be related to their degree of specific knowledge in each area, both by virtue of training and of experience. It implies that graduate training programs for directors and supervisors of special education should provide some background in general education of curriculum and administration, but that the major emphasis might well be on providing comprehensive knowledge of the major ideas and techniques in each area of exceptionality. Such a training program would require a minimum of two years of graduate study and makes it necessary that a graduate faculty be made up of several persons, each of whom is a specialist in his area.

INCLUSIVE PREVALENCE STUDIES

One duty of the administrator of special education is to determine the probable number of exceptional children in his community so that his district can more accurately plan programs for them.

Farber, B. The Prevalence of Exceptional Children in Illinois in 1958. *Report of the 1958 Illinois Census of Exceptional Children, Circular—Census 1A.* Springfield: Superintendent of Public Instruction, State of Illinois, 1959.

Purpose: To indicate needs for special education services in Illinois.

Subjects: All children of school age in Illinois who were identified as exceptional in a state-wide census in 1958.

Procedure: Each county superintendent of schools was responsible for the collection of data in his county. Each child designated as exceptional in the census was reported by his teacher, his parent, or a social agency. Each person who collected data was provided with a list of attributes to guide him in his classification.

Results: 11 percent of all of the children in Illinois were enumerated as exceptional. Most of the prevalence rates were similar to theoretical estimates reported in the literature and to those of other prevalence studies. Within the expected range of prevalence were speech defects, visual handicaps, socially maladjusted and emotionally disturbed, educable and trainable mentally handicapped, the gifted, and those with multiple handicaps. Reported prevalence was below theoretical expectancy in the areas of physical handicaps, hearing impairment, and slow learners. The authors suggested that teachers may have reported only the more severe cases in these categories. The data suggest that about one-fourth of the exceptional children in Illinois were currently receiving special education services. Almost 50 percent of those with speech problems were being served; services for the slow learners (10 percent) and multiply handicapped (17.5 percent) were the lowest.

Comment: This study suggests that teacher identification yields a fairly accurate estimate of the number of exceptional children, at least on a state-wide basis. This degree of accuracy might or might not hold in one county or one school system. The only accurate way to check the validity of teacher identification would be to conduct a study in which the criterion measure of exceptionality was established by teams of experts examining a random sample of the same population from which the teachers derived their data.

Wishik, S. M. Handicapped Children in Georgia: A Study of Prevalence, Disability Needs, and Resources. *American Journal of Public Health,* 1956, 46, 195-203.

Purpose: To determine the prevalence of handicapping conditions among the child population of Georgia and to assess the adequacy of existing resources to meet those needs.

Subjects: A 10 percent sampling of the child population of two counties in Georgia considered to be representative of the state in urban-rural distribution and in racial pattern.

Procedure: Diagnostic criteria were drawn up defining each of 12 types of exceptionality. During a three-week period, everyone in the community (schools, agencies, physicians, parents, etc.) was asked to refer children who seemed to fit the definitions. At the end of this period of voluntary reporting, an independent sample canvass of the community was made by selecting every tenth household. The last phase of the study involved drawing a sample from the children reported as exceptional and then obtaining a confirming diagnosis from specialists from different disciplines.

Results: Accuracy of this voluntary reporting was surprisingly high, with an average of about 64 percent. Speech, hearing, and vision were least accurate; epilepsy, orthopedic conditions, mental retardation and personality disturbances were most accurate. The canvass reporting discovered children overlooked by the voluntary survey, but also yielded a higher percentage of over-referrals. Overall accuracy of the canvass was

51 percent. Ten percent of all children under 21 years of age were estimated as exceptional.

Comment: This study is important in that it attempted to validate the accuracy of prevalence figures gathered by survey and referral techniques. The only major weakness in the study is that it leaves unanswered the question of how many exceptional children were missed by the survey. Of those reported, confirmation by diagnosis was surprisingly high. One might surmise that this was because only the more obvious and severe cases were reported, but the reported incidence of 10 percent approximates the estimates of exceptionality made in other parts of the country.

Summary

The one most significant generalization on the present status of research would be that substantial behavioral research studies have not been done in the area of administration and supervision of special education. An encouraging note is provided by the studies done by the Los Angeles School Districts and the U.S. Office of Education. Guidelines for future research are provided by these two studies.

Certainly research is needed, because the administrator of special education assumes a very important role in determining the direction which programs for exceptional children will take in the future. Directors and supervisors are cast in the role of leaders and molders of public opinion, but in the past they have often been less well-trained in special education than the staffs they have directed.

The following are some projects and research problems which could yield useful information regarding the administration of special education:

1. Studies of role perception or role discrepancy of the administrator of special education. Such a technique might yield very useful results as to how both superintendents and the special education staff visualize the role of the director of special education, and how this perception actually affects the role that the director plays.

2. How do the type of college training and prior experience affect the functions which an administrator performs when he actually assumes the working position as director of special education? Should he be a generalist or a specialist? Can he realistically be both?

3. How many teachers and what conditions require the presence of a supervisor in a department of special education?

Index of Names